FOGG IN THE COCKPIT

FOGG
IN THE
COCKPIT

HOWARD FOGG
Master Railroad Artist, World War II Fighter Pilot

Wartime Diaries,
October 1943 to September 1944

RICHARD FOGG

AND

JANET FOGG

CASEMATE
Philadelphia & Oxford

First published in the United States of America and Great Britain in 2011.
Reprinted in 2018 by
CASEMATE PUBLISHERS
1950 Lawrence Road, Havertown, PA 19083, USA
and
The Old Music Hall, 106-108 Cowley Road, Oxford, OX4 1JE, UK

ISBN 978-1-61200-004-6
Digital Edition: ISBN 978-1-61200-015-2

Cataloging-in-publication data is available from the Library of Congress and
the British Library.

For a complete list of Casemate titles, please contact:

CASEMATE PUBLISHERS (US)
Telephone (610) 853-9131
Fax (610) 853-9146
Email: casemate@casematepublishers.com
www.casematepublishers.com

CASEMATE PUBLISHERS (UK)
Telephone (01865) 241249
Fax (01865) 794449
Email: casemate-uk@casematepublishers.co.uk
www.casematepublishers.co.uk

CONTENTS

"One of the greatest hazards in flying is
fog in the cockpit."

*As told to Richard Fogg by his father Howard Fogg, this phrase was
uttered by a meteorology instructor to a class of student pilots in 1942.
A gale of laughter, led by Howard, followed this pronouncement.*

Air Cadet Howard Fogg at Parks Air College in East St. Louis, June 1942.
Lettering on Fuselage reads:
U.S. ARMY-PT-I9
AIR CORPS SERIAL NO.40-2609
CREW WEIGHT 400 LBS
Courtesy of Peter Fogg

INTRODUCTION

Described for decades as the world's foremost railroad artist, Howard Fogg's fascination for railroading began early. He sketched his first train when he was only four years old.

After graduating from Dartmouth College with honors in 1938 with a degree in English Literature, Howard attended the Chicago Institute of Fine Arts. Appreciative of the many ironies in life and politics, he hoped to pursue editorial cartooning, though he also painted, which is where his talent ultimately led him.

Howard's career as an artist has been explored in radio and television interviews, magazine articles, newspapers, and books, but that is not the primary objective of this book. Here, we focus on his military service as chronicled in his personal wartime diary. Written during 1943 and 1944, it offers a unique perspective into the life of a fighter pilot with the Army Air Forces. Although principally concerned with his experiences as a pilot, it is inevitable that his love of railroading and his enthusiasm for painting is also reflected in these pages.

Drafted into the Army on May 15, 1941, Howard was assigned to the 4th Armored Division at Watertown in upper New York State—but the December 7, 1941 Japanese attack on Pearl Harbor changed his life. The Army Air Corps needed pilots, so with his keen vision and sense of duty, Howard requested a transfer. He received basic flight training at Parks Air College in St. Louis, primary training at Vance Air Base in Enid, Oklahoma, and finished his schooling at Foster Field in Victoria, Texas.

Commissioned as a second lieutenant with pilot's wings on November 11, 1942, Howard's first flight assignment was at Westover Field in Springfield, Massachusetts. There, he flew P-47 Thunderbolts under the leadership of Lieutenant Colonel Avelin P. Tacon Jr., who commanded the 359th Fighter Group, comprised of the 368th, 369th, and 370th Fighter Squadrons.

Lucky Howard.

The Westover assignment allowed him to travel regularly to New York City, where he continued to court the vivacious, beautiful, and unconventionally determined Margot Dethier, daughter of a Belgian concert violinist. Smitten by Margot when they met at the Dartmouth-Yale football game in 1934, Howard patiently pursued "Maggie" throughout her college days, despite her initial disinterest in his romantic declamations.

Following her 1942 graduation from Bryn Mawr College, Margot accepted her own new challenge. She returned home to New York and became one of the first female railroad ticket agents, a high-pressure job requiring a prodigious memory as well as patience with those who viewed the position as one that should only be held by a man. But women were filling men's jobs all over the United States, and Margot persevered.

So did Howard.

That fall and winter Margot realized how strongly she returned Howard's affections, and on April 10, 1943, they were married at the Madison Avenue Church in New York City.

After a brief honeymoon, Howard's flight training again became the young pilot's priority. Assigned to Grenier Field in New Hampshire, the 368th and 369th Fighter Squadrons continued their training in P-47s, though a shortage of planes limited each pilot's flight time. In May, Howard was transferred to Republic Field on Long Island where his squadron received new Thunderbolts, and training intensified. Howard then returned to Westover Field in August, while Margot stayed with his parents in Summit, New Jersey. On October 1, 1943, he received his combat orders and traveled to Camp Kilmer, New Jersey to await his transfer overseas.

Richard Fogg and Janet Fogg

Captain Howard Fogg. *Courtesy of Richard Fogg*

*We begin this transcription with a note penned by Howard
on a "Memoranda" page within the diary.*

Smorgasbord
This is not intended to be the intimate "lock and key" type of diary, but
rather a cumulative digest of events, incidents, and personalities recorded
by date and concerning the 368th Fighter Squadron, and especially "D"
Flight. No style, no planned form, merely enough notes to refresh the
author's dull memory should that anticipated day of writing a book ever,
by good fortune, arrive and become an actuality. Personal philosophizing
and opining will colour much of the record, and why not, since any facts
are made human and alive and vibrant by the personal touch, be it biased
or open-minded.

Howard Fogg

Fogg Mission Destinations Map. Western Europe in 1944. *By Janet Fogg*

1.

OCTOBER 1943

England at Last!

Friday, October 1: Westover Field, Massachusetts—Oh memorable of all Fridays when, unwittingly, and with promises of seeing her in Summit soon, I gaily kissed Margot farewell for the last time prior to shipping. Of course we'd have time off from Westover Field. Yes? Who dreamt that a week from tonight we'd be on the high seas Europe bound, with the family still waiting in Summit. Such is fate. But perhaps it was easier this way. No parting tears. No grief of certain parting. In any event, all was excitement and confusion as we prepared to board the train for Kilmer. Nineteen cars and B&M *(Boston & Maine railroad)* #4114 at 2:30 A.M. All aboard!

> [World War II rages. As Howard and his 368th Fighter Squadron begin
> their journey to England, the US 5th Army enters Naples, facilitated by
> Italy's September 3rd signing of a secret armistice with the Allies.]

Saturday, October 2: Camp Kilmer, New Jersey—Our route was varied to say the least. First, we traveled to Greenfield, thence Troy, thru Albany, down the West Shore to Weehawken, thru the yards to a junction with the Pennsylvania at Jersey City. A GG1 *(Pennsylvania Railroad electric locomotive)* hauled us into Kilmer at 4:00 P.M.

To call this place huge is rank understatement. It's breathtaking, with huge loading platforms, miles of buildings, and more. There are thousands and thousands of men. Every PX is jammed and every theatre full. Really an impressive array of manpower surrounds us, and, for once, efficient Army organization. Excellent food albeit cafeteria style. Good Bachelor Officer Quarters, better than Westover. There's gambling and cards, galloping dominoes, and streams of whiskey.

Pre-1949 U.S. Army photo of Camp Kilmer, New Jersey. Camp Kilmer was a staging area and part of the New York Port of Embarkation for troops heading to the European Theater of Operations. The wooden buildings were painted bright contrasting colors for camouflage, similar to the Dazzle camouflage used on ships during World War I. Over 2.5 million soldiers were processed through Camp Kilmer to the ETO or back home.
This photo is in the public domain as a work of the United States Federal Government.

Sunday, October 3: Camp Kilmer, New Jersey—We were alerted at 8:00 A.M., thus destroying any dreams we had of a final visit home. No telephoning, no contacts outside, all mail censored.

Poor Margot. God how I miss that girl already. It drives me nearly crazy being so near to her.

The hills against the northern horizon, beyond which lie my home, how ironic to be sent here to await shipment. But we're busy repacking and inspecting equipment, and having meetings.

We are very, very hot! All spare time is used for heaving the dice and money is changing hands rapidly. A good bit of "Prestone" flowing at night.

[The Greek Island of Kos is captured by 1,200 German paratroopers. About 900 Allied and 3,000 Italian troops are taken prisoner and the Germans execute 90 of the Italian officers for fighting against Germany, their former ally.]

Monday and Tuesday, October 4 and 5: Camp Kilmer, New Jersey—Hunter really tied one on, as did Taylor. They put

Margot Dethier in New York City on April 9, 1943, the day before her wedding to Lieutenant Howard Fogg.
Courtesy of Richard Fogg

Hunter in a cold shower and he just stood there blinking his eyes, completely unmoved by the icy stream. Amazing.

Some hot rummy games are being played. I lost three bucks to that dog Hagan, this morning.

We're busy censoring the enlisted men's mail. A strange new task that brings a clear picture of the human side of an army, all the emotion, the warmth and coldness of feeling, the gay and sad, poor and rich, ignorant and scholastic, a revealing cross section of the average American boy. His chief thought is of home, his meals, and his money. He reassures loved ones. Each is sublimely optimistic as to his future. The censors' job requires the strictest kind of confidence and complete seriousness of approach.

Morale is ace high. To a man all are anxious to get going and all are confident we are the best damn outfit in the Army, myself included. I never have seen a finer group of enlisted men. They are grand guys, intelligent, ambitious, and unquestioning in their faith that we'll be successful. Surely I am lucky to be a part of such a squadron.

[British Prime Minister Winston Churchill announces that in September, the Italian fleet surrendered at Malta.

Expelled from Corsica by French troops, Germany completes their evacuation of troops from the island.]

Wednesday, October 6: Camp Kilmer, New Jersey—We leave tomorrow, and all but our field packs and valpaks have gone already along with the advance party of officers and men. Tonight, the lid is off. "Prestone" and coke floweth as water in the halls. A fine sextet is born out of a bottle: Perk, Doc Duennebier, Wiley, Forehand, Taylor, and myself. Our rendition of "Down by the Riverside" a tremendous choral achievement worthy of public acclaim.

Joe Arthur was positive he could liquidate the entire BOQ barehanded. Joe was put to bed by Forehand who applied pressure to Joe's toes to achieve same. Forehand's foot lock proved to be a good dissuader.

[Valpak was the common pronunciation of Val-A-Pak, zippered travel bags that could be carried folded or hung from a hook.]

Thursday, October 7: New York Harbor—Goodbye New Jersey and, incidentally, the United States of America. We entrained at 1030, boarding the CNJ *(Central Railroad of New Jersey)* #827 pulling 12 cars. Traveled branch lines to Port Reading, then straight in to Jersey City and the noble ferry *Bayonne* to 43rd Street.

Boarded the U.S.A.T. *Argentina.* She's a good veteran of many war trips and a few running fights. Originally designed for 500 cruise passengers, she was enlarged to hold 4,000 troops, yet we find ourselves double-loaded with nearly 7,000 men. Conditions are really crowded. Men on all the decks, in the scuppers, men everywhere, but no one seems very upset except the second lieutenants. Poor guys.

[The USAT Argentina *(originally the* Pennsylvania*) was built in 1929 for the Panama-Pacific Line, sailing from New York to San Francisco via the Panama Canal. Following a remodel in 1938 she was re-christened the* Argentina *by the American Republics Line and in 1941 she began Atlantic convoy duty.]*

Friday, October 8: At Sea—1:00 A.M.: The Empire State Building and all that is New York loom enticingly against a crisp half moon. A beautiful final glimpse of much that we know and love. And so to bed.

7:00 A.M.: We're at sea, heading east northeast to England. It's a thrilling sight to see our 15 to 20 ships in wide formation. The battleship *Texas* is flagship and a group of destroyers ring us. Ours is a fine ship, one of the largest in the convoy. She displaces 22,000 tons; 33,000 tons loaded. The dining room steward tells me he has been on the *Argentina* since she was built. He provides a marvelous officer's mess. Sets a nice table.

We have beautiful weather and calm sailing.

I stood the 1200 to 1800 hold watch with the men. Terribly stuffy down there and cleanliness is a problem, yet morale is still very high.

Saturday, October 9: At Sea—Another bunch of ships joined us this afternoon. I now have identified the *Kungsholm*, and three of the Grace Line Santa liners, sister ships of the ill-famed *Morro Castle*. The old *America* has been on our starboard beam all the way. Some trim freighters and tankers. Estimate 30 to 40 ships and a rumored 15 destroyers.

PBMs and PBYs have paid us frequent visits. What a thrill to see them overhead.

Monopoly is the game of the day and fortunes are being made and lost. I spent most of today reading Edgar Wallace's *Face in the Night*.

Cater, Donohue, Forehand, Arthur, Hagan, a Lieutenant Lee (Med. Adm.), and myself are bunking in #47. A good gang. Cater, the old salt, who has four years in the Navy at Lexington as a Ranger, is kidding and advising the boys. Great time. We're the focal point for all games and bull sessions.

Another fine smooth day.

[Christened in 1930, the Morro Castle *sailed between New York and Cuba. On September 8, 1934 a fire broke out with the ship about five miles off the Jersey shore. Many of those aboard perished and roughly half of the crew were accused of cowardice, sensationalizing the tragedy.*

The PBY Catalina (Patrol Bomber by Consolidated Aircraft Corporation) was one of the most famous "flying boats" of World War II. This reliable seaplane was primarily used for rescue and reconnaissance, but also participated in bombing missions.

The PBM (Patrol Bomber Mariner by Martin), while lesser known than the PBY, was bigger, faster, had better range, and carried better armament.]

Sunday, October 10: At Sea—A helluva wind blowing today, with low, grey clouds, much white water, and half the ship's populace draped over a rail despite the increasing raw cold. Not terribly rough, but a nice pitch and roll and an ugly looking ocean. This old battlewagon really buries her nose in the green water. Several of us felt rather lousy. I was lucky and got a kick out of the rough day.

Donohue and I had the 1800 to 2400 shift. Most of the gang in bunks, although spirits still good despite "recent illness." A great bunch.

Monday, October 11: At Sea—Beautiful, cloudless day. A crisp, sparkling blue ocean, and PBYs overhead several times to say "hello." It's much colder as we get north and east of Nova Scotia. The ocean is a beautiful thing; its colours and contours are an unending fascination.

All quiet in #47 today. Everyone is sleeping or reading, although we held the usual abandon ship drill at 1400. No more advance warning from here on in.

After supper we had a big bull session in #47. Donohue read passages from the *Bible*. Sex entered the scene inevitably. Joe Arthur expounded on his military career with gestures. We, in turn, reminisced on our flying at Grenier and Farmingdale. Bed at 11:30 P.M.

[*In a message to Congress, President Franklin D. Roosevelt requests the repeal of the Chinese Exclusion Act, stating, "It would be additional proof that we regard China not only as a partner in waging war but that we shall regard her as a partner in days of peace. While it would give the Chinese a preferred status over certain other oriental people, their great contribution to the cause of decency and freedom entitles them to such preference."]*

Tuesday, October 12: At Sea—A beautiful day, but we made little headway due to the destroyers refueling from a tanker in the convoy. Spent most of the daylight hours at it.

Little to record. A few PBYs overhead. Boat drill. Rather monotonous so I slept most of the day.

Donohue and I were on the 2400 to 0600 shift in the hold. I had the damnedest time trying to keep awake, even wrote a poem in desperation. Went on deck awhile to let Stewart have a smoke only to find a gorgeous moonlight night. Ships silhouetted against silver tipped waves. A wondrous sight.

Too clear though; we make good targets.

[Convoys were the lifeblood of the American war effort in Europe. As such they were a high priority for the German war machine with the infamous U-boat its principle weapon. Although sub-hunters like the PBY were always a welcome sight, a convoy relied heavily on its warship escort. With destroyers and even battleships pulled from other duties to fill this defensive role, the Navy recognized the need for a smaller, less expensive purpose-built ship. The result was the destroyer escort, which entered service in January 1943. Since a convoy could only travel as fast as its slowest ship, a destroyer escort did not need the speed of a destroyer, and its weaponry could be specifically tailored to the task at hand. Although it is 3,000 nautical miles from New York to London, convoys routinely took indirect routes to avoid detection. While a Buckley class destroyer escort had a range of 5,500 nautical miles at 15 knots, it was common practice to refuel during the voyage, even though valuable time was lost in the process.]

Wednesday, October 13: At Sea—Forehand appeared to relieve my feeble body at 0700. Whew. Bathed and shaved. A big breakfast then into the sack! Hot dog.

We enjoyed another beautiful day, clear and quite calm. We've had great weather for this time of year.

Lost $3.90 in rummy, dammit. Rotten cards all the way. Had a big bull session again last night, until 2:00 A.M. An intelligent and dispassionate discussion of sex, mostly by Donohue. Amazing difference in outlook.

The ship seems to be rolling more as I drop off to sleep, hmmmm?

["I take great pleasure in informing you that His Majesty the King of Italy has declared war on Germany . . . By this act all ties with the dreadful past are broken and my Government will be proud to be able to march with you on to the inevitable victory . . ."—excerpt from a message to General Dwight D. Eisenhower from Marshal Pietro Badoglio and the new Italian government.]

Thursday, October 14: At Sea—Our seventh day out and we're into rough weather; it's been increasing all day. Squalls of rain scud, and now, at 1600, a solid leaden overcast with big waves coming at our rear quarter to give pitch and roll. Why we're not all sick I don't know, although Pino was this morning. Thomas rigged up a protractor showing degrees roll and pitch. Roll ten degrees and pitch five degrees.

It's fascinating to watch the other ships, an advantage of company on an ocean cruise. Damn near go out of sight then loom up. Even our ship and the *Kungsholm* are really rolling. The Grace liners look like they'll tip over.

Dirty weather, but fun, and spoils the tin fish's aim. Let her blow!!

[The 8th Army Air Forces carries out Mission 115, a massive attack against the ball bearing works at Schweinfurt, Germany. B-17 bomber losses are horrifying and the United States halts daylight raids into Germany that exceed the range of fighter escort. The deployment of the long range P-51 Mustang will allow the resumption of bombing missions deep into Germany, starting with "Big Week" in February 1944.]

Friday, October 15: At Sea—Really rough yesterday, smashed dishes in the dining room, library a mass of books, terrific waves running as high as "A" Deck. Other ships' whole hull would disappear. One roll was 14 degrees, or 28 degrees, total. Never imagined big liners rolled so much. Thought the *Oriente* was gonna capsize once behind us.

Today is still rough, but not quite as violent. A few rain squalls.

Saw our first Royal Air Force Coastal Command Sunderland today. Quite a thrill, we're really getting there. Perhaps Monday.

I was on duty from noon to 1730. Then I read Dos Passos' *The Big Money*. It was good, but disturbing in its hardboiled realism. A big rummy game in #47 tonight.

[Carrying 10 crewmen, the Sunderlands entered the Royal Air Force Command Service in 1938 as long-range reconnaissance and anti-submarine aircraft.]

Saturday, October 16: At Sea—The dirtiest weather yet, really vicious looking. Not as rough as Thursday, but a low thick overcast and driving rain with sea a white angry froth and decks deserted, cold and raw and wet.

Played rummy, read, slept, and ate candy. The meals are still terrific. Gus, our room steward is a great entertainment. We're getting more restless now that the trip's end is in sight. The men are still bearing up pretty swell. Much equipment has "changed hands" but our boys won't come out short if I'm any judge.

Sunday, October 17: Arrive Liverpool Harbor—Gus woke us at 8:00 A.M. He opened the porthole. <u>Land</u>. Saw beautiful rugged hills, although quite barren, like the hills of California only green. Ireland. A few sections like mesas. Way off to port the Outer Hebrides looked quite mountainous, like New England.

A beautiful clear day with clouds ahead. Two Spitfires buzzed the Hell out of us in the morning. Some thrill. Our first Spits. Beautiful.

We spent all day sailing down between the Hebrides, through the Firth of Clyde, Isle of Man, past Belfast and the Antrim Plateau of Ireland. A beautiful coast, a thrilling sail. The convoy is gradually breaking up. Boats dropping out for Glasgow, some of us on to Liverpool, others will go on down into the Irish Sea. We anchored in Liverpool Roadstead shortly after dark.

Monday, October 18: Liverpool Harbor—At anchor 'til after noon. The *Kungsholm* and the *Monterey* are still with us. Into the Mersey River and docked at Mersey floating dock about 4:15 P.M. with the *Kungsholm* ahead of us.

Liverpool looks big, filled with drab brick buildings. Rows of warehouses, docks, ship cranes, little river boats, church and government buildings, towers, no lights, very smoky, and the whole scene transcended into shadowy substance by a gray-pink tinted sundown haze, reducing everything to mere bulk and outline, like a Turner landscape. Very fascinating.

Stout little tug brought Port Officer and Pilot aboard out in Roadstead. Several British officers were also on board.

I'm in charge of clean up of men's area. Whew!! All packed, and in the hold with the men most of the afternoon and night. A grand final supper on board.

[J.M.W. Turner was an English artist whose landscape paintings in the

first half of the 19th century influenced the rise of Impressionism in the 1860s.

Chiang Kai-shek is sworn in as president of China.]

Tuesday, October 19: Debark. England at last!—The men debarked at 5:15 A.M. I signed clearances, checked with the Port Officer, and was last 5418M off ship. The train shed by the dock was about a 300-yard walk and everything was dark, in a blackout.

My valpak is in a goods van, with two vans on the back of the train. I sat in the first class LNER *(London and North Eastern Railway)* car with Colonel Tacon, Major Tyrrell, Thomas, and a warrant officer, our guide.

Fascinating trains. Smooth riding. Comfortable seats, fast. Beautiful ride. A grand clear day as we traveled around south of Manchester to Stockport, up a valley climbing over the Pennine Range. Four mile tunnel at Summit. Down into Sheffield. Coal, coal! Into level country of Lincolnshire. Coffee at Lincolnshire.

Then onto branch lines to Wretham and Hockham at 3:30 P.M.

Wretham and Hockham Train Station, Norfolk.
Courtesy of Thomas P. Smith: Archived by Char Baldridge, Historian, 359th Fighter Group Association

Two miles by Jeep to Wretham Hall, a 52-room estate. So this is it. We're in England. I like it.

Wretham Hall, one mile from East Wretham Airfield USAAF Station Number 133,
six miles northeast of Thetford in Norfolk.
Courtesy of J. McAlister: Archived by Char Baldridge, Historian, 359th Fighter Group Association

Wretham Hall, one mile from East Wretham Airfield. "D" Flight occupied the 2nd floor room to
the right of the entrance.*Archived by Char Baldridge, Historian, 359th Fighter Group Association,
from records at HQ USAF Research Center, Maxwell Air Force Base, Alabama*

[Northeast of London in Norfolk, the heart of East Anglia, East Wretham airfield was rapidly built in the early days of the war and became operational in March 1940. It consisted of grass runways, the northeast to southwest measuring 5,640 feet and north-northwest to south-southeast at 4,200 feet. The Royal Air Force requisitioned Wretham Hall, located approximately one mile from the airfield, for use as an officers' mess.

East Wretham and its various hangars and buildings, as well as Wretham Hall, officially transferred to United States forces in July 1943 with the three fighter squadrons arriving that autumn. East Wretham was assigned USAAF designation Station 133.

As the 368th Fighter Squadron settles into its quarters at Wretham Hall, bad weather and unwavering German defenses bog down the US 5th Army's offensive along the Volturno River in south central Italy.]

Wednesday, October 20: Wretham—Rooming with Baldy, Wiley, Davis, Renken, Doc, and Stewart. Very nice and we have plenty of room. Some house, with its marble floored hall, wrought iron banister, and fine inlaid hardwood floors. We have two dining rooms, the Red Room and the

Green Room. Two servings. Food is better than expected. Coffee!

We drew our bicycles in the afternoon. Seem like good bikes. Great sport riding around. Lovely grounds, woods, like a forest preserve in northern Illinois. Two little ponds. A ruined abbey in vines, hundreds of years old.

Little stone cottages, barns, hedges, lanes, and local country folk are all quite fascinating. A grand spot.

Played Ping-Pong and drank English warm ale.

"Abbey" ruins near Wretham Hall.
Courtesy of Thomas P. Smith: Archived by Char Baldridge, Historian, 359th Fighter Group Association

There's one C-5 *(P-47 Thunderbolt)* on the field about a mile away. Little hope of flying now. Grass field looks pretty good, though.

This place is really blacked out at night.

Thursday, October 21: Wretham—English rain! Got soaked going to the cycle shop to have pedals tightened. Nice wood fires burning.

Major Stewart and good old Fieg were here. Flew over in the afternoon from Bodney. Fieg the same swell redhead. They've been here four months. The 352nd is about eight miles from here. Hope to see Brown, Gates, Davis, and Gerst soon. Major Stewart swell as ever.

Alm is gone. His oxygen gave out over the Channel. Eacker spun in when overshooting.

Received a lecture on Negroes. English treat them as our equal, a ticklish situation.

This place is still amazing, like a big fraternity house. Played more Ping-Pong, drank ale, and did a bit of reading: *Punch* and *Illustrated Post.*

Searchlights and flares at night, .50 cal firing southwest of us. Jerry overhead in overcast somewhere. A bit spooky.

Friday, October 22: Wretham—Beautiful day. Quite mild and sunny.

Davis flew over and phoned me from line. I rode down to the airfield and had a good chat. He's the same as ever. Gave us a good buzz when he left. Good pilot.

Had tea and cakes from YMCA wagon at 11:00 A.M. English women run it. Very nice. Rode into Hockham with Smithy, Forehand, and Hunter in

Bicyclist approaching Wretham Hall. *Courtesy of Thomas P. Smith; Archived by Char Baldridge, Historian, 359th Fighter Group Association*

the afternoon via Wretham, about five miles.

Lovely countryside. Quaint, tiny town. Bought cycle lamps in a little shop next to a garage. Saw school children dancing to Victrola. Very picturesque, a few thatched roofs. Good time.

Played Hearts after supper and some Ping-Pong.

Many group changes announced today. Swanson swaps with Gray. We lose Taylor and Downing and get Mosse and McGeever. No one is very happy about it. Why wait until now to switch around?

Saturday, October 23: Wretham—Whitey Gerst was here today. He too, looked mighty good and is the same old guy. Sure great seeing these guys.

Didn't do much. Bicycles, Ping-Pong, and cards the order of the day. We all saw a swell stage (mobile unit) show. Darn good singer, a boy magician, a <u>real</u> violinist, some beef trust dancers, piano, and drums. And an English version of Betty Hutton. Really the best such show I've ever seen. Interesting to note that the men liked the violinist best and requested several encores of classical, serious playing, a high tribute to the calibre of our enlisted personnel.

[*Howard's in-laws, Edouard Dethier and Avis Putnam Dethier, met at The Juilliard School in New York City where Edouard taught violin and Avis studied voice, hence Howard's interest in classical violin and his notation about a real violinist.*]

Sunday, October 24: Wretham—Another day as the others. Jamison popped in, in a Spitfire V much to our amazement and delight. Came down from Wing. I sat in the Spit's cockpit. Very small. <u>Very</u> comfortable. Feel just like you're part of the plane. Jointed stick. Whole ship very small, smaller than I'd imagined. Looked like a toy next to our C-5. Gave us a swell show buzzing Hell out of us after lunch.

We saw "Ball of Fire" at night. A very good movie but it made us all quite nostalgic for New York.

[*The Spitfire was a fast, light, highly maneuverable short-range fighter that rose to fame during the Battle of Britain in the summer of 1940. The "Spit" was powered by the same Rolls Royce Merlin V-12 engine that was later licensed to Packard for use in the P-51 Mustang.*]

Monday, October 25: Wretham—Gates and Brown over this afternoon. Haven't changed a bit. Brownie full of the devil. They really worked us over proper! Below tree line!

We're having ground school now, about two and a half hours, daily. Good stuff. Studying everything from aircraft recognition, to flight control, to air-sea rescue, to R/T, and so on. It's important that we know all this.

Wiley, Donohue, and Shaw in London for four days of school. Bet they have fun.

I left for Cambridge on the 558 train with Janney, Burton, Baldy, Stearns and Doc. Third class, nice coach. English Speaking Union. Six girls. Had supper at King's Parade. Good! Walked to Rex and it was just closing, but lots of fun wandering around in blackout. Bed at 51 Jesus Lane.

Tuesday, October 26: Cambridge—A swell day, foggy but we had fun. Ate a nice breakfast, wandered through bookshops looking at train books. Found more shops in the pipe-narrow streets. Went to The Union, had lunch at Toni's, drank a wonderful sherry.

Took a walk for an hour alone, to King's College Chapel. King's College, Trinity College, The Backs along River Cam, beautiful parks, really an impressive place. Saw bicycles, bobbies, uniforms, market baskets, lines at stores, six cadets marching down Trinity Street. The public washrooms are underground. Very high buses dwarfing all else. A kind old engineer offered me a ride in his engine, a 4-4-0 of the older vintage.

A foggy blackout, then back to Thetford Square, caught the bus, into bed at midnight. Fun!

[In the United States the accepted standard for classifying steam locomotives is the Whyte notation of wheel arrangement. A 4-4-0 would have four leading wheels, which help support the front end and negotiate curves, four driving wheels, and in this instance no trailing wheels, which would otherwise help support the cab if necessary.]

Wednesday, October 27: Wretham Hall—Have a helluva head cold and the weather is lousy to match.

Classes in Hall, very swell.

Drew an engine in brown ink. Didn't go out at all. Very dull day.

McGeever is back in "A" Flight. Downing sent to Group. Swanson commanding officer of 369th. Gray, to Group Operations. Charlie Mosse (captain from 369th) takes over "B" Flight. He's a good, quiet, regular little guy from Arizona.

[Promoted to first lieutenant on July 24, 1943, as flight leader of "D" Flight, Howard held a position usually assigned to a pilot with the rank of captain.]

Thursday, October 28: Wretham—Same as Wednesday. Wrote some letters, drank a bit of ale.

The boys from London returned. Some stories they had to tell. The Piccadilly Commandos are really wild. Underground bars. Women. Women. Women. All lonely and eager.

My principles will meet the acid test in London, I imagine. Dammit! I sure deny myself a lot of fun. Guess it's worth it, tho.

[Dedicated to one another for 53 years, Margot returned Howard's sentiment. In a January 18, 1943 letter to her best friend, Margot wrote, "You ask me if I'm really in love with him, well, it's not quite the way I've always thought was the way one felt when in love, but it's something a little difficult to explain. The feeling I have for Howie is somehow more secure and quiet. I just know that I want more than anything to be his wife and to be the mother of his children (imagine me wanting kids!). I know that I miss him simply horribly and just live for the days when we're together. When I'm with him I feel a peace and contentment I've never known before. When I go to the station to meet him I'm as excited and nervous as a kid on her first date and when I say goodbye, I just leave a part of me behind. If that isn't love, I guess I'll never know what love is. Maybe this sounds like a lot of slush, and maybe it doesn't make any sense, but I don't know how else to try to explain. I just know.*"]*

Friday, October 29: 65th Wing HQ—Another lousy day of weather.

Took the liberty bus to the 65th eight miles past Cambridge. Nice sightseeing fun via NewMarket. Ate a good lunch.

A swell S-2 *(squadron intelligence)* colonel spoke and I watched flight control set up. Then an air-sea rescue lieutenant lectured. Really a marvelous set up. House buoys, speedboats, airplanes. They pulled 114 men out in a 24-hour period, four weeks ago. Have also pulled men off the French coast.

Bought some real honest-to-god milk chocolate at their PX. Returned at 5:15 P.M. Forehand and Simmons were dropped off at Cambridge and reappeared about 10:00 P.M. with a few weeks old puppy, one-half cocker and one-half wirehair. Butch. Perfect. Also a Victrola. Great time.

Saturday, October 30: Wretham—Nuttin' to report. Same as a dozen other lousy days.

> [*The Tripartite conference in Moscow concludes, where the United States, Great Britain, and the Soviet Union are unanimous in their determination that it is essential to continue their close collaboration and cooperation into the period following the end of hostilities.*]

Sunday, October 31: Cambridge—Borrowed five pounds from Doc and Baldy and headed for Cambridge again, this time with two other officers in a command car minus curtains. Made the trip in one hour flat. We hit 60 and nearly hit trees, tanks, and trucks. Some ride! Frozen when we arrived.

Had a good room at the Blue Boar. Lousy supper, tho, went to a pub, The Volunteer, run by a former heavyweight who is quite a character. Drank some ale. Dropped in at The Union for a while. Saw Janney and Burton with dates. Sunday night very quiet. Turned in at 10:30 P.M. Wonderful beds!

Air raid alarm sounded, some spooky sound. We rolled over and went to sleep.

Thetford Station, Norfolk. *Courtesy of Elsie Palicka, wife of Ed Palicka, 370th Fighter Squadron Photographer: Archived by Char Baldridge, Historian, 359th Fighter Group Association*

2.

NOVEMBER 1943

The Calm Before the Storm

Monday, November 1: Cambridge—Breakfast stunk. Th' Hell with the Blue Boar.

Found a fine book on watercolours and more ink and some pen points. Ate lunch with Burt and Janney at K.P. Walked through St. Johns, Kings, and Trinity Colleges, the chapel, and back again.

Still drizzling. Got fed up and caught the 430 train to Thetford.

Rode in a 1935 Ford V8 cab to the Hall in time for second chow at 6:30 P.M. Good time, but oh this weather.

Tuesday, November 2: Wretham—Back to the daily routine of sketching, Ping-Pong, and reading. Little to report. Vicious volleyball games after the afternoon lectures.

Lemmens, the junior officer, gets the first plane. He's excited, got a D-5 *(P-47 Thunderbolt)*, and they have 'em at Wattisham depot, a 10 minute flight from here. They're working rank backwards, a good deal.

The Colonel was lost coming back. Andy said they landed at the wrong field. Navigation is really rough. When in doubt, land anywhere.

Got paid in pounds 22/11/10.

[The P-47 Thunderbolt was built by American Republic. The D series was first put into service in February 1943 and by September had reached version D-25. Effective in air combat and adept in a ground attack role, this large, single-engine fighter plane also served as a medium range bomber escort when fitted with external fuel tanks.]

Wednesday, November 3: Wretham—Painted a watercolour.

Thursday, November 4: Wretham—Weather is much better.

Painted a good scene of a B&O *(Baltimore & Ohio Railroad)* in the Alleghany hills. A pretty, nostalgic look. That new book helps a lot.

Kibler won the toss and flew. It was some sight, him tearing down the line on his bike in full flying equipment, parachute bouncing on the fender.

More planes coming in. Hyland and Hudelson got D-5s. Lane has a D-10. He's proud. No one else will fly those ships.

[Newer versions of the Thunderbolt, such as the P-47D-10, incorporated changes such as additional cooling flaps around the back of the cowl to reduce overheating of the turbosupercharged, air-cooled radial engine. A bubble canopy was adapted from British modifications to the plane, replacing the original design which had impaired rearward visibility.]

Friday, November 5: Wretham—Bull shit!

[The Senate passes the Connally resolution in which it is "Resolved . . . that the United States, acting through its constitutional processes, join with free and sovereign nations in the establishment and maintenance of international authority with power to prevent aggression and to preserve the peace of the world."]

Saturday, November 6: Wretham—It's cold as Hell out and sparkling clear.

No more single days off. Two days off in 14 instead, which is much better. Will go to London the 13th and 14th.

Major Tyrrell and Botsford have planes now. Sam White has his, was ferried in here. We also have a Fairchild C-61, a sweet little plane with a "Scarab" engine. Nice.

Tonight saw Fred Astaire in "Sky's the Limit."

Sunday, November 7: Wretham—Baldy and I took a bike ride around the estate, very pretty. Nice day. Fall colouring at its height here. Woods are lovely.

Wretham Hall estate (note ruins in lower left corner). *Courtesy of Elsie Palicka, wife of Ed Palicka, 370th Fighter Squadron Photographer: Archived by Char Baldridge, Historian, 359th Fighter Group Association*

Wiley returned from a week with Eagle Squadron (334th) 4th Group. Some outfit! He had a wonderful time. He's our G-2 *(group intelligence officer)* now. Donohue has shifted to Group. I rarely see him anymore.

Monday, November 8: Wretham—We went for a ride in a C-47 30218 this morning, landed at Wattisham to drop Shaw, Baldy, Perk, and Hawk. Randy was already there with Burton to pick 'em up. Good pilot, sweet landing. Great fun riding in that big crate.

Very hazy, tough to pick up check points on our maps. Woods are well indicated. Railways and roads are tricky. This damn East Anglia looks like Long Island in miniature, individual dimensions. Loads of big air fields. Really enjoyed the flight.

Had tea at tea wagon on our return at 11:00 A.M. Volleyball and a half mile run with Bo in the afternoon. Painted "Wiley's Commando." A rough babe!

[The C-47 or Gooney Bird was the military version of the Douglas DC-3 passenger plane and was used to haul troops, carry tons of equipment, or tow troop-carrying gliders.]

Memo: Have had nearly 40 V-mails from Mom, Dad, Margot, and Auntie Bert. Christmas package arrived with two books from Harrie and Betty. Received a few regular letters and a cute birth announcement from Beanie Herway, a son. Card from Marybelle Webb. Card from Grandma.

Our V-mail must be slower than Hell. They haven't even seen my new Army Post Office number as of October 27th. What a rotten break for the family, waiting so long.

[V-mail was based on the British "Airgraph" system, whereby censored mail was photographed, reduced to finger-size onto reels of microfilm, and then shipped overseas. Developed at a receiving station, the correspondence was then printed at about 25 percent of actual size on lightweight photo-paper. This miniature mail would then be delivered to the recipient.]

Cartoon from a V-mail re: Weather. By Captain Howard Fogg
Courtesy of Roy C. Weiss: Archived by Char Baldridge, Historian, 359th Fighter Group Association

Tuesday, November 9: Wretham—Spent entire day painting:
1) Hagan's Hosters
2) Train Busters
3) Doc Duennebier's Adv

Lots of fun, but tiring. No ground school, hence the amount of work. Too damn cold out to sketch the scenery about the place. Didn't even drink any port.

All the second looeys save Hunter and Simmons now have their planes, all D-5s, 6s, and 10s. Shaw and Major also have theirs. Damn!

Broach (369th) piled up our Fairchild in a ground loop. I had a chance to fly it, too, as it was available to flight leaders. Hell.

Colonel Woodbury (Wing P/O) *(Pilot/Officer of the Royal Air Force)* dropped in. A good guy, it seems.

[With the exception of a few cartoons and paintings that he mailed home, Howard gifted his paintings to fellow pilots and friends or discarded the examples that didn't fulfill his expectations.]

Wednesday, November 10: Wretham—P/O Lyne lectured on the African campaign and Malta. Very interesting. He's our RAF liaison S-2 officer. Recently returned from Malta.

Changed days off with Hunter so three of us could get our planes. Went to London with Perkins and Stearns on the six o'clock.

The London train. *Courtesy of Elsie Palicka, wife of Ed Palicka, 370th Fighter Squadron Photographer: Archived by Char Baldridge, Historian, 359th Fighter Group Association*

Arrived Liverpool Street 10:00 P.M. Wonderful visibility, a big moon and haze, which caused diffused light. Could see people a hundred feet away. Cab to Reindeer Club, then billeting office, then to Regis Hotel on Russell Square.

[General Eisenhower announces formation of the Allied Control Commission for Italy. The Commission is tasked with aligning the Italian economy in complete support of the fight against Germany.

The War Department announces that the Army Air Forces have withdrawn from anti-submarine operations and that the United States Navy has assumed full responsibility, with a mission to seek out and destroy hostile submarines wherever at sea, in three different theaters of operations.]

Thursday, November 11: London—Went sightseeing, then to the Reindeer Club. Bought railroad books, browsed shops. Took a cab to "Strike a New Note," a wonderful musical with Sid Field. Two bars in Piccadilly then dinner at Prince's and listened to music. Bed at 10:30 P.M., dead tired. Swell time.

[With "Strike a New Note," Sid Field struck the funny bone of war-weary London audiences, achieving the success he'd sought for decades. His comedic prowess and acting skills took him from the Royal Palladium to film and television. Bob Hope once remarked that Sid was "probably the best comedian of them all." Sadly, Sid's career was cut short in 1950 when he died from a heart attack at age 45.]

Friday, November 12: London—Up at 10:00 A.M. Breakfast at Reindeer Club.

Me to Waterloo, took train to Clapham Junction then underground to Paddington, Euston and King's Cross. Back to the Club at four. Tea. Train from Liverpool Street at 5:46 P.M. Thetford at 9:30 P.M. Beautiful moon. Cold as Hell.

[Czechoslovakia and the Soviet Union sign a treaty in Moscow pledging mutual aid in prosecuting the war, no separate peace, and mutual respect for each other's sovereignty.]

Saturday, November 13: Wretham—Got my plane!
Captain Pezda of the 370th and I went to Wattisham in the command

car. Captain Irvine flew down to lead us back. I have a P-47D-10, 275104, with a P&W *(Pratt & Whitney)* R-2800-63 engine. Eleven hours on the ship. Flies beautifully. It's a thousand pounds lighter than the D-2s.

Lieutenant Howard Fogg's P-47D-10 Thunderbolt CV-T 42-75104. *Courtesy of Peter Fogg*

I landed at dusk with field lights after coming in Xtee *(cross-wind)* first try. First pilot to land with lights here. Captain Malley (Control) all excited. Me too!

Sunday, November 14: Wretham—Lousy day.
   Nothing done on my plane with my mechanic, Freddy Gall, on leave.
   Painted a picture or two, wrote a few letters.

Monday, November 15: Wretham—Plane needs lots of attention. Gall's unhappy. Need hydraulic relief valve, new accumulator. Lord knows when we'll get 'em.
   Listened to a wonderful lecture by Lieutenant Colonel Heinrichs, A-2, Wing. He's a professor from Middlebury, Vermont and a flier in the last war. Lectured on Russia and Italy. Really an eye-opener. Very good!
   Getting a nice cold again.
   Started a locomotive model out of cardboard today.

[The Allied Expeditionary Force for the invasion of Europe is officially formed.]

Tuesday, November 16: Wretham—Head cold.

No parts for my plane.

Worked on locomotive model.

Took aircraft recognition tests.

Had meeting of Flight. Good bull session, elements sort of formed. Me and Baldy, Kibler and Hunter, Hag and Randy. Use of nicknames rather than code numbers agreed on.

[In German-controlled Tinn, Norway, 160 US bombers strike the Vemork hydroelectric power facility and heavy water factory.]

Wednesday, November 17: Wretham—Still have cold.

No parts for my plane.

Worked on locomotive model.

Talked to Colonel Tacon about compressibility. Very enlightening.

Baldy and Davis really tied one on tonight. The rum here is poison. Baldy was wild, mad drunk. Threw a glass of rum at the ceiling. Fell over furniture. Really a rough time.

Talked to P/O Lyne, very nice chap. Oxford graduate who teaches in a big public school. Wants to take a group of us through Oxford and Colonel Tacon sez okay. I'm all for it.

[Compressibility can occur when high-speed airflow over the aircraft's control surfaces impairs their function. Usually associated with a high-speed dive, severe compressibility can result in a total loss of control.]

Thursday, November 18: Wretham—Baldy doesn't remember a thing.

Painted on plane insignia in cold canvas hangar all day. Hands nearly numb. Paint equipment is poor but it looks fair.

Gall is still fighting trouble in the hydraulic system on my plane.

My cold is worse.

Worked on the locomotive model.

Had tea at eleven. Hit the spot. No wonder the English drink tea:

1) to keep warm

2) to prevent starvation

Friday, November 19: Wretham—Cold as Hell. Frost. Clear. I feel lousy. Painted all morning, stayed in all afternoon working on the locomotive.

Have had letters from Gross, Kiel, and Paul.

Heard that Kim Urion was killed ferrying a Grumman Avenger from Floyd Bennett to Knoxville. Engine failure. Jumped too late. A helluva shock. He was a swell kid, good pilot. I'll get one for Kim. Paul *(Kim's father)* asked me to!

Saturday, November 20: Wretham—Cold as Hell. Fog. Damp. Frost.

"D" Flight to Saffron, Walden for dinghy drill in school pool. Cold truck ride, used blankets. Fun with dinghies in warmed pool water. Great dinghy battles. They're a wonderful institution. Lunch at Duxford (78th). Nice set up in an old RAF Station. Cold ride back.

Roast pheasant in Room 215. The boys (Hunter, Perk, Simmons, Randy) bagged a half dozen. Cooked 'em in the fireplace.

There was a helluva brawl here. About a dozen guys expected gals. Everyone skunk drunk. Fights. Broken glasses. A rough night. Wild tie cutting. Colonel Smith mad!

Sunday, November 21: Wretham—Miserable foggy day.

Really feel lousy. Everyone is half sick with colds and sore throats.

Worked on locomotive engine. Didn't go out.

Three hour bull session by Major to us flight leaders. Pretty sickening crap on combat, tactics, blah blah.

Very dull day.

Lieutenant Colonel Grady L. Smith, Station Executive.
Courtesy of Paul D. Bruns, 369th Fighter Squadron Flight Surgeon: Archived by Char Baldridge, Historian, 359th Fighter Group Association

[Field Marshal Kesselring is designated commander-in-chief of German forces in Italy.

The Royal Air Force begins a series of concentrated night attacks against Berlin.]

Monday, November 22: Wretham—Still lousy weather. Still feel like Hell.

Lecture on S.D.158 by P/O Lyne in the morning. Good job on a dull subject.

A little flying late in the afternoon, didn't even go to the line myself.

Everyone disgusted with weather and food, which is quite poor and monotonous. Boys hunting pheasants this afternoon.

Ettlesen blew in today. Four days and 18 hours on the *Queen Mary* to Scotland, a record run. Looks fine. Good to have him back in the gang.

Don't know what my status will be now. Here's hoping against hope I can keep my flight.

[Entering British airspace, pilots were required to comply with Secret Document 158; flying at 5,000 feet or immediately below the cloud cover, whichever was lowest, so that their plane could be readily identified by ground observers.

A conference between President Roosevelt, Prime Minister Churchill, and Generalissimo Chiang Kai-shek begins in north Africa. The three allies discuss future military operations to restrain and punish Japanese aggression and to restore those territories that Japan has taken by violence since the First World War.]

Tuesday, November 23: Wretham—Same old story. Lousy day. Feel like Hell.

Excellent lecture on geography of Continent's coastline, flak, landmarks, and so on by a captain with 50 missions out of the 56th Group. Damn good.

Flying in the afternoon but the field closed in 15 minutes. Worse than Suffolk. A wonder everyone didn't spin in. Cater landed at Walton. Baldy and Hagan at Hemphall. Really had us worried due to poor phone. We had to sweat 'em out for four hours.

Flight meeting regarding our plane numbers, etc.

Went down to line, my first time outdoors since Friday. Plane in good shape, all painted. Only needs sump #10 rocker box. Gall in better spirits.

[Adolf Hitler watches a demonstration flight of the Me 262, a prototype jet airplane.]

Wednesday, November 24: Wretham—Pretty good day.

Still feel rotten, though. Goddam this head of mine!

Hag and Baldy flew back in the morning. Seems they landed immediately as the weather got bad, at 1520. Good headwork.

Part for my ship came in this afternoon. She'll be ready in the morning but Doc has grounded me. Dammit.

Thanksgiving, November 25: Wretham—Beautiful day.

Nose packs in my nose. Went down to line. Everyone flying. Not me. Hell! Cater flew my ship. Hydraulics out again. Double Hell!

Turkey for dinner.

Our "Yanks" GI team beat the "Rebs" in the squadron, in a hot touch football game.

I went to bed at 6:30 P.M. Bound and determined to go to London tomorrow.

Curse this weather, the dampness, cold rooms, poor ventilation.

[Likely precipitated by the clammy, cold English weather and flying at altitude in icy, unpressurized cockpits, Howard struggled with regular bouts of painful, chronic sinusitis both during and after the war.]

Friday, November 26: London—Caught the 933 from Thetford via a Jeep with Sergeant Rocher at the wheel. Rode down with Gall and Hightower. Reached Liverpool Street at 1:30 P.M. "Lunch" in station. Cab to Red Cross billet for a single room at 105 Gloucester Place W.I. in a nice old home like the Millikens'.

Reindeer Club for tea. Bought Christmas cards and a ticket to "Hi-de-Hi" in the seventh row. A spotty, at times funny musical with Flanagan and Allan, much like Olsen and Johnson, in a huge theatre (Stoll, an old opera house). Cold.

Rode the Underground to Piccadilly, walked to the Reindeer Club to eat, walked back to room. Black as Hell out. Foul weather.

Bed at 11:00 P.M. Very comfortable.

Saturday, November 27: London—Lousy weather. Mist, fog, rain.

Breakfast in bed, some class! Up and out at 10:00 A.M. Cab to Reindeer Club. Bought a book for Davis. Cab to Basset-Lowke. A few wonderful railroad models on display. Bought a 4-4-0 live steamer second-hand for six pounds, cute as Hell, and will she run! Wow!

Lunch at Liverpool Street. Caught the 233 Saturday train, pulled by 3-cylinder 4-6-0, Bastwick Castle, 1930. Good engine. I reached Thetford at 6:00 P.M.

Truck ready and waiting. Reached Wretham Hall at 6:40 P.M., in time for supper.

Ran the steamer to the amazement and delight of all. A wild time in 207. "Master Mech" Stuart fired her up. She ran for 35 minutes.

[The British 8th Army offensive across the Sangro River in southern Italy begins.]

Sunday, November 28: Wretham—A lousy day.

I felt good in London. This room is poisonous. My head is awful again, just awful. Goddam this Hall to Hell!

My plane is being modified for belly tank. Hydraulics still out.

Rained so I slept all afternoon. Went to bed again after supper. Wot a day!

[In his November 1944 Informal Report of Morale, after Howard had returned stateside, Chaplain Wilbur C. "Chappie" Ziegler reports on the 359th's new commanding officer, stating, "I guess the one thing that made him immediately popular was that he thought the barracks were too cold." The following month's report states, "thanks to Colonel Randolph's interest, the Hall is much warmer than it has ever been before."

Howard's diary entries now begin to include daily notations of those he wrote letters to. Although most of those daily notes are excluded from this text, it was his habit to write a V-mail or Airmail to his beloved Maggie at least three times a week, or daily when extraordinary events took place. Howard also wrote faithfully to his parents and other friends and family.]

Monday, November 29: Wretham—Clear visibility, 5/10ths clouds, rest of squadron flying all day.

I feel good again. Hallelujah! Got <u>un</u>grounded by Major Hiles (Doc has gone to school in Bristol for a week).

Plane is still out, needs hydraulic pump and relief valve. Gall is pissed off, no one to work on my ship. Hope I can fly tomorrow.

Boys are still bringing in pheasant every night. They're some gang of hunters. Hunter's gun jamming, Perk and Simmons shooting over Forehand's head, Forehand chasing an old hen through the woods with a club. The cooks breaded it tonight, simply delicious! Zombie is getting fat on pheasant scraps.

Oh these pilots, all nuts!

[Pilots referred to the amount of cloud cover in 10ths, with 10/10ths being solid overcast.

President Roosevelt, Prime Minister Churchill and Soviet Leader Joseph V. Stalin meet in Tehran, Iran, to discuss the future of postwar Poland and Germany.]

Tuesday, November 30: Wretham—Flying again today. I feel more like myself, a little pep. My ship is still out though, dammit.

Went to Yarmouth this afternoon. Saw RAF air-sea rescue with HSLs (Hi-speed launches). Great little boats, 63 feet long, wood hull, powered by three 500 horsepower Napiers, maximum of 35 knots, cruise at 27. Carry a crew of 12. Number 2551 has picked up 29 plane crewmen. We had tea on her, nice skipper. A wonderful service, coordinated with Navy.

Major Richmond is here from the 352nd to lead our first operation. Looks like we'll be operational this week. And me with a goddam lousy 20 minutes.

Letter from Bob today, he's in P-38s now.

Brownie is missing. Their flight was jumped by Me109s. Last seen, Brownie was chasing a 109 down through overcast at 25,000 feet. Goddam it! Hope he bailed out. Crazy little guy, sounds just like him. Wish I could see Gates. He must feel awful.

[Every new fighter group had to be led into combat by experienced pilots. Senior flying officers of the 359th were assigned to Duxford on detached service to the 78th Fighter Group while Major Luther H. Richmond of the 352nd Fighter Group arrived at Wretham to act as temporary group commander.

The Lockheed P-38 Lightning was a fast, powerful, twin boom aircraft. Major strengths in combat included superb maneuverability at low altitudes, concentrated firepower, and a terrific rate of climb. Early versions of the P-38 were especially vulnerable to compressibility.

The Messerschmitt Me109 was the standard fighter of the Luftwaffe. The most advanced fighter in the world when put into service in 1937, this lightweight, all-metal design received a constant stream of refinements to the powerplant, armament, and other areas that kept it competitive with Allied fighter aircraft until the end of the war. Weaknesses included its short range and a very narrow track which made it unstable during take off and landing.]

Beginning with Chapter 3, December 1943, each chapter will be followed by excerpts that have been selected from transcriptions of the original monthly narrative History of the 359th Fighter Group, archived at HQ USAF Historical Research Center, Maxwell Air Force Base, Alabama. The complete documents were transcribed by Char Baldridge, Historian, 359th Fighter Group Association, from reports filed from December 1943 through September 1945 by Maurice F.X. Donohue, 359th Fighter Group historian and combat intelligence officer.

3.

DECEMBER 1943

Operational!

Wednesday, December 1: Wretham—Goddam sonafabitch! Woke at 4:00 A.M. in real pain, left jaw, teeth, eye. Here we go again.

Had a practice Field Order at 0600. Cancelled at 0800. Staggered down to line at 0830. Went to Major Hiles at 0900 and he slapped me in quarters. He packed my nose again. Ouch. I hit the sack at 4:00 P.M. and stayed! God, I'm sick of this business.

My ship is all ready, belly tank installed. Baldy flew her in the afternoon. Said she handles sweet.

Cater to hospital for observation for stomach cramps, vomiting. Hiles thinks it may be "air nerves." Hmmm??

[The Tehran Conference ends with consensus achieved amongst the three Allies on how to divide postwar Germany and the westward re-alignment of the Polish eastern and western frontiers. The Soviet proposal to execute 50,000 German officers is rejected by the Allies.

The following statements are released:

"No power on earth can prevent our destroying the German armies by land, their U-boats by sea, and their war plants from the air.

"Our attack will be relentless and increasing.

"Emerging from these cordial conferences, we look with confidence

45

to the day when all peoples of the world may lead free lives, untouched by tyranny, and according to their varying desires and their own consciences."]

Thursday, December 2: Wretham—Raining.

Not much better although I got up to hear Bolefahr lecture on the Dutch coast in the morning.

Major Hiles had a Jeep pick me up for more nose treatments. Felt some better in the afternoon.

Took a sleeping pill tonight and dropped off early. All the gang went to a USO show, said it was darn good. Wish I could have gone.

[German forces launch significant attacks against Josip B. Tito's partisan army in Yugoslavia.]

Friday, December 3: Wretham—Received packages from Grandma, the folks, and from Nadine's mom.

[Edward R. Murrow describes a Royal Air Force nighttime bombing attack on Berlin in his classic "Orchestrated Hell" broadcast over CBS Radio, after receiving permission to accompany the crew of a four-engine Lancaster.

Early in the war the British engaged in daylight bombing, but with no long-range fighters to protect the bombers they suffered terrible losses. In 1940 the Royal Air Force started conducting long-range strategic bombing missions at night, and continued to do so until the end of the war. Pathfinder aircraft would go in first and mark the target(s) with flares, giving the bombardiers a point of reference. This strategy dovetailed nicely with the USAAF preference for precision daylight bombing, thus keeping the Germans on the defensive 24 hours a day.]

Saturday, December 4: Wretham—Weather is bad, no flying, Major Hiles off.

I feel much better. Washed 14 handkerchiefs and wrote letters. Packages arrived from Gross and Bairstows.

Major Tyrrell, Shaw, Bo, Mosse, and Forehand to Duxford tomorrow to fly their first mission. Here I sit, oh curse the luck!

I was to be commanding officer, then Major decided Kibler should since he's been commissioned longer. Major wants to separate us, says, actually, I can't rank Kib. Why in Hell didn't the damn fool think of that eight months ago instead of the evening of going operational? I'm really fed up with that screwball. So is everyone!

[Bolivia declares war on the Axis powers.]

Sunday, December 5: Wretham—Feel fine and spent all day on the line. Mosse checked my ship at 30,000 feet this morning. She's ready for combat, belly tank and all. Sure wish I could fly her.

Bo is sick. Pino is going in his place. What a goddam lousy outfit. That brown-nosed bastard oughta be a tail-end Charlie, but he's in precious "A" Flight so Heaven can wait. Crap!

368th Boy Scout Troup took off at 4:00 P.M. How I hated to see my ship going off without me. That really hurt!

Headache returned tonight. So what, let it ache!

Doc returned from Bristol. Good to have him back.

Monday, December 6: Wretham—Mist and fog. No flying.

Still feel pretty good. Drew some maps. Wrote a poem about the Thunderbolt.

There's lots of sickness with a mild flu epidemic in England. Sam White, Burton, Hagan, Bo, and myself all grounded.

I've been reading Clifford Odets' plays. *Waiting for Lefty, Paradise Lost, Rocket to the Moon, Golden Boy*, and *Awake & Sing*. It's ironic to read his philosophy of middle-class decadence in the Thirties, the grim portent of war. Mebbe he was right, but he's pretty rugged.

[The Cairo conference between President Roosevelt, Prime Minister Churchill, and President Ismet Inönü of Turkey concludes with an affirmation of the traditional relations of friendship between the Allies and Turkey.]

Tuesday, December 7: Wretham—Fog and mist all day. No flying.

Really feel good now, the best in three weeks. By god, I think this cursed sinus is licked.

Listened to a couple of lectures, did a watercolour of Margot.

Kib and Hunter are in London. Burton is running around the halls in his fur-lined flying jacket and shorts. Some picture.

Botsy and Simmons GI'ed the floor of 215 today, too much "Zombie" and pheasant grease. Zombie is quite a pup now, still cute as Hell and full of the devil.

The boys are still at Duxford. Haven't flown yet.

Wednesday, December 8: Wretham—Lousy weather. Feel swell.

Studied the Belgian coast with Bo all morning. Some good poop available.

Clayton Davis here this afternoon via Jeep. Good to see him, to talk about Brownie. We hope he bailed out. There's a good chance of it.

Left for London on the 556, one hour late. Baldy's and Davis' first trip. Misty moon, good visibility. Made up five minutes.

Took the underground to Oxford Circus, walked to the Reindeer Club. Ate. Checked into #93, a room for three. Hit the sack at 11:30 P.M.

Thursday, December 9: London—Slept until 9:30 A.M. Breakfast at the Club. I got a haircut and shampoo and rub. Wonderful. Lunch at 12:30 P.M. Bumped into Louis Cross, Duxford DFC in the morning. Good to see one of the old Foster Field gang.

Spent the afternoon at Keith Prowse's listening to records. Swell fun.

Baldy and Dave toured via cab. Met at the Club at 4:30 P.M. Ate. Went to "Strike a New Note" again and thoroughly enjoyed it. Supper at Prince's. Talked to bull fiddle player. Walked to the Club. Had coffee, bed about 11:00 P.M. Good fun, a restful, lazy day. Feel swell.

Friday, December 10: London—Dave left at 8:20 A.M. to meet a major back at Wretham. Baldy and I slept until <u>11:30 A.M.</u> Wow!

Lunched. Saw Dick Gates. He, too, thinks Brownie may be alive. His brother and Tom Fox were in the same squadron when Gordon was killed. Dick the same as ever.

Baldy and I window-shopped all afternoon along Bond Street, Oxford Street, and Piccadilly. Walked through Selfridge's. Reminded me of Fields.

Tea at Club, cab to station, caught the 546 train in the blackout. Arrived an hour late to Cambridge. Moonlit night and the truck was waiting. Had coffee in the kitchen. Bed at midnight.

Saturday, December 11: Wretham—Today, I <u>flew</u>. Yes, flew. Had Randy's ship up for half an hour and then snow socked in tight. Barely saw the field to get in. Really good to fly again.

Our gang at Duxford went to Emden today, should be back with the hot scoop tomorrow.

There was plenty of activity here last night. The boys saw an enemy knocked down in flames over toward Wattisham. Flares.

Field is on Air Raid general alert tonight. Gas masks and helmets ready, hmmm? Wot's up?

Sunday, December 12: Wretham—No flying. Too overcast.

Called for 1300 briefing. Colonel Tacon gave a swell talk, with questions and so on, discussing operational flying.

The gang returned from Duxford. The Major in usual form. All military courtesy, blah blah blah! Crap!!

Pino really got in a tangle with some 190s. They went nearly to Emden with the 78th. Mosse said my ship was swell but his flight aborted.

Gall happy about the ship but feels lousy because ship out for 25 hour inspection now.

[*The Focke-Wulf Fw190, powered by a BMW radial engine, was considered one of the best fighters of its era. After a Luftwaffe pilot mistakenly landed on a British airfield in June 1942, British testing found it superior to their Spitfire MK V in many respects, hastening development of the MK IX.*]

Monday, December 13: Wretham—Operational!!

We were briefed at 0900 and took off at 0950 leading element in #3 flight, lead squadron. Me, Shaw, Hunter, 'n Kib. I took Baldy's ship, very good engine. Took off in four ship formation, full belly tank, some thrill, what with me with one hour! Climbed to 29,000 feet in a two hour run. Good formation. Swell to be up high again.

Landed at 1200, briefed at 1245 for our first real mission: sweep to France (Cassel, St. Omer, Le Tréport). I didn't go. Baldy went instead. No excitement, not even flak.

Great fun we're operational at last. Everyone tired tonight. Wish my ship was in shape.

I'm up in the morning. "D" Flight rides again.

368th Fighter Squadron dispersal area, East Wretham Airfield.
Courtesy of Alfred M. Swiren: Archived by Char Baldridge, Historian, 359th Fighter Group Association

[Howard's fighter squadron, the 368th, one of three in the 359th Fighter Group, initially included A, B, C, and D Flights, which were identified on the radio as Red, White, Blue, and Yellow. Black or Green identified extra flights. Each squadron contained at least sixteen fighters.

Men from the 824th Air Engineering Squadron, the 648th Air Material Squadron, the 3rd Gunnery and Tow-Target Flight, and the 448th Air Service Group provided ground and combat support to the 359th Fighter Group.

Aircraft of the 359th Fighter Group were under the command of the 67th Fighter Wing of the USAAF Eighth Air Force VIII Fighter Command. The unicorn, considered a symbol of strength and integrity, became the group and squadron insignia.]

368th Fighter Squadron Coat-of-Arms. With a background disc of yellow, the squadron color designation, the white unicorn head holds a red thunderbolt firmly between his teeth. Its one horn indicates that the squadron flies single engine planes. *Image from the archives of Howard Fogg.*

Tuesday, December 14: Wretham—Ground fog and broken overcast. No flying.

Released from the line at 3:00 P.M. until 8:00 A.M. the 16th.

Had a rip-snorting volleyball game in the afternoon then a hot shower. Damn good snack bar at 10:00 P.M. I ate French fries until I was blue in the face, and greasy.

Renken bought me a leather belt in Thetford. Now have very inconspicuous uniform, no insignia, no tags, just shirt and pants, GI shoes, sweater, first aid kit, gum, cigarettes, and a pocketknife.

Took "Mike" down and installed him in cockpit by (*gun*)sight. Looks cute. "*Clumpy II*" is ready to ride again!

[*"Clumpy" adorned the side of Howard's P-47 Thunderbolt. The original Clumpy was a cartoon character, a naughty but beloved puppy Howard created before 1942. After the war Clumpy's cartoon adventures decorated an occasional gift for family, and the pup's antics ultimately graced a series of bank advertisements.*]

"Caught in the Act—!" Valentine's Day "Clumpy" Cartoon for Margot Dethier. 1942 cartoon by Howard Fogg. *Courtesy of Peter Fogg*

Wednesday, December 15: Wretham—Solid dark overcast, no flying.

Two hour gas session by Little Caesar this morning; two hours more this afternoon. A wonder to me the pilots don't openly rebel against this guy. He is absolutely hopeless. A tough break to have him at the top of such a grand squadron.

"D" Flight, as usual, was moved down into a separate dispersal area which is good in that we're close to the field and off by ourselves. Transport for crew chiefs the main problem. Tallyho, goddam it.

A big poker game tonight in #215: Shaw, Randy, Hawk, Wiley, Botsy, and Perk. Randy started off with three Kings at five-card draw.

I painted a little P-47 watercolour.

[Subsequent to breaking off diplomatic relations with the government-in-exile of Yugoslavia, the United States, the Soviet Union, and Great Britain recognize Tito's Communist Popular Liberation Committee as the future government of Yugoslavia.]

Thursday, December 16: Wretham—Overcast.

Big briefing at 1045, we're to provide withdrawal support for first wing of 700 Forts from Bremen. Start engines scheduled for 1215. Mission scrubbed at 1210.

Really a let down. We were top flight. Nerve tension terrific. Cussed for five minutes.

Only 12 out of 48 P-47 Thunderbolts of the 355th returned to base.

Colonel Tacon sure used his head! Would have been suicide to take this green bunch thru that overcast and over past the Zuider Zee with 10/10ths cover. The preparation was good practice however, served to take the edge off.

Lunch at Hall. Played volleyball.

Saw six Forts circle the field. Two landed. Nice jobs, with ceiling and visibility terrible. Pilot Halcott and Co-Pilot Bradley rooming in 207 with us. Good boys. Their first mission and they're happy to be here.

[The B-17 Flying Fortress, or Fort, represented the first mass-produced four-engine heavy bomber. Boeing's prototype first flew in 1935 and following the attack on Pearl Harbor production accelerated. Revered for its rugged ability to reach its target, sustain battle damage, and still bring home the crew, the aircraft served in every combat theater of World War II.]

Colonel Avelin P. ("Hardtack") Tacon Jr., Commanding Officer, 359th Fighter Group. Flight gear includes RAF 1940 Pattern boots, A-2 jacket, B-3 life preserver, Type C British helmet, US A-14 oxygen mask, B-7 goggles with R/T lead, and seat parachute harness.
Archived by Char Baldridge, Historian, 359th Fighter Group Association, from records at HQ USAF Research Center, Maxwell Air Force Base, Alabama

Friday, December 17: Wretham—Weather very poor. At line all morning drawing charts and signs for Captain Shaw.

Spent nearly two hours in B-17F of Halcott and Bradley. Some ship, a maze of equipment and gadgets. Randy (Bradley is from Asheville and knows Randy) and I stayed in the cabin while they preflighted. Fascinating to watch the kids' teamwork with the controls. Really impressive, reminded me of "Air Force." All the drama is there. <u>Hats off to the bomber pilots</u>.

Bo, Mosse and Doc went to see Colonel Smith about the Major, Doc talked. The Major, like a man, is doing an about face. He's mixing and friendly, have to give him credit for trying. He's got guts. Sure hope the situation improves.

["Air Force" was a Howard Hawks film released in March 1943, and featured the B-17 C and D models in the Pacific Theater of Operations. President Roosevelt signs the bill repealing Chinese exclusion laws.]

Saturday, December 18: Wretham—Rotten weather, rain and drizzle.

Bombers are still here (Halcott from the 360th, and Molesworth from the 303rd).

Worked in the shack all day. It's really swell now, with furniture, a Victrola, and radio. Tonight about twelve of us, and the <u>Major</u>, waxed the floor then went to squadron mess for coffee. Great time. Major really putting out. I'm all for him, hope he can keep it up.

Nice V-mail letter from "Hoppie" at Dartmouth to all overseas Alumni, really heartwarming.

Hagan still grounded (sixth day) for sinus, like I was. He's sore as Hell, do I appreciate it!!

There's a good volleyball court right outside the ops shack. Darn handy and some wicked games. Spirits high. A great gang.

[From 1916 to 1945 Ernest Martin Hopkins ("Hoppie") served as the eleventh president of Dartmouth College.]

Sunday, December 19: Wretham—Rain all morning, cleared in the afternoon. Getting cold.

Our B-17 guests finally got off late.

Wiley lectured on escape this afternoon.

Volleyball game. Ping-Pong with Major last night, and he's a pretty good player. He's sure making an effort to be friendly. A good man for trying, I can't deny it!

Hagan's sinus still has him grounded.

Another poker game in 215 tonight.

Weather supposed to be good tomorrow. I hope. Clear and cold out!

Monday, December 20: Wretham—Beautiful, cold morning. Clear.

Wakened at 0700. Briefing at 0830. We're to pick up Forts over Texel and escort them 70 miles at 29,000 feet. I'm top flight.

Start engines at 0950. Took off at 1005. My ship felt dead, had no pep. Pulled 40" and couldn't catch Shaw. Engine cut out a lot and finally quit cold over the Dutch Coast. That's some feeling at 28,000 feet with 120 miles of water behind and enemy in front. I aborted with Randy as escort. Wheezed back across the Channel and found the field. Landed at 1150, very mad.

There were 22 aborts in group. That's what comes of a week's standing on the ground. Damn *Clumpy II* anyway.

All rid of my nervousness now. It's a real thrill up there with the bombers.

[Pulled 40" refers to engine manifold absolute pressure measured in inches of mercury (Hg). This would equate to roughly 5 psi of boost from the turbosupercharger.]

Tuesday, December 21: Wretham—Clear with clouds, becoming overcast.

At 0920 Wiley hollered for us to stand by without briefing. We grabbed our stuff. At 0935 we got a start engine for 0940. A mad scramble to ships, no belly tanks. A sweep over France.

I flew #3 for Shaw and Hunter with Baldy. Good flight at 21,000 feet over Calais and the St. Omer region. Medium flak that was damn accurate; one burst less than a hundred yards behind the Major's flight, to our left. Those Heinies are good! Too good. Lots of bogeys high and low but no action. Good look at French coast. Helluva good mission. Colonel Tacon pleased. No abortives in squadron and only one for group. Morale high. Everyone rarin' for action.

Wednesday, December 22: Wretham—Fast moving overcast, broke by noon. Briefing at 1100. Took off at 1215 with Major Richmond, Baldy, and Hagan. Major really flies smooth. I had Randy's ship, which is damn good. Enjoyed successful ascent thru the clouds. What a gorgeous sight on top. We essed over the second box of 18 B-17s at 27,500 feet. Impressive to see hundreds of B-17s below you against the dazzling white clouds.

Colonel is really happy about the mission. Four aborts in squadron. Whole group off in 6 minutes 35 seconds. Baldy was low on gas, so he peeled off near Yarmouth.

Downing and Hollis saw a couple of bombs yesterday by their ships. Said, "Hell let's put 'em on," so they had 'em put on. That was crazy-nuts when they were on sweep as spares. They turned around, got lost, landed with the bombs twice, and finally brought 'em back here. What a crazy outfit.

Got a new pilot today; Drake, from Palisades Park, New Jersey. 43-G *(pilot training class)* in "C" Flight. He's bunking with us.

[*A box, or combat box, was a tactical formation of heavy bombers designed to maximize their defensive machine gun fire. Pioneered by the 8th Air Force, a box kept the bombers in close proximity and allowed interlocking patterns of machine gun fire against enemy aircraft. Three combat boxes would often join up to form a combat wing.*]

Thursday, December 23: Wretham—I'm not scheduled, taking the day off. Painted night train scene and loafed around Hall all day.

The squadron ran a practice mission with some B-24s. No one enjoyed it.

Simmons spun out of a turn in the clouds. Great sport.

Baldy returned this afternoon; he couldn't get any gas at the field yesterday. He spent the night with the bomber crews of two B-17s and a 352nd pilot who got two yesterday. They went to a pub and got tight, couldn't find the field again, wandered around until 2:00 A.M.

We had English orphans here today. Ate lunch, took them sightseeing. Great time had by all.

Received Christmas cable from Mom and Dad.

Drake is a hot Ping-Pong player.

[*The Consolidated Aircraft B-24 Liberator became operational in 1941, and by the end of the war it had been produced in greater numbers than any other American combat aircraft. A faster, more modern design than the B-17, it failed to achieve the B-17's iconic status. The B-17 was easier to fly and proved to be more rugged in combat, but the greater range of the B-24 made it a valuable asset in the Allied war effort.*]

Friday, December 24: Wretham—Briefing for huge show at 1100. All bombers and fighters in ETO *(European Theater of Operations)* to northern France to knock out rocket gun emplacements. Our group patrolled for one hour at 14,000 feet, and me not scheduled. Hell!

We sat by the radio, more nervous than if we'd been flying. Lots of bogeys and a little flak but there was no action anywhere. I was a nervous wreck just listening in. Believe me, you can really lose fingernails sitting by a radio listening to your pals on a mission.

Only Captain Shaw's flight and three spares got back to our field. All the rest ran out of gas and landed in Manston, south tip of Thames estuary.

Gall is working hard on my ship.

Christmas Eve. Some joke. Hardly any of our pilots are here. Renken brought up a radio and we listened to that, read, visited, and finally turned in about 11:00 P.M.

Waiting for the return of fighters at East Wretham Airfield Control Tower.
Courtesy of Elsie Palicka, wife of Ed Palicka, 370th Fighter Squadron Photographer:
Archived by Char Baldridge, Historian, 359th Fighter Group Association

[General Eisenhower is named Supreme Allied Commander of the Allied Expeditionary task force for the invasion of Europe.]

Christmas Day, Saturday, December 25: Wretham—A lousy, grey day. No visibility.

Sketched airplanes and opened Christmas presents. I painted two watercolours, a PBM and an A20. Gave Gall my P-47 picture. He liked it. Ate a wonderful Christmas turkey dinner, with seconds, wine, candy, and cigarettes.

Our boys all returned about 4:00 P.M. Really sore. They spent the night at an RAF station, cold, no turkey. RAF guys snotty to 'em, raised Hell 'cause four Spitfires had been shot down. The cooks here loaded 'em with turkey, and then they felt better.

Everyone kinda moody, what with the grey day, Christmas carols on the radio, and thoughts of home. We have it soft here compared to some theatres, but it still isn't any fun sitting in this damp hall on Christmas Day.

Sunday, December 26: Wretham—Weather stinks.

All of us at line in the morning. I copied an article on aerial gunnery, typed it up in the afternoon.

Big volleyball game. Good dinner with ice cream.

Saw "Casablanca" last night, finally! Swell picture.

Ettlesen finally had to move out with his own squadron upstairs. We'll miss him.

Zombie is now "owned and operated" by the cooks, too much bladder trouble for room 215 to handle. He's still a cute pup and squadron mascot.

Gall has *Clumpy II* ready for a test hop. Hope all is okay. I'm still in an ornery mood, seems no one cares whether we fly or not. Christmas blues or somethin'.

Monday, December 27: Wretham—Still overcast, but field is on green so Baldy and I went on a cook's tour of East Anglia. He led, we flew all over, buzzed an airdrome, trains, had a good time. *Clumpy II* seems fine, although we went only to 2,500 feet.

Took 'er up to 30,000 feet alone this afternoon thru break in overcast. She runs like a top. Perfect!! The sweetest I've ever flown now. Gall happy. Me too.

Couldn't see the ground above 20,000 feet. Got good and lost. Wing controller "fixed" me 60 miles south of here. Steered me home right over the field with 40 gallons to spare! And visibility down to one and a half miles. Really accurate. Up for three and a half hours today. Reminds me of Farmingdale and feels swell. Ole *Clumpy* is rarin' to go. Have all my back flying pay now.

Tuesday, December 28: Wretham—Bad weather so no flying until the afternoon. A little local stuff then.

Spent all day working on the status board, they'll make a sign painter out of me yet.

Had an interesting show by the 8th Air Force traveling company on

German uniforms, rank, and insignia. Very good.

For Captain Shaw's birthday had a <u>big</u> cake and beer in Bo's room in the evening. Shaw really surprised. A swell show for a swell guy.

The squadron is really solid now, one big happy family, full of pep and eager for anything. The Major has been really doing a conscientious about-face. More power to him.

Wednesday, December 29: Wretham—Practice mission at 1300 but I stayed on the ground painting status board. Very uneventful, tiring day and I'm sick of lettering.

Painted Captain Shaw a B-25 watercolour, night scene, one of my best plane pictures. He liked it a lot.

Enlisted men had a beer party with beer, cokes, and sandwiches in the post library. A good time. Sang songs, accompanied by two guitars and an accordion. We all went down for about an hour, very informal. They are, as I've often said, a great gang. Couldn't ask for a finer bunch of men. Gall all decked out in blouse, cigar, and mess cup full of suds. He's a swell little guy.

Weather should be good tomorrow.

The original Briefing Room (or War Room) at East Wretham Airfield. *Archived by Char Baldridge, Historian, 359th Fighter Group Association, from records at HQ USAF Research Center, Maxwell Air Force Base, Alabama*

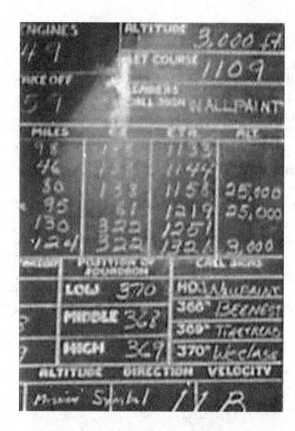

Detail of chalkboard from
photo of the original Briefing
Room, believed to be from the
December 30, 1943 mission.
*Photo archived by Char Baldridge,
Historian, 359th Fighter Group
Association, from records at HQ
USAF Research Center, Maxwell
Air Force Base, Alabama*

[*British General Bernard Montgomery, leading the British 8th Army,
captures Ortona on the Adriatic coast of Italy.*
The Royal Air Force launches a heavy raid on Berlin.]

Thursday, December 30: Wretham—A beautiful, clear morning.
Briefing at 0930.

We escorted a combat wing over northern France today at 25,000
feet. Took off at 1100. Never saw a thing. No flak, no enemy <u>and</u> no
bombers?? Went a helluva ways into France on a tail wind, and then
came back on a reciprocal.

Baldy, Hag, Randy, and I (Blue Flight) ran low on gas over Dover.
We went to Bradwell Bay and set down. I had 10 gallons left! Swell field,
runways, Mosquitoes. Took off at 1445 in swell two ship elements, flew
tight formation.

Haze very bad. Good old Fine boy brought us home to land on our field on the dot. A damn good flight all the way! Over 600 miles, 3 hours 35 minutes total.

Nine V-mails to greet me here!

[The de Havilland Mosquito was originally conceived as a twin-engine light bomber with a two-man crew. Made almost entirely out of plywood, it was nicknamed the "Wooden Wonder" and "Timber Terror." It proved to be a versatile and adaptable aircraft and in modified form served as a fighter, photoreconnaissance aircraft, and pathfinder.]

Friday, December 31: Wretham—What a mission! Colonel led first, Major second. I led Yellow Flight with Hunter, Kib, and Hagan (Kib out, Hawk in #4 slot). To Paris, support into, at, and out of target area, at 27,000 feet! Bombers in good form. Major did a wonderful job of essing the whole time. I gave good support. We were hot!

Encountered terrific flak over Paris. My wing went thru the smoke from one burst. Paris was clear, saw the Eiffel Tower, and boy did those bombs blast the smoke! Bogeys everywhere! We could have jumped four bandit decoys (three o'clock low) each, but escorting the bombers came first. Colonel took a crack at four, but they beat it. A swell, exciting mission. We really protected those bombers!

Landed at Manston, refueled, smoked a cigarette, looked at some Typhoons. I'll take a 47! Major Simmons, McGeever, Botsy and my flight back here at 1545.

[The Typhoon was a British single-engine fighter-bomber.]

History of the 359th Fighter Group, December 1943

Two days less than eleven months after its creation, the 359th Fighter Group became operational on 13 December 1943.

By the end of the month (and of the year) the 359th had flown seven missions against the enemy: an introductory shallow fighter sweep into northern France, two penetration escort flights over Holland, two long area support missions against the vital Crossbow targets of the Calais area, a Ramrod escort assignment from north France into Belgium, and, on the last day of the year, close support of 64 Flying Fortresses before, at, and after an assault on the C.A.M. ball bearing factories in Paris.

All aircraft dispatched returned from these missions and although the pilots received a thorough introduction to the German's flugabwehrkanone, otherwise knows as flak, there were not encounters with enemy fighters until the seventh and final mission of the month and the fleeting contacts that day were inconclusive.

Their effect in sum was a general conviction that the 359th had come of age, had begun to justify the fact of its existence, could face the future with confidence in its training for combat, and pride in the men it sent searching for the Hun.

Taken as a whole, the month provided excellent weather: crisp wintry days that came as a welcome respite from the chilling drip of November. But haze and morning ground fog in the early part of the month sharply curtailed flying. As a result, 17 officers of the 359th had an extended tour of temporary duty at Duxford, one of the RAF peacetime stations made famous during the Battle of Britain, and, in December 1943, home of the 78th Fighter Group.

VIII Fighter Command policy required that each unit in the growing roster of Thunderbolt groups be led into battle by pilots experienced in the theatre. This objective was achieved by sending a new group's senior flying officers to fly on the wing of combat-tested pilots in an older organization, while a veteran of the theatre was detailed to lead the new group in its first missions.

Thus, during the first 10 days of December, Colonel Avelin P. Tacon Jr., Majors William H. Swanson, John B. Murphy, Albert R. Tyrrell, Rockford

V. Gray, and 12 captains and lieutenants waited at Duxford for an opportunity to fly operationally with the 78th while Major Richmond, commander of the 486th Squadron, 352nd Group, moved from nearby Bodney to Wretham Hall to act as flying group commander of the 359th. Command of the 359th Group devolved upon Captain Chauncey S. Irvine, operation officer of the 370th Squadron, promoted to major later in the month.

The contingent at Duxford had a lazy time waiting for a break in the weather, but the activity at their home station continued at a pace only a little less than feverish as all departments checked their readiness to undertake operations.

Major Richmond in this period made an unobtrusive but thorough study of the Station's operational scheme. He also demonstrated the necessity of personally digesting all available information on the enemy and the war, an attitude that made a lasting impression on the pilots and tactical sections of the 359th Group.

On 11 December 1943 the waiting ended for the command detachment at Duxford. The 78th flew withdrawal support for the 2nd Bomb Division after the attack on Emden that day and the 359th's pilots flew with elements in each of the two tactical groups Duxford put in the air. The group in which Colonel Tacon flew destroyed an Me109 in the course of escort.

Our pilots played a role in the combat: the flight led by Captain Irvine with Colonel Tacon on his wing, made an unrewarded bounce of an Me109, and a top cover flight including First Lieutenant James R. Pino, 368th Squadron, was bounced, also unsuccessfully, by enemy fighters.

There were no losses on the mission and on the night of the 11th the 359th officers returned from Duxford with their ground crews. The atmosphere resembled a swimming pool after the bathers' first plunge, with general announcements that the water felt just fine.

A practice mission was planned for 12 December 1943 but weather forced cancellation. It was flown the next morning, the first assignment of a day momentous in the story of the 359th.

Take off was at 0945 on a flight over the Wash and up the Northern Coast over Flamborough Head to a point east of Hartlepool and home via Nottingham to a landing at 1200. Before take off, Colonel Edward W. Anderson, 67th Fighter Wing commander, had given a telephone warning to Colonel Tacon that if the weather held, the first mission would come that afternoon. Accordingly, when the 42 planes had taken off, orders were passed to the squadrons to begin refueling as soon as they returned.

Field Order 200 arrived in the intelligence teletype room at 1155, while the aircraft were still touching down. The pilots were at once taken to

Wretham Hall to lunch and 30 minutes later were at the briefing room. There Major Richmond's easy poise and quiet confidence did much to relieve an inevitable tension.

The plotting was necessarily hurried, and extra time was inadvertently allowed to gain altitude before the first penetration of the enemy coast. Major Richmond was informed of the error before take off and in consequence, flew a somewhat deeper and wider sweep than had first been contemplated.

Inadequate refueling facilities reduced the number of airplanes which could be prepared after the morning mission. Of these, four aborted, so that 37 sorties were flown in this first mission, which was without incident save for six contrails seen at 1451 at 31,000 feet at a point which was estimated to be about 10 miles north of Abbeville. The Continent was totally obscured by 10/10 cloud.

The whole mission was crisply summed up by VIII Fighter Command's Narrative of Operations: "according to plan and uneventful." The pilots who flew the show remembered it chiefly because one of them left his microphone button on and "breathed down everyone's neck" throughout the whole ride.

That night, Lieutenant Francis W. Hankey, station transportation officer, called a meeting of all transportation personnel at which Lieutenant Maurice F. X. Donohue of the combat intelligence staff described the mechanics of a mission, stressed the importance of immediate and fast intra-station transport and at Lieutenant Hankey's suggestion, laid down the principle that a pilot could commandeer any car any time. A schedule was later worked out by which trucks accompanied each squadron's pilots wherever they went, standing by in readiness for a mission.

The 359th Group was warned to mount belly tanks for an escort mission on the 14th, but this Field Order (201) was canceled at 0511 on the 14th and the day's next bombardment mission (FO 202) included no assignment for the 359th. This second order was also canceled at 0826 on the 14th.

On FO 203, received at 0231 on the 16th, the 359th briefed its pilots to fly escort from Kijkduin to Dekkaveen, returning via Texel, but Major Richmond expressed doubt at the briefing if the weather would permit take off at 1225 as scheduled, and it so developed. Twelve combat wings of bombers assaulted Bremen, but base weather permitted only the 4th, 55th, 354th, 355th and 356th Fighter Groups to get off in escort, the 56th, 78th, 352nd, 353rd, 358th and 359th all scrubbing.

The 18th of December was a dull day although Group Intelligence began a policy of lecturing ground crews on the technique and status of the war;

40 mechanics from the 369th Squadron were the first audience. On the 19th, Plan Eye Que was received, and the 359th found itself assigned a tactical role in a massive strike by the Eighth Air Force.

This second time of waiting ended on the 20th with the receipt of FO 204, which called for escort of four combat wings of B-17s from Texel Island inland en route to Bremen. Major Richmond, who had returned to his living quarters at Bodney, flew to Wretham at dawn to take the briefing at 0830, and 59 airplanes were up at 1000.

A spasm of abortives followed, with 22 aircraft returning early. Five of these flew home as escorts. The abortives, including spares were: engine troubles, 8; failure of belly tanks to release, 7; radio, 1; and supercharger, 1.

The mission itself was flown without combat; the bombers, which were 5 minutes late, were seen tightening formation over the North Sea. The escort was taken up 2 minutes from Texel at 1101 at an altitude of 29,000 feet, and was continued until a point southeast of Zuidlaarder Lake. The reciprocal was flown back to Texel to afford protection to the second task force which was then arriving over enemy-held territory.

An unidentified but suspicious P-47, marked MV, flew near and behind the 368th leader for five minutes on the return route, and the top cover flight, at 32,000, saw six enemy aircraft at 35,000 during the escort. Both of these facts, missed in interrogation, developed at a critique called by Colonel Tacon immediately after landing, and were reported at once to Fighter HQ. The result was a "smack the Hun" order, instructing groups to pursue and destroy the German high altitude reconnaissance patrols.

The critique was notable mainly for Colonel Tacon's pronounced dissatisfaction with the number of abortives. On the technical side, the improvement in take off procedure, which cut the 15 minutes required to get off on the 13th to 7 minutes, was noted and the meeting ended on a generally happy note, a feeling later fortified by the congratulatory vein of Issue 85, VIII Fighter Command Narrative of Operations: "an excellent job," by all fighter groups.

The most complete test materialized on 21 December, in the shape of a hurried scramble in support of a B-26 operation against Crossbow targets in the Calais area.

A warning order stipulating no tanks was received at 0815. Major Richmond at once came to Wretham. At 0912, Wing checked receipt of the warning, and could add no details. The squadrons were told to keep their pilots ready for take off in a hurry. At 1013, S-2 was informed that the FO was in the teletype room awaiting corrections, and work in the plotting room began at once on penciled notes. At 1020, Wing was told that start engine time figured at 1007 and every minute take off was delayed meant a minute more late arrival. No decision on whether the mission was on or off was forthcoming until 1032, when Wing ordered: "get cracking."

Start engine time was fixed at once by Colonel Tacon at 1040, take off 1050. Squadrons were briefed on the intelligence conference phone circuit on times and courses, and got away at 1052, making Gravelines landfall at 1130, 30 minutes late but 30 minutes before another group confronted by the same problems managed to reach its patrol area.

No Marauders were seen although Major Richmond led five orbits over the assigned patrol area. The 359th also saw from some distance, without at once realizing what was occurring, the incident in which a Spitfire exploded under P-47 attack. This led to a check when the mission returned to ascertain that no 359th guns were fired.

Lieutenant Herman B. King of the 370th Squadron crash-landed in a field near Manston, and, since a suspected sabotage of his airplane had been discovered earlier, a new investigation was begun. The pilot was unhurt.

In this hurried effort, 57 aircraft (including two spares) got up in 7 minutes 25 seconds. There was only one abortive, due to a defective propeller. Accuracy of the flak at Gravelines was the principal subject of conversation at mess that night.

Although everyone associated with the effort believed the 359th Group acquitted itself well, the generally breathless effort to get into the air obviously presented dangers, and Colonel Anderson advised Colonel Tacon to hold a briefing no matter how late a field order was received in the future.

The third mission in three days came on 22 December: FO 207, in at 0230. Major Richmond came over from Bodney for the last time and flew as section leader while Colonel Tacon for the first time took over as flying group commander.

The job, escorting 220 B-17s and 120 B-24s from the Dutch Coast to Zwolle on the way to Osnabrück was, VIII Fighter Command later said, carried out "according to plan." There were four abortives: one pilot error, one escort and two belly tank release failures. Take off required 6 minutes 20 seconds for 53 airplanes.

At the critique that afternoon, squadron leaders complained that it was impossible to distinguish "Beesnest" (368th call sign) and "Weelass" (370th) in the air. Wing was asked to effect a change and new names—Jackson (368th) and Wheeler (370th) were assigned for use beginning 4 January 1944. At the end of the day Major Richmond informed Colonel Anderson that he believed the 359th was ready to operate on its own. The Major accordingly was ordered back to duty with his own squadron at Bodney.

Having flown four missions and still waiting for a chance to fire its guns, the 359th was a trifle abashed on the 23rd to discover itself assigned as shepherd to B-24s on a training mission over northern East Anglia. Self-esteem was restored by the discovery that the veteran 78th and 20th Groups were also on the mission order, which was completed in an uneventful flight, although loose bomber formation made proper escorting difficult.

That evening Colonel Tacon called a meeting of all officers of the command in the lounge at Wretham Hall. There he read and discussed two letters from General William E. Kepner, one on the subject of poaching (dated 16 December 1943) and the other on the need for better military deportment, dress and discipline (dated 8 December 1943). Colonel Tacon also read and explained his policy re: promotion of officers. The broad lines of the plan, he said, were to prevent "F.C. trouble" from preventing promotion of an able officer and to assure that assignment and promotion would be on "a scale of fairness and equality." To this end officers who demonstrated outstanding ability would be reassigned to position vacancies for the next higher grade in organizations in which a vacancy exists.

Creation of a Promotion Board to determine efficiency ratings and assignments of flying officers was announced at this meeting.

On December 24, Plan Eye Que came into operation. This bomber assault-by-squadrons on the special objectives in the Calais area required endurance and a medium altitude performance of the Thunderbolt not contemplated when the aircraft was designed, but, although the 359th patrolled its assigned area at 14,000 feet for 65 minutes, it met, in common with the other fighter groups, no enemy opposition.

FO 209 was received at 0230, and at 0800 Wing informed the duty intelligence officer to brief completely: tell the pilots the whole story. In consequence, Colonel Tacon ordered the briefing closed to all save pilots, flight surgeons, and intelligence officers, and the usual other attendants were informed that their invitations were canceled for the day.

IX Bomb Command's FO 208, throwing Marauders and Spitfires into the area, was received five minutes before "start engines," after all pilots had left for dispersals, but group and squadron leaders were informed by courier.

Take off (56 aircraft) required 6 minutes 25 seconds. There were no abortives (Colonel Tacon, emphasizing the importance of the targets, had warned "anyone who feels an abortion coming on, say so now") and the flights stayed so long in the area, as cover for the 724 bombers, that 28 aircraft had to land for refueling at advanced bases. One of these, piloted by Lieutenant Charles V. Cunningham, was "a belly landing at Reigate;" the pilot was unhurt.

From the fighter pilot's point of view there had been an unconscious build-up to a relative letdown: the mission, the targets, the striking force, the use of genuine precision bombardment technique, the required staying time, the required altitude, all had captured the imagination of the pilots. They were convinced they would be rewarded by their first combat, and the German refusal to fight was a disappointment.

A worse disappointment was to come on the next combat mission, but Christmas (saluted with a teletype greeting and an all-day release "for maintenance, training and a Merry Christmas") intervened. The mess, for officers and men alike, was outstanding, all diners agreed.

There was no mission on the 26th, and 27 December's FO 210 for the 28th was canceled quickly. On the 29th, Wing Operations Order Number 2 put the 359th up in support of B-24s again in company with the 352nd Group. Major Swanson conducted the briefing and led, with Colonel Tacon flying independently as an aerial observer. His only criticism was that the middle squadron essed so widely that a safe, if momentary, bounce at the bombers could have been made straight down at the moment the essing sections were farthest apart.

A take off record was set this day: 48 ships up in 5 minutes 45 seconds. The Colonel meanwhile had devoted a part of the morning to considering matters for the coat-of-arms mottos evolved by group intelligence officers and Flight Lieutenant R.O.N. Lyne, RAF Liaison and a Latinist of apparently hair-trigger ability. "Cum Leon," referring to the 359th Group's heraldic unicorn, and thus, indirectly, to the crown of England, in token of the association with the RAF, received most favorable attention, though lacking the bloodthirsty touch of "Ad Caedeneum," "Caedendo Vivemus," and "Inventi-Detine-Trucida." Other ideas were "Lupus Custodit" and "Lupus et Pastor," as well as "Pastores Coeli."

The year was fast ending. Two days remained. They produced two missions. FO 210, in at 0230, 30 December, was the first. It required escort of "the rear unit" of the second ATF (air task force) bound for Ludwigshafen, from Roye in France to Belgium. Rendezvous times were given for the front of the task force, which the order said would be "approximately 30 minutes" ahead of the rear unit. Wing, queried on the point early in the morning, said the plotters should accept 30 minutes as being the actual "plus plotting time" in the problem.

The 359th, as it turned out, flew a lonely 81 minutes in enemy territory since the bombers, apparently flying tighter formations than expected, were nowhere to be seen when the rendezvous was reached on course and on time. The bombers' track was searched in vain.

The 358th Group, flying a similar assignment on the same FO, had a similar experience, but the failure to effect a rendezvous nonetheless nettled the 359th Group, which had determined to meet all its commitments and felt it had so far succeeded.

The year's last mission erased all thought of this disappointment. FO 211 gave the 359th what it considered a jewel of an assignment: close escort of a single wing of 64 B-17s almost from the French Coast directly up to and around Paris (where the C.A.M. ball bearing plants were the target) and out again. Not only was there again the virtual certainty of combat but there was also sole responsibility for the bombers, plus a chance to see the bombing itself, and, because of the small numbers involved, every tactical opportunity to provide effective protection.

All expectations, save that of combat, were amply realized. The bombing was theatrically compact, with satisfactory billowing smoke. Paris, and the Eiffel Tower, was an unforgettable thrill, as was the famous Parisian flak barrage. More important, none of the 64 bombers were lost, their bombing results were officially "good," and the Fortresses' own verdict of the support was "excellent."

Six Fw190s were seen and pursued, but Colonel Tacon, leading a flight, and Major Gray, leading a section, drove the aircraft into steep dives for the deck, but neither were ever in range. Still, it was a jubilant group which came back from the show.

The mission was planned by Colonel Tacon to provide as continuous an escort as could be managed, with the result that all aircraft, save his, landed at Manston for refueling. His own airplane, using a 75-gallon belly tank, was in the air a minute more than 3 hours before he landed at Wretham for interrogation.

"We get closer every time. Next time is it," was the general declaration at the end of this mission on the 31st. There was no formal New Year's Party largely because of transportation troubles, the distance of the Station from Cambridge, and more fore-handed stations, but the bar remained open past 2000, and a festive time was had by all visible participants.

A moderate chill was cast upon the proceedings by the arrival of Flight Lieutenant A.E. Boming, there to deliver an interrogation lecture the evening of 31 December, but this was first rescheduled for the morning of 1 January 1944 and later canceled.

The Officer Candidate Board did not meet and the Flying Evaluation Board met once to consider the case of Second Lieutenant Robert D. Hall. Recommendations were sent to Fighter Command. The station's first general court-martial was held 7 December. The accused Private Edward E.

Koberski was sentenced to two years imprisonment and dishonorable discharge in a sentence approved by VIII Fighter Command GCMO 24, dated 17th December.

Ground training was hampered by disrepair of the opeidoscope. An elaborate program of chess, bridge and cribbage tournaments also was put under way by Second Lieutenant Irvan Segal, 368th, but no clear-cut winners had appeared in any of these events by the end of the month.

The chapter may very well close with the language of Chaplain Wilbur C. Ziegler at the briefing of 30 December, the first briefing at which prayer was offered:

"O God, we humbly ask Thee to bless our day's work, so that following Thy Holy Will, we may help to bring peace and liberty to all men. We pray that Thou wilt forgive us our trespasses, and pray that now as we fly into the future, we may know that we are never alone—but that Thou art always with us, giving us strength, courage, faith, and Thy divine protection. Amen."

4.

JANUARY 1944

Oh, This English Weather!

Saturday, January 1: Wretham—Happy New Year! A nice lazy day. Rain and a warm front. I slept until 10:30 A.M.! Some treat, boy it was fun! Had a good shower then a swell turkey dinner.

Painted a dame for Room 205 in the afternoon. Played Ping-Pong with Doc and some new signal corps officer. Lost to both. Grrr! A quiet, but pleasant beginning to the New Year. Poker games going again tonight, payday was yesterday.

Our raid yesterday was damn good. We didn't lose a bomber or a fighter. The 358th lost two bombers and six bellied in. Colonel Tacon is well pleased and so is Wing. We have a good reputation already and the Colonel is really the fair-haired boy. Why not? He's wonderful!!

[Field Marshal Erwin Rommel is named Commander of German forces north of the Loire Valley in France.]

Sunday, January 2: Wretham—Clear as a bell, fooled the weatherman for a wonder.

Nothing doing in the morning. A volleyball game.

Flew this afternoon with Baldy. Range estimation at 200 yards astern,

71

plenty rusty too! Then to 15,000 feet and practiced diving at 60 degrees left leveling at 8,000 feet. Looks like they're gonna make bombers out of us. Swell time anyhow. Hit 400-410 IAS *(Indicated Air Speed)* pulled out in 2,000 feet. Down to 500 feet at 400 IAS after last dive. Rear hurt like Hell. Hope it's okay. Tried a couple of rolls, first since Westover, sure am rusty. But fun. *Clumpy II* is really hot without that belly tank.

Baldy has his first real cold now and a bit of sinus but okay.

Copied McClelland Barclay's Ziegfeld Girl of 1941 tonight, sure a wonderful picture (his I mean). Learned a lot.

Monday, January 3: Wretham—Lousy weather, with rain and wind.

Worked on status board in the morning. Loafed in my room for the rest of the day, no pep, touch of a head cold. Oh this English weather! Nuts.

No excitement, just some of the usual poker games raging in 215 and the Major's room.

Major Rockford V. "Rocky" Gray, Group Operations Officer. *Courtesy of Alfred M. Swiren: Archived by Char Baldridge, Historian, 359th Fighter Group Association*

Davis leaves for Halesworth and the 56th Group on Wednesday, guess he hates to leave the gang. Hope he makes good there. He's a funny guy. Not too impressive a record here but he had two strikes against him.

[The US 5th Army begins an offensive against German forces at Cassino, Italy.]

Tuesday, January 4: Wretham Received the Air Medal.

Called at 0615 for 0730 briefing. Beautiful <u>cold</u> morning. Still dark when we went to the War Room. Bombers already up shooting colored flares like a Fourth of July celebration, a beautiful sight against the cold dawn. Took off at 0900. Me, Shaw, Hagan, 'n Baldy: Red Flight, top squadron, to 30,000 feet over Frisian Islands thence R/V *(aerial rendezvous)* and southeast 15 minutes with B-17s. Thence home. Two hours 45 minutes and no excitement.

Cold as Hell. First time I ever got so cold in a P-47. Felt lousy and flew lousy. Still feel lousy. Not on flight schedule tomorrow.

Meeting tonight with Shaw and pilots to discuss too many North Sea abortions. We gotta start using our heads, not our emotions. Why worry? You either make it or don't.

[Established in May 1942 by President Roosevelt, the Air Medal is awarded to individuals for distinguished, meritorious achievement while participating in aerial flight on a regular, frequent basis in the performance of primary duties. It may also be awarded to those who perform a particularly noteworthy act while performing as a crewmember, even though not on flying status, if a discernable contribution is made to the mission of the aircraft in flight.]

Wednesday, January 5: Wretham—Cold, frost, ground haze, broken overcast.

Briefing at 0845. Escort 120 B-17s from Flushing area southeast toward Ruhr area, about 20 minutes. Baldy took my ship. I laid off today, no pep and I'm having my chute repacked. *Clumpy* came back okay, Baldy satisfied.

They flew an uneventful mission, including no abortives, which is good. No bombers lost, but no enemy lost either, dammit.

Watched volleyball this afternoon. Got paid. Wrote letters tonight to Mom, Dad (Airmail) and V-mail to Margot, then played Ping-Pong with Doc. Still can't beat the old man. He's good.

Hagan and Randy are in London. I'll bet they're tighter 'n Hell. Baldy broke loose and went to Norwich with Burton on liberty run. Hope he gets plastered. He's in too much of a rut. Perk has a good case of sinus.

Thursday, January 6: Wretham—Bad weather over the Continent. Scrubbed a mission. No flying save for a few test hops.

Kibler got a bad ear testing at altitude.

Played volleyball. Talked to Gall a while. We waxed *Clumpy's* whole fuselage, looks good. Sketched in the afternoon. Played some lousy Ping-

Major Harold W. "Doc" Duennebier, 368th Flight Surgeon.
Courtesy of Anthony C. Chardella: Archived by Char Baldridge, Historian, 359th Fighter Group Association

Pong with Doc. Lousy! Read Marco Page's *Fast Company*, a darn clever yarn. Enjoyed it.

This damn room is like a dispensary, guys wander in up 'til midnight expecting Doc to paint a throat or pack a nose. I don't see how he stands it. They drive me nuts, far into the night.

Bed about 11:00 P.M.

Friday, January 7: Wretham—Overcast.

Briefed at 0930. We're heading southeast at 1125, Sedan-Bapaume escort. Colonel is White Flight. I'm leading Blue Flight, with Shaw, Kirk and Hunter.

Colonel flew under the weather at 3,000 feet to the coast, then thru holes to 25,000 feet and found bombers R/V on time. Nice job of flying.

Plenty of bogeys and our first withdrawal escort. Spits and 38s everywhere but we saw no action as we were close cover. Kirk flew his usual lousy position, made me work to keep in. Came back down thru overcast tops to 12,000 feet, with layers underneath. Broke out at 900 feet in rain, homing to field, in pretty rugged weather. Glad I was with the Colonel. We landed okay. Three hours.

Hag had Green Flight. He landed elsewhere. So did Randy and McGeever, in Black Flight. Twenty-two ships were up with no abortions. A good show, good experience in bad weather. *Clumpy* fine. Tired!

Saturday, January 8: Wretham—Poor weather. Overcast.

Went down to line as usual but released until tomorrow. Sketched, read, wrote letters. Weather broke a little in the afternoon. Hagan came back with Green Flight. Randy and Mac showed up later.

A B-24 crashed near the field Randy was at. He fished out the remains through the flames. The 24 fell out of formation at 1,000 feet. Very odd. A grim time for Randy.

All pilots in "D" Flight have received the Air Medal now. Party scheduled here tonight with women, likker, and GI band.

A very dull day, until tonight! Some wet party. Everyone drunk, loads of wimmin (bunch of bags). Even Colonel Tacon was pleasantly lit. Dames all over the building until 1:00 A.M. I had a few drinks m'self.

Sunday, January 9: Wretham—Cloudy and rainy.

Released until tomorrow, a good thing after last night, as a real drunken stupor prevails. About 12 guys ate breakfast. I wobbled down at 8:30 A.M. to French toast, coffee, and fruit juice, lots of fruit juice. Bunky sicker 'n a dog all day. Baldy slept until noon.

I tried to paint a train and got quite disgusted. Sure don't like any of my stuff lately, goddam it, guess I'm fed up with this rut-like existence. Same old grind, same people, same room, it sure gets tiring. And my drawing really gets me down. My god it's lousy. I'd better quit now before I throw all my paints away. Very fed up.

> *[Prime Minister Churchill and General Charles de Gaulle meet at Marrakesh, Morocco to discuss inclusion of a French expeditionary force in the invasion of Europe and the degree of authority of the French committee over civil affairs within France subsequent to the invasion.]*

Monday, January 10: Wretham—Bad weather breaking in forenoon.

I censored mail in the morning at line.

Three Spits (two Mark IXs and a XII) and two Typhoons came in, worked over the field and landed overnight, for our study and observation. Canadian and New Zealand pilots, good guys all. One big blond New Zealand guy looks like a Dartmouth tackle, flying a Typhoon. Did rolls off the deck at 350 IAS. Those Typhoons are hot! The Spits do pretty well too! Wow.

Kibler was transferred to the 370th, has "B" Flight, Lancaster out. A nice break for Kib but I hate to lose him. He's really a great kid and going places too. Hope he makes a good record. I'll miss him.

Lieutenant Ralph E. "Kib" Kibler with dog "Flak."
Photo courtesy of Anthony C. Chardella: Archived by Char Baldridge, Historian, 359th Fighter Group Association

[President Roosevelt and Prime Minister Churchill report that merchant shipping losses attributable to U-boats are 60 percent less than losses for the preceding year.]

Tuesday, January 11: Wretham—Warm front coming in, overcast.

Briefed at 0930. Carrying 108-gallon tanks, we're protecting withdrawal of B-17s from Germany. Major Gray leading our section. Me, Hunter, Hag, and Randy: Yellow Flight; Forehand leading Green Flight. Hag aborted, had no oxygen.

Major Gray got behind the first section and lost 'em. We wound up between 15,000 and 10,000 feet, 11 of us, and never saw the B-17s or the rest of the group. Stooged around, picked up two boxes of B-24s and brought 'em home. Landed early in rain. Pissed off.

Bo's flight, Blue, while at 23,000 feet with B-17s, was bounced by Messerschmitt Bf109s. Hyland spun out after three, went down into overcast with a 109 on his tail. NYR. *(Not yet returned).*

Some goddam mess! Where was Major Tyrrell with White Flight?

Three 370th boys gone. Buckley into drink. Tucker crashed in Wales and may be okay, but we don't know. Batch bellied in, in Scotland off Air Relay (RT) patrol. Our section never saw ground or sky. Mission should've been scrubbed. Now we have 4 NYRs. Even Colonel Tacon aborted. Nuts! Major Gray can go to Hell!

> [*During World War II aluminum was in high demand. Rather than use it for a fuel tank that would be carried once and discarded, the P-47 and other Allied planes used a 108-gallon drop tank made from laminated paper.*
>
> *Leighton McCarthy presents his letters of credentials to President Roosevelt as the first Canadian Ambassador to the United States.*]

Wednesday, January 12: Wretham—Weather bad, no flying.

Spent the morning at line, censoring, talking to Beck, Gall, and so on. We now have Homeyer in "D" Flight. He'll be element leader, Hagan the deputy.

Baldy, Renken, Downing, and I left for London on the 334. Rode in compartment with two greyhounds and a huge woman with a terrible cough. Some ride. No rooms at billet but finally found a place.

Thursday, January 13: London—Up at nine for a lousy breakfast. Downing slept in a burned out room (they had a fire yesterday). Baldy and I slept in the owner's room. Renken in service quarters in basement. Some night. To Hell with the Mandeville Hotel.

We got new rooms at 105 Gloucester Place. Nice place. I met Gates and Fieg for lunch, movies, tea, and supper. Had a swell visit.

Me to bed at <u>8:30 P.M.</u> Read, drew, <u>slept</u>. In the morning went to the bank to get dough from Mom. Baldy, Renken, and Big Dog sight "saw." Went tea dancing, got looped, warmed up with Baldy and a blonde in room, then Renken walked in and took the "swing shift." Some night!

Friday, January 14: London—Wakened by Renken and breakfast tray at 9:30 A.M. Ate, went to PX, bought coat and gloves. Had lunch with Renken and others at the Reindeer Club. They took the 220 train.

I went to Winsor-Newton and Reenes looking for art supplies but no success. Wound up out in Camdentown area at Roberson's. Bought Whatman paper and brushes.

Tea at Withers on Baker Street. Caught the 546. Here at 1015. Helluva nice sunny day in London. I enjoyed it, and I enjoyed being <u>alone</u> for a change.

Mission here. Randy flew my ship, couldn't trim it.

Bolefahr transferred to 370th. "A" Flight gets Bach. Maybe this shifting is good, but I don't see it. Bo was a swell guy and invaluable! Nuts.

Saturday, January 15: Wretham—Terrific fog, can't see a hundred yards.

I worked on status board all day.

Most of 'em sacked in all day. Group is one year old today.

Bolefahr's ship bellied in by Rodeheaver yesterday. Bet he'll be surprised, he's in London.

The Major, Joe, and several others are drunker than skunks tonight. Never seen the Major so high.

Wrote a long letter to Maggie about London. Saw "The Ghost of Frankenstein" in the lounge. A good deal, movies here at 7:00 P.M. Monday, Wednesday and Friday. Very nice. Bed about 11:00 P.M.

[French troops capture Monte Santa Croce in Italy.]

Sunday, January 16: Wretham—Same as yesterday.

I worked on status board then played darts. Got beaten in Ping-Pong tournament by Lochnaine. He's plenty good, really beat me, 17 to 21, 21 to 17, 21 to 15. He'll hit the finals or I'm mistaken.

Painted a train with my new #8 sable brush and Whatman paper. Turned out fine, good to have decent materials again.

Service for Hair and Tucker. Prayer for Hyland and Buckley. Very impressive and human. Chaplain Ziegler (now captain) is a swell guy.

Monday, January 17: Wretham—Same as yesterday, some heavy fog that broke into a light overcast in late afternoon.

Finished status board, looks good.

The 370th came over for volleyball in the evening. We beat them five straight games. Really have a hot team.

Show tonight is "Honeymoon Lodge" with Ozzie Nelson and Harriet, Veloz and Yolanda. Not bad. A light comedy.

Sketched another train, may paint it tomorrow.

Homeyer moved into 207 on Saturday. He's from Houston, Texas.

First lieutenant. Good pilot. Funny guy, kinda egotistical, but a good, dry humor. Room 207 is now Doc, Renken, Stewart, Drake, Homeyer, Baldy, and I.

[*In an Allied attempt to break through the Gustav Line, British forces in Italy cross the Garigliano River, pushing northwest to the Aurunci Mountains and Liri Valley. The Germans transfer two armored divisions to oppose their efforts.*]

Tuesday, January 18: Wretham—Same as yesterday, a very dull day. Wrote letters. Painted another watercolour of a train. It's okay. Leaves starting. White and McGeever off tomorrow for seven days. I'm off the 26th. Scotland here I come.

Wednesday, January 19: Wretham—Fairly clear this morning. Pretty sunrise. Briefing scheduled for 1200. Scrubbed at 1030 when weather socked right back in. Nuts.

Another volleyball game today. The 368th hasn't lost a game yet. Throwing darts daily.

Got a letter of commendation from the Major for my work on the status board. Darn nice of him! He sure has improved 100 percent. Morale is damn high and he's really winning some friends.

Letter from Dick Webb today, he's been in Newfoundland, Iceland, and Scotland, now back in the States.

Movie tonight.

[*During a speech to the House of Commons, Foreign Secretary Robert A. Eden warns the Spanish government against continued aid to Germany.*]

Thursday, January 20: Wretham—Same old story, fog, fog, fog. Warm and wet.

Went to line and there was no heat or light. Came back to Hall for the rest of the day. Wrote letters to George, Lester, Charlie and Webb. In the afternoon I painted what is probably the most realistic locomotive in watercolour I've yet done. One thing the English can do is make wonderful Whatman paper and paints. Terrific brilliance and light. Swell painting!

English winter so far has been very gentle. Grass has never lost all its greenness, no freezing, very few frosty mornings. The temperature is usually from 30 degrees to 45 or 50 degrees. Okay by me, snow here would be lousy.

Shot the bull all evening. Shower and bed.

[Royal Air Force bombers drop 2,300 tons of bombs on Berlin.]

Friday, January 21: Wretham—Weather finally broke beautifully. Warm, sunny, with good visibility.

Briefed at 1200 after early lunch. Colonel had a wonderful briefing. His humor, his quiet assurance, he really can give a pep talk, has a natural gift for real leadership. We have the "milk run" again, Calais-area patrol for low bombing of gun emplacements, etc.

Hunter flew my ship with Hag leading. Homeyer and Baldy flew element. Beautiful group assembly. No excitement on the mission. Some of the boys aren't back. Hunter and Hag at Manston. The group was out for three and a half hours.

Movie tonight. Party tomorrow night. Received my other blouse today, also a letter from the Scarletts.

Saturday, January 22: Wretham—Another front. Lousy weather, overcast with high winds.

Usual day of censoring mail and playing darts. Read, sketched.

Hag and Hunter came back from Manston in the afternoon during a lull in the weather.

Another party tonight. Better than last one, some fairly good women. Jitterbug contest. Doc Jones sang "Handlebars in the Moonlight." He's nuts, but funny. Pretty well behaved bunch, until the girls left at midnight, then the fun really started. Me 'n Baldy besieged the first floor from the balcony. "Balloons" full of water.

Chauncey (Major Irvine) joined in with a fire extinguisher. Doc Jones with a bed roll. Oh, we had a great time. Hiccup!

[The Allies begin Operation Shingle, the four-month assault on Anzio, Italy.]

Sunday, January 23: Wretham—All very quiet in Hall this morning. Only

Wretham Hall Interior.
Courtesy of Thomas P. Smith: Archived by Char Baldridge, Historian, 359th Fighter Group Association

a handful for breakfast. I got up at 8:00 A.M., why, I don't know. Sat around until 10:00 A.M. and then <u>walked</u> down to line for fresh air. Weather breaking.

Flew a practice mission dive-bombing off Cromer with 100 pound practice bombs. Me, Baldy, Randy, and Hag were Red Flight. They flew beautiful formation! Really good. We Split S (*half-rolled*) at 15,000 feet out of squadron Lufberry, dove at 60 degrees left to 10,000 feet and released. Captain Shaw led the squadron for the first time. Did okay. Clouds over water prevented our using a "slick" target, we just dumped 'em into the soup. Good to fly again.

Good chicken dinner. Wrote a letter to Margot. Received warning order for tomorrow morning, good weather predicted.

Monday, January 24: Wretham—Briefed at 0930. Flying area patrol instead of weaving escort. Each group assigned an area along bomber's route to clear out, result of success of milk run, at bombers request. Heading 142 degrees to southeast of Brussels, patrol to Dinant, German border.

Me, Randy, Hag, and Baldy took off in beautiful formation. Those guys are terrific!! Whole squadron talked about us. I love those guys!

Mosse led Red Flight, I led Yellow, Hawk led Green, a good section of 12 ships.

The bombers were called back due to bad weather. We never saw them, or anything else. Controller sent us all over central Belgium looking for any bombers who hadn't returned. All we saw were loads of P-47s from 25,000 to 30,000 feet. Stratocumulus to 29,000 feet, 8-10/10ths below. Warm front and rain at base. No trouble.

Tuesday, January 25: Wretham—Spent morning at line reading *God is My Co-Pilot*. Pretty good. Briefing at 1230. Scrubbed at 1235.

Hag and Randy took off on local flight to visit friends nearby.

We tried to take off again at 1515, actually taxied up by ops shack, but Homeyer waved us back. We never did fly. Heavy cumulus and showers were responsible.

Played badminton with Tommy Lane in the new hut across the road. Great sport.

Very nice letter from Sid Field yesterday, wants me to look him up in London, guess I will, too.

I'm sleepy as Hell tonight, and so to bed early for a change.

[After seeing Sid Field perform in "Strike a New Note" in November, Howard dropped the actor a note, complimenting Sid on his talent and the success of the show. The gracious actor responded personally to Howard's letter, inviting the young fighter pilot to "look him up" when he next returned to London.]

Wednesday, January 26: Wretham—Briefing scheduled for 0800 scrubbed at 0630. Briefing at 0915 scrubbed 10 minutes before start engines. A bomb mission, too, dammit, with 500-pound bombs.

Flew locally at 1,100 to 1,200 feet, alone in *Clumpy*. Buzzed all along the canals west and north of Ely, swell time. Cruised 275 IAS at 40" at 100 feet. Not bad!!

Big volleyball battle in the afternoon between "A" & "B" Flights and "C" & "D" Flights. We lost the third game by two lousy points.

Packed for leave tonight. Hope to get out of here tomorrow if Group ever cuts the goddam orders. Meanwhile here I sit wasting time.

Lemmens and Renken left tonight. Guess I was dumb not to do likewise. Oh, well, tallyho, a week is a week.

[President Pedro P. Ramirez of Argentina informs President Roosevelt that he has signed a decree of breach of diplomatic relations with Germany and Japan.]

Thursday, January 27: Leave, Wretham to London—A <u>very</u> warm, cloudy, windy day, which found me awake at 7:30 A.M. for a quick shave, breakfast, a call to Group to check my leave orders. Left the station at 9:15 A.M. with the courier in a 2-1/2 6 x 6, the driver, Nick, 12 years a cab driver, made that truck purr. We made it to Thetford in 12 minutes, hit 55mph.

Caught the 932, it was running 10 minutes late, rode comfortably in third class compartment in first car. Read a mystery book. Pleasant, slow journey. Arrived London 1315. Talked with the engineer, looked over the 2800 Cl. 4-6-0 three-cylinder. A nice guy. Said our USA 280s are great.

A cab to 105 Gloucester. Delightfully warm and clearing fast, took lining out of greatcoat. Helen greeted me. Room 11 again. Nice. Went 'round the corner to the Angelo, a Greek restaurant, for a <u>delicious</u> lunch of Brussels sprout, soup, macaroni, cheese, chips, and jam pudding. Then to movie on Baker Street, "The Little Foxes" with Bette Davis. Good but heavy. The theatre (Classic) is very modern. Out at 4:30 P.M. took cab to Reindeer for tea.

Walked to Piccadilly and saw "And the Angels Sing" with Dorothy Lamour, Hutton, and MacMurray. Screwy and good! Out at 7:30 P.M., took cab to the Greeks and a good supper of Vienna steak.

Very warm and clear with a new moon. Searchlights were cutting weird patterns above London, heard airplanes but no alarms. In my room at 8:45 P.M. Read in bed 'til nearly 12. Lights out. Grand sleep. Relaxed. Happy. Free as the very air which carries spring's advance messenger outside.

[On January 19, 1944, the Soviet's Second Shock Army, 59th Army, and 42nd Army link up near Krasnoe on the Eastern Front, crippling German forces in the Petergof and Streina areas. German forces fight on, but on January 27 a 324-gun salute announces the end of the siege of Leningrad.]

Friday, January 28: London—Slept until 9:00 A.M. Ate breakfast in room and finished painting C.P.R. *(Canadian Pacific Railroad)* double-header. Bathed, shaved, shampooed, went for lunch to Swedish restaurant on Crawford Street, delicious Swedish dish, gnocchi, cheese covered hominy-like stuff. Swell.

Walked to Bond Street and bought a Frank Wootton print of some Mosquitoes and a diary for Hagan. Went to Reindeer Club to check train schedules. Cab to Euston. Saw "City of London" 1943, 4-6-2 Streamliner. Nice engine. Got LMS *(London, Midland & Scottish Railway)* locomotive booklet.

Cab back to 105 Gloucester at 3:30 P.M. Cleaned up, cab to Slaters for good tea (Welsh rarebit).

Walked to theatre and was advised to go to the stage door. Caught the end of the afternoon performance. Sid came out to meet me in a golf outfit, was very cordial. Went up to his room and met another looey, Eldon Mills.

Sid loves that letter I sent him. Had tea and met "Goofy." She's nuts! Saw show, left after "bells" number. Met Sid and Alec Pleon at theatre bar. A nice visit over good Scotch. Saw rest of the show then met Sid and Miss Dorothea Martin (wow) in dressing room. To the Trocadero for several drinks in little bar, just we three. Fun.

Sid is very nervous, energetic, always the actor, and very pleased with his success. He's anxious for Hollywood but a regular guy, sincere, friendly, good hearted, and one constant laugh. His energy never ceases. He is big and strong but dissipated and older in appearance. He had a dinner date at 9:30 P.M. so I went to the Reindeer Club afoot. Walked to Swedish snack bar on Crawford Street for a snack. Room at 10:30 P.M. Bed at 3:00 A.M. Some day!!

Saturday, January 29: London—Waked at 9:00 A.M., breakfast of oatmeal, tea, toast and jam. Shaved leisurely, checked some sketches, phoned up Glasgow for a room at Central Hotel (LMS) tomorrow. These English operators are friendly, informal. When I got the room, the operator broke in and said "my, aren't you the lucky one." I nearly died laughing.

Another warm (March, NY) day. Cab at 12:15 P.M. to the Trocadero. Sid and William Stiles (Show director) at bar. A quick Scotch, then a Mister Barry (theatrical agent and a helluva nice man) joined us. Four for lunch right past the long queue for private table. Some fun. Sid has a lousy cold but still peppy. Interesting visit. Stiles is a well-educated, likeable chap. All are very cordial.

Went round to theatre, spent entire afternoon and evening in Sid's room "soaking" it up. Visited with him between numbers. Met Triss Henderson and had tea around the corner with Jerry Desmonde who was in the RAF but has a bad gut (he invited me, was I surprised) a helluva swell guy and good looking. Talked with Alec Pleon and of course Dorothea Martin. Owen Price (Secretary) also there. Don't get the Martin angle.

Sid hurt his toe on a rolling prop (rolled over it) in the drunk scene. Poor guy can hardly walk but the show must go on. Not such an easy life!!

After matinee, Laurence Olivier and Vivien Leigh came up. Both are charming and she is beautiful. I've never seen such eyes in a woman, sparkling green. Gawd, what a temper I'll betcha! Very lovely and cordial to me. They don't want Sid to go with MGM, say contracts tie you down and you don't make any money. Have to pay English and US taxes. Camera no fun compared to audience. Had scripts with them, offered very interesting comments. They both should know.

Went down to bar with Sid and "Dotty" after the bell scene for several Scotches. Some guy named Tony Bizell and an actress named Margaret Miles visited with us. She was very dramatic. Also met Pasqual, a big London producer!

When the show finished and Dotty was gone, Sid and I went up to Fred Pollit's office (the theatre manager). A US Sailor was visiting with Fred, so amidst an air raid, flak, bombs near and mucho Scotch we had four rather high people. An unforgettable hour. Oh, Gawd that Scotch. Fred quite a guy. Sid nearly missed his train home.

I staggered to Reindeer Club at 9:30 P.M. Ate in a daze, nearly passed out, and (god knows how) walked to 105 Gloucester. Staggered upstairs, really drunk, and fell into bed. Why I didn't heave I'll never know. Wot a day! Wot an unforgettable day.

[Eight hundred US bombers launch attacks against Frankfurt and Ludwigshafen.]

Sunday, January 30: London—Up at 7:30 A.M. to pack. Helen brought me breakfast and two cheese sandwiches to take on train. Left 105 Gloucester at 8:45 A.M. in a cab to Euston. Aboard the once "Royal Scot" third class carriage with good big windows. Thirteen cars, #6223 4-6-2 all the way. Nice sunny/cloudy day. Lovely.

Left at 10:00 A.M. Rugeley first, then Crewe (huge engine sheds), thru "Ruhr Valley of England" to Carlisle via Preston, Lancaster and over famed Shap Summit. Lancaster to Carlisle a beautiful ride up over barren moors and steep hills, a bit like those "open faced" coast mountains near San Luis Obispo coupled with Vermont. Blackout at Scottish border, arrived Glasgow at 8:00 P.M. in 10 hours. Traveled 401 miles and made 6 stops. Good!

Nice room in the Central Hotel. Very old, typical American room, a bit like Copley Plaza. Served a delicious dinner in very lovely, richly appointed Malmaison Restaurant in hotel. Beautifully served. An exact duplicate of a smart New York restaurant. One surprising thing, no tipping in hotel, service charge added for everything even bellhops. A very nice day. Loch Lomond tomorrow.

Monday, January 31: Glasgow—Up at 7:00 A.M. Breakfast at 7:30 A.M. Left Hotel at 8:15 A.M. for Washington Street Bus Terminal in grey drizzle. Glasgow is like Chicago, brick streets, streetcars, warehouses. Central Station elevated like C&NW *(Chicago & NorthWestern)*.

Bus (like Thetford Bus) at 8:45 A.M. Twenty miles to Balloch at foot of Loch Lomond. Up west shore via Luss to Arrochar, cut over hill to Loch Long, thence after 15 minute stop, up "Rest & Be Thankful" pass over craggy moors and down into Loch Fyne valley and Inveraray. Four hours there, coffee at Junior Officer's Club. Sketched, ate lunch (lobster pie). Painted in the rain until MPs said no mo' pitcher. Balls!

Walked about. Had tea at JOC, snotty English looeys. Very homesick all of a sudden. Th' Hell with the whole British Empire, I'm an <u>American</u>!

Bus back at 4:30 P.M. via same route. Arrived here at Central at 7:30 P.M.

Nice scenic day, rain showers, low scudding clouds on mountaintops. Some sunlight, nice light and dark patterns, like New England minus the trees, all yellow ochre and rich brown tones, trees along waters, not high at all. Very old hills. Rugged granite outcroppings. Loch Fyne and Long empty into Firth of Clyde, navigable to all ships.

Dinner in Malmaison. Braised goose excellent but felt lousy since 3:00 P.M. Same old gut trouble. Me for bed and the Hell with everything, especially the war!

Excerpts from the January 1944 Informal Report of Morale for the 359th Fighter Group, submitted by "Chappie" Ziegler indicated that: "The month of January saw the high morale suddenly waver, momentarily falter, and then soar up again, as these men for the first time felt the full lash of war. On the 11th, four well liked pilots failed to return from a mission. Each man down to the lowest private, suddenly fully realized, perhaps for the first time, that we were a part of this war, and began to work with just a bit more determination.

"On the 4th of the month this group went on record as being one of the few fighter groups to begin each mission with a prayer by the chaplain. The suggestion was put to a vote among the pilots and was unanimously accepted by them."

Captain Wilbur C. "Chappie" Ziegler (left) praying with pilots.
Photo courtesy of Thomas P. Smith: Archived by Char Baldridge, Historian, 359th Fighter Group Association

HEADQUARTERS 359TH FIGHTER GROUP
Office of the Group Historian
APO 637 / US Army
4 February 1944

History of the 359th Fighter Group, January 1944

January 1944 produced the 359th Fighter Group's first victories in aerial warfare, and its first combat losses. Ten missions were flown against the Luftwaffe and of the 557 aircraft dispatched in the month, four did not return.

These losses were suffered 11 January when bad weather, a partially executed recall, and a violent reaction by the German Air Force resulted in one of the great days of air combat in the history of the war, with 60 bombers being lost in assaults on Oschersleben, Halberstadt and Brunswick. The German Air Force lost more than 247 fighters.

Of the four pilots lost by the 359th that day, one was last seen entering cloud over enemy territory at 15,000 feet with Me109s on his tail; one fell off into a compressibility dive near the English Coast, apparently a victim of anoxia, and two were killed in bad weather crashes in England.

The 359th had to wait 10 days before beginning to avenge those men. A single enemy aircraft was destroyed on 29 January—more than a dozen Thunderbolts collaborated in a savage and overeager assault which resulted in claims by four separate pilots for credit for the victory, and the next day the numerical score against the Luftwaffe was equaled by a claim of 3-1-3: two Me109s and a Junkers Ju88 destroyed, another Ju88 probably destroyed, and three other enemy aircraft damaged.

In another direction, the 359th prepared rather apprehensively for its first dive-bombing, but since these missions invariably were improvisations arranged when bad operational weather scrubbed larger enterprises, an atmosphere of comic opera crept into the general attitude toward this part of the fighters' job.

Although sweating ground crews repeatedly "bombed up" for thunderbombing assignments, and the 359th even flew 330 miles to Leeuwarden on 28 January (to find the target obscured by cloud), the month ended without any of its 500-pound bombs being cast upon the enemy.

Life in the ETO began to be both simpler and more complex as personnel completed acclimatization, broadened the social base of their off-duty life, and found their menus improving on the station. In token of their status as semi-veterans, by completing three months ETOUSA service, they also began to go on seven day leaves.

East Wretham was invaded by determined parties of engineer corps officers planning its transformation into a bomber command station, and the usual rumor of imminent departure freshened anew, but life in Wretham took on a new blossom. Ground officers encountered hardships in new Nissen hut quarters but those remaining at Wretham Hall had more room.

Two Saturday night officers' parties were held, and both of those were considered smashing shows. Motion pictures began to be shown thrice weekly for the officers. Restrictions on leave, which had been limited to 48 hours off the station per month, were relaxed, and partly because of the introductions achieved at the 2 dances, social life on leave noticeably improved for the pilots.

The weather defied the gloomy prophets of misery and remained good on the ground, although cloud made missions a matter of hours of instrument flying. Nevertheless, as the season marched toward spring and the gloom of the late mornings and early afternoons of December began to vanish, the spirits of all Yanks throve. Health generally was good and the mess improved, enhanced by the supply of all the thousand varied items needed to keep the 359th Fighter Group functioning.

Feeding the station was a major operation. First Lieutenant David Steine, the station quartermaster, reported that foods consumed at Wretham from 1 January to 31 January involved these totals: chicken, 3,807 pounds; turkey, 1,800 pounds; steak, 6,644 pounds; other beef, 20,409 pounds; pork, 6,134 pounds; frankfurters and other luncheon meats, 3,363 pounds; bread, 27,900 pounds.

Fowl and fresh meats were served at 34 meals, as against 22 in December (partially invalidating the general unofficial nomenclature of "Spam Medal" for the ETO ribbon) and fresh eggs and fresh oranges were twice served to all station personnel, while pilots continued to receive their normal issue of 3 fresh eggs and as many fresh oranges per week.

Since the combat efficiency in the air depended, in the final assessment, on the efficiency of all the varied activities on the Station, a brief statement by Lieutenant Steine of the supply situation as of 31 January, 1944, may be of interest:

Class II and IV (Clothing, Stationery, Cleaning & Preserving Materials, etc.)
1. Organizations on the Station currently reports a combined average percentage of 93 percent for T/BA equipment received and on hand.
2. Individual clothing and equipment is currently reported by the same organizations as approximately 99 percent complete. All personnel on the station have their complete modified clothing allowance for

this Theater of Operations as authorized under Amini. Cir. No. 97, HQ, ETOUSA, dated 18 December 1943.

3. Office supplies, stationary and cleaning and preserving materials are requisitioned on a 30-day basis. Items generally in short supply in these categories are mimeograph paper, envelopes, brooms, brushes, and insecticides.

4. This station has on hand all barracks equipment laid down in RAF Scales of Entitlement (with the exception of 100 Officer's Mattresses, which are no longer in production) to which it is entitled.

Class III (Petrol, Coal and Coke)

1. During the month of January, 20,956 gallons of MT Petrol were issued compared with 20,936 gallons issued in December 1943.

2. Inventory, or stock on hand, of coal and coke, as of 28 January 1944, totaled 470.13 tons of coal and 278.13 tons of coke respectively. During January 138.10 tons of coal and 121.40 tons of coke were received. Total issues of coal and coke for the month totaled 230 tons. Based on inventory, a continuance of the present rate of consumption, this station has approximately 12 weeks supply on hand.

Similarly, with air corps supply, the position was much improved over December. Processing efficiency improved with a move of new offices next to the warehouse. The depot at Wattisham inaugurated a daily delivery service, and although aircraft parts remained closely controlled, they could, with persistence, be obtained.

There were sundry exceptions to this general rule: winter flying jackets for pilots, for example, were unobtainable. The squadrons remained short of both hydraulic pumps and aircraft jacks, but most things could be found if one looked long enough.

An example of a supply problem not recently encountered arrived on 25 January, when Colonel Tacon was notified of his promotion from lieutenant colonel to a full colonelcy. At a meeting of officers where Lieutenant Colonel Grady L. Smith, the station executive, announced the fact, Colonel Tacon made a somewhat oblique reference to the "chickens" which would now adorn his shoulders.

But the eagles were, in fact, nowhere to be found. The officer most intimately concerned had not protected himself against the requirements of promotion, and there were not other budding colonels storing insignia against the happy day. A number of volunteer missions to London began to be organized to obtain the silver birds.

At this point Lieutenant Duane H. DeMarcus, supply officer, went to work, and 24 hours later turned up with eagles obtained from the 359th's neighbors at Bodney, where the insignia had been reposing in an air corps supply stockroom.

Of the other officer promotions of the month, most were in the 368th Squadron.

Briefing developed a new aspect; the award of medals and decorations by the group commander, in token of past combat duty, occurred just before announcement of the new mission for the day.

At this period the Air Medal was awarded for a single victory or, in the ETO, for ten sorties against the enemy. By VIII Fighter Command standards, a belly-tank mission to the limit of endurance in support and escort of heavy bombers counted as a double sortie.

The first victory came on the 17th mission flown by the 359th. Claims for this first victory were filed by four pilots, but many hours of hard flying were first recorded.

January 1st was a rare day, since a release until 0800 2 January arrived late on 31 December. The pilots relaxed, but the next day there was considerable, and, as it turned out, unfruitful activity, revolving around a proposed practice dive-bombing on the southern sands of the Wash. This was eventually scrubbed by the 67th Wing before the aircraft took off. Also that day, new call signs ("Jackson" for the 368th and "Wheeler" for the 370th) came into effect, and Colonel Tacon confirmed selection of "Cum Leone" as the 359th's motto.

The first mission of the year did not materialize until the fourth day of the month, when an early (0730) briefing arrived for a Ramrod penetration on the way to Münster.

The 359th's share of the mission was unremarkable. Colonel Tacon, who led, was displeased by the 12 early returns, bad formation flying, and the general snafu condition of the mission when the 359th arrived to take up escort of a scattered bomber task force. This displeasure was increased by the pride with which he had complimented the performance in the 31 December assault on the Paris ball bearing works.

Mission No. 9, 5 January, was a better show, though, as it turned out at subsequent critiques, the bombers were lost and never sure of their positions or targets. The official story of the mission ended with bombs away on five targets of opportunity.

But Mission No. 10 on 7 January was generally regarded as a good job of work: shepherding five scattered combat wings of bombers along their withdrawal from Ludwigshafen. The VIII Fighter Command FO was 215.

The mission report perhaps does not sufficiently emphasize the achievement of leaving the briefed course to duck and dodge through holes in the overcast, arriving at the rendezvous at the scheduled time. Spitfires were late in arriving, so the 359th Group stayed with its big friends until the RAF did appear.

The weather was very bad and the conventional FO injunction "remain to the limit of endurance" had been scrupulously obeyed, with the result that 30 of the 59 aircraft which flew landed at other fields, and it was hours before the welcome "all accounted for" could be circulated through the squadrons.

Weather now restricted operations, but a RAF circus of Typhoons and Spitfires visited Wretham, as did Captain Jorgenson, AJAX. For both pilots and ground defense crews manning machine guns, aircraft recognition was a constant anxiety.

The mission of January 11 was defined in FO 216 of the VIII Fighter Command: to support the rear elements of 300 B-17s from Diepholz to the Dutch Coast as the bombers returned from attacking the Focke-Wulf 190 plant at Oscherleben and the Ju88 wing manufacturing factory at Halberstadt.

There resulted one of the great struggles of the air battle of Germany. And this battle was fought by the Americans under a grave handicap; the weather "socked in" at the bombers' home bases, and the recall signal was given by the controllers while the Liberators of the 2nd Division had just crossed the Dutch frontier entering Germany. As a result, all the carefully arranged schemes of escort and support had to be jettisoned and combat decisions made in midair.

Visibility aloft was poor due to a heavy haze hanging from 20,000 to 27,000 feet and there was 10/10 cloud from the English Coast all the way to the Continent and inland. Colonel Tacon's blind flying instruments went out and he was forced to abort near the Dutch Coast, command passing to Major Swanson. The group was broken up by a combination of the overcast and the bombers in distress, encountered soon after landfall, and elements of the 359th helped protect bombers in every one of the three divisions, driving off a number of enemy attacks.

Major Tyrrell of the 368th Squadron led a section of eight ships into the briefed rendezvous, while Major Swanson's section escorted first B-24s and then, returning inland, B-17s out of the enemy-held area.

The only combat casualty of the day was Second Lieutenant Edward J. Hyland who spun out of a Lufberry after a bounce by Me109s and disappeared into the overcast with enemy fighters pursuing him.

But there were three other losses. One was Captain James E. Buckley, a West Pointer and like Hyland, a Philadelphian, who was last seen in a compressibility dive from 22,000 feet over the North Sea. The other two were victims of the weather and of their inability to get satisfactory homings under the ceiling that at times was down to less than 500 feet.

Lieutenant Lynn W. Hair crashed into a tree in the middle of England, near Chipping Warden, miles past and south of his base. Flying with Lieutenant Ray S. Wetmore, he obviously had decided against reentering the overcast to gain altitude for a fix, the course adopted by Lieutenant Wetmore, and crashed soon after he peeled off from Wetmore's wing. The latter testified his altimeter "showed 300 feet" when he landed at Molesworth, and this may have deceived Hair.

Lieutenant William N. Tucker Jr., equally lost, flew west into Wales where he crashed near Rednal Shropshire in the Shrewsbury area.

A light on Captain Buckley's character and worth is given by a poem found in his effects:

"Thoughts"

The green of the grass, the glitter of lakes,
The things I call my own
Are gone away, nor will return
Till the seeds of faith are sown.

The sun that shines, the trees that sigh,
The loves that I have known
Will never smile or speak again
Till I am heading home.

The peace I know, the faith I have,
In which I'm not alone
Will stay within all of us
Till from this Hell we've flown.

Please God that we may leave this place
As swift as we have come
To find the things we love the best,
When here our work is done.

Another difficulty with the 67th Wing homing system developed in the case of First Lieutenant Glenn C. Bach, assigned to a relay patrol over the

North Sea. An incorrect vector sent him on a course out in the North Sea for 35 minutes before he decided to fly due west, which he did for half an hour, eventually crashing, gasoline almost gone, in a sheep field in Northumberland near Hexham. He was reported as NYR until 1813 on the 11th, when, within 15 minutes, the news of his crash and those involving Hair and Tucker were relayed to combat intelligence by Captain Robert F. Malley, flying control officer.

Only two of the four losses on the 11th were officially listed as missing in the air combats of the day, but the 359th Group felt that it had lost all four men to the Germans, and as Colonel Tacon said at the next briefing, that they would get their own back and some more from the Luftwaffe. They felt also that their share of the escort was well done, finding testimony thereof in the official story of the mission, and in the official tributes to the work of the Eighth that day, including General James H. Doolittle's view as given in General Kepner's letter of 27 January, 1944.

The next chore tackled was the assignment that came to be known as the "milk run," which is to say Plan Eye Que and its constant, dull patrolling of the Pas de Calais area. This time, 14 January under FO 217, the 359th stayed in the area for 97 minutes until the bombers made their final run over the last patch of woods and all bombs were away and bombers out, 36 minutes late.

There was intense flak, which hit and caused minor damage to Colonel Tacon's airplane, as well as the ship flown by his wingman, Lieutenant Cunningham. Otherwise the only interest of the day focused on the identity of the airplane bounced at 7,000 feet by a section of the 368th led by Major Gray. Major Gray fired nine rounds from each gun before he saw an American insignia on the aircraft and he returned home still not sure of its type, although the other pilots believed it a P-51. His gun-camera film showed no image.

Bad weather scrubbed operations immediately thereafter. Major John R. Fitzpatrick, combat intelligence officer, warned unit commanders to prepare for biological warfare by the Germans. The long-delayed arrival of an opeidoscope allowed the launching of Lieutenant John E. Regan's recognition training schedule. Investigation of the "sabotage" incidents of the previous month continued and FOs were scrubbed with great regularity.

The first mission flown after this period was again an Eye Que patrol on 21 January under VIII Fighter Command FO 221. The feature of this assignment was the launching by the gunners at Clacton-on-Sea of a somewhat personal vendetta against pilots of the 359th Group, although Zed Battery rockets fired at the bombers in France were reported by the flights for the first time. The patrol time in the target area, 115 minutes, also was a new high.

A dive-bombing practice was run on 23 January. During the run Major Sam R. Marshall, ordnance officer, and Second Lieutenant John L. Downing saw from a Lysander a submarine that hurriedly submerged. Coastal Command was notified through Wing A-2.

On the 24th the patrol technique extended to deep penetrations. Another innovation was the creation of a "bouncing squadron" to attack enemy formations some distance from the bomber course. An order had already been received to take down signs declaring the fighters' first objective to be the number of bombers safely brought home, and this obviously was the beginning of a new and determinedly offensive fighter policy.

It received no very fair test on the 24th, since once more the weather closed in unexpectedly and the bombardment formations were recalled. The fighters, however, patrolled their assigned areas. Neither bombers nor enemy aircraft were seen and the 359th spent an uneventful 86 minutes over enemy-held land.

On 25 January a fighter sweep was in prospect until 1003, when Wing told the 359th to practice dive-bombing. Uncertainty about cloud over the practice ranges lasted until mid-afternoon and then, with the group "bombed up" and ready to go, difficulty in effecting a clearance through the 12th Group of the RAF led Colonel Tacon to scrub the whole show. It was, all hands agreed, a wearing day.

Equally so was the 26th, when two bigger shows were ordered and scrubbed by 0640. At 0806, Wing ordered thunderbombing on a Dutch airdrome and the 359th briefed on this mission, only to have another scrub message at 1007. That afternoon, John Houbolt, chief of the OWI section on Holland, talked to the pilots on his native land: a part of the general reemphasis on geography in pilot training.

Next day, Flight Lieutenant Clifford A.S. Anderson, 401 RCAF Fighter Squadron, talked about night fighting to the pilots in another meeting, emphasizing the lay-out of the Drem System.

The 359th Group once more briefed for thunderbombing on the 28th. This was another hurry-up job with considerable uncertainty about the weather. A four ship weather reconnaissance got off at 1305 to look over Leeuwarden, but they were still on their way home when the Group, carrying 500-pound bombs, took off on the main run. The Group found the target areas obscured by cloud, and never did see the 352nd (based at the neighboring station of Bodney) which had flown over Wretham during our take off. A rendezvous 19 minutes after our take off had been scheduled.

Wing reported the 359th south of its briefed course, in the middle of the Zuider Zee, and then at 1603, over Leeuwarden. This was an anomaly, since no port turn was made. Equally mysterious was the exit of the four weather ships, which landed at Manston after finding themselves far south of course. Flak hit Lieutenant Lester G. Taylor's airplane. His knowledge of geography had prevented him from going in for a landing, although he had for a moment believed he was nearing the southern edge of the Wash.

The 359th Group's first claims were made as the month ended. The first score was on 29 January, when an errant Me110 was savagely attacked and destroyed in a wild melee which made prophetic an amusing cartoon First Lieutenant Howard L. Fogg Jr., the 368th's artist-pilot, had drawn weeks before: P-47s converging from every altitude and heading on a stunned enemy pilot. A dozen men took squirts at the Me110. Claims were filed by four. The enemy was, in any event, thoroughly destroyed, one pilot going into and below the overcast to take pictures of the pilot bailing out and the aircraft crashing.

The claimants were Captain Clifton Shaw of the 368th (who had first crack at the 110) and Major Gray, First Lieutenant Clifford E. Carter and Second Lieutenant John H. Oliphint, all of the 369th.

This Me110 was the only enemy airplane sighted. The mission was otherwise uneventful, the by-now-customary overcast delayed our setting course five minutes and the bombers were five minutes late.

Next day produced more claims. A flying visitor that day was Lieutenant Colonel Harold J. Rau, A-3 of the 67th Wing, but he flew the mission with the 370th top cover squadron and saw none of the action found by the 369th, which bounced eight Ju88s forming a line abreast to the left rear flank of the bombers, and also attacked 6 Me109s which dove headlong through the bomber formation. Three were claimed destroyed, with another a probable and three others damaged. That day, incidentally, 49 aircraft got off the ground in 5 minutes 40 seconds.

The month ended with another day of indecision forced by the weather. The penetration originally listed was canceled early, at 0710. Orders to bomb up were received at 0955, and briefing was held at 1330. The lights had just been flashed on after viewing the target and bomb runs on the opeidoscope screen in the briefing room, when word was sent to Colonel Tacon that this mission, too, was scrubbed.

"Chaplain," he called at once, and Chaplain Ziegler gravely walked to the briefing dais to notch, with his ticket-taker's punch, the T.S. card that the Colonel, like every other pilot, had providently been equipped with by the Chaplain for just such contingencies.

News later that day that another group had gone in and bombed the same target with good effect (fires visible 50 miles with a 3,000 foot pillar of smoke) and had, in addition, shot down six enemy planes, did not improve tempers that evening.

But the teletype message of congratulation from General Kepner on the achievements of the 29th and 30th, fortified the 359th Group's conviction that it was in fact ready for the hazards of the future.

5.

FEBRUARY 1944

The Bombing Intensifies

Tuesday, February 1: Glasgow to Edinburgh—Called at 9:00 A.M. Shaved, down to breakfast of sausage and scrambled eggs. Packed, checked out, caught a cab, he drove me about to Sauchiehall Street, the Art Museum, University Hill, Park, and the Auditorium. Glasgow is very plain and ordinary. Typical business city, but withal I like it, and the Scottish people who seem more like our own.

Caught US Train LNER 1120 Queen Street 4-4-0 "Peeble's Shire." Nice comfortable ride to Edinburgh arriving at 12:40 P.M. Into Edinburgh and out of Glasgow the line tunnels under the city. Waverley Station is huge and confusing. Lies in narrow "gulch" of town. The great castle looms up across the gulch from busy Princes Street with its spotless double-deck trams on <u>four</u> wheels.

Edinburgh is terrific! All the picturesque aspects a visitor could wish. Hills, monuments, schools, broad streets, winding alleys, cathedrals, the great castle. A clear, windy day. Perfect. I love it. Durable stone architecture. Rugged!

Tried LNER N. British Hotel. No! Royal British. No! Tram up Princes Street to the LMS Caledonian. Yes! Nicer room than Glasgow. Behold, Renken and Lemmens greet me exuberantly! Good to see them. They've been here the whole time dating the Scottish female populace. They love the women here and they <u>are</u> pretty.

I painted the castle from my room (418) window. Pretty soft. No lunch. Went out at 5:00 P.M. and rode cab around city to Holyrood Palace, Castle, Observatory Hill (fine view) for an hour. Nice cab and drive, more like an American cab.

Ate dinner at L'Apertif on Frederick Street, just off Princes, #24. It's a charming place, modernistic mode with little rooms and alcoves. Intimate and luxurious, the finest restaurant I've struck in Britain. Everything right. A half-dozen oysters to start, macaroni and cheese pot, and Brussels sprout. Followed by caramel custard and coffee, all delicious with good bread and butter. A lovely meal for 12 shillings or $2.40, about like New York, not bad. Supposed to be the best in Edinburgh and I believe it.

Back to hotel on a windy, moonlit night with the Castle silhouetted against scudding silver fringed clouds, beautiful. Here's to Edinburgh, Britain's finest city. "Home" tomorrow.

Wednesday, February 2: en route to Wretham—10:10 A.M. caught LNER first class. A beautiful coach. Eighteen cars with a pusher *(extra locomotive at back of train)* from Dunbar to Berwick. Four cylinder Pacific, changed at Newcastle to a four cylinder #2545 "Diamond Jubilee." Arrived Peterborough at 5:22 P.M., 12 minutes late. Change stations to 705 Lowestoft train. Comes across from Rugby on LMS. Thetford at 9:30 P.M. Truck to field.

Main Gate and MP Station, East Wretham Airfield. *Courtesy of Elsie Palicka, wife of Ed Palicka, 370th Fighter quadron Photographer: Archived by Char Baldridge, Historian, 359th Fighter Group Association*

Notes of happenings at Wretham while I was on leave: Changes in rooms, each flight has a room now. "D" Flight in 207. Me, Hag, Home-yer, Randy, Baldy, and Hunter. Good deal! Shaw and Tyrrell and Doc in 206. Stuart is with "B" Flight, Renken with "A" Flight, and Wiley with G-2 boys. Nelson is in Group and Major Wallace is squadron ex, some good deal! Doc on DS *(Detached Service)* at Bodney.

Gall has *Clumpy* all Simonized, looks wonderful. Also new plugs again.

Group has 3-1-3 *(3 enemy aircraft destroyed-1 probable-3 damaged)* now. Captain Shaw and three others an Me110. Thacker one destroyed, one probable. Four missions while I was gone, dammit.

Some Lysanders on the field, mebbe to tow targets?

Two new pilots in "A" Flight: Beaupre and Ashenmacher. Green.

[The Lysander was a British single-engine high-wing fixed-gear STOL (short take off and landing) multi-purpose aircraft.]

Thursday, February 3: Wretham—Briefing at 0830, took off at 0954. Me, Colonel, Hawk, and Randy. We were on instruments from 18,000 to 22,000 feet. Wow! 10/10ths to Wilhelmshaven/Emden as B-17 escort, sweep area, no bandits.

Two 190s jumped Les Taylor and Thompson. Thompson shot up but landed okay at another base.

One hundred and fifteen mph wind at 28,000 feet over top of soup. Airborne 3 hours 20 minutes. Everyone had gas trouble and a couple bel-lied in. Simmons nearly bailed out in drink. Colonel and I made base. Hurrah for *Clumpy*! Still had 50 gallons!

Colonel complimented our flight. Boy, I was a wreck after leave. Nerve strain. Slept all evening after writing V-mail to Mom, Dad and Margot.

Red Alert tonight. Moonlit night, flares, a distant fire, and a bomb or two. A bad day, overall for us. Terrible weather. Lost 12 USA versus 5 Nazis.

Glad I flew okay.

[Fuel consumption was measured in gallons per hour (gph) and could change dramatically depending on operating conditions. A 1942 test by the War Department Air Corp, Material Division, found that at Military

Rated Power (full throttle 51" Hg, 386 mph at 15,000 feet) a P-47B
burned 250 gph. Republic Aviation tests in 1944, at 75 percent Normal
Rated Power (360 mph at 32,000 feet) resulted in consumption of 135
gph. A postwar Flight Test Division memorandum showed a Maximum
Air Miles per Gallon rating of 51 gph, this at 15,000 feet and an indicated
air speed of 185 mph. In that test, the additional drag and weight of two
165-gallon wing tanks increased fuel consumption to 65 gph.]

Friday, February 4: Wretham—Beautiful day.
Briefing at 0840. Take off 1006. Top squadron, Yellow Flight, with
me, Homeyer, Hag, and Hunter. Shaw section. Goddam good section formation. Picked up bombers okay. Took 'em to Aachen (en route Frankfurt), then swept north and west and home in 2 hours 40 minutes. No
sign of enemy but a little flak around bombers. Cold as Hell. 8-10/10ths
on ground, cumulus at 26,000 feet.

Went up again at 1350, no lunch. Me, Hag, Hunter, and Homeyer.
"D" Flight alone to Calais up coast to Oostende and back at 16,500 feet.
Each flight took off as they gassed up. Fun being all alone above heavy
overcast and cumulus. Big thrill to be boss, set course, go through overcast and find way back. We went to pick up returning bombers. Only
saw some stragglers.

Twenty-two sorties.

[Argentina severs diplomatic relations with Hungary, Rumania, Bulgaria,
and Vichy France.]

Saturday, February 5: Wretham—Briefing at 0830. Take off. Me, Hunter,
Homeyer, and Baldy: Yellow Flight. Shaw section. Beautiful formation.
Eighteen ships all the way! Really lovely. Nice escort over B-17s to
Orleans, Tours airdromes, France, west of Paris southeast of Cherbourg
peninsula. Swept back north at 18,000 feet. Three hours and ten minutes.

Really tired today. Lunch, hot shower, bed! Woke at 5:15 P.M. and
dressed for supper. Wrote letter about leave but didn't finish it. Party
tonight.

C.C. Davis over here. Visited, ate, and had one drink. Dave has two
Fw190s now and 60 sorties. Nice going, but that 352nd sure has lost a
lot of men.

By the way, Crawford (Bird Dog) has been missing since that windy raid on Thursday. Dammit, a good guy.

I'm not partying tonight, have warning order for tomorrow morning. Pretty drunk out there. Hope we don't fly.

Sunday, February 6: Wretham—Briefing at 0815. Take off at 0915. Shaw, Baldy, me, and Homeyer. Shaw blew a tire taxiing so I took over. Burton joined Homeyer in #4 slot from Green Flight. Blue Flight had Colonel leading. Baldy flew beautiful, was Blue Two. Good section; good formation

To Romilly-sur-Seine, escorting B-17s into target at 25,000 feet. Clear above 10/10ths over France. Our section bounced about eight Fw190s at 9,000 feet, but the bastards hid in the clouds. The Colonel's flight fired. We were covering so out of range, no shots. Swell dive and run though. Hit 450 IAS. Gave good cover. Joined fast. Climbed back up. Four P-47s bounced us on the way up. Fw190s all over but we couldn't get 'em. Makes ya mad as Hell.

Kidded with bomber boys. A good mission. Shaw still mad about tire. We all got our Air Medals this afternoon.

Show tonight. Letter from Margot.

[Under heavy German counterattacks, Allied troops withdraw from the beach south of Rome and the Cassino front.]

Monday, February 7: Wretham—Warm front, slight rain, but cleared beautifully about 4:00 P.M. No flying for a change.

Spent morning at line. Played a volleyball game. Sat in on an informal talk by Major Wallace on his trips to Europe while at Dartmouth.

Lectures and movies on weather and aircraft identification at Hall all evening. Very dull. Went to PX and got paid afterwards.

After supper we really cleaned up 207, swept, dusted, threw out furniture, got two wicker and two straight chairs, and a new table. Baldy and Hunter completed their damn fine map of operational area. Re-hung pictures. Room is really nice now, quite livable. Finished long letter about leave. Lazy day.

Shaw made Major tonight. Everyone very pleased!

Warning order so bed at 10:45 P.M.

Tuesday, February 8: Wretham—Wakened at 0620, breakfast at 0640,

Major Clifton Shaw, Operations Officer, 368th Fighter Squadron.
Archived by Char Baldridge, Historian, 359th Fighter Group Association, from records at HQ USAF Research Center, Maxwell Air Force Base, Alabama

briefing 0740, take off at 0910.

Shaw led our squadron, with Hag, me, and Randy. A short 2 hour 20 minute mission to northern France escorting two boxes of B-24s all the way to Crossbow targets, thru 9-10/10ths cumulus.

Beautiful day, a bit hazy here, clouded up in the afternoon. Local flying. Released from line, however. A goddam dull milk run this morning.

Had picture taken with Wallace and Fitzpatrick by a P-47 for Alumni Magazine. Fun! Nothing else.

Major Robert A. Wallace, Lieutenant Howard L. Fogg, Major John R. Fitzpatrick, with P-47. February 8, 1944 photo for Dartmouth Alumni Magazine.
Courtesy of Dartmouth College Library

Felt kinda rotten tonight. Sat by the fire all evening and shot the bull about flying, cadet days, and so on. It was fun looking back, though. Smitty is a riot when telling of his experiences.

Shaved, bed at 10:30 P.M. Wrote to Sid Field and a V-mail to Mom and Dad. Hope I get some pep.

[The Allied "Crossbow" campaign ran from August 1943 to March 1945. A total of 68,913 aircraft took part in missions against experimental stations, production facilities and deployment sites for the German V-1 and V-2 long-range weapons. The V-1 is better known as the buzz bomb, after the distinctive noise of its pulse jet engine.]

Wednesday, February 9: Wretham—Had a briefing for a double mission, they scrubbed that. Changed to a bomb sweep, we got out to our ships, and they scrubbed that. So we quit. A warm front caused all the trouble.

Spent the afternoon sacking in and writing letters. Received airmail from Margot and Mom, V-mail from Dad.

Show tonight. Bread, jam, and butter in 207. Bed at 11:00 P.M.

Thursday, February 10: Wretham—Terrible snow squalls, 300-foot clouds. Briefing at 0815. Take off 0945.

Me, Randy, Hunter, Baldy (Baldy didn't get off, trouble with belly tank): Yellow Flight. Whole group scattered into flights, attempted to form above. We lost everyone.

Climbed for 10,000 feet through snow and soup to 15,000 feet. Windshield iced up badly. Went on across, picked up bombers, many fours of P-47s all over, couldn't identify 'em, picked up Cunningham of 370th but then lost him again.

Went in to Lingen, Germany. Stayed with B-17s the full time, turned back singing "We Three Are All Alone." Hit vicious squalls off and over Yarmouth, made landing field at 400 feet. Wow. Glad to get back. <u>Hardest</u> flight I <u>ever</u> made.

370th had a field day. Kib, Major, and Hodges got one Me109 each. Brown got two Me109s. Ettlesen got one Me109 (369th). No losses. Sure wish the 368th would get in on the fun.

[With the 369th and 370th engaging the enemy and the 368th successfully rendezvousing with and maintaining escort in horrific weather

conditions including cloud formations reaching to 20,000 feet, the 359th Fighter Group received a letter of commendation for this mission from Lieutenant General Carl A. Spaatz, commanding general of US Strategic Air Forces in Europe.]

Friday, February 11: Wretham—Beautiful, warmish day. Cumulus not bad. Briefing at 1015. Take off at 1157.

Me, Shaw, Homeyer, and Baldy: Yellow Flight, close squadron. Baldy aborted mid-Channel, belly tank again. Perk and Downing were the only two in Green Flight to take off.

The five of us tried to cover the B-17 stragglers from Frankfurt (St. Michel to Coast 300 degrees). Prowled around behind the main boxes. We'd go to one B-17, a couple of 109s would pop up from clouds beneath another. We'd chase 'em, they'd Split S down to 14,000 feet. We saw three B-17s go down due to lack of sufficient cover over stragglers. Really pissed off.

Spitfires everywhere made recognition hard. Two Spits jumped us twice, damn 'em. Was ready to shoot them!

Saturday, February 12: Wretham—Weather poor.

Lazy day. Volleyball, wrote letters to Margot, folks, Gil, Rudy. Sack time. Homeyer left on day off, the Norwich gigolo.

Spent evening drawing whacky cartoons. Major Shaw and Colonel Tacon got a kick out of them.

Sunday, February 13: Wretham—No mission. A day of rest per order of 8th Fighter Command. Now they're getting smart!

Everyone slept late. No reveille for enlisted men.

Down to line for geography class.

Wiley is a first lieutenant at long last. He's sure earned it.

A big battle in Room 207. Beds torn up, pillow fight, tables and chairs upturned. Swell fun. All started when I decided Hagan should not sleep after lunch. Wot a mess.

Had fried chicken for dinner. Showed a good movie tonight, "Background to Danger," with George Raft.

Monday, February 14: Wretham—Solid overcast. Cold and raw. Feels like snow.

"The Group Returneth to the Fold," by Captain Howard Fogg.
Courtesy of Elsie Palicka, wife of Ed Palicka, 370th Fighter Squadron Photographer:
Archived by Char Baldridge, Historian, 359th Fighter Group Association

No mission. Released until tomorrow at 0900.

Volleyball game in the morning. Aircraft recognition in the afternoon. Wrote V-mails to Margot and folks (Valentine's Day) and then sack time. Poker game in our room at night. I listened to records in Forehand's room for over an hour.

Note: This business of scrubbing missions is quite the group joke. Three scrubbed in one day last week. Two on the 15th. Colonel Tacon bore witness while Captain Brown presented Mike Donohue with the Royal Order of Scrubbers, a fine scrubbing brush on a ribbon worn about the neck. 8th Fighter sure dreams 'em up fast.

Tuesday, February 15: Wretham—An uncertain day, warm, partial overcast, slight haze.

In readiness all morning. Order to put on bombs.

Ate lunch then back to shack. Released until tomorrow at 1330.

Played volleyball then stopped by PX at 3:00 P.M. Reached Hall.

Ordered back to line to move to advance base overnight for long mission. Got all ready, went to briefing room, and waited. At 1600 still no dope. Finally Colonel Tacon came out, picked up a pointer, looking very serious, and said, "Gentlemen, our paratroopers landed at St. Omer at 3:15 A.M. We are to land there in one hour, refuel, and stage a night fighter sweep at midnight. Any of you that believe this will now stand on your heads, the mission is scrubbed." Some joke! The place went crazy! Laughs, hoots. And so to supper.

Wrote V-mail to Margot, Allie, Auntie Bert.

[Bombers of the US 15th Air Force drop thousands of tons of bombs on the monastery located at the top of Monte Cassino in Italy. President Roosevelt declares that such monuments cannot be spared when American lives are at stake. The attempt to capture its ruins fails despite united attacks by British Commonwealth and Polish forces against the defending Green Devil paratroopers of the Fallschirmjäger Division.]

Wednesday, February 16: Wretham—The worst day of weather yet! Socked in, grey and drizzly all day into the evening.

No mission for the fifth day. Nuts! Getting too darn rested.

Spent the morning at the line. Hawk called the pilots to attention this morning and presented Captain Piazza with a ribbon and cartoon, order of Furlined Pot with Cover, for his retrieving of 'chutes. A swell soldier and he sure was surprised. Some fun.

Painted a train this afternoon. First picture since I did the "Castle" in Scotland, a darn good 4-8-4, Lehigh Valley #5105.

Baldy and Hunter left for London on the 334. Wot a duo!! Wow!

Lieutenant Burgess (from Nashville, 38 years old), who has replaced Harry Scharoff as Wiley's assistant (Scharoff to 78th Group) is a good guy. Reminds me of Ed Holland. Burgess is interested in my painting, and his wife works for the NC&STL *(Nashville, Chattanooga & St. Louis)* railroad.

[In Italy, the German counterattack against the bridgehead held by the US 5th Army at Anzio fails.]

Thursday, February 17: Wretham—My god, another grey drizzly day. This ceases to be funny. This forced "rest" is nuts. A week tomorrow since we've had a ship off the ground.

Again at the line all morning. An escape story by Lieutenant Sheehan (56th) this afternoon. He had quite a time!

Nothing else to mark the day. A poker game in 207 tonight. Doc Jones and Pino rendered a snappy piano duet of "Ida" tonight. Doc really funny, as usual. Wrote V-mail to Margot, Mom.

Randy and Hag and Homeyer are really first class sack artists now. I always know where to find them, anytime.

Balls, think I'll load up on Port. Platt sez tomorrow's weather will be bad too. England. Phttt!

Friday, February 18: Wretham—Still bad weather. Grey, snow today, ground nearly white. At line all morning.

Loafed around later. Painted a fair CNW *(Chicago & North Western)* 4-6-4 in the afternoon.

Movie night.

Baldy and Hunter are back. They had a good time. No rough stuff.

Doc Duennebier returned from his three weeks DS at Bodney. Glad to see him back.

Shaw told Randy if he got up for breakfast tomorrow he'd ground him for two weeks. Randy, "the sack artist."

Oh this confounded weather.

Saturday, February 19: Wretham — What a siege of bad weather.

A good movie on POWs at 0830, then I headed to line for censoring.

After lunch finished painting the CNW 4-6-4. Then started an old-time scene, 4-6-0 at country crossing, wagon hit, farmer punching engineer, with horse running away. Randy loves it, it shall be his.

Yesterday was Hagan's twentieth birthday. Sure seems strange, I'm nearly seven years older than he is. Wow.

Party tonight, so of course we got a goddam warning order. The Hell with these corny parties. I'd rather have a good snack bar. Food has really improved lately, though.

Sunday, February 20: Wretham—Briefing at 0930.

Me, Shaw, Hag, and Randy: Red Flight, high squadron. Mission, to escort seven wings of B-17s from Lingen to Dümmer Lake en route targets near Berlin. Also 15th Air Force up from Italy and 8th Air Force B-17s to Berlin, Poznan, then Russia! Big day in ETO.

Took off on runway four for the first time. Overcast stratocumulus from 2,000 to 5,000 feet but no trouble. No action, a little flak near IJmuiden Landing Field in and out of vicinity. Landed at 1340, 3 hours 5 minutes flight time.

Got terrible gas pains in stomach during flight. Really pained me for a while. Ship ran beautifully after our long layoff. She now has 23 missions. Had a nice squadron formation the whole time.

Brigadier General Edward W. Anderson presenting the Distinguished Flying Cross to Lieutenant Benjamin M. "Hag" Hagen III. *April 13, 1944 photo courtesy of R. Hatter: Archived by Char Baldridge, Historian, 359th Fighter Group Association*

Good chicken dinner on return. Leaving for London on the 556 train alone.

[Hamburg, Leipzig, and Braunschweig are attacked by 970 US 8th Air Force bombers, on this first day of "Big Week."]

Monday, February 21: London—Quite a raid over London last night. Walked from the Reindeer Club to 105 Gloucester. Fires in all directions, heavy ack-ack sirens, streets deserted. There were hits all over the city, from #10 Downing to Paddington and so on.

Spent the night in Room #2 with First Looey Andy Straun, a B-17 pilot. Helluva nice guy. We sat up 'til 2:30 A.M. "bulling." Swell visit. Slept until 10:00 A.M. in #2, a swell room. Nice breakfast.

Went to PX and bought ribbons for Hag and Randy. Lunch at Reindeer. Played records. At 105 Gloucester I moved to Room #8. Cleaned
myself up.

Went to Slater's for tea then to the theatre at 5:00 P.M. Met Dorothy
at the entrance, then Sid, Owen, Styles, Barry, and Desmonde. Went to
the bar as usual. Wickcliffe showed up, some surprise! Been here two
weeks. Sid, Dorothy, Wick, and I went to supper and dancing at the Trocadero. Swell time.

Cab to bed at midnight. Wick really excited, his first visit. He's near
Reading. 570th getting P-38s from the 9th Air Force. Sid and all were
very cordial to him.

*[Jerry Desmonde regularly played straight-man to Sid Field's comic
characters.]*

Tuesday, February 22: London—Breakfast at 0900, loafed, dressed. Cab
to Roberson, bought more watercolour paper. Cold as Hell out.

To Trocadero at 12:30 P.M. to have lunch with Sid and Barry. Sid really likes his watercolour of the C.P.R. Pacifics double-heading. Owen
likes his gloves. Says everyone likes me; he sure is a swell pal. Went 'round
to the theatre and stayed an hour before saying goo'bye.

Back to 105 Gloucester. Read *Perry Mason* for a while then caught
the 546. Damn good meal in the first class diner. Comfortable car, nice
easy trip. Only 15 minutes late. (On time going down.)

Sure enjoyed dancing with Dorothy on Monday, she's a Helluva nice
glamour girl, whatever she does with Sid. Damn nice gal.

The boys had a big day. Colonel Tacon and Doersch shared one.
Mosse's flight jumped three 109s, all pilots bailed out. Mosse, Lemmens,
Cater victorious.

Wednesday, February 23: Wretham—Briefing scheduled but they
scrubbed it at 0930.

Censored mail. Went down to dispersal. Gall changing plugs on
Clumpy, doing 100 hour inspection, sez ship is okay. Has 25 straight
missions now.

"Sid" Brown, Big Springs, Texas, 43-I, Aloe Field, has joined us here
in "D" Flight. Good boy. Has about 95 hours in 47s. We went up this

afternoon. I had Botsy's ship, a <u>sweet</u> D-6. Flew local around rain showers, bombers, buzzed the canals, clouds, etc. Lot of fun, all below 3,000 feet. He did quite well, stayed right along with me, nice crossovers in steep turns. He'll be okay, I think. A good guy and a worthy addition to "D" Flight.

Major Shaw and Pino off on their leave tonight. Hawk and Botsy returned. Had their usual swell time in Scotland.

Movie tonight. Wrote airmail to Margot.

Squadron Recapitulation:
Commanding Officer: Major Tyrrell
Operations: Major Shaw
"A" Flight: Captain Bolefahr, Pino, McGeever, Lane, Keesey, Hudelson, Ashenmacher
"B" Flight: Captain Mosse, Cater, Janney, Lemmens, White, Burton, Beaupre
"C" Flight: Captain Forehand, Smith, Hawk, Perkins, Simmons, Botsford, Drake
"D" Flight: First Lieutenant Fogg, Hagan, Homeyer, Hunter, Baldy, Randy, Brown
S-2: Wiley, Burgess
Engineer: Stuart
Supply: Arthur
Exec: Wallace
Adjutant: Stearns
Armament/Ordnance: Thomas
Comm: Renken, Segal
Doctor: Duennebier

Thursday, February 24: Wretham—Gorgeous <u>cloudless</u> day. Some ground haze to 2,500 feet.

Briefing at 0915. Start engines at 1024. Take off at 1034. Colonel Tacon with us. Me, Baldy, Hag, and Randy: Yellow Flight. Baldy had to come back due to rough engine, just after we left. Major Tyrrell led Red Flight. We escorted 300 B-17s from Egmond to east of Zwolle.

A few bandits. Major Murphy got one but lost Niccolai, his second man. Major Tyrrell climbed us up to 30,000 feet chasing six FWs into

Germany. The group Xmas-ed, Hag and Randy turned, Major kept on and got two of 'em. McGeever got another. Goddam the luck!!

Landed. Grabbed a sandwich. Crews were waiting for us with tanks, ammo, and so on. Fast work!! Took off again in 20 minutes at 1356. Major Tyrrell, Randy, me, and Baldy. We went in at Knocke to Brussels for withdrawal support. No action. Swept all over for an hour, out way down at Le Touquet. It was a rat race coming home, loops, rolls, and so on.

I flew rotten today. Really pissed me off. Tired.

Friday, February 25: Wretham—Take off at 1112. Prop out on take off so I circled and returned. Very mad! P-47s are <u>heavy to land</u> with <u>400 gallons</u>! Grease on brushes only trouble. Gall is pulling 100 hour inspection now. Okay!

Homeyer, Baldy, Hunter went on as Blue Flight. No excitement on the mission. They went way in to Saarbrucken, saw the Alps in far distance. Three and one-half hours. All returned okay. Charlie Mosse led squadron. Swanson led group, Forehand the section. A little flak was all.

Movie tonight was "Iceland" with Sonja Henie and John Payne. Phooey!

Big argument in 207 about coming out on deck, gunnery, etc. Very healthy occupation, providing they don't drive me crazy. Bed at 10:00 P.M. Bad weather forecast for tomorrow.

Saturday, February 26: Wretham—A lousy day with fog and rain but warm.

Went to line for censoring mail and shots (ouch). My typhoid is a little bastard this time!

Slept all afternoon after aircraft recognition at 1330. Good steak supper. Wrote letters most of the evening.

Feel very dull and listless. Guess it's the weather and the shots. Received a swell letter from Webby today, sure would love to see that guy.

Doc is playing the piano. He's good. I'll learn yet!

Released tomorrow for "rest and maintenance." And so to bed.

[US forces in the European Theater of Operation received immunization shots for smallpox, typhoid, tetanus, and typhus. Shots for plague, cholera, and diphtheria were given "when necessary" or in the "presence

of danger." The frequency of booster shots was adjusted during the war years as was the mix. For example, the diphtheria immunization became a theater requirement in 1945.]

Sunday, February 27: Wretham—Everyone slept late, no reveille. I got up for breakfast, loafed around, went down to the photo lab and copied a photo of four P-47s taking off for a watercolour.

Fried chicken dinner was good.

Went to Bodney in the command car with Tyrrell, Swanson, Forehand, and Orwig. Saw Fieg, Gates, and Davis. Don't like their layout. Hi-ridged grass field and their hall is way off from the field. Things are scattered all over. Good visit, though. Fieg all shot up by 20mm when their four were jumped. Only he and the other wing man came back. Some luck. Fw 190s are still tough!

Quiet evening reading. Poker game in 207. Brownie is married. Bed at 1030.

Monday, February 28: Wretham—Good weather, snow squalls in heavy cumulus.

Brownie "soloed" in Hag's ship. Mine is back in shape. Flew down to see Herway in the afternoon. Klein off course, landed at 363rd P5/B (Rivenhall). Cleared, took off, and found Wormingford okay. Nice field and runways, made a good landing.

Saw Herky (captain) 377th, APO 638. He's fine. Had cocoa and sandwich at squadron pilot's room. Took off, came back at 1,000 feet, 45", 2500 RPM, at 295 IAS. Damn good! Peeled off at 300 IAS, whee! Had fun today.

Movie and haircut tonight. Two letters. Warning order. London with Randy tomorrow night. Christmas package mailed last October came today. Wow!

Tuesday, February 29: Wretham—Good clear day, 3/10ths billowy cumulus.

Briefed at 0920. Take off at 1040. Blue Flight, middle, led by me, with Baldy, Randy, and Hunter. Randy did a damn good job, a beautiful flight, completely uneventful. We escorted five wings of B-17s in their withdrawal to Egmond from near Appeldoorn 120 miles east. P-38s and P-51s were also there. Followed Major about, lost him in terrific sun, so came home alone. Buzzed clouds west of Yarmouth in tight formation. Out 2 hours 45 minutes. "D" Flight sure flew swell.

Randy and I are leaving for London at 1756. We wonder whether or not to take our helmets in light of last week's raids. We are taking our gas masks.

Good ride, four in our compartment, train on time all the way. Took underground then cab to 105 Gloucester. Room #2. Ate supper at Binn's Snack Bar, bed at 11:00 P.M.

[*The US 5th Army's bridgehead at Anzio, Italy, is attacked by the Germans yet again.*

The Soviet government confirms the Finnish-Soviet peace rumors and reveals the conditions demanded by Finland.]

Excerpts from the February 1944 Informal Report of Morale for the 359th Fighter Group, submitted by "Chappie" Ziegler stated: "As I understand it, a man's morale is an intangible something within his mind. Here is what I have observed on morale during the last month. The morale of our pilots is excellent. They are like a well coordinated team approaching a victorious season. They are confident of their own abilities, their planes, and each other. They have complete confidence in and respect for their commanding officer, Colonel Tacon. They are an experienced, mature team. They know there will be times when they will lose ground, but in the end victory will be theirs. They have lost friends like Lieutenant Cosmos, Lieutenant Niccolai, and Lieutenant Crawford, yet go on to knock more enemy planes from the skies. From a chaplain's point of view, here is an interesting bit of "morale" I have discovered in talking with the pilots who have had victories credited to them. Very few of them, in fact only one, have felt any exultation in shooting down an enemy. More than once I have heard them say, "you'd be surprised how the memory of killing that enemy pilot stays with you." As a chaplain I was glad to find that they feel it is a dirty job, but one that has to be done effectively if the world is to be free. A died-in-the-wool militarist would perhaps scoff at that attitude, but I see it as the basis of the peace that is to come.

"Morale among our ground personnel officers and enlisted men is not as high as that of our pilots for one reason: they are not directly engaged in war in the strictest sense. Each man understands his work is vital to

the keeping of planes and pilots in the air, but he has not seen an enemy plane, has not shot a gun, has not been exposed to bombing, or even seen the enemy in the distance. Lacking that direct contact with war, other problems loom large before him: furloughs, passes, food, etc. As a unit, however, the morale of this field is to be commended, and each man is doing the job expected of him."

HEADQUARTERS 359TH FIGHTER GROUP
Office of the Group Historian
APO 637 / US Army
4 March 1944

History of the 359th Fighter Group, February 1944

Sixteen enemy aircraft were destroyed by the 359th Fighter Group in February 1944 as a hard year of work and preparation paid off in results: a high standard of combat efficiency.

Out 16 times in 14 days, the 359th distinguished itself twice in getting its Thunderbolts back into the air quickly to fly double missions. Although never up to its rated strength of 75 aircraft, it consistently put more fighters over enemy territory than any other single group in the theatre and its pilots demonstrated a remarkable ability in instrument weather flying.

February saw the launching of a savage Anglo-American effort to knock out the Luftwaffe—its factories, air parks, control stations, ground installations and airborne strength—before the invasion. To that effort, the 359th Group contributed 766 sorties.

Two pilots were lost in action. A third was killed in a local flying accident. Flak was the deduced cause of one of these losses, and almost every combat pilot had one or more close calls from the German anti-aircraft artillery. In consequence, a declaration frequently heard in training, "Flak never bothers fighters," became quite the favorite epigram, if delivered with a properly satiric sneer.

The 16 claims of victories, averaging one a mission, were achieved in four days. There were also claims of two enemy fighters damaged, but major emphasis, as always, was in complete fulfillment of the specific mission stated in the FO, and here the 359th believed it had acquitted itself well.

Although flying conditions were all too often barely operational, ground weather was remarkably fine for East Anglia in February. Health improved and so did the food. No Spam was served at East Wretham throughout the month, in itself a high point of the war in the ETO.

Scotland, and more especially Edinburgh, became the standard place for leaves by both officers and men, while London, hitherto the immediate goal of almost all personnel on pass, lost popularity as the tempo of German raids increased and German raiding efficiency improved.

Two tiny items in "Stars and Stripes" monopolized conversation among enlisted men for a period. One was the announcement by a Tennessee farmer-prophet that the war would be over by 9 April. The other was a declaration by the Surgeon of the Navy that he was preparing for five years more of war.

Merits of both these views were sagely debated, as was the prospect of more and better food. The food did improve, Captain Steine reporting that fowl or fresh meat was served 38 times (four more than in January) while fresh oranges were served thrice, fresh apples once, and fresh eggs once to all station personnel. Pilots continued to receive their normal issue of three fresh eggs and three fresh oranges each per week.

Chicken, ice cream and cake became normal for Sunday dinner. For the month, 3,989 pounds of chicken were served. Other food poundage were: steak, 6,944; other beef, 8,924; pork, 7,758; frankfurters or luncheon meats, 3,220; bread, 21,272; potatoes, 27,600.

Menus at Wretham Hall improved noticeably with the accession of First Lieutenant Roger Van Gorder, 369th Adjutant, as mess officer there.

As for quartermaster equipment, Captain Steine said units on the station reported a combined average of 95 percent for T/BA equipment received and on hand, and 99 percent of individual clothing and equipment. Another record of a kind was established when, for the third consecutive month, no shortages in laundry and dry cleaning for the enlisted personnel of the station were reported.

Efforts of Colonel Smith to conserve use of transportation, involving a return en masse to bicycling and emphasis on use of bus-trucks running 'round the field on 30-minute headway, were reflected in the reduced issue of MT petrol: down to 18,143 gallons as compared with 20,958 gallons in January. Although the national coal crisis reduced delivery of coal to 44 tons and coke to 106 tons, stocks on hand on 29 February were 440 tons of coal and 210 of coke, a 10-week supply.

Lieutenant DeMarcus reported more efficient service from the Wattisham depot which had canceled all obligations and required resubmission of all requisitions. In consequence, the number of aircraft grounded because of lack of parts, which had averaged 3.5 a day in January, was reduced in February to 2.6.

The U.K. battle jacket issued to pilots, and very popular with them, was supplanted in their affections by a new issue late in the month of the Armored Force combat suit, relieving the shortage of flying clothes. The battle jackets were issued to enlisted men in lieu of the D-1 mechanics jacket, in short supply because of lack of repair facilities and lack of zippers.

A critical shortage of bolts, straps and channels for the 108-gallon belly tank developed in the last 10 days of the month, and all such expendable items for the droppable tanks were placed on the controlled list by the depot.

Installation of water injection systems in the aircraft, assuring 15 minutes of extra power for combat, was completed under direction of First Lieutenant George M. Hesser, engineering officer. Throughout the month a constant average of 10 aircraft were at modification centers being fitted for wing tanks.

Higher HQ notified Lieutenant Hesser that complete drainage of water from all aircraft would be necessary nightly to avoid freeze-ups. His answer, characteristically, was to suggest that the station at once be supplied with "the necessary equipment to turn the airplanes upside down in order to get all the water out of the lines." The result was that alcohol was made available for use in all aircraft.

Lieutenant Hesser's wrecking crew, which had engines running during all take offs and landing, also gave a good demonstration of fast work on 11 February when Lieutenant Carter hit a tree on take off. A great gash was torn in the wing of the aircraft near the root and a tire wrenched off the landing gear, but the rugged P-47 staggered around the landing pattern and Carter bellied the plane in just as the last ships took off. Hesser's crew got the airplane off the landing ground in quick time.

The Air Medal was awarded during the month to 10 officers, and 29 other pilots received clusters to previously awarded Air Medals. These medals and clusters were presented by Colonel Tacon during briefings. All were awarded on the basis of an Air Medal for 10 sorties, belly tank bomber escort to the limit of endurance being counted for this purpose as a double sortie.

Ground training went on, especially for the new pilots from the replacement pool at Atcham. Lectures included a discussion on recent German fighter airplane development, and showing of the new RAF POW picture, "Information Please." Flight Lieutenant Anderson, the courteous Canadian, who had smilingly wiled away his two years as night fighter without ever firing a shot, became moderately famous soon after his talk. He shot down two raiders on London in a single night, was promoted squadron leader and had his picture played prominently in the grateful London newspapers.

Two of the now regular fortnightly officers' parties were held at Wretham Hall. Blackjack remained a constant part of every evening, as did intra-squadron poker games in bedrooms. The chess tournament ended with First Lieutenant Donohue winning, Colonel Tacon runner-up, and Captain Carey H. Brown defeating Captain Edwin F. Pezda, a West Point classmate, in the table tennis finale. Bridge and cribbage tournaments were abandoned because of dispersal of many ground officers to the 370th communal area, more informally known as "the disciplinary barracks." The original settlers there organized a bar, improved the furnishings and at the end of the month were almost belligerently boastful about their superior accommodations.

In the 16 missions flown in February, 804 aircraft were airborne and early returns totaled 48, or 5.9 percent. The 766 complete sorties flown averaged 47.8 aircraft per mission, with the 16 victories representing 2 percent of that total and the two combat losses .26 percent.

The month opened with a general belief that six or seven operational February days was all that could be hoped for. Actually, the Eighth Air Force, flying in the most rugged weather imaginable, was operational on 19 days. This successful attempt to maintain the grinding pressure of January on the Luftwaffe involved a certain degree of improvisation, as fighter sweeps and thunderbombing efforts were arranged at intervals when heavy bomb shows were canceled. And this led to a series of scrubbing of these minor enterprises, with the result that the 359th Group ended the month without having dropped a bomb.

The first scrub arrived on 1 February when a heavy assault on Frankfurt was scheduled for withdrawal support; vide FO 230, in at 0122, was canceled at 0740. A release until next day came early, 0855, which was a novelty, and the balance of the day was taken up with a variety of enterprises.

Technical Sergeant Walter E. Koehler arranged for station-wide distribution of the stenographic summary of the 0800 BBB news bulletin. The squadrons were asked, at the request of Wing, to be particularly watchful for the daytime appearance of radar-equipped night fighters, an eagerly awaited evidence of strained German Air Force resources. At 1600 that afternoon, Major Gray went to Horsham St. Faith and Bomb Division HQ, for a critique on the last four missions. Captain Malley, meanwhile, talked to new pilots on Secret Document 158; the bible of identification. The warning order to FO 231 was in at 2155. A direct telephone ran from the combat intelligence office to Major Fitzpatrick's room at Wretham Hall, and the "drill" on such orders was to circulate the word via squadron intelligence to commanding and engineering officers.

The next day, 2 February, was a harried one, as was usually the case when the job involved VIII Fighter Command support to IX Bomber Marauders. Colonel Tacon was at a conference at AJAX, Bushey Hall, outside London. Major Swanson made what decisions were open, such as position of the squadrons and plan of escort; but the order did not arrive until 1150, when 67th Wing telephoned that the mission was high cover for B-26s attacking Triqueville in the Le Havre area, zero hour 1410.

Briefing was called for 1220, but mild hysteria ensued. By the time

Second Lieutenant Ralph A. Platt, weather officer, had been called, had bicycled to his office and computed the winds aloft, it was 1220. It was quickly obvious that start engine time should be 1235, an impossibility, so that the waiting pilots were sent back to their dispersals to pick up chutes, Mae Wests and other flying gear, while Wing was informed we would be at least 10 minutes late. This, Wing said, was satisfactory. But the weather had coarsened and a final decision was not had until 1240. The 359th briefed hurriedly, pilots were trucked to dispersals, engines spun at 1300, and 45 aircraft got off at 1310.

The bombers were seen leaving the target area, a vision denied the 20th Group's P-38s, scheduled for close escort, but the only incident of real note was reported by Lieutenant Oliphint, 369th, whose aircraft collided in bad weather with a barrage balloon cable at 100 feet near Southend. The P-47 won the collision and the balloon, hidden in the overcast, was freed. The aircraft was almost unmarked, save for minor dents and a skinned propeller.

On Mission 20 against Wilhelmshaven for the next day, the 359th lost a pilot to intense flak over Emden, and won a victory in isolated combat between an element of two aborting Thunderbolts and two Fw190s. The victory was not discovered until the next day, as the claimant, First Lieutenant Robert C. Thomson, landed at Woodbridge with battle damage.

Lieutenant Cecil W. Crawford, flying on Major Swanson's wing, ran into heavy flak at 24,000 feet at Emden. He did not return from the mission, and all three other aircraft in the flight suffered flak damage. The weather was brutal, the flights stayed to the limit, and 23 of the 54 on the mission landed at other fields.

On 4 February, the 359th Group was congratulated by AJAX for its fulfillment of an impromptu second mission. The congratulations, for getting five flights back into the air, was delivered with 12 flights actually up!

The first effort was normal enough, save for a last minute warning of a 160-mile-an-hour wind aloft on the return home. Take off of 52 ships required only 5:47. The group was down at 1248, and as Colonel Tacon left his airplane, combat operations telephoned instructions to fuel and take off by flights as soon as could be. Courses were passed to the squadrons at 1305, and the first flight of four was off for Dunkirk to sweep the area for stragglers at 1328. By 1355 46 ships were on the way. The patrols, which covered as far south and west as the Pas de Calais, were without incident. Command's sweet words for managing to get as many as 20 ships back up reached the station at 1400.

Six airfields in France were the targets on 5 February. The 359th Group's order was not until 0650, annoying for intelligence staff since the dispersed targets made the briefing one of the most complicated yet encountered. Take off was at 0958 as a light snow fell but the mission went very smoothly, the bombers' excellent formation helping greatly, and after escort, the flights swept uneventfully from La Ferté-Bernard north to the French coast.

Four French airfields were again bombed next day, when 10/10 cloud concealed primary targets. The 359th part of the show involved escort for the first ATF. Colonel Tacon and two 368th Squadrons flight-bounced 20 Fw190s flitting in and out of a low overcast. The encounter reports relate how Second Lieutenant Howard E. Grimes, going home alone, found he could outdive three pursing Fw190s but could not outrun them in level flight.

7 February was a busy day, since a release to the 8th was on the station at 0830, giving the harried ground crews a full day in which to work on their aircraft.

Next day, 8 February, the 359th provided sole support for 110 Liberators which attacked military installations in the Pas de Calais. No B-24s were lost, which was splendid news, but the mission itself was a headache, since distress calls on C radio channel, the frequency common to fighters and bombers, were heard throughout the run yet no bombers could be found in trouble. Men in the bombers guarding C channel complicated the job by neglecting to identify the box from which they were calling.

Another early job came up the next day, and pilots were awakened early for an 0740 briefing, which involved a rendezvous at Egmond at 0955 with 360 B-17s bound for Leipzig. Eighteen minutes before start-engine time, the whole show was scrubbed, and the 359th was put on readiness. At 0942, Wing ordered two squadrons to "bomb up," the third to be top-cover, and the "off-with-the-tanks, on-with-the-bombs" routine was on. The 359th Group briefed for the job, dive-bombing Gilze-Rijen airfield at 1000, and was unsurprised when this show was scrubbed at 1148 because of cloud over the target.

The following day was 10 February and very different. The FO stipulated a milk run with 169 bombers against Brunswick, but the Luftwaffe reacted violently; 10 of the 11 fighter groups had combat, knocking down 55, probably getting two more and damaging 42 for a loss of 29 bombers and 11 fighter pilots. A letter dated 12 February from General Kepner forwarded commendations from Generals Spaatz and Doolittle.

The 359th's share in all this was six victories and 26 more minutes of escort of 180 3rd Division B-17s than had been planned. The day began with a headache (the teletype machines went out) and ended with a heartache; the death, after evil weather and all the kindred hazards of combat had been surmounted without loss, in a local flight of Lieutenant Alexander M. Cosmos.

Lieutenant Cosmos, one July day in 1943 over Long Island, had dived a Thunderbolt longer and faster than any other human being, a dive that began above 30,000 feet and ended at 3,000 in a whistling shriek heard for 10 miles. That was a distinction of a kind, but the 359th thought mostly of the black-haired, serious-browed California boy in terms of his quiet unvarying courtesy and determination to do his job as well as he possibly could.

Snow was falling as the pilots rode to the line in their trucks from Wretham Hall but the day cleared just before briefing began at 0815. In token of the preceding day's miscarriages, Captain Brown presented Lieutenant Donohue with the Royal Order of the Scrub: a GI brush, but there was more serious news a moment later from Colonel Tacon.

The 359th Group, he said, had achieved the worst accident record of the command with 17 separate accidents, most of them due to fast taxiing. He complimented the 368th Squadron, which had a spotless accident record, and announced that fines would be imposed for fast taxiing as well as for unauthorized low-level rhubarbs.

A total of 51 aircraft got up at 0942. Low cloud at base interfered with setting course, but there was worse to come; cumulus beginning at 8,000 feet in which the flights flew for 20 minutes before breaking cloud at 20,000 feet. Five pilots never did find the rest and were among the nine early returns.

The 359th was down at 1237 but it seemed hours before the 13 aircraft that landed at other stations were accounted for, and a report was even prepared listing Major Irvine as NYR. He was almost within shouting distance, at Horsham St. Faith, but could not get through on the overloaded telephone lines until 1410, when all were safe and six good claims in.

A jubilant group went to supper, to be saddened at 1825 by the news that Lieutenant Cosmos had gone into the ground from a 300 foot ceiling near Somersham. He had taken off at 1645 for an hour's test flight, and was overdue 29 minutes when killed.

"Pick and shovel work," in Colonel Tacon's phrase, comprised the 27th mission, on 11 February. Lieutenant Carter's tree-surgery marked the take off, in which 52 ships got up in 7 minutes, and on arrival in the rendezvous area, where 4 combat wings of B-17s were supposed to be returning from Frankfurt, the 359th found bombers scattered in gaggles over an area of 200 square miles with 2 and 4-plane enemy elements nipping up and down from the undercast for quick darting pecks which could not all be countered in time. Fifty intriguing minutes were spent in this will-o-wisp hunting, and two B-17s were seen to stumble out of their formations and unload their crews by chutes—next to a bomber explosion an escort fighter's most discouraging sight. There was consolation in the fact that other groups assigned the same job could not find the bombers at all, so our escort undoubtedly had saved some big friends.

A warning to FO 241 was canceled at 0554 on 12 February, and there followed nine non-operational days, as weather interrupted the air assault on Germany. FO 243 was scrubbed early (0400) on the 14th, a day on which Wretham was socked in under a 500-foot ceiling. On the 15th, Captain Niven K. Cranfill and Second Lieutenant Charles H. Kruger flew a weather recco into the Le Havre area where a B-26 show was proposed, and the predicted order from Wing to bomb-up arrived later in the day. The 369th and 370th Squadrons were to bomb, but Lieutenant Platt told Wing the weather was 10/10 over the Dutch targets, and the bomb order was eventually reduced to readiness, waiting for a break in the target clouds.

The weather did not clear but new excitement appeared in the shape of a warning at 1500 to prepare to move to a forward base at 1630. Pilots were sent to Wretham Hall for musette bags, returning to the briefing room to learn the news. The move was scrubbed at 1720, but briefing proceeded in strained solemnity as Colonel Tacon announced that parachutists had captured St. Omer and the group would at once fly there. The atmosphere relaxed when he gravely proceeded that on landing at the French airdrome, the group would at once refuel for a fighter sweep, take off time: midnight. Though our part in the move was scrubbed, Bodney did make the ride, and was marooned in the South of England by socked in weather the next day.

Wing called at 2024 that day to say that "the confusion of this afternoon was unavoidable, occasioned by a combination of circumstances, which we'll try to avoid next time." The 359th considered it all a fairly routine bad weather day.

The orderly calm of the major effort assault in FO 245 on 20 February, was a welcome relief. The most interesting point, from the pilot's point of view, being the success of the anti-jamming device built into their radios by Captain Alfred M. Swiren, group communications officer. The jamming whine created by the Germans (generally read as "Goering says you'll never get back") had imposed a heavy strain on concentration in the air and was now practically eliminated.

First Lieutenant Ralph E. Kibler, flying radio relay, thought he saw a strange daylight focusing beam, and this was reported, although later observations tended to confirm the first analysis, that it was simply reflected light from the Dutch greenhouses four miles below.

On the 21st, the 359th saw Bramsche and Diepholz well hit. By accident, Lieutenant Paul H. Bateman fired a brief burst on one of the 56th Group's erratic yellow noses during the continuing attacks by the Halesworth pilots, who during this month told one of our airmen that the way to get victories was to stooge around like a German and thus attract Nazis to their doom.

Early next morning, the 22nd, Major Fitzpatrick and Lieutenant Donohue went to Snetterton Heath, 7 miles away, to watch the 96th Heavy Bomb Group brief for a return to Schweinfurt. They were greeted with shouts of joy from the bomber navigators, who urged immediate nomination of a P-47 pilot for President. The 96th's share of the show was scrubbed, but the 359th had a highly exciting time.

To begin with, the 359th Group was introduced to "Happy Valley," the Ruhr, as the bombers were south of briefed course, with the result that many pilots were under accurate and intense gun fire for 10 minutes without a break. Colonel Tacon with his wingman, First Lieutenant George A. Doersch, shared a long-nosed Fw 190 destroyed, and was so pleased with Doersch's performance in the violent flak-evasion and combat that he nominated Doersch his permanent wingman. Doersch, "Pop" to the whole group, was promptly dubbed "Floorpaint."

Captain Abbey was present at the interrogation in which Colonel Tacon described how the P-47 had outperformed the long awaited new Focke-Wulf, the tables between lecturer and lectured being thus reversed. Major Tyrrell, whose 368th pilots scored three of the day's five victories, filed another protest against the romping playfulness of the 56th Group's pilots.

Another show at Schweinfurt was projected on the 23rd, and the 359th was asked to fly two missions. This was abandoned an hour before briefing on the first effort, and at 0908 a release came through, permitting work on water injection installation.

The best performance of the month materialized on 24 February. On their third try, the B-17s got to Schweinfurt, where 263 bombed the remaining ball bearing works with excellent effect. They were taken into the Continent by the 359th Group, which destroyed four enemy fighters in the process, and, 3 hours 18 minutes later were escorted out.

According to plan, the 369th left the bombers seven minutes before the bulk of the Group, which continued on to the German frontier. As a result, the 368th was on the way to Belgium in its second mission of the day six minutes after the last airplane of the other two squadrons touched down at Wretham from the first ride.

After clearing the briefed withdrawal area of all visible stragglers, Colonel Tacon made an elaborate sweep of the Pas de Calais, staying in until convinced that no staggering Fort or Lib was still exposed to enemy fighters.

Two victories by Major Tyrrell ended a climbing chase in which he and his flight accepted heavy odds, but the general satisfaction at the results of the day were tempered by the absence of Lieutenant Albert T. Niccolai. Big, dynamic, aggressive, he had been grimly determined "to score," and disappeared on the tail of an Me109. The men who knew him were confident that if he had not run into a low-level booby trap, he would come walking back to them over the Pyrenees, burly confidence and sardonic humor intact.

Mission Number 33 on the 25th was noteworthy because Colonel Tacon began a policy of giving squadron commanders experience in conducting the briefing and leading the group.

Major Swanson was in command of an uneventful FO 251, but there was anxiety for some hours about the whereabouts of Second Lieutenant William E. Simmons, a spotter who overshot the field and could not be plotted by the Wing's "fixer" system on Channel D. The last fix placed him near Nottingham and it was 1550 before news that he was safe came in.

Next day, Colonel Tacon led a section, Major Murphy conducting the briefing and leading the hard work done shepherding stragglers across Holland. An unsolved mystery was a 7.0 mm bullet hole in the Colonel's airplane cowling when both he and his section were confident no enemy aircraft had been within five miles, up, down or sideways.

There was no mystery, however, about the feeling of the 359th on its month's work. The results, they felt, showed the fruit of devotion to duty, air discipline, and untiring emphasis on tight formation flying.

The future held much: Wing authorities permitted revelation of the news communicated to Colonel Tacon that the 359th Group would be re-equipped with P-51B aircraft.

The response was conflicting. The P-47 was never popular with pilots fresh out of flight schools where AT6s were venerated. Ten weeks of combat flying had proved its solid worth, its near invulnerability, its combat superiority to German equipment. But the P-51 had been the dream airplane of most of the pilots before they ever had a P-47 cockpit check. It was "good downstairs as well as up," the pilots knew, and basic fact, it had the range.

There had been jealousy about deep withdrawal assignments going elsewhere. With P-51s that would be no more, and as for the losses other P-51 groups had suffered, the 359th Group felt that formation flying was the cure for that.

Anyway, the future was going to be new and different.

6.

MARCH 1944

First Ground Attacks

Wednesday, March 1: London— Slept 'til 9:00 A.M. Ate breakfast, went to PX then 9th Air Force Art Show. Good watercolours.

Ate lunch at Veeraswamy and it was damn good! Watched matinee of "Strike a New Note" and then met Sid, Triss, et. al. at Trocadero for drinks afterward. Randy and I stayed for supper alone there. <u>Good</u> service. Mucho Scotch. Cab home and bed at midnight.

Thursday, March 2: London—Breakfast at 10:30 A.M., went to PX then the Trocadero for lunch with Mr. Barry. Then theatre until 4:00 P.M. Triss there again. Cute gal!! Reindeer Club for tea, underground to station.

Took the 546 and rode in first class restaurant car. Ate a good supper. Cold and clear as Hell out. A bright moon.

Swell time. Randy really enjoyed being behind the scenes.

We're definitely getting P-51Bs. Tech Orders are in already and a few ships due any day now. I have mixed feelings, curious yet leery. I love old *Clumpy* with her big radial engine.

Bath here at 10:00 P.M. then to bed.

[The North American Aviation P-51 Mustang was a sleek, fast aircraft originally developed in 1940 to British specifications. It was a tremendous success as a long-range bomber escort, and many experts regard the Mustang as the finest fighter of World War II. Powered by a Packard-built version of the Rolls Royce Merlin water-cooled V-12, the P-51 had a range in excess of 1,600 miles when equipped with external drop tanks, and could protect bombers deep into Germany and back, a major advantage over the P-47. In early 1944 the 8th Air Force began to transition to the Mustang, with 14 of its 15 groups ultimately flying the P-51.]

Friday, March 3: Wretham—Clear, cold, cloudless morning. Some cumulus later in the day.

Briefed at 1145 after morning at line and lunch at 1100.

Took off at 1312 for Type 16 Patrol *(a flight guided by ground-based radar)* under controller. I led Randy, Homeyer, and Baldy in Yellow Flight. Bo led section, Shaw led squadron and Swanson led group. Flew at 20,000 feet in the Brussels, Leuven area. Heavy, beautiful cumulus to 17,000 feet.

No action, but damned accurate flak. Botsy and Forehand were both hit near Ghent. They had to return. Holes in windshield and fuselage. Boy were they lucky. Target was Berlin today. Eight hundred and forty heavy bombers, but rumor has it they aborted. Hell!

Show tonight. Beaupre and Ashenmacher on first in the morning. Good!

[President Roosevelt announces that the Italian Fleet will be equally divided between the United States, Great Britain, and Russia.]

Saturday, March 4: Wretham—Briefing 0845. Terrific snow squalls. We hardly believed we'd take off. But after three time changes we did take off at 1035. It cleared and we got above the stuff.

Me, Major Shaw, Baldy, and Randy: White Flight. Bombers aborted so we picked up stragglers. Solid cumulus to 20,000 feet so we went up to 25,000 feet.

Major Shaw's controls started to freeze and mine were stiff. We started home. Cold as I've ever been in a P-47 with ice inside the canopy. Cleared up over base. Flew 2 hours 30 minutes. Nearly frozen when we landed.

Bo was supposed to lead the squadron but ended up leading an element. Went as far as Aachen. 370th had a swell scrap. Three enemy aircraft destroyed, one probable, and three damaged.

Party tonight and the 368th is raising Hell. Wow!

Sunday, March 5: Wretham—Released at 0700. Good thing, wot a night, with the whole damn squadron drunk on wine. Sacked all morning. Wot a head! The Hell with wine!

Flew local four ship formation this afternoon. Me, Brown, Baldy, and Randy. The most beautiful day in England. Spring air, warm sunlight, gorgeous, billowy cumulus, like a Texas sky. We rat-raced through clouds, really wonderful, carving tunnels, caves, and canyons. A P-47 from Bodney jumped us. We split up and murdered him. Hit the deck down the canals. It was wide open from Ely to Thetford, 56", 320 IAS, 200'. Number one formation really moving. A swell ride and the most fun in England. Everyone satisfied, for a wonder! Brownie is <u>damn</u> good.

Movie tonight, "The Moon is Down." Excellent!

Monday, March 6: Wretham—Seventy-seven enemy aircraft downed by our fighters. A record. Beautiful morning, a layer of cumulus from 3,000 to 7,000 feet. Briefing at 0815. Took off at 0950.

Colonel Tacon led first section. Major Shaw, Hagan, me, Hunter: Red Flight. Good formation.

A good run to Egmond. Five wings of B-17s to escort from there to east of Zwolle en route BERLIN! They made it today! No action for us. Good view of Amsterdam. Landed at 1210.

Took off again at 1300. Me, Randy, Homeyer, and Hudelson: Yellow Flight. Reached English Coast off Yarmouth then burned out RT dynamotor. Returned to base.

Bolefahr's and Bach's Section went down to 4,500 feet and tangled with 109s and 190s. Bo got a probable 109. Cater fired, Janney too. Booth and Pherson in '69th got one each. Lots of stragglers, some dinghits, a big show.

Someone in group has a stuck transmitter and he raises Hell breathing and singing. Very bad. Colonel is investigating. He aborted twice today because of radio problems.

Group missions total 39 now.

Tuesday, March 7: Wretham—Bad over Continent. A little rain in the morning then cleared beautifully, like Sunday.

No mission.

Homeyer took *Clumpy* on cross-country flight. Baldy and Hunter took Colonel Tacon's and Tyrrell's ships for radio checks (ha ha). Baldy chased a P-51 over Bodney on the deck. Came back here and found out Colonel was at Bodney. Some joke.

Hag, Randy, and I walked down to line in warm sunshine to look at a visiting P-38J-10 and a P-51B-7. Both interesting and tempting but I loves dem 47s!! Also had an A-20 drop in for a while.

Sky was full of planes, bombers practicing formation, fighters dog-fighting, all raising Hell.

Brownie moved in to 207 today. After the way Baldy, Hunter, and Randy fixed Hag's bed last night I doubt that he'll be safe. Oh this bunch of maniacs!

Wednesday, March 8: Wretham—Beautiful morning.

Briefing 0945. Took off at 1107.

Me, Hunter, Hag, and Baldy: Yellow Flight. Penetration area escort from Zwolle to Dümmer Lake at 25,000 feet.

Shaw sent our flight down to bring home an aborted B-24. We had a great time. Chased a contrail, got bounced twice by P-47s. Brought the bomber out over Valkenburg, came home to find an 800 to 500 foot ceiling. Landed at 1335.

Ate sandwiches and coffee. Took off again at 1450 with Shaw leading squadron (Hag, me, and Randy) through overcast. We split up and Janney, Burton, and Cater came with us. Chased five contrails to 30,000 feet near Zwolle but couldn't catch 'em. Flew all over that area but couldn't find any bandits. Started after some P-47s once. Came home, found a nice hole over Ely.

Quite a day, 5 hours 15 minutes flight time. Tired. Ran train on new track tonight.

Thursday, March 9: Wretham—Solid overcast at 500 feet.

Briefed at 0845. Took off at 1010.

Me, Hunter, Hag, and Baldy: Red Flight. Had to turn in overcast with ships on right. We followed group over to Zuider Zee then took off on our own. Bounced three P-47s (damn) at 10,000 feet. Horsed around and finally came home. Found a hole at Yarmouth, came in under the clouds at 300 feet. Landed at 1340.

Some ceiling!

Took off again 1350. Me, Randy, Hag, and Hunter: Yellow Flight. Flew through holes in overcast at 600 to 700 feet. Shaw, Smith, Bolefahr, and me, leading flights in starboard squadron. Goddam good squadron formation. We left 'em over Zuider Zee. Chased bogies over B-24s coming out but were our own P-47s again (dammit). Stooged around at 18,000 feet over B-24s out into North Sea, cruised around, but no luck. Landed at 1625.

Really dead! Not <u>one</u> claim in 8th Fighter today, even at Berlin!!

Memoranda: The 4th, 354th, 357th, and 363rd now have P-51Bs. The 20th, 55th, and 364th have P-38s. They provide target support, even on the three recent Berlin raids. One P-51 outfit destroyed 21 for no losses on Monday, March 6th. A terrific fighter team has developed now. P-47s with 100 gallon tanks penetrate and withdraw. P-47s with wing tanks provide intermediate cover, and P-51s and P-38s provide deep cover and target support. Also some Royal Air Force Mustangs are now working at deep ranges and Spits stay at close range. The strength is terrific.

On March 6th, 77 enemy aircraft were downed by our fighters. On March 8th, we downed 80-odd enemy aircraft, and not <u>one</u> claim was made on the same route today, even at Berlin.

Friday, March 10: Wretham—Foggy day.

We were released and everyone slept late. A welcome rest. I wrote some letters. Randy fixed my railroad track. I cleaned "Casey Jr." and polished the boiler. We ran 'er dry of fuel and even tried hundred octane but that made too much smoke. Track is okay now.

Sat in Bo's room all evening and shot the bull, talked about the Army, flying, etc.

A very lazy quiet day. In bed at 1045.

Saturday, March 11: Wretham—Wakened at 0600. Briefing at 0700.

Shaw is leading group, gave a good briefing. Two missions set for today, with one or the other or none for us. We got none. Released at

0900 so came back to Hall. Just relaxed, and bang! Mission. Back we went to start engines at 0945. Some mess. I had no guns in my ship. The schedule was messed up, we had no maps and no course cards, but away we went. Me and Randy tagged on behind the 370th, then pulled 40" hg. and caught our own Yellow Flight. Met bombers returning from Münster, only 120, no trouble thru three layers of clouds.

Whole mission, whole morning all screwed up. Oh well, we had fun flying.

352nd Fighter Group out of Bodney sent three squadrons (12 planes) on deck to strafe airdromes in France. They never found the airdromes but lost two pilots. Colonel Anderson (Wing CO) is mad as Hell. Sez no more of that crap. I still bet those guys had fun flying, though.

Painted a watercolour of four P-47s in the afternoon. Show tonight, "Meet Lily Mars." Good.

We were released and then scrubbed for tomorrow. Nuts!!

Sunday, March 12: Wretham—Warm front. Briefing at 0845. Scrubbed.

Nothing else all day. Loafed. Wasted time. Bull sessions. Sketched. Very dull. No movie. Poker game in 207. Bed at 11:00 P.M.

Monday, March 13: Wretham—Briefing at 0800. Swanson leading. Albertson with us now. Took off at 0945. Me, Baldy, Hag, and Hunter, but Baldy aborted. Lane filled in, had a nice flight. Shaw aborted. Al took over. We changed Yellow to Blue in nice aerial teamwork.

Flew to Pas de Calais to escort seven B-17 squadrons and 21 groups on separate targets. We gave area support above overcast at 24,000 feet.

I took our flight to 19,000 feet as we escorted seven Forts while they dumped eggs, then we brought them back to the Coast. A lot of fun and we really covered 'em. No action and just a little flak. Hellish <u>rough</u> air though, under soup from off Dover to base at 2,500 feet.

Brownie checked out with Trigger in the afternoon. He did okay, a good job, and he'll go with us tomorrow.

I sacked early. I'm tired.

Tuesday, March 14: Wretham—A beautiful day. Clear, some cumulus, and quite cool.

No operations anywhere.

Hunter led the 368th Flight of Brownie, Lemmens and Ash on a 12-ship practice escort for some new B-17s. Brownie and Hunter flew again in the afternoon.

We loafed around the line all morning. I read *Vayenne* in the afternoon. Had aircraft recognition at 4:00 P.M. "Duffy" Burgess broke the projector.

Tonight, Homeyer returned. He had a good time, mainly in Cambridge.

We ran "Casey Jr." for 45 minutes on Doc's alcohol. Ran out of water and melted the steam dome solder. Pow! Off she blew. Ran beautifully otherwise, with a slow chug like a real engine. The alcohol is better fuel than the spirit. Hurrah for Doc.

I wrote the wackiest letter of my career to Margot. Really nuts! Woof!

Wednesday, March 15: Wretham—Briefing at 0800 for a deep job, withdrawal from east of Dümmer Lake to Zwolle. Target is Brunswick. Me, Brownie, Baldy, and Randy: Yellow Flight. Albertson aborted with his whole flight. Smitty and Simmons aborted, too. Also Lane. So Forehand flew my #4 and Hawk was Bo's. Eight ships.

Over Dümmer Lake behind the bombers we found 12 Me109s. Bo missed his chance by not breaking into them on his right fast enough. Result, we climbed up under them in spirals, jockeying for position, neither side opening the attack. We were desperate for gas so I finally beat it. Dodged flak over Zwolle and hit the Zuider Zee with 80 gallons. Made the first field west of Yarmouth. Seething mad. Landed with 25 gallons at 1315. Brownie had 20 gallons, Randy 20 gallons, and Bill 40 gallons. Whew! Must respect the P-47. Oh, for some gas!

[Allied bombers level Monte Cassino with a 3,500 ton assault.]

Thursday, March 16: Wretham—Wakened at 0530 by "Duffy" Burgess.

Briefed at 0700. I sat out the first mission. They provided penetration escort from Compiegne to Nancy en route Munich and Augsburg. Ran into some Me109s like yesterday. No claims for us. 370th got three. Nuts!

Sam White flew my ship and he landed low on gas but okay.

I took up Bach's H D-5, a nice crate, beat-up looking but ran beautifully. Me, Brownie, Hag, and Baldy: Blue Flight to Colonel Tacon. Good formation. We found bombers west of Chalons, took 'em out to the landing field near Dieppe. Ran into some flak at Beauvais and Creil but no enemy aircraft.

Colonel had me cover rear while he went ahead. Some Spits made us break once but we really escorted well, flew nice esses right over the bombers. Very hazy so we flew down at 15,000 feet all the time. A good job for "D" Flight.

[On the Italian front, attempts by the British 8th Army to break through at Cassino fail.]

Friday, March 17: Wretham—Very heavy fog all morning. Had aircraft recognition at 0900 then read all morning. Lunch at 11:30 A.M.

Fog burned off, briefing at 1230. We're to strafe the airport at Beauvais, north of Paris, with an eight-ship section from each squadron led by Colonel Tacon. Major Cranfill leading five flights for top cover. Albertson leading Yellow Flight. I led Green Flight, with Baldy, and Staley from the 369th.

Terrible haze and cumulus (like Farmingdale) up to 7,000 feet. Hazy over France. Reports of bandits from "Fire Bay" had us excited so we climbed to 27,000 feet. No sign of 'em. Back down to 15,000 feet to protect striking force. They dove to the deck but missed their target in the haze. No firing, no losses. Beat it back to 10,000 feet and home. We picked up wicked flak at Dieppe. I could hear it!

Saturday, March 18: Wretham—Two missions again today. Penetration and withdrawal in northern France, route to Augsburg area target. I didn't fly. Hag, Brownie, Homeyer, and Hunter flew first. Homeyer, Baldy, and Randy flew second. No fighters but terrible flak both times.

Albertson was hit coming home from second show. Bailed out as his plane caught fire. Had Randy and Baldy with him, near Abbeville. Tough break. They said his chute opened okay. Hope he can evade successfully.

I spent some time with Platt in the weather room. Also visited our tower.

Stinko party tonight! Didn't even go downstairs. No drinking for "D" Flight. We're all out of sorts and everyone went to bed around 11:00 P.M. The Hell with these lousy parties.

Captain Ralph A. "Stormy" Platt, Weather Man. *Archived by Char Baldridge, Historian, 359th Fighter Group Association, from records at HQ USAF Research Center, Maxwell Air Force Base, Alabama*

Sunday, March 19: Wretham—Cold front went thru and it cleared nicely.

Released 'til 1200. Slept all morning.

I got up for breakfast, went down to line and read P-51 tech orders.

Briefing at 1530 by Major Tyrrell. Type 16 area support at Pas de Calais, in at Gravelines to Lens, out Cayeux.

Me, Baldy, and Homeyer (Brown got stuck in the mud), so Cater joined us over St. Omer. Major aborted. Bo took over.

Terrible flak at Calais all over us at 18,000 feet. Hit Ashenmacher. He came back, Lane with him. Landed near Romney. He's in hospital with hand and arm wounds. No details yet.

Saw a Fort blow up. Silly goddam mission.

Got lucky coming back, had a Helluva time finding base. Overcast at 25,000 feet and ground haze. Came back at 40" to beat the dark. Just made it. Nuts!!

Monday, March 20:Wretham—Warm front moving in fast.

Briefing at 0830. Only 12 ships are available. I'm not scheduled.

Major Tyrrell, Brown, Hag, and Hunter took off at 0957. They hit instruments at 18,000 feet and were still on 'em at 31,000 feet. They aborted and so did the bombers. One and one-half hours instrument time. Wow! Were they mad.

Rain in the afternoon. Sketched a bit, showered. Painted engine. Wrote letters tonight. Today is one-year anniversary of 43-C. A party going on, mostly in 207 as is usual. Wot a gang! Brownie went to London today.

Ashenmacher, so it is said, lost his left index finger. A tough break. Damn that flak! Was bad again this morning, they said.

*Tuesday, March 21: Wretham—*Bad weather over Continent. No mission.

To line in the morning to censor mail. A very good talk in Hall at 1000 by RN *(Royal Navy)* lieutenant on experiences in the Mediterranean.

Drew new flying suits after lunch, real beau-

Lieutenant Joseph M. "Ash" Ashenmacher. *Photo courtesy of Anthony C. Chardella: Archived by Char Baldridge, Historian, 359th Fighter Group Association*

ties, best stuff the Army has ever issued me.

Aircraft recognition at 4:00 P.M.

Supper, sketched, and loafed in the evening. Went to bed quite early. Weather should be good out tomorrow. A damn nice letter from Conny today.

Sketched a cartoon. Situation: Two MPs caught swiping apples from fruit stand by a cop. No caption necessary.

*Wednesday, March 22: Wretham—*Had lunch at 1100.

Briefing 1130. Murphy leading. Took off at 1310. Me, Randy, Homeyer, and Hunter: Blue Flight. Overcast from 3,000 to 5,000 feet. Clear above. To near Dümmer Lake escorting three wings of B-24s in with-drawal from Berlin. Loads of bombers and fighters in the air, all ours. No action, no nuttin!

However, today's box score was rough. We lost 12 to 1. Wot's the story here? Rough! Dammit!

Brownie returned. He had a good time. Randy and Hunter on leave tomorrow, going to London.

Damn good movie tonight, "Dr. Gillespie's Criminal Case." Haircut coming up. Two boxes of food arrived today. Boy, do these Hershey Bars taste good.

Thursday, March 23: Wretham—Wakened at 0600.

Briefed at 0715. Took off at 0845 with a thin overcast from 3,000 feet to 5,000 feet. Me, Brown, Hag, and Baldy: Yellow Flight in low squadron. Tacon and Tyrrell also leading flights. East to landing field at Egmond then on to vicinity of Dümmer Lake to pick up four wings of B-24s.

I was assigned area <u>below</u> the front two wings at 15,000 feet. Dodged lots of flak, saw bombs drop, saw targets demolished. Some excitement, though no enemy aircraft in vicinity, but dodging bomb bays and flak was enough. They hit one town northwest of Osnabrück, Bramsche, and virtually obliterated it. Wow!

Left at "Xmas" and met Major Tyrrell (Red Flight) at Zuider Zee. Some coincidence. Both flights above and we'd been miles apart, then back together and home. Three hours of flying.

Hunter and Randy left on leave today. Pretty quiet here.

Friday, March 24: Wretham—Up at 0500!

Briefed at 0600. Scrubbed as we started engines.

Re-briefed at 0815. Scrubbed as we left pilot shack. Nuts.

Pea soup weather, visibility a thousand yards at best. Four decks of cloud. Silly bastards at AJAX *(Headquarters of the USAAF Eighth Air Force VIII Fighter Command)* sure missed the boat! Censored mail.

In the afternoon we got the ball club rolling and 20 men "reported." Shaw pitches a beautiful fastball. Hawk to catch. Colonel Tacon on first base. Had a practice game. Good fun.

Playing ball at East Wretham USAAF Station Number 133.
Courtesy of Alfred M. Swiren: Archived by Char Baldridge, Historian, 359th Fighter Group Association

Movie tonight, Donald O'Connor in "Mr. Big." Quite good. The kid's clever.

Swell letter from Kiel today. Still in Wyoming, has the 676 Salvage Collecting Company. Ran "Casey Jr." tonight. Good!

[The Luftwaffe bombs London with 90 medium bombers.

The Royal Air Force bombs Berlin with 810 heavy Lancasters.

In Italy, the bridgehead at Anzio held by the US 5th Army is bombarded by long-range guns and aircraft.

The ongoing attacks by the US and British against the Gustav Line at Cassino continue to be repulsed by German defenders.]

Saturday, March 25: Wretham—A warm hazy spring day. Darn nice out. Released until tomorrow for rest and maintenance.

Wrote letters this morning while everyone sacked in. Walked down to line, censored a little mail. Lecture in briefing room at 1400 by RN Lieutenant Chaplin on air-sea rescue. Good.

Then another practice ball game. Aircraft recognition at 1645. Test. Easy.

Steak for supper. Homeyer on Norwich "run" as usual tonight. Brownie and I ran "Casey Jr." again. She's in good shape since we "back-stopped" her with a re-soldered steam dome. A nice easy day, no flying at all here.

Zero hour at 0800 in morning. Hit the sack early.

Sunday, March 26: Wretham—Up at 0615.

Mission scrubbed at 0616. Balls!

Spent morning at line. Ground fog dissipated by noon.

Briefing at 1250. Squadron headed southeast at 1320, Pas de Calais area, to escort 120 B-24s. A milk run. I feel poorly and didn't go. Hag, Brown, Homeyer, and Baldridge were Blue Flight. Hag came back with a broken belly tank.

We had a "pick up" ball game. I pitched and Smith caught. Some battery! The first really swell, warm spring day. Shirtsleeve weather is delightful, but I still feel poor.

Gang came back okay. Saw lots of flak and no enemy aircraft.

Movie tonight and good fried chicken dinner. I still haven't much pep.

[*A B-17 from the 452nd buzzes the base, dropping a bottle attached to a handkerchief parachute. In the bottle, this message:* "To the P-47 boys, to you who fly and keep them flying. Many thanks for the wonderful work you are doing for us who are up here in the big ones. You are to all of us a million-dollar sight when you help us on every mission. Again, we the boys of this Fort SUNRISE SERENADE want to thank each and every one of you for your protection of us as we make each mission. Thanks a million. Signed, the crew of the SUNRISE SERENADE"

Although the "P-47 boys" continued to do their job of protecting the SUNRISE SERENADE *from enemy fighters, she was brought down by flak over Brussels, Belgium on May 1, 1944. The pilot was killed and the rest of the crew sent to a POW camp.*]

Monday, March 27: Wretham—Fog and overcast to the deck all morning.

They scrubbed one briefing. Had one at 1015. Called us back from ships. We ate lunch in flying clothes and finally took off at 1255, flew straight out through overcast to 5,000 feet and assembled as we flew course. A nice job in incredible weather. Three hundred foot ceiling, 1,500 yards visibility, and 48 ships assembled on top. Beautiful.

Flew south to Chartres and spotted our bombers, two wings of B-17s.

Me, Baldy, Hagan, and Homeyer, with Perk and Drake: Red Section.

370th and 369th Flights took a bounce on 109s and FWs at 5,000 feet. A good fight and Fearson and Fong got one each. McKee and Cunningham received battle damage. 370th new boy shot down. Cater outran three 109s on his tail.

We six were the <u>only</u> ships to escort bombers out to Le Havre.

Tuesday, March 28: Wretham—Three briefings scrubbed, six courses drawn and scrubbed, and they finally took off about 1530 on a Type 16 in the Paris area, at the landing field at Cayeux.

Homeyer, Burton, Keesey, and Cater were Yellow Flight. The rest of "D" Flight were off. Yellow Flight didn't see anything, not even much flak. Landed at 1800.

Major Tyrrell is raising Hell about our sloppy formation (Colonel too), and rightly so. We're getting too complacent. Need brushing up.

I stayed at Hall all afternoon with a bit of a cold, but seems better. Brownie and I ran "Casey Jr." Wrote a couple of letters.

We have two P-51s in the squadron now. One is painted and one is silver. Wroe and Bisher in charge, both quite happy. They have swell cockpits.

Wednesday, March 29: Wretham—Overcast stratocumulus at 1,000 feet. Visibility okay. Briefing at 0945.

Me, Brown, Baldy, and Hag: Yellow Flight, high. Bo leading and we assembled underneath. Red Flight shuffled above me in the soup. I headed left out of the way, ran through soup, solid to 8,500 feet. Bad rime ice on wings and prop, 35", 170 IAS, 300'. Climb was sluggish. Dangerous!!

Met bombers off Dutch coast ahead of group. Couldn't climb up to them. Finally got up to 25,000 feet around Lingen to escort rear of four wings of B-17s going to Brunswick. Left them east of Dümmer Lake. Bounced two 47s at 9,000 feet on clouds coming back. A beautiful bounce. Two of us on each one. Really snuck up on 'em.

Hag and Brown landed for gas. Baldy and I made base with a 600 foot ceiling and rain. Three hour 20 minute mission. Whew!

Got a bad ear.

Made captain today.

Captain Howard Fogg. *Courtesy of Richard Fogg*

Thursday, March 30: Wretham—Cold, beautiful day. Heavy cumulus "buzz" clouds.

My head and ear are all stopped up. Went by dispensary for nose packs in the morning.

Censored mail. Briefing at 1230. Twelve ships bombed up for a 24 ship escort to hit an airdrome south of Zuider Zee. No action.

Colonel and Major Tyrrell checked out in P-51 today. Both simply raved about it. Major like a kid with a new toy.

Hunter, Randy, and Homeyer returned tonight. All had a good time. Randy and Hunter saw Sid, Triss, and Barry.

My head is still plugged, goddammit. Feel pretty good, but I sure wish my ear would clear up.

Friday, March 31: Wretham—Couple of briefings, but missions scrubbed. Released about 1000.

Good local flying, heavy cumulus, clouds, squalls, snow. Clear.

Forehand, Bach, and Bo checked out in the P-51. They liked it.

Hunter test hopped Forehand's 47(O) and came in to land with no oil pressure. Had to crash land near the Hall. Damn lucky to escape with a bruised head and backache. Damn plane really went haywire, and he did a good job of walking her down, 95 IAS, staggered over trees. He was lucky!

My ear is still plugged but I feel pretty good. Had nose packs again. Played bridge with Doc, Keesey, and Bunky. Good fun. Bed at 11:00 P.M.

A lack of oil pressure caused Lieutenant John B. Hunter to crash-land near Wretham Hall in Captain
William C. Forehand's P-47(O). Lieutenant Hunter escaped with a bruised head and backache.
Courtesy of Elsie Palicka, wife of Ed Palicka, 370th Fighter Squadron Photographer:
Archived by Char Baldridge, Historian, 359th Fighter Group Association

Captain John B. Hunter. *Photo*
courtesy of Marvin Boussu: Archived
by Char Baldridge, Historian, 359th
Fighter Group Association

Excerpts from the March 1944 Informal Report of Morale for the 359th Fighter Group, submitted by "Chappie" Ziegler stated that: "Last month we said that morale was an intangible something within the mind of a man. Being intangible then, how is one able to observe whether that man's morale is high or low? The answer is that it gives expression in the man's daily life. Therefore let me show you where I have observed the morale of the men of this field and what I have observed.

"As far as the pilots are concerned, the most important barometer to me is their action at briefings. When you see them push each other around: when you hear them kidding one another about their girls and the time they had on their days off; when you hear them laugh heartily at the antics of their dog mascot named "Flak"; when you see them kid Lieutenant Platt, the weather officer about the 200 foot ceiling; when they are seen bowing their heads quietly as Chaplain Ziegler gives the prayer before briefing; when you watch them sitting confidently listening to the C.O. telling of the mission for the day and then watch them get up and go to their planes, every move giving expression to long training and complete confidence, when you can see all these things, as we can see them in our pilots, then you know morale is at a high level."

History of the 359th Fighter Group, March 1944

Twenty-six missions against the Luftwaffe were flown in 20 days of March 1944 by the 359th Fighter Group, plus two weather-reconnaissance penetrations of the Continent, one in strength.

Of the 1,222 Thunderbolts put up from the rolling grass field at East Wretham, 1,157 sorties over Europe were completed. A total of 20 combat claims, 13 destroyed, 5 probably destroyed and 8 damaged, were recorded from the month's gross of 300 enemy sightings.

Two pilots were lost. Two other pilots were wounded by flak, and there were 13 cases of battle damage in airplanes which returned to their home field. Three ships were washed out in take off and landing crashes.

Three of these 13 battle-damaged aircraft came home after hitting trees and high tension wires in a locomotive-strafing spree inside Germany on the 13th, and another, piloted by Lieutenant Cunningham, staggered back for 190 miles on the deck with a cylinder blown out and wing mauled by 15-plus enemy aircraft hits in combat, on the 28th.

These statistics do not include the achievements of four buzz-artists who went on detached service on the 17th to a special coterie of ground attack enthusiasts organized at Metfield, where they soon distinguished themselves. Pleased as the 359th Group was at the achievements of this quartet, there was a more solid pride in the mature high escort performance of the Group, including the five double missions flown in the month, three of these in the successive assaults on Berlin.

The patience of Captain Hesser in distributing engineering personnel among the three fighter squadrons, and in organizing ten separate refueling and re-servicing dry runs, paid a large dividend in these harried days of double missions. Thirty minutes ground time between the landing and re-dispatching, including 10 minutes taxiing, was the fruit of this preparation, a record in the theatre.

The month had many high points. These included the first strafing assignment, an attack 17 March on Beauvais airfield, which was a failure; the first completed thunderbombing mission, a raid 30 March on Soesterberg airfield, which was a success; and the arrival on 26 March of the first six P-51Bs, which scored a triumph.

But the real story lay in the never-ending defiance of almost incredible flying weather, a defiance, literally of "snow, wind, rain, dark of night," in which pilots achieved in the language of Herodotus "swift completion of their appointed rounds" despite every hazard of a murky English spring.

As the rather complicated statistical summary of the weather compiled by Lieutenant Platt shows, there was no officially "clear" day in the month, and the field was "Green" (meaning visibility 2,000 yards minimum, ceiling 1,500 feet minimum and not raining) for only 34 percent of all the daylight hours.

In these circumstances, 26 missions in 20 days meant one scrubbed mission after another, much hasty improvisation as scheduled take off hour passed with the field still socked in tight, many briefings with fog kneading the windows of the briefing room, and the unlimited serenity of soul and confidence born of skill on the part of the pilots.

This is not to say the English sky lacked its billowing glory of strata-galleons afloat in a sea of dreamy blue, there were such afternoons, but a low and glowering overcast was the more usual celestial setting at take off time, and there was frequently every doubt that the mission could get off until in fact it did get off, with consequent worry about conditions at touch-down time.

The casualty rate, 1.7 per 1,000 sorties, and none of it attributable to weather, demonstrates the superb quality of the bad weather flying which the pilots contributed to in this crisis-assault on the fighter strength of the German Air Force.

The composite track of missions shows an almost exact quadrant radiating from Thetford Wood, and the railroad track from Norwich which was the clear-weather pointer home, to an area southwest of Chartres, west of Mainz, and to Steinhuder Lake. This was the 359th Group's arena in March of 1944, but two chutes predominated. One was the alley from the familiar flak-free coordinate of 5237N-0437E due east to Dümmer Lake. That was for penetration of the Reich. The withdrawal corridor led from below Chalons northwest toward Amiens. And of course, there was the milk run in the Pas de Calais, where the steadily-strengthened German flak defenses cost the 359th Group Captain Albertson.

In the frenzied pressure days of OTU at Grenier and Republic Fields, he had played a large role as operations officer of the 369th Squadron in conditioning pilots fresh from school for the arduous demands of combat formation-flying. In the ETO reshuffle of flying officers according to relative rank, he had gone to the 370th Squadron as flight commander. And, as assistant group operations officer, he was flying with the 368th Squadron the day flak smashed the right wing of his aircraft and he went over the side. So everyone knew and missed him and hoped he would come walking back before the war was over.

Lieutenant Kerns, NYR on 27 March in a confused combat was in a different category. He was a replacement pilot, just up from the pool at Atcham. And the circumstances of his loss offered no such easy grounds for hope of a successful bail-out and evasion as in Albertson's case.

Small and dapper, Kerns was a sensitive and gifted young man with much promise. A copy-boy of the Kansas City Journal, he had forsaken that paper for journalism school and returned to become its night club editor, curious preparation for a fighter pilot's life. He was full of plans at Wretham for a musical show he had well on the way to writing and producing himself, full of gags and quick clean judgments on the humor (or lack thereof) of offered contributions.

In his mind, there was more than that. There can be no sacrilege in quoting an unmailed letter found in his effects and written four days before he went missing in action. The poem echoes Magee's "High Flight" but has its own value. The pilot to whom he refers is Lieutenant Hair, killed 11 January in a bad weather crash in England.

"23 March 44
"Dear . . . .
"A month ago one of our pilots was killed while letting down through some messy weather on return from a mission. I didn't know the boy, because he had died before I came. I expect it happened two months ago. I heard about him though, and got his locker. The guys all liked him, but that is no indication of a special significance, because everyone likes everyone here, mostly. There are cases of greater respect and lesser, of course.

"Our Major received a letter from the boy's wife a few days ago, and gave it to us to read. It was a fine example of courage. I wish I could send it to you. I was moved by the sincerity of her letter. It was fairly long. She wanted to know how it happened, wanted to know things he had written about, like how to get his medals because he had written that "They were for nothing spectacular." She wanted to hear from some of the boys she had known who were with him in the States. She wanted them to write and wanted to send them packages—cookies and the like.

"He left two little children, girls, behind, who were too young to know their father well. His story, in short, is much the same as most these days. But her letter had a touch of something in it which fascinated me by its sad beauty.

"So I wrote a poem. It isn't good, though not bad. I showed it to my buddy Callahan, who suggested it might be sent to her as a memoriam to his memory—something she could read to the children when they were old enough to understand that their father had been a fighter pilot in the great war. Major Murphy read it, and is going to send it to her, from one of the fellows in his outfit. What do you think of it? I can't decide if it is a good idea. Here is the poem.

"We speak not in sorrow that he died,
Though we miss him sorely—there are some who cried
Because they like the man. They knew
His quirks, his laughter, and the way he flew.

"His was not a gesture to vain strife.
He died pursing that which filled his life;
He loved to fly and to his flying gave
A mastery that made the sky his slave.

"He knew the breathless beauty of the Air—
Towering clouds the Heaven fashion there.
He rolled and tossed o'er fleecy stratus fields
And drank the flaming glory flying yields.

"His heritage was but a pilot's right
Out soaring mighty Eagles in their flight,
You zoom and play mid sunset's golden mirth
High beneath the wispy roof of Earth.

"And though his taste for life was justly sweet,
He laid this precious gift at freedom's feet;
And when he left, he went still in the fight
To keep intact all that he held as right.

"The least we owe is faith, the best a smile.
A faith that what he did was worth the while;
A smile we owe because he left us one,
A fitting tribute to the job he's done.

"Apart from all the day's question of right or wrong, there is the more intimate problem of the heartbreak of today's conflict. Though some, and perhaps myself, might question and give reason for fighting a war, and try to affix some logical economic source to it, this becomes relatively unimportant in this more personal problem. Certainly we cannot disregard the causes of war, and we shall never end them, unless we see them in the light of truth.

"But who am I to say such things to this young widow? Can she be told or convinced that he died needlessly? Further, should she be robbed of what small consolation she derives from her bitter pride in his sacrifice—her conviction that what he did was that "full measure of devotion."

"Perhaps there is some good in the veil we sometimes hide behind. Perhaps the defense against unhappiness we build up has its points. There must be something to what a lad we knew once called Bourgeois sentimentality.

"More and more I realize how clearly true it is that "They also serve who stand and wait." What we accomplish here—our daily pursuit—occupies our minds as well as our physical bodies.

"Odd though, how far distant such a thing seems from the rest of us. We expect such things, and when they come, a few words are said, but mostly it is forgotten quickly, or even made a joke of. We have lost others besides this lad, and there was no poem. It was only when this lad became connected through this letter with a living existence in a world of the past, that we fully realized what his loss meant.

"Surprisingly enough, the weather is good today. Stormy, the weather man, began the briefing today with the quip, "That clear blue overcast you see, gentlemen, needn't alarm you. It's the sky."

"Still haven't been off the base since I last mentioned London. Expect to take my next pass, though, and drop in on a nearby village. I haven't had any fish and chips for over a month now.

"Give . . . . my best regards."

This was the kind of young man who made up a terrible bludgeon and magnificent shield that was VIII Fighter Command in the spring of 1944. This was the kind of young man who made up the 359th Fighter Group.

They won 16 Distinguished Flying Crosses and innumerable clusters to the Air Medal that month. They gambled furiously, mostly at blackjack. They had magnificent fun in London. They were full of wonderful stories of leave in Edinburgh. They said farewell to Captain Malley, detailed for duty in the United States after almost two years in Britain, and said it cheerfully. They were fighting a professional war, with an amateur's zeal.

Life on the Station improved, product both of the 359th's "settling in" as it began Month Number Six in the ETO, and of the rapidly expanding tempo of work on the new installations designed to make Wretham a RAF Bomber Command station for two heavy squadrons, 36 aircraft and 2,400 men.

Chaplain Ziegler, a shrewd observer, found the station satisfactory in his monthly evaluation of morale, and a reinvigorated special service and athletics program was launched by Lieutenants Edward W. Devine and Robert C. Payton.

Though the 11-team station basketball tournament was a large success, the arrival of softball weather, in conjunction with the opening of the gymnasium, was the most potent new morale development. The most devoted of all physical culturists, the weight lifters, found 15 adherents.

The number of liberty runs to nearby towns was halved, and Norwich was chosen as the single city to be visited on these evening excursions. In the same attempt to conserve transportation, the number of dances for officers was reduced to one a month, and further emphasis was laid on use of the intra-station bus-truck system.

Mileage was reduced by these measures, the March figure of 77,659 comparing with 82,531 miles clocked on the motor pool speedometers in the shorter month of February, but, largely because truck use increased as Jeep use diminished, total petrol consumption increased from 18,143 in February to 20,052 in March. Of this increase, 1,030 more gallons were used by the motor pool, the rest of the spread going to ancillary base services and transient vehicles.

The most important improvement of the ration, as is shown in Captain Steine's summary of quartermaster supply, was the weekly issue of fresh eggs on Sunday mornings. Spam again was not served; and there were four additional servings of fresh meat or fowl. Supply of fuel became more difficult, and Captain Steine described the steps taken to meet the general coal and coke crisis throughout the Kingdom.

Air Corps supply continued in a favorable position, so far as the P-47 was concerned. The daily average of planes grounded for lack of parts rose slightly, to 2.9. Captain DeMarcus also reported concern at the relatively bad supply situation on the P-51, because "quantities of these planes were shipped to this theatre before the parts projects left the States."

Another new combat costume was issued the pilots on 23 March, a fur collared intermediate flying suit which replaced the Armored Force outfits issued the preceding month. The new jacket was a great popular success and was worn everywhere during duty hours by flying personnel.

Intellectual stimulation was provided by a renewed drive to make the Army Talks series of discussions a vital factor in all units. A series of weekly "open forums" on problems of the war was launched for officers, with Colonel Smith acting as moderator at the first sessions. On a more mundane level, the ground officers quartered in the communal area achieved an especially handsome collection of murals, both blonde and brunette, painted by Staff Sergeant James F. Makoffke on the walls of the lounge, now known, and proudly, as "The Purple Shaft Club."

As usual, the hard work of the month was done by the unsung heroes of the line, the mechanics, armorers, and specialists who kept a record number of ships in commission during a grueling month. In theory, the 359th had 70 aircraft. Actually, 10 of these were always away at Burtonwood for installation of wing tank shackles.

As part of a scheme to keep all groups operational while quickly producing completely re-equipped groups, as quickly as they arrived here the wing-shackled ships were sent off the Station in exchange for unmodified Thunderbolts. That meant a constant succession of acceptance checks and work on unfamiliar planes. There were rarely more than 50 ships on the field, and the averages for the month, 47 airborne a mission, with 2.5 returning early for 44.5 effective aircraft over the Continent, were eminently satisfactory, especially since these statistics include the prescribed 36 plane mission of the 30th, in addition to the five days on which double missions were flown with no time to do any maintenance in the hurried minutes for refueling.

Typically, the month began with a bad weather day and a certain amount of confusion. The weather was too bad for the heavies, which, by ETOUSA logic, made it ideal for fighter bombing. At 0830, Wing warned it would ask for a weather recco in preparation for an attack on Melsbroek airdrome.

Again typically, Melsbroek was not one of the hundreds of targets on which Wing had distributed target information and pictures, which fact was a source of grief to the S-2 section, but the three-ship weather recco, led by Captain William C. Forehand, found the Brussels-Antwerp area covered by 10/10 cloud at 14,000 feet. This was duly reported at 1304, and 20 minutes later Wing was asked for a release which arrived at 1330. A new priority list of airfield targets was supplied and at 2045, Walcott warned of a maximum effort mission on the morrow.

This was FO 257 against Frankfurt and Chartres. Captain Daniel D. McKee claimed an Fw190 in a 3 hour 14 minute mission. Briefing for this was reasonably late, 0845. The take off, at 1037, was delayed by sheets of snow lashed up by prop wash, 49 aircraft requiring 7 minutes 30 seconds to get up.

The attack on "Big B," Berlin, was scheduled to begin on 3 March, but bad weather forced the 14 combat wings to abort, only some 79 attacking Wilhelmshaven. The 359th's share of the show was to have been withdrawal support over Belgium under direction of Type 16 control, the portable three-dimensional radar plotting room at Hythe. FO 259 was in at 0500, but our amendments arrived before take off and as late as 1250, Colonel Anderson, (promoted Brigadier General during the month) warned to hold pilots at their dispersals until the last moment for possible changes, but the 359th got off on schedule and was over Louvain at 1415 as originally planned. The bombers, off course, did not use the briefed withdrawal corridor and the only interest of the mission was in the discovery, by Captain Mosse and Lieutenant Kerns, of five dinghies with a B-17 crew aboard 50 miles northeast of Lowestoft. Air-sea rescue aircraft were guided to the area by Mosse and Kerns.

One of the fine performances of the 359th Group's history was recorded on 4 March. This was a gallant intervention over Germany by 24 outnumbered Thunderbolts, led by Major Murphy, which drove off 100 enemy aircraft and saved an aborting and turning (and consequently disorganized) B-17 wing from attack.

This was a second attempt to get to Berlin, and again fiendish weather interfered. As on the 3rd, a P-38 group had managed to reach the capitol of the Herrenvolk; on the 4th, one combat wing of bombers got in to the target, but the rest aborted on weather.

At Wretham there was every doubt, because of a genuine snow storm, that the 359th could do any flying whatever. Major Murphy briefed, which originally called for a rendezvous at 1117, later revised to 1142, but snow was still falling at start engine time and it was 1021 before Wing could inform Major Murphy that the 359th was needed and must get off when it could, late or not.

The snow providentially stopped, and after mechanics had wrestled desperately to free frozen control surfaces, especially ailerons, the group got up at 1045. Near Hachenberg the 368th Squadron had been detached to examine aircraft near stragglers and two 370th flights had been sent back to cover other stragglers. The result was that only 24 P-47s were on hand when Major Murphy saw 50 Germans diving in on the aborting B-17s, with 50 more Huns top cover. The Major confessed later he had not expected to come back from the duty-required bounce of the attacking Germans.

Why he and his small force was not boxed in and destroyed by the Huns who outnumbered him 4 to 1, and had every advantage of altitude and initiative, no one will ever know. Instead, the top cover enemy moved off and only later devoted itself to a running, and unsuccessful, pursuit, and the gaggles attacking the bombers broke at the threat of Murphy's attack, and went for the deck. The Major destroyed two and three others were damaged. In view of the hundred hazards of the takeoff in the snow, the 359th felt it had justified itself at Hachenberg about as completely as any fighter group could.

There was no flying on the 5th, although 200 bombers attacked French airfields, but the 6th produced the first double mission of the month.

The pertinent references are FO 262; the first large-scale assault on Berlin. The fighters had a big day, claiming 82-8-33, and the 359th scored 3-1-3 of these. Neither of the assignments was a good one; initial penetration and final withdrawal with the Luftwaffe massed at Berlin itself. Colonel Tacon tried to lead both efforts but his radio transmitter failed on each sortie, and Major Murphy took over the first job (53 up at 0952) and Major Shaw assumed command of the second (48 up at 1306). This take off was 46 minutes after landing, an interval of 36 minutes from last ship touching down to start engines. The 359th Group went in deeper than briefed on this second effort, was bothered by an open transmitter all the way, and also made its debut, through Lieutenant Carter, in steamship strafing. He beat up a 350-foot ship near Den Helder.

That afternoon when Captain Swiren reported that the "breather" on the open transmitter had interfered in every homing and resulted in Captain Pezda being given a wrong course home by 200 degrees, a critique was called by Colonel Tacon. Particular emphasis was paid to the danger of a "professional" attitude, too easily induced by the low casualties and comparatively easy victories.

7 March began at 0515 with a Wing request of a weather recco, but this was canceled before the pilots got off and the day was notable chiefly for ground school security training and, at 1645, official news that the B-29 was in the theatre and might be seen.

Berlin was again the target of the 8th, and successfully. Erkner was demolished. The 359th flew its second double mission, going in to Steinhuder Lake on the first run and to Emlichheim on the second. First Lieutenant Raymond B. Janney II scored a probable, and Lieutenant Grimes survived a Category E (salvage) crash landing at Bungay on the first effort, from which the 359th Group was down at 1402. Second take off was 1449.

Next day was an almost exactly similar story: Berlin, two efforts, 41 minutes on the ground between missions.

The weather was execrable. Colonel Tacon recommended that the mission be scrubbed. A Lysander at 700 feet couldn't see the ground. AJAX replied to take off when take off was possible, and to leave early so as to have plenty of gas to find a field; so, wing lights on, the 359th did get off at 1016, 15 minutes late, under a 600-foot ceiling into a lowering overcast with a light ground haze. The planes pulled vapor trails as they went up. As it turned out, the bombers were late too, so the first rendezvous was as planned. The second effort was without special incident.

The weather prevented operation on the 10th. Major Fitzpatrick talked to the station staff on the function of his section; part of a weekly series of such familiarization talks.

There was complete confusion on the 11th which began with receipt of FO 265 at 0338. It called for two alternate missions; prepare to replace P-51s going on a Münster attack if the 355th Group could not take off, or to substitute for P-38s on a Pas de Calais operation if the 364th Group were earthbound. The plotters were called at 0410 and Major Shaw briefed at 0700, but both the other outfits were airborne. Then Wing told the 359th Group to be ready to take over the 356th's share of the plan. That was scrubbed too, and at 0845, with pilots still standing by, red flares arched up from the control tower to signal the whole deal was off.

But the fun was not over. Wing, also at 0845, released the 359th until 0730 next morning, and the pilots, up since 0600, dispersed to Wretham Hall, to basketball games and to the ends of the 'drome. At 0915, Wing rescinded the release and ordered start engines at 0945. Somehow, this was done, and the 359th Group got up at 0954 with 51 ships, flying an uneventful withdrawal assignment on the Münster attack.

At 1812 on this day, Wing released the 359th to 0730 on the 14th. It seemed too good to be true, and it was entirely that, because at 2150 this release also was rescinded, the 359th to be available if 364th Group could not take off next day. That group was tied in by weather on the 12th, and 52 Liberators bombed Pas de Calais unescorted, but the 359th was not ordered up.

A release was once more rescinded at 0215 on the morning of the 13th; FO 267 turned out to be a milk run in the Pas de Calais, with 48 aircraft in the area east of Cayeux for 69 minutes. The overall mission was a failure, weather shielding all primaries and only seven bombers attacking a target of opportunity, Poix airdrome, while three were lost and 45 suffered minor flak damage.

The routine of rescinding releases continued on the 14th, when a release until 1100 was voided at 0515, but FO 268 was scrubbed at 0648, 3 minutes after it came off the teletype machines, and the morning, after much telephoning from Wing, degenerated into a practice mission, with 12 369th aircraft taking off to escort and attack 18 new bombers. At 1140, Colonel James Ferguson, commander of the 405th Fighter-Bomber Group, arrived from Christchurch with three members of his staff to renew a friendship with Colonel Tacon and inspect the 359th Group's method of operation. Colonel Ferguson returned later in the month to fly three missions with the 359th.

The mission of the 15th afforded a number of highlights. All escort that day, the bombers said, was superlative and the 359th did its share, going well beyond its briefed rendezvous point to find the Liberators and returning to spend an additional 23 minutes with them when they asked for help as we left. The 368th Squadron duplicated its previous feat of climbing 5,000 feet to meet and disperse enemy ships waiting to attack the bombers. This combat was at 28,000 feet.

At the other end of the scale a section of the 369th Squadron fought 10 Me109s from 26,000 down to 12,000, with Lieutenant Kruger destroying one. Kruger came out on the deck with Lieutenants Robert L. Thacker and Frank S. Fong. On the way they strafed two locomotives. All three had a difficult time getting home as all hit trees and/or high tension wires inside Germany. But the Thunderbolts again behaved like homing pigeons despite battered wings and torn propeller blades.

Three more claims of destroyed Germans were filed after the first effort on the 16th, two of them by Lieutenant Wetmore, after a busy 39-minute escort, 19 minutes longer than briefed, in the Chalons area under Major Tyrrell. Some 40 Hun fighters made passes at the bombers, diving from 33,000 feet and going straight for the deck. One of these, a decoy, was destroyed. The other two kills were made from the belly shot artists, driven off the bombers' lower hemisphere by the 370th Squadron. A remarkable feature of the escort was when the 67th Wing controller, sitting in Walcott Hall near Peterborough, England, could correctly warn the group leader over Chalons that the contrails visible 30 miles away were enemies. Pilots also saw flak that broke into eight glowing "balls of fire."

The 359th Group was down at 1216 and up again 34 minutes later with Colonel Tacon leading an uneventful withdrawal mission. Ground haze and cloud complicated everything including the bombing, but the heavies let go their loads on instruments, and 18 of them found and smashed a fire-fighting equipment plant at Ulm.

FO 271 was in at 0500 on the 17th, St. Patrick's Day, and was scrubbed at 0620, to be succeeded at 0645 by FO 272, which survived until 0808. The field was socked in under a gray haze but no release was forthcoming until 1000, and 30 minutes later that release was rescinded and the 359th was ordered to strafe Chartres and Beauvais.

Colonel Tacon, who elected to lead the strafing himself, prepared a careful briefing based on his own early attack-aviation training. Soon after noon, General Anderson arrived, saw the orders, decided that the plan of having the 359th and 361st Groups both attack the two targets destroyed any possibility of surprise for either. So he assigned us to Beauvais and the 361st to Chartres. Briefing was accordingly changed. Squadrons were not allowed to schedule both their commanders and operations officer for the show, one of each pair being required on the ground.

After all the planning for a coordinated strafing, the mission turned out badly. In addition to poor visibility, which also prevented the 78th Group from finding its assigned airdromes, Wing diverted both the 359th and the 361st Groups from their briefed approaches to their initial points to search for bandits. These were not found.

By that time the planned runs were impossible, as was surprise, and after twice finding and losing Beauvais airdrome in the haze, the 359th, when it went to 150 feet for the strafing run, was improperly orientated, and did not get over the target. In obedience to General Anderson's instructions, no second pass was made.

Pilots could report only that French peasants seemed delighted as well as startled to find American aircraft thundering over their fields, and had saluted with vigorous arm-waving.

The last double mission of the month was flown on the 18th. Two FOs were teletyped and the decision to use 273A (an assault on eight aircraft factories and airdromes in south central Germany) was not had until 0830.

The FO's assignments gave only nine minutes to refuel, but Wing could only suggest one squadron be sent home early to refuel. This was done. Flying conditions were again miserable, with three separate decks of cloud, and on the way out after the first mission the 359th was on instruments at 28,500 feet, and these conditions were reflected in the splattered formations of the bombers. On the second effort, the assigned Libs were 44 minutes late, but valuable work was done nonetheless taking out unescorted B-17s. Captain Albertson went over the side at Aux Le Chateaux at 1705 at 7,000 feet after the right wing of his aircraft was smashed by flak.

A party at Wretham Hall that night was a success, so it was pleasant that at 0100 on the 19th FO 274 was scrubbed and the 359th Group released until noon. Lieutenant J. B. Chaplin RNVR, arrived for lectures on the Mediterranean Campaign and air-sea rescue work, and the Group relaxed for a beautiful Sunday's flying. It was a lovely day, so at 1140,

Wing alerted the station for a late afternoon assignment. Briefing was at 1530, and take off at 1657, after much emphasis on night recognition systems and landing procedures.

These, as it turned out, were not needed. The 359th held formation on the way home and down just at dark, at 1930, to report a patrol of the Pas de Calais notable only because of another flak incident—Second Lieutenant Joseph M. Ashenmacher, badly hit in the left hand, had managed to get to Romney with Lieutenant Thomas S. Lane. There Ashenmacher, a new boy and well-liked, was hospitalized at Winchester, Hunts, where it was found necessary to amputate his left index finger.

High dense cloud spoiled the attack on Frankfurt set up on 20 March in FO 275, but Major Cranfill, leading his first mission, stayed in cloud that ran 10/10 from 19,000 to 31,000 feet until 1110, when his "C" Channel listeners (the men flying position #2 in each Blue Flight) reported the bombers were aborting. Some bomber formations did, in fact, continue, the fighters' usual problem of the "heroes" going on in the face of a recall, but most came back with their loads.

There was no mission on the 21st, and 22nd March was the day that the Luftwaffe would not fight over Berlin and let eleven combat wings bomb their capital through the overcast. The 359th was on withdrawal support. Six enemy aircraft dove for cloud before they could be bounced, and the highlight of the ride was a mid-air collision northwest of Meppel between P-47s piloted by Lieutenant Kerns and Captain Pezda. Kerns' ship needed a wing change but got home. Pezda's airplane was less seriously damaged.

On the 23rd, the bombers' indecision as to their position and schedule delayed rendezvous but ultimately meant we escorted them around Handorf airdrome and saw the bombs fall, a novelty.

On this day also, the 359th Group was informed that the DFC would be issued for conspicuous achievement on single flights, such as "doubles" scored against the enemy. Preparation of a number of such recommendations began.

24 March was a headache. Eventually, nothing came of it, the field was closed in tight and it was impossible to get off. For literally hours, Wing, AJAX, and Bodney were on the phone, reporting who was getting off and who wasn't and asking weather sequences on Wretham. At 1055 Wing abruptly said to forget the whole idea. Two other groups also were unable to get up. There was little enemy reaction.

Aircraft recognition tests were given on the 25th, and on the 26th, after pilots were awakened early and breakfasted at 0615, FO 280 was scrubbed. Major Irvine briefed on a milk run to the Pas de Calais and led the show, but there was little of interest in an 88-minute patrol. Bomb results were better than usual on these targets.

On this day Captain Charles C. Ettlesen, and Lieutenants Thacker, Carter and Oliphint, who had gone to Metfield for the strafing experimental group known as "Bill's Buzz Boys" (referring to Colonel Duncan, in command at Metfield) began to distinguish themselves, with an expert job on Châteaudun.

The 359th's 57th mission on 27 March cost Lieutenant Kerns his life in a muddled combat by Captain McKee's flight which the rest of the group never could find.

There was much initial doubt if we could get off that day on FO 282, an attack on Chartres. Zero hour was delayed 60 minutes at 1100 but at 1145, Wretham still had only 1,100 yards visibility and a 300-foot ceiling. The weather cleared slightly, and the 359th Group got up at 1257 with 47 aircraft.

Lieutenant Fong, who knocked down a Focke-Wulf 190 was the only Chinese-American pilot in the theatre the day he scored this victory on his seventh mission. Lieutenant Robert L. Pherson also scored that day, and Captain McKee claimed two damaged. The mission was part of a general assault on Luftwaffe installations in west and northwest France.

Four more airdromes were successfully bombed on 28 March. The 359th Group's part in it was not eventful, though three briefings and two red-flared scrubs preceded take off, and the Group did plenty of looking under vectored control once it got in its area. 900-yard visibility and 600-foot ceiling were the cause of the morning scrubbings.

Brunswick and the MIAG plant was the target on the 29th. Escort was longer than usual, from off Egmond at 1220 to Steinhuder Lake at 1310, but all else was as usual in this penetration run up the flak-free alley into central Germany.

In sharp contrast, the 30th was a red letter day. It began with Colonel Ferguson, who had flown the Brunswick job the day before, making a deep weather recco of the Low Countries in an 8-ship sweep commanded by Colonel Swanson. This was at 1000. They reported that the target areas were clear and Soesterberg was selected by Wing as the objective.

Twelve ships of the 369th Squadron were bombed up, with a dozen escorts each scheduled from the 368th and 370th. Briefing was a much more informal affair than previous thunderbombing attempts, but this time all worked perfectly. Much rank flew in the bomb squadron; the flights were led by Colonel Tacon, Colonel Ferguson, and Colonel Swanson, and the whole mission went off with great éclat, the Eighth Air Force summary describing the bomb results as "excellent."

Colonel Tacon celebrated this first bombing after so many disappointments, by leading the 359th Group in review at low level over Wretham on his return, and taking the same formation-buzzing show over to Bodney. Happiest of all, probably, were the ground crews who had so frequently and futilely loaded and unloaded bombs in the past.

At the briefing that morning Colonel Tacon reported to his pilots that he had flown the P-51 the day before and considered it the finest fighter he had ever been in. He announced a plan of checking squadron leaders, operation officers and flight commanders out in the new ship first, to insure adequate instruction for the pilots in the flights.

Another show was scheduled for the 31st but that was canceled at 0855, and taking advantage of good weather, pilots hastened to get in needed non-operation time. At 1100, First Lieutenant John B. Hunter came in to land and found himself without power and bellied in a mile north of the field. The aircraft was wrecked by the crash and fire but Hunter, save for scratches on his forehead and a bad jarring, was unhurt, a tribute to the rugged construction of the P-47 which had brought so many pilots unscathed through so many bad situations in 60 combat missions.

7.

APRIL 1944

The P-51s Arrive

Saturday, April 1: Wretham—Briefed at 0635, mission scrubbed. Briefed at 0900, mission scrubbed.

Damn these guys. Don't they ever read weather reports? Five hundred yards visibility and fog. Warm front moving in this afternoon.

Spent morning and afternoon at line. Tried to paint but messed it up. Not in the mood.

Wrote statement of accident for Hunter. He feels pretty good, slept all morning, and has a beautiful black eye and stiff back.

Major Shaw returned from a week at gas school. He was <u>not</u> at "Flak Home" as he'd kidded us. He'll go to Group now and Mosse will return as operations officer.

Got a new railroad magazine. Feeling much better, my ear is mostly clear. I received boxes of food from home.

[In 1942 the Stanbridge Earls estate became the first "Flak Home" and Roke Manor later served in a similar capacity. "Flak Home," or "Flak Shack," was a quiet, rest and relaxation home for USAAF Officers.]

Sunday, April 2: Wretham—Warm front with rain and a 500 foot ceiling.

Stanbridge Earls "Flak Home" or "Flak Shack" near Romsey, Hampshire. *July 1944 photo courtesy of Anthony C. Chardella: Archived by Char Baldridge, Historian, 359th Fighter Group Association*

Slept until 11:00 A.M. Ate lunch then played bridge until 4:00 P.M. Wrote letters. Ate supper. Bridge again until <u>1:45 A.M.</u>! Hagan and Randy's first attempts with me 'n Sam White. Coaching by Janney, Homeyer, and Shaw. Wot a night.

Monday, April 3: Wretham—Weather like yesterday.

To line at 0845. Censored mail. Released at 0930.

Brownie and I taxied the two P-51s, one to, and one back from the steel hangar. Noses are being painted green. Nice feeling ship. Trim and light, a real fighter.

Ate lunch then back to shack for aircraft recognition with Duffy. Then bridge again. Me and Hag versus Keesey and Randy.

Hunter feels pretty good now with no stiffness. His black eye is receding. Shaw to Group. Mosse to us.

London tomorrow for me.

[In addition to the green noses, rudder colors varied among the various fighter squadrons. Rudders were painted yellow on planes for the 368th, red for the 369th, and dark blue for the 370th. Code letters, painted

forward of the national insignia on the planes, were CV for the 368th, IV for the 369th, and initially CS for the 370th, although this changed to CR mid-March of 1944.

Radio call signs also varied and were changed regularly. When the 368th first arrived in England, their call sign was Beesnest. This changed to Jackson in January of 1944, Sonnet on April 17, 1944, and Jigger on April 23, 1944.]

Tuesday, April 4: Wretham—Same weather.

Censored mail. Played bridge, sketched, cleaned up for London.

Took the 556. A comfortable ride all by daylight. Arrived in London at 9:10 P.M. Took underground to Oxford Circus. Walked to 105 Gloucester by moonlight. <u>Very</u> warm. Took off topcoats and carried them.

No room at 105 Gloucester for me. Damn fools forgot. Went to Reindeer Club and ate. No rooms at Simond's Hotel. Brook Street, no luck. Phoned several others. Finally hit a good room at Ford's Hotel on Manchester Street, #40. A couple of good Scotches in the lounge then bed at midnight.

Wednesday, April 5: London—Breakfast in room at 8:00 A.M. Went to Boat's Chemist, McVickers for ribbons, Basset-Lowke, and Roberson. Then to 105 Gloucester Place to clean up. Lunch at Veeraswamy.

Went to the matinee then backstage. Met Mr. Barry at the bar for Scotches. Ben Eaton was there. Also saw Triss. She stopped by in her street clothes and said goodbye to me. Very cute.

Ate supper at the Trocadero with Barry, Sid, Eaton, and Hag. Fun. Sid was in rare form, told dirty jokes. Good food. Broke up at 11:00 P.M. Barry's car took us to our rooms, in bed by 11:30 P.M. Good time.

Thursday, April 6: London—Up at 9:00 A.M. Breakfast in bed. Packed, went to PX, took cab to station. Coffee on the 1150 train. Arrived Thetford at 1500. Truck at 1545. Hungry as Hell as I had no lunch.

Ate a good supper, watched a lousy movie, then played bridge. Took a walk alone. Feel kinda moody, restless, and fed-up. Wrote some letters.

Pino came back from hospital yesterday, his infected ear is okay. Hunter is okay but has a sore rib.

They've painted the ship's noses a vivid green. Looks okay. Sure haven't done much flying lately. Been a week now.

Friday, April 7: Wretham—Still bad weather. Cold as Hell out with rain. They tried to run a strafing mission at 1045 but scrubbed it right in the middle of the briefing. Good! 10/10ths at 800 feet. Sun came out a while late this afternoon but it's supposed to be bad again tomorrow.

Started my painting this afternoon, not too bad so far. Worked on it for an hour after supper. Bridge and basketball tonight.

Major Shaw is pitching for Group now, a major catastrophe to our baseball team. Brownie, however, has taken over and is doing okay. They beat the 369th today. Lost to Group yesterday. The 370th beat Group today. And so to bed.

Saturday, April 8: Wretham—I checked out in the P-51 #6775, CVY. A B-7. Wot a plane! Never felt such turns, rolls, or handling. Stalls beautifully. <u>Flies</u> right down the landing approach at 115 IAS. Really sweet.

Worked a bit more on my painting in late afternoon. Slow drying. That bar we're working on is really gonna be something! Bill Simmons is in charge of the shack, a good man for the job.

Movie tonight starred Sinatra. "Higher and Higher." Not bad. "Frankie Boy" wows 'em. Should have heard the gang screaming and cheering in falsetto voices. Really a riot. Bridge afterwards.

Easter Sunday, April 9: Wretham—Socked in 10/10ths. One mile visibility. Briefing at 0945. Rain at take off so moved back one and one-half hours.

Me, Randy, Hag, and Hunter: Blue Flight. Major Shaw leading. Broken cumulus and haze, pretty clouds, not much in the way of instruments needed. We headed to Egmond, thence 33 minutes inland 100 degrees. No bombers, no nuttin! So we turned around and came back. Three hours flight time using 150 gallon belly tanks. Not bad. Quite stable, but heavy.

Another movie and then played more bridge. A.G. and I versus Randy and Hag. We get a day off a week <u>on post</u>. No passes but leaves continue.

Went to 10-minute special Easter service before briefing. Chaplain Ziegler is swell!

Monday, April 10: Wretham—Beautiful spring day. Blue sky with some fair weather cumulus.

First mission took off at 0810. Withdrawal protection, Pas de Calais to the Reims area.

Second mission took off at 1415. Escort P-38s bombing south of Bremen. Then a P-38F-6 flew in here and picked up a flight of four for escort to photograph damage on second mission. A hot ship, sans armament. All blue. Nice.

I didn't go on either mission. Flew the P-51 CVY again for an hour and a half. Loops, rolls, sweet ship.

Drew pencil outlines for a painting.

Bridge and letters tonight.

[US and British Air Forces begin an offensive against airfields and communication centers held by Germans in France and Belgium.]

Tuesday, April 11: Wretham—Briefing at 0745. Took off at 0915.

Me, Baldy, and A.G.: Yellow Flight, high, with Bo. Shaw leading squadron.

Escorted B-17s penetrating Zuider Zee past Hanover! One hundred fifty gallon tanks on ships. We were up for <u>four</u> hours. The 370th got in a fight with 190s near Hanover, up front and low. Pino lost oil pressure, bellied in near Zwolle. He's okay, landed in a haystack. Bo, Mac, and Keesey shot up his plane. Mac got a big flak hole in his tail. We left Bo and brought home a lone B-17 on three engines from Steinhuder Lake almost to Zuider Zee. Left him when low on gas but made base okay.

The 370th strafed airdromes. Took out 88s. Smith bailed out over Holland when he ran out of gas. Dunlap not yet returned, also ran out of gas. Quite a day!

John Dilling from the 320th–352nd, evaded safely on December 30th when he went down. Gave a good talk to us in the afternoon.

Movie tonight. Pretty tired.

["88" was the Allied designation given to a series of German artillery guns with a bore of 88mm. Originally designed as an anti-aircraft gun, its 20-pound shells produced the flak that proved effective against both bombers and fighters. Variations of the 88 were feared and respected as anti-tank weapons.]

Wednesday, April 12: Wretham—A beautiful, clear spring day. Warm. Flowers. Birds. Whee!

They had a good mission all set, withdrawal protection from near Hanover, and they scrubbed it <u>in</u> the air, so Major Shaw took the group on an uneventful fighter sweep.

The flights were all reshuffled today. We lost Hag to "A" Flight and got Tommy Lane for "D" Flight. A good guy, but I hate to lose Hag. McGeever is now assistant ops officer. We have two new boys as of yesterday but don't know their names yet. Everyone is flying the P-51s now.

I painted all day. Nearly finished the picture and it nearly finished me, too. My back aches and my head aches!

Captain Howard Fogg painting a P-47 shooting down an Fw 190. *April 14, 1944 photo courtesy of Anthony C. Chardella: Archived by Char Baldridge, Historian, 359th Fighter Group Association*

Thursday, April 13: Wretham—Feel lousy. Stayed in bed until after lunch. Got up to get a haircut in squadron area.

Group took off at 1345, escorting withdrawal from Frankfurt (the target). Major Tyrrell, Lane, Homeyer, and Brown. Brown's engine quit twenty miles off Knocke. He was in my ship. *Clumpy* is at the bottom of the North Sea. A.G. and Major gave a good fix to Air/Sea Rescue. They saw him in the water splashing around but with no dinghy? No trace of him since. A/S Rescue found the oil slick 20 minutes later. Piss poor visibility, they said, less than a mile. I feel doubly queer since I was scheduled to fly and took myself off the schedule. I should be in the drink instead of Brownie, goddamit.

Squadron Recapitulation:
Commanding Officer: Major Tyrrell
Exec: Major Wallace
Operations: Captain Mosse
Assistant Ops: McGeever
"A" Flight: Captain Bolefahr, Beaupre, Hagan, Hudelson, Cater, Keesey, Lambright
"B" Flight: First Lieutenant Bach, Lemmens, Janney, Burton, White, Hawkinson, Hatter
"C" Flight: Captain Forehand, Simmons, Smith, Botsford, Perkins, Drake
"D" Flight: Captain Fogg, Hunter, Homeyer, Randy, Lane, Baldy
Missing in Action: Pino, Holland, April 11, 1944; Brown, Channel, April 13, 1944

Friday, April 14: Wretham—Released until tomorrow. Swell spring day, so why the release? Felt good for a change, though.

No more word on Brownie. He had it. Goddam *Clumpy* to Hell!

Spent all day at the line painting my new ship, *The Saint*. She'll be okay and I'm glad it <u>isn't</u> a D-10. Gall feels pretty good, glad he had another plane right away to ease his mind.

The Colonel's D-22 is a dream with her paddle prop and new sight.

The bar looks beautiful, with waxed floor, paint, and so on. All set by tomorrow night.

The "new" bar at Wretham Hall.
Archived by Char Baldridge, Historian, 359th Fighter Group Association, from records at HQ USAF Research Center, Maxwell Air Force Base, Alabama

Movie tonight was "Behind the Rising Sun." Jap propaganda but had a swell fight in it.

Painted gold stripes on "Casey" last night. Pretty snappy.

Saturday, April 15: Wretham—Jackpot number two.

Each flight went after a different airdrome. Six flights took off between the 368th, 369th, and 370th. 369th got top flight. Me, Randy, Hunter, and Baldy: Blue Flight with Bo leading. Randy headed back, had an oil leak. Hawk in to replace him.

To Paffenburg at 15,000 feet, 3/10ths cumulus down on deck 35 miles northeast to Wittmundhafen drome. Missed by one-quarter mile. IAS 450.

Got four cracks at locomotive and train. Destroyed it. I damaged a radar tower. Some thrill!! Picked up a slight hole in right wing from small arms.

First second of video clip, U.S. Government Archive Number [342 USAF 17629 R11 MPPS] from VIII Fighter Command, Combat Film No. 2912, Capt. H.L. Fogg, 368th Sqdn., 15 April 1944, 359 F.G., Attacking Ground Targets.
Courtesy of CriticalPast

VIII FIGHTER COMMAND
COMBAT FILM No. 2912
CAPT. H.L. FOGG   368 SQDN.
15 APRIL 1944   359 F.G.
ATTACKING
GROUND TARGETS

Wide open with water injection climbed back to 10,000 feet in four and one-half minutes. I flew Lane's D-10(G). She's a good 'un. Some ride.

Sinus hurt all day. Dammit!

Party tonight. The bar is beautiful! Picture looks swell. Pretty wet out!

[Operation Jackpot was initiated by the 8th Fighter Command on April 15th and was directed at Luftwaffe fighter bases. Later expanded to include railroad infrastructure and trains, these missions were dubbed "Chattanooga."

Water injection was employed at wide-open throttle to cool the combustion chambers and reduce the risk of detonation, which could damage or destroy an engine.]

Gun camera view of locomotive being strafed by Captain Howard Fogg. Tenth second of video clip, U.S. Government Archive Number [342 USAF 17629 R11 MPPS] from VIII Fighter Command, Combat Film No. 2912, Capt. H.L. Fogg, 368th Sqdn., 15 April 1944, 359 F.G., Attacking Ground Targets. *Courtesy of CriticalPast*

Gun camera view of radar tower being strafed by Captain Howard Fogg. Fifteenth second of video clip, U.S. Government Archive Number [342 USAF 17629 R11 MPPS] from VIII Fighter Command, Combat Film No. 2912, Capt. H.L. Fogg, 368th Sqdn., 15 April 1944, 359 F.G., Attacking Ground Targets. *Courtesy of CriticalPast*

Sunday, April 16: Wretham—No mission, low ceiling all day. Went down to line and painted airplane again. Everyone else slept. Loafed later like it was a typical Sunday afternoon. Bridge and movie at night.

Got a 36" x 26" piece of canvas duck from the parachute department for future oil painting.

There's trouble with *The Saint.* Her water injection is screwed up. RPM surges. Needs new engine, but engineering sez no, just fix it and the Hell with the pilots. Sure fed up with their damn attitude. Stuart is a bastard! Soft soaping, smug, self-centered, he's not fooling anybody but himself.

Monday, April 17: Wretham—No mission. Weather the same as yesterday only colder.

I censored mail in the morning. Painted the fireplace in the afternoon.

Baldy, Randy, Burton, Lemmens, Hudelson, and Botsy all promoted to first lieutenant. Party last night. I got stinking drunk, worst I've ever been. Sicker than a dawg, drinking Scotch, brandy, port. Ugh. No wonder. Whew!

Word arrived from Ed Hyland's sister, he <u>was</u> killed, the International Red Cross confirmed. Bad, but expected.

Baseball league starts tomorrow. Boy, do we need a pitcher! We play the 369th tomorrow night.

Plane still out.

Tuesday, April 18: Wretham—The most beautiful day since I've been in England. We laid in the grass by the Ops shack and soaked up sunshine.

Mission was a penetration escort from landing field to southeast Hamburg, a long water hop clean past the Frisian Islands. Our flights saw Denmark.

Eleven ships took off at 1216 but three came back early, between problems with oil leaks, superchargers, etc. These ships are all beat up, and they need new engines. Goddam engineering department really gripes me. They'd squeeze blood out of a turnip. Flights landed at 1545.

Got a 9' x 12' rug from salvage today, really improves our room.

Got track from home and ran Casey tonight.

369th beat us in baseball 7 to 4. We played from 1800 to 1930.

Wednesday, April 19: Wretham—Up at 0600. Briefed at 0700.
Cold and clear.
Nine ships took off at 0825 on penetration escort from Zuider Zee to Dümmer Lake. Randy was the only "D" Flighter to go. Saw heavy flak but no enemy aircraft. Three hour flight.
I had a headache again. Went to Doc, he did nose packs. Grounded me to Hall.
After lunch I went back to line with field equipment on for alert.
Homeyer finally got a brand new silver, hydro prop D-22. A sweetheart and is he happy. Randy's and mine are in for engine changes. Good!
Baldy test hopped Colonel's new D-22. Prop out. Two A-31s came in here today for tow target duty.
I headed back to Hall, painted blue panels on Casey with red and gold striping. Got the rest of the track from Dad today.
Movie was "Shadow of a Doubt." Excellent.

Thursday, April 20: Wretham—Day off. Stayed in the sack all morning. Wrote letters, read magazines in the afternoon.
Squadron practiced strafing an airdrome. At 1725 took off to Pas de Calais for the good old area support milk run. Landed at 2015. Homeyer, Baldy, Lane, and Hunter all went, 10 ships in the squadron. No action and little flak.
Randy flew the P-51B-7.
"D" Flight now has: T-engine, X-engine, U – D-22, G – D-10.
Forehand got a D-22 today. Pulled his rank on Keesey in typical Forehand fashion. That bastard sure irritates me. He has a mouth like a wind tunnel.
Head feels okay. Hope I can fly tomorrow. Weather was cool, but nice.

Friday, April 21: Wretham—Grand spring morning. To line at 0830. Painted on *The Saint* most of the morning then walked to Hall for lunch.
Briefing at 1315, took off at 1510. Me and Lane: Red Flight. Bo led. Took off, set course. Wing called and scrubbed it as we neared Norwich. Warm front was too bad for late returns, and there were rain showers already in the area. So we all practiced ground strafing, hit the deck, and flew the best part of an hour. I finally lost the others behind some trees

and Lane and I came in alone. Sloppy landing with 150 gallon belly tank.

Major Shaw got a D-22 today. Gave Keesey his D-10. Janney gets Pino's old ship when it returns. Drake got a D-2. Mosse has a D-21 Curtiss semi-paddle with Wroe as his crew chief, in "D" Flight. V his letter. We now have five ships. W & Y also should return. Wow!

Saturday, April 22: Wretham—Another beautiful spring day, the warmest and sunniest yet.

Fooled around line all morning. Censored mail. Mac talked about night flying.

Had Doc pack my nose after lunch. Felt better. We had an intra-squadron ball game at line. Nice warm sun.

Briefing at 1600. To Hamm, Germany as target escort. Took off at 1730, landed at 2040. Homeyer and Colonel flew Red Flight. D-22s were good.

My ship's new engine froze. Mechanics couldn't even start it or pull it through the hangar. Gall very pissed off. Me too. So they hauled her back into the hangar and will change the engine again. Lane gets his new engine tomorrow.

370th reported five enemy aircraft destroyed, 369th got two. 368th had zero, as usual. Nuts!! 370th lost a pilot though, a new boy on his first mission.

Supper at 2130. Sleepy.

Sunday, April 23: Wretham—Still another grand sunny day.

Went to the dispensary for more nose packs. Head feels okay, but Doc said no flying.

Squadron briefing at 1300, take off at 1406. The 368th and the 369th sent up 12 each for bombing mission. The 370th got top flight to airdrome south of Leuven, Belgium. No action. They were gone two hours.

Went to line for a while. Spent the afternoon painting a watercolour sketch of operations shack. Not too bad. Good fun.

Ate second chow. We played with Renken's cannon, used shotgun powder. Not so hot. Ran train, wrote a letter, and so passed another "quiet" evening in the goddam ETO.

Forehand goes to dive-bombing school for three weeks on Tuesday and he's taking the P51 B-7(Y) with him. Phooey!

Monday, April 24: Wretham—A bit cloudy and cooler.

Briefing at 0945, took off at 1100, landed at 1415. No action. Flak hit Janney and Lemmens as Mosse's flight strafed an airdrome, hangars, etc. Found 15 holes in Janney's plane. They were on escort near Metz.

Doc on courts-martial duty so I went to base dispensary and had Doc Kendall pack my nose. It's still inflamed but draining. Wish it would quit.

Spent the afternoon making notes of missions for a talk to enlisted men. Looked at new engine change on *The Saint*, coming along okay. "D" Flight is back in its own area now, and that's much better.

Seventeen pilots checked out on night flying from 9:00 P.M. to 11:30 P.M., in two shifts. I went up into the tower. Hot coffee, sandwiches here at midnight. Beautiful, cold, starry night. All okay.

Tuesday, April 25: Wretham—Duffy woke me at 0515.

I woke Lane and Hunter but let the others sack in. Five hours sleep! Wow. Breakfast at 0530.

Briefing at 0600. An uneventful mission as penetration escort, south Abbeville to southeast of Paris.

Cater had gas fumes, hit the deck with his flight. Hag, Hunter, Lane, and Lemmens crossed the French coast at zero altitude. Broke up a German soldier gym class on the beach.

Second mission at 1300. Pas de Calais milk run as the 359th escorted 30 B-24s.

Me to Doc as usual in the morning and now I'm officially grounded, goddammit! Feel okay. Dull headache now and then is all. Hell!

Forehand took off with the wing tank packed with clothes.

Movie and lecture by MC, then shower and sack this evening.

Wednesday, April 26: Wretham—Wakened at 0500 again. Me and Baldy got up.

Briefing at 0600, took off at 0724.

Penetration escort to north of Hanover. Tacon and eight ships, quite a squadron. No action.

Squadron practiced dive-bomb mission in the afternoon. Homeyer flew over to Halesworth (56th). My ship ready this evening. Baldy got her up for three hours, sez she's okay. Whoopee.

I went to the base dispensary and Doc fixed me up with packs. Beautiful day again so sat in the sun the balance of the afternoon. Head has the same dull ache, dammit. My leave starts May 4th. Hooray.

Good supper. Practice baseball game with '69th, we lost 11 to 5. Played bridge until 10:00 P.M.

370th practicing night flying tonight.

Thursday, April 27: Wretham—Briefing at 0730.

Squadron took off at 0820 for Pas de Calais to Dieppe. No action. Landed at 1200.

Briefing at 1730.

Took off at 1900 for Type 16 for Charleroi, Belgium, bomber withdrawal. No action. Landed at 2130.

The most perfect day of weather yet. Almost hot and sunny.

My head seems much better. Got nose packs, then flew (yes <u>flew</u>) for two hours slow time below 3,000 feet in *The Saint*. She's sweet to handle and the engine is fine. Like her characteristics better than *Clumpy*. Randy checked 'er at 32,000 feet. She's ready to go.

Bo's new D-22 caught fire on the line, leaking gas onto hot exhaust. Had to use the fire truck. Tough luck. The 369th got 12 P-51s today. We have 14 ships in commission now.

Took off my four-day moustache. Hag and Lemmens on leave now, me and Lane next.

[An Allied convoy sailing west of Start Point along the Channel Coast is spotted by German pilots. Covered up by the Allies during the war, the convoy was making a secret practice run for the planned invasion of Normandy. The Allies lose 197 seaman and 441 soldiers when the Germans attack the convoy at night.]

Friday, April 28: Wretham—Nice day again, although a bit cool and windy, but we were released until tomorrow. Most everyone sacked in all morning.

I went to line at 0830, took Janney's (<u>B</u>) D4 up to check fuel consumption. Very strong gas fumes so I landed after 20 minutes. Looks like the fuel injection nozzle connection is spraying raw gas all over accessory section. Nice material for a fire. Whew!

Had aircraft recognition at shack at 1300. Took wax down to Gall. Got rations. There were chips in Lane's new engine so they're changing it again. That makes three for "D" Flight. Nice engines they're giving us. Nuts.

League ball game with the 85th after supper. We won with a "comedy of errors" 21 to 6. Wiley "pitched."

Then watched "Slightly Dangerous" with Lana Turner. Wow!

Saturday, April 29: Cambridge—Briefing at 0715 for a penetration escort east of Hanover, 15 miles, to target Berlin. The 370th shot up railroad yards at Münster, claimed seven trains. Cunningham got an Fw 190. No other action. We put up 17 ships for a change. Not bad. Lane flew mine and said it was okay.

Janney and I went to Cambridge on the 1125. Ate lunch at Tony's, then went to pipe store, jewelers, then to movie, "Flesh and Fantasy." Damn good!

Took a walk along River Cam. Beautiful green lawns, tulips, jonquils, and trees all blooming and green. Really is a lovely town. Had supper at English Speaking Union. Then took the 722 back. Met Ashenmacher returning from hospital. Rode in V8 cab back to base.

Sunday, April 30: Wretham—Had an early briefing for a three and one-half hour escort mission to central France (Orleans). B-17s are targeting airfields. No excitement. "B" Flight strafed a field, got several planes and an ammunition dump.

Released until 0600 tomorrow.

All P-51s here now, we received 76 of 'em in three days. This field is loaded with ships; they're all over. I have a B-15, silver, 19:10 #1026879. A honey. All of "D" Flight has new ships, the only flight that does. Nice break.

Mosse is with us. Has Wroe with him. We get Sage from "C" Flight for A.G. We also got a new boy, Bob Addleman, from South Bend, Indiana, 43-D. Flew at Wright Field in P-39s, P-47s, and P-51s. A nice quiet guy, either a bit stuck up or hot, but okay.

Seven of us flew from 1930 to 2030, practicing night flying. Nice lighting system.

Excerpts from the April 1944 Informal Report of Morale for the 359th Fighter Group, submitted by "Chappie" Ziegler indicated: "The morale of the men on this field reached a new high during the month of April. I was never more convinced of this than on last Friday evening as I took a tour of the field for the express purpose of measuring our morale. Let me tell you what I found.

"Let's start our tour at Wretham Hall. It is just 1830 hours. The bell for the second sitting of supper has just rung. The usual mad dash for the dining room is in progress as we begin our tour. There is plenty of friendly ribbing, pushing and shoving, laughter about "chow-hounds" and "wolves," all tokens of the strong friendship that binds all these officers together into the best fighting group in England. In the main lounge the seats are already drawn up for the evening show at 1845. Each chair has a slip of paper on it reserving it for someone. Some chairs are already occupied by men reading the "Stars and Stripes" or listening to the radio as Frank Sinatra "sends" them. The show tonight is Lana Turner in "Slightly Dangerous." With Lana performing, both the 1845 and 2045 shows are sure to be packed. Passing through the lounge we enter the bar. Since it has been decorated, our bar must be one of the most enticing in all England. The room is flooded with indirect lighting and the color scheme is blue with gold trimming. The bar is complete even to the "brass" rail, only ours is an iron pipe. On the wall is an oil painting of a P-47 shooting down an Fw 190, done by Captain Fogg of our group. Major Tyrrell and Lieutenant Simmons deserve the credit for the tremendous improvement in the attractiveness of the bar room. Passing from the bar we enter the game room where Lieutenant Downing, amidst cries of "that's a low blow," is taking a beating at the hand of Captain Swiren on the dart board. The Ping-Pong table is put to hard use as Lieutenant Drake and Captain Smith battle it out. From the game room we step outside, walk across the rose garden, and come to the officer's baseball diamond, located in the middle of a cow pasture. A League game is in progress. We have an Officer's Softball League with five teams in it: HQs, 359th Fighter Group, the 368th, 369th and 370th Fighter Squadrons and the 85th Service Group. Tonight the 368th and 85th are playing. We can't stay to see the whole game but find out later that the 368th wins to the tune of 21 to 8. At least 20 other men are watching the game. I might say here that nothing has contributed to the morale of this station during the month as has softball."

Group HQ ball club. Photo taken August 1, 1944. Standing (left to right): Lieutenant Wiley, Major Fraley, Lieutenant Englund. Kneeling: Captain Fogg, Major Cranfill, Lieutenant Renken, Captain Platt. Sitting: Colonel Tacon, Major Pezda, Lieutenant Major (former pitcher for the NY Giants), Lieutenant Swaney. *Courtesy of Peter Fogg*

Office of the Group Historian
APO 637 / US Army
4 May 1944

History of the 359th Fighter Group, April 1944

April of 1944 was the last full month in which the 359th Fighter Group flew the Thunderbolts in which it trained for combat. Replacement of the P-47s, long delayed, was achieved with a rush at the end of the month, when ferry pilots flew glistening new silver Mustangs into the field at East Wretham by the dozen.

April essentially was a month of waiting: waiting for the arrival of the P-51s, waiting for the Luftwaffe to give battle, waiting for the day when strafers would find an airfield loaded with enemy aircraft, and, most of all waiting for the invasion of Festung Europa.

This was the month when the US Strategic Air Forces in Europe cascaded more than 40,000 tons of bombs upon the enemy and his installations: a larger tonnage of explosives than was achieved by the RAF Bomber Command in that magnificent organization's systematic destruction by fire and bomb of the German and his cities, factories, and railroads.

England blossomed that month. Rain fed the earth (and restricted flying) during part of the first fortnight but then the apple trees flowered, cherries bloomed, the shrubs 'round Wretham Hall blazed in glory. And, as the days lengthened, so did the intensity of the preliminary bombardment of the Nazi system of communications, and concomitantly, the demands upon the fighter groups became larger.

The pattern was erratic. Good flying days passed without missions, target selection wavered and swung between assaults on the enemy capital, upon his airfields, upon railroad choke points, upon his rocket installations on the French coast, but as April ended the 359th found itself flying 13 full dress missions averaging 3 hours 23 minutes each in 11 days, including 5 missions in 3 days, a foretaste of the work to come when assault by sea and land would require dawn-to-dusk air support and attack.

In sum, the month of April meant 23 missions in 20 days, in which 1,010 airplanes were flown, 81 returned early, for a total of 929 sorties. 87 airborne enemy aircraft were sighted (the Luftwaffe then was hoarding and husbanding its resources for the climacteric struggle over the beaches) and of these 10 were destroyed, as well as 24 others set afire on the ground.

These successes, plus the further score of one probable and 21 damaged, cost the 359th Group five pilots; two comparative novices believed lost to enemy action, two MIA in the culminating incidents of oil-pressure diffi-culties in the 368th Squadron, and one who parachuted over enemy territory after a strafing attack left him with insufficient petrol to get home.

The oil pressure troubled airplane, which Lieutenant Pino belly-landed successfully in Holland, normally flown by Lieutenant Janney, had gone 55 missions without aborting. The airplane from which Lieutenant Brown parachuted into the North Sea also had a successful record for Captain Fogg, to whom it was usually assigned. The loss of these five pilots gave the 359th a five month record of claims in combat and on the ground; of 63 enemies destroyed, eight probably destroyed and 42 damaged for 14 losses, of which 12 were in combat, one a non-operational accident and one on DS with Bill's Buzz Boys.

The claims summarized do not, of course, embrace the ground successes scored in strafing. Ettlesen on 19 April led a successful attack on the special stretch of track between Osnabrück and Bremen. His encounter report casually mentions that his attack this day wrecked his 18th locomotive on that particular bit of track. On the 29th of April the 370th Squadron ran a gunnery pattern over the yards at Hanover, blowing up 14 locomotives and damaging seven others.

The eight .50 calibre guns of the big Bolts were useful, as was the rugged construction of the airplane, which again saved lives. Captain McKee on 29 April brought a P-47 back from Germany with a blown cylinder, in itself a remarkable tribute to the airplane as well as pilot, then found himself in flames at 600 feet. He shot an emergency landing at Framingham with an oil obscured canopy, nosed over, and the airplane flopped on its back. He crawled out unhurt, and returned to Wretham to find that before the mis-sion he had been put on orders for a week at the Flak Home at Alton Dorset! Lieutenant Robert V. Beaupre of the 368th Squadron, in one of the 3rd Gunnery's older P-47s, crashed because of a sheared oil shaft pump. His airplane broke into four pieces; the engine was hurled 60 feet by the impact and the pilot escaped with a broken leg. An additional tribute to the P-47 was the fact that as the month ended and the 369th gave up its P-47s, that unit had flown 83 missions over Europe with one loss.

A combat loss outside the 359th Group which touched every pilot closely was the death in action 14 April of Lieutenant Colonel Richmond, of the 352nd Group at Bodney. Leading his squadron strafing, he went into the ground after being hit by light flak only moments after he had scored his first victory over a Focke-Wulf in the air.

Quiet-voiced, massively calm, the kindly, balding Richmond had been, in a real sense, foster-father in the nervous days of December when the 359th went operational, and his loss was keenly felt.

Two generals visited, and the month was notable also for the improving assignments consequent to the issue of 150-gallon belly tanks. This extra petrol allowed Captain McKee to prolong the assigned penetration support well beyond briefed limits in the attack on Hamm, 22 April, and a consequent engagement with 15 enemy aircraft, of which seven were destroyed in the air.

The most important social event of the month was abolition early in April of all off-station passes and leaves for non-combat crews. This focused attention on the developing life in the new communal area, as the Red Cross Aero Club opened, as was the gymnasium. Softball sprouted into feverish activity (Colonel Tacon organizing and catching for what appeared to be the best club) and almost all officers, save pilots, moved to the new area.

In day to day summary, the month began with rain and fog, which did not deter an early start 1 April. Breakfast was at 0530 and fog was so heavy at briefing at 0630 that the whole show was generally regarded as an April Fool's joke. Tempers were not improved by a decision to re-brief on the 56th Group's mission, and this briefing was duly held at 0900. At 1020, the mission was scrubbed, the pilots were put on "available" at their dispersals, and finally, at 1050, the whole show was canceled.

Next day it rained, and there was more gloom at news of the decision to re-equip the 339th Group with P-51s before the Mustangs were sent to Wretham. 3 April was also un-flyable, but steps were taken to correct an injustice done to Lieutenant Colonel Murphy, awarded a "damaged" by the Assessment Board at AJAX, although his wingman had seen the enemy pilot bail out in a fight 24 February over Hardenburgh. The award eventually was corrected.

There was more rain on the 4th but by evening it was a brilliant example of a late English spring afternoon at its best. At midnight Wing inquired if the 359th Group possessed a copy of the Plan Jackpot, mass strafing by all groups. Wretham had no copy but the whole plan was teletyped; Lieutenant Gilbert Jamieson flew from Walcott with the latest flak information on targets in the assigned Oldenburg area, and there was an exhaustive 80-minute briefing. All went for naught, as the weather was non-operational for strafing, and although the 359th penetrated to its area, it could not, like most others, identify its target, and the opportunity for mass surprise and mass destruction of enemy aircraft parked wing to wing throughout northern and western Germany was wasted.

The 6th was notable chiefly for the 7-5 victory pitched by Major Shaw for HQ over the 368th Squadron, where he had been for 10 months operations officer, and the same squadron's bitter complaint that the delivery used by its ex-star was, in objective fact, illegal.

There was another Jackpot briefing on the 7th, but the show was scrubbed (these fighter attacks en masse were scheduled only when the weather was not good enough for heavy bombers, a fact warmly resented by the fighter pilots) and Colonel Tacon indiscreetly fell to boasting in the briefing room of the victory over the 368th. Whereupon the 370th challenged, and won a rousing ball game.

Mission 62 was flown on the 8th, a day when mist and fog at briefing turned into clear, bright sunshine at take off, which was 1229. The 359th had the pleasure of seeing enemy airfields at Quackenbrück, Bramsche, and Salzbergen well bombed, but no Germans were seen, although flights dropped back to shepherd stragglers to the enemy coast.

The weather was miserable on the 9th. The morning was good, suspiciously good, with a fine blue sky before briefing at 0945, when it rained so hard that a Miles Master, sent up as local weather recco, couldn't get back to the field and had to land in a cow pasture. Most of the bombers scrubbed but some went on in against Greifswald. At Wretham, a 15-minute postponement of takeoff pyramided into a second 45-minute delay. Then the briefed mission was scrubbed at 1140 when Colonel Tacon informed AJAX there was steady rain, 900-yard visibility, and 1,000 feet of ceiling. The pilots were put at available, and at 1305 were ordered off to pick up stragglers. The group was airborne at 1324 under a clear blue sky but the weather again worsened abruptly and it was a gloomy day, with a lowering overcast, when the mission was down at 1630.

On the 10th there were two shows; one a take off at 0817 to escort heavies who abandoned their primaries and wandered above France and Belgium before striking at Eekloo airdrome, and the second, an escort to the 20th Group's droopsnooting. This idea, mounting a bombsight instead of guns in the long snout of a P-38 had taken, with good results. The 20th Group bombed the airfield at Gütersloh that day. The 359th was irked because the Kings Cliffe fighters, who were early at the enemy coast, did not wait for their escort but steamed on in to the target where the Wretham fighters eventfully rendezvoused.

On the 11th, Lieutenant Doersch knocked down an Fw 190 in a long chase at 50 feet altitude, and the day was notable also for the thorough beating up of airfields at Volkenrod and Bielefeld, blowing up one enemy plane at every pass. Total claims were 13-1-14.

Three pilots were lost that day and there was a worry about five others for hours, especially Doersch, who had a long lonely ride home on the deck. Pino, it developed, had bellied safely when his oil pressure quit, waved to Captain Wayne N. Bolefahr and the rest of his flight, then had run to a Dutch outhouse, only to run out again and burrow into a haystack. Bolefahr's flight strafed and destroyed the grounded P-47. Thomas P. Smith, a fanatic Crossbow enthusiast, bailed out over Belgium when he ran out of gas while strafing. Lieutenant Elmer N. Dunlap, one of the first two replacement pilots, was last seen in the combat area over Fallersleben. Lieutenant Will D. Burgsteiner, star of the show, later was lost when a weapons carrier pinned him against a wall and shattered his arm on the 25th.

The bomber effort against Leipzig on the 12th aborted just as airborne, but the controller ordered a sweep anyway, and the patrol deep into Germany and the Hanover-Steinhuder Lake area was uneventful.

The weather was glorious these days, completely atoning for the worst days of the winter. On the 13th, General Anderson appeared at briefing to present 11 DFCs. He told the pilots that strafing would continue so long as the results warranted it and so long as losses were not excessive, and he urged them to make sure airfields had profitable targets before going down, to attack only if aircraft were visible, and to avoid the civilian strafing which had brought the Luftwaffe into bad repute.

Another pilot was lost this day in a long 61 minute escort of four B-17 combat wings from Pronsfeld to Nieuport that was distinguished otherwise only by the number of bombers seen destroyed by flak. Lieutenant Cecil R. Brown, star pitcher of the 368th, bailed out 20 miles north northwest of Knocke on the way home. Major Tyrrell gave a complete Mayday; a flight remained over the area 5 minutes before dwindling petrol forced them to leave, and Air-Sea Rescue was on the spot in 10 minutes. But Lieutenant Brown was not recovered, though there was a faint hope that the Germans might have gone out in response to a distress signal flashed in the clear on the International Morse frequency. Brown had dinghy drill in the pool at Saffron Walden but his dinghy, it was believed, did not inflate. At least he was never seen to climb aboard although he was seen in the water.

Next day there was another Jackpot. The 359th Group was one of the two in the Fighter Command which did not lose one or more pilots, as bad weather and alerted German defenses cost the VIII Fighter Command 30 MIAs. Few aircraft were found in the buzzing of Oldenburg, Kayhauserfeld, Varel, Wittmundhafen and Hagan. The flight assigned to attack Jever aborted. Among the claims of the day was a locomotive destroyed by Captain Fogg, a notorious lover and brilliant painter of trains, whose room at Wretham Hall contained not only dozens of watercolors of locomotives but a scale-model steam loco which lustily puffed around the room for the fascination of all observers. Fogg also executed his first oil of the month, an air combat scene for the redecorated fluorescent-lighted new bar at Wretham Hall.

17 April, dull and cloudy, was the effective date for new radio call signs. The group leader became "Chairman," the 368th Squadron "Sonnet," 369th Squadron "Tinplate" and 370th Squadron "Tailer." Two of these were later changed again, 368th Squadron going to "Jigger" and 370th Squadron to "Red Cross." Controller, long familiar as "Fine boy" was now "Pickaxe." The bombers became "Vinegrove" instead of "Goldsmith" and the fighters became "Balance" instead of "Denver."

Announcement of Major Murphy's promotion to a lieutenant colonelcy was received on the 17th also, and he was to have briefed for a late mission in southern France but this scrubbed at 1545. A rush of activity followed until the end of the month, however, including missions on each of the next 11 days.

On the 18th Colonel Murphy led a penetration escort job along an entirely new route to Berlin, slicing across the Danish Peninsula. The mission was enlivened by attacks on our airplanes. Next day, another effort was made by the bombers to get to Berlin, this time along the normal Egmond alley.

Because of the night-and-day attempt in the 368th Squadron to locate the cause of its oil pressure failures, plus an abnormal number of engine changes and the constant shuttling in and out of aircraft assigned for wing-shackle conversion at Burtonwood, the number of P-47s available for operations sank to 34 and only 32 flew the mission. Captain Ettlesen and his flight strafed locomotives, concentrating on tracks in the town of Bad Oeynhausen.

On the 20th, 95 weary minutes of Crossbow patrol were unrewarded by any incident of note, and the 359th Group was airborne on the 21st only to be recalled at Norwich.

On the 22nd, General Kepner described to the pilots the constant attempt to bring the Luftwaffe to battle, and said he was convinced it required at least 10 missions before a fighter pilot began to see with his eyes what the old timers saw, that good vision was a great part of the secret of good air fighting. The mission to Hamm produced a double victory in the air for Lieutenant Kibler, among total scores of 7-0-1. Second Lieutenant Earl W. Thomas of the 370th Squadron was lost in action on his first mission. He had been originally scheduled when the squadron thought another Crossbow patrol was coming up, was kept on the lineup when the mission changed, and was last seen in combat over Hamm at 24,000 feet. The 359th Group also sweated out Lieutenant Harry E. Cuzner, of the 369th Squadron, who staggered back over the North Sea to the emergency strip at Woodbridge with a bad oil leak.

On the 23rd the 359th dive-bombed Le Culot and Eekloo. Lieutenant Luster H. Prewitt brought an armed bomb with a broken vane and jammed release gear home with him but it was successfully handled by a RAF bomb disposal squad after he negotiated the ticklish job of landing.

There was also perspiration, to a milder degree, about Lieutenant Andrew T. Lemmens, on a test hop above the field. A strut broke on his landing gear but after much climbing and diving Lemmens made a successful belly-landing at Wattisham.

The 24th was a day of mild hysteria. To begin with, briefing was originally scheduled for a leisurely 1200, but as the early morning grew it became obvious that the stations on the south of England were weathered in and the 359th Group was abruptly switched to the 405th Fighter-Bomber Group's earlier mission. So briefing was at 0945 in a rush.

The mission was a success, with seven airplanes being destroyed in ground attacks after leaving the bombers, but pilots saw dozens more on French airfields around Nancy, and as soon as the 359th Group was down Colonel Murphy asked for permission to go back and strafe these targets. This came down from AJAX via Wing later in the afternoon, but by that time it was obvious no one was very sure just where the airdromes were and the freelance volunteer job was scrubbed.

There were two shows on the 25th. Briefing for the first was at 0600 and the 359th had the satisfaction of breaking up an attack on the bombers; Lieutenant Robert J. Booth scored his fourth air victory. That afternoon there was another Crossbow escort job, in which the bombers distinguished themselves by remaining in the overcast at 27,000 although they had good conditions 5,000 feet lower.

26 April was the day when all the bombers that had assaulted Brunswick through the clouds returned safely, but from the fighters' point of view, it was a snafu show from start to finish, with combat wings everywhere flying on un-briefed headings, off course, and late. Fortunately, the Luftwaffe didn't fight. That afternoon, Colonel Tacon sent the 359th out to practice dive-bombing, as Colonel Swanson had come back from fighter leader school at Milfield with the word that every available fighter would be used as heavy artillery in the first two days of the invasion.

The weather had now turned cold and chilly, and the sun on 27 April was a relief, as was the fact that briefing, consistently at 0600, was delayed until 0730. Colonel Tacon read a summary of the dramatic interior story of the Crossbow war, but this did not make the old job any more palatable, especially since one group of bombers made seven passes at one patch of woods without, apparently, bombing.

That afternoon, Captain McKee led a straggler round-up in the Charleroi area on a late afternoon show, with the result that since his section essed behind the bombers all the way to England to guard against Hun intruders, who had a field day over England a fortnight before, the last fighter was not on the ground at East Wretham until 2146 when dusk and haze made conditions worse than straight night flying.

P-51s began to arrive on the 28th; they arrived in swarms so that there were 41 on the station that night. They were flown in by ferry pilots, the 359th Group losing its wingshackled P-47D22s to the Ninth Air Force. All of this put a heavy burden on the ground crews.

Lieutenant Cunningham claimed an Fw 190 on the 29th. This was the Berlin attack in which 66 bombers were shot down, but no attacks were made on the second ATF during the period of the 359th's escort. Cunningham's section had gone up on the first ATF and ran into enemy aircraft at Gehrden. Lieutenant Charles W. Hipsher accounted for seven locomotives at Hanover, out of the 21 hit.

Bricy was strafed on the 30th, adding two more destroyed on the ground to the 359th's claims. The P-51 complement of 76 now was complete, and there were more than 140 aircraft on the station as April ended, so many that Major Norvil T. Hinds, station defense officer, had all ground defense guns manned all night. But the Hun did not come.

8.

MAY 1944

The War Hits Home

Monday, May 1: Wretham—Hazy and warm.

Briefed at 0615. Two Pas de Calais jobs today, one area and the other withdrawal. No action. Landed at 1030.

Briefed at 1700. No action. Landed at 2030.

Shaw timed me in Randy's ship for one and one-half hours, from 1930 to 2100. A bit hazy out still, but fun. Flew to 5,000 feet, dove, made my head and ears hurt. Hell!!!

Carey Brown killed in P-51 engine failure this evening. A sad loss!!

Beaupre bellied in on gunnery flight in P-47. Ship a total wreck. Threw him 60 feet still strapped to chute. Ship a junk heap and he busted one ankle, boy was he lucky!!

The 369th is off operations with P-51 training. Five of us to Wymondham for dinghy drill in pool. Cold but fun. Those dinghies are wonderful! Sam White off to A/S Rescue school. Cater to P-51 school yesterday. Forehand dropped in from Milfield (dive-bomb school), sez it's fine up there at the RAF base. Stearns is mess officer here now. All ground officers moved out. Bob Addleman in Brownie's sack with us.

Painted stars on my P-51 this afternoon. Blue enamel looks good.

Tuesday, May 2: Wretham—Cloudy and windy as Hell.

Released all day. Went to hospital and Doc gave me the heat treatment. Felt better.

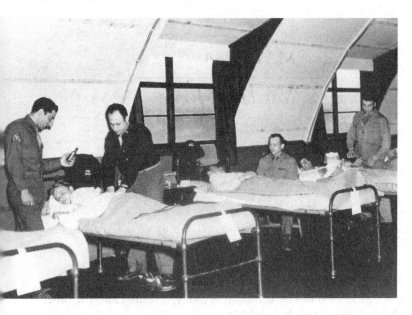

Station Hospital. *Courtesy of Elsie Palicka, wife of Ed Palicka, 370th Fighter Squadron Photographer: Archived by Char Baldridge, Historian, 359th Fighter Group Association*

Went to bomber critique at Elveden Hall in the afternoon. Had my own Jeep. Interesting. 3rd Bomber Division HQ was full of colonels, majors, and generals for the big bull session about previous missions.

Botsy killed in his P-51. Took off to fire guns and the gas selector valve didn't seat when he changed tanks. He tried to belly land near Thetford and overshot, hitting trees. He was thrown out and broke his neck.

Found out that Brown's death was due to power spin, from top of loop at 10,000 feet.

Wednesday, May 3: Wretham—Clear, cumulus, and windy as Hell out. Rained last night.

Released. Headed to hospital for heat treatment again, really opened me out today. Was there all morning.

Colonel Meyer (352nd) talked to us about P-51s in briefing room this afternoon.

Got haircut, pay, and rations. Went to movie at the new port theatre, a damn good deal, with a big screen and good sound. Colonel Tacon, Trigger, and 60 of us walked back nearly two miles. Great sport. We marched into bar in formation. Tacon sure is a regular guy.

Colonel Avelin P. "Hardtack" Tacon Jr., Commanding Officer, 359th Fighter Group. *Courtesy of Elsie Palicka, wife of Ed Palicka, 370th Fighter Squadron Photographer: Archived by Char Baldridge, Historian, 359th Fighter Group Association*

Scott replaces Loverro. I'm glad, never liked that little wop, he's too sloppy.

Wrote letters after show. Leave, tomorrow.

[The US 8th Air Force, led by General James H. Doolittle, launches a major bombing raid against Berlin with 1,500 bombers.]

Monday, May 8: London—Group had a big fight near Brunswick in P-51s. They encountered 75 109s. We got 14 of 'em! Hagan got one. Homeyer got one. Bolefahr got one and damaged one. Posty Booth got three. He has seven now (369th). Nice shooting!

Lost Sackett (369th) though, and a new boy.

Squadron Recapitulation:
Commanding Officer: Major Tyrrell
Exec: Major Wallace
Operations: Captain Mosse

Assistant Ops: Janney
"A" Flight: Captain Bolefahr, Keesey, Cater, Lemmens, Ashenmacher
"B" Flight: First Lieutenant Bach, Burton, Lane, Hatter
"C" Flight: Captain Forehand, Perkins, Simmons, Hunter, Marcinkiewicz
"D" Flight: Captain Fogg, Homeyer, Randolph, Lambright, Beaupre
"E" Flight: Captain McGeever, Smith, Bunky, Addleman
"F" Flight: First Lieutenant Hagan, Hawkinson, Baldy, Drake

Tuesday, May 9: London—Sam White transferred out of 368th to A/S Rescue along with Kirk, which is bad and good. Addleman gets White's plane. Lemmens and Drake have theirs. More damn planes here than operational pilots.

[In preparation for D-Day, Allied air forces launch large-scale raids against German airfields and rail communications in France.]

Wednesday and Thursday, May 10 and 11: London—Lost Hodges from the 370th. He bailed out over France. Kibler and his new wingman disappeared strafing. Bad! Everyone landing anywhere for gas, four and one-half hours without wing tanks!! Rough day.

[The US 5th Army and British 8th Army begin an offensive to take the Gustav Line at Cassino, Italy.]

Friday, May 12: Wretham—Beautiful morning. Warm.
Back in harness again. Up at 7:30 A.M.
Bolefahr and I to plotting rooms to help prepare the mission. Very interesting. We're heading in to near Leipzig for target support. I flew Bunky's ship, a B-10(G). Feels sloppy at altitude with wing tanks. Good to fly again although we didn't do much. No action. Flew for 5 hours 35 minutes. Head felt okay.
I'm scheduled to fly tomorrow and Randy sez my ship is swell. Colonel is raising Hell about poor formation again.
The 369th beat Group at ballgame tonight.
The boy's butts are really tired. Five and one-half hours on a dinghy for training is rough. They like the P-51s though.
Hag is swell as a flight commanding officer. He's a good man. It's tough about Kibler. This ground strafing is dangerous!

[P-51 losses from ground attacks were significantly greater than from bomber escort duties. The engine cooling system was vulnerable to ground fire and even a single rifle round in the wrong place could cause an engine-seizing loss of coolant.

The fighting along the Gustav Line at Cassino, Italy escalates, with furious German counterattacks.

The Allied Governments warn the Axis satellites of Hungary, Rumania, Bulgaria, and Finland to withdraw from the war, cease collaboration with Germany, and resist the forces of Nazism, or suffer the consequences in rigorous peace terms.]

Saturday, May 13: Wretham—Wot a ride to break in on!

Lunch at 1115.

Briefing at 1145. Headed to the Polish border, 80 miles northeast of Berlin, to provide withdrawal protection for bombers targeting Poznan. Me, Burton, Randy, Simmons, and Hunter: Yellow Flight.

Lousy haze and poor squadron formation. Trigger lousy too. Mosse led our section. Flew course of 97 degrees over, 250 degrees back, from Heligoland. Headed out to sea east of Denmark, crossed till we saw Sweden. A 1,400 mile trip. Intense flak at Stettin ripped through Mosse's flight and they're not back.

Out 5 hours 25 minutes in all. We were over water for 1 hour 5 minutes coming home.

These P-51s are the world's greatest fighter! Marvelous. Two hours 43 minutes on wing tanks. Cruise an easy 230 IAS at 27,000 feet. My ship's a honey, with a wonderful cockpit, a great ride. Boy, I love my ship, she's sweet!!

Sunday, May 14: Wretham—Cold, clear and windy out. Some cumulus. Released until tomorrow for rest and maintenance. Slept until 10:00 A.M. It was a swell morning to sack in.

In the afternoon we had a formal presentation of Distinguished Flying Crosses by General Anderson.

General Anderson is a good guy, but it was cold as Hell standing out on the field. A nice medal. I'm proud to get it. Poor Botsy got his posthumously.

They raised so much Hell in the bar last night that Colonel Tacon closed it. Fun's fine, but some of these guys don't know when to quit.

Brigadier General Edward W. Anderson presenting the Distinguished Flying Cross to Lieutenant Arlen R. "Baldy" Baldridge. *April 13, 1944 photo courtesy of R. Hatter: Archived by Char Baldridge, Historian, 359th Fighter Group Association*

Now we all get to pay.

Stearns had a swell snack bar for us tonight with coffee, sandwiches and French fries. A good man!

Saw "My Gal Sal" tonight. A fair movie.

Still cold tonight. Brrrr!!

[The Distinguished Flying Cross is awarded to those who, while serving with the Armed Forces of the United States, distinguish themselves by heroism or extraordinary achievement while participating in any capacity in aerial flight. The act of heroism must be voluntary, above and beyond the call of duty. The extraordinary achievement has to result in an accomplish-

Lieutenant Raymond L "Botsy" Botsford.
Photo courtesy of Marvin Boussu: Archived by Char Baldridge, Historian, 359th Fighter Group Association

*ment so exceptional as to clearly set the recipient apart from others in
similar circumstances.]*

Monday, May 15: Wretham—Weather is bad over the Continent. Cold,
windy, cumulus, and showers here.

To line at 0830 for flight leaders' meeting (Me, Bolefahr, Bach, Forehand, Smitty, McGeever, and Hagan).

Aircraft recognition at 0930. Released at 1200.

I wrote a long letter describing leave on typewriter at Ops shack.

We need <u>300</u> hours for a tour now. Makes me sort of mad. Just like
the Army, promise one thing, do another. Where's the honor in that? Sort
of makes you wonder what th' Hell you fight for. Wot th' Hell's the use
of worrying. They want 300, we'll give 'em 300, but then, by golly, I'm
going home!

*[A fighter pilot's tour of duty was 200 hours of combat flight time prior
to this increase to 300 hours.*

*German troops begin withdrawing from the Gustav Line north to-
wards Rome.]*

Tuesday, May 16: Wretham—Weather just like yesterday, no flying at all.

Today I was transferred to the 370th Squadron along with Burton,
Lemmens and Les Taylor of the '69th. Hell! It's tough to leave the 368th
after a year with the same gang. Hate to leave Freddy Gall, too. He felt
terrible. Everyone seemed sorry, even Trigger. I take my ship with me
though, which is one good break.

I have "E" Flight here, leading Callahan, Andy Lemmens, "Hammy"
Newberg, and Kirby Baker. The last two aren't operational yet, but seem
okay. Colonel Murphy and Captain McKee were very cordial. Our flight
is in Room 305, over Bo's room. Not bad, with five single beds, a good
fireplace, and the southern exposure is nice.

Smitty gets my old flight, lucky bum. Gee, I feel lousy tonight.

*[The Royal Air Force Coastal Command sinks five U-boats off the Nor-
wegian coast.]*

Wednesday, May 17: Wretham—Today worse weather than the others,
with rain, low grey clouds, etc. Released until Friday at dawn. Quite a
lay-off.

Spent the morning at line, censored mail, played volleyball, and met my new crew chief, Sergeant Clampitt from Newcastle, Indiana. Seems okay but quiet. To line again in the afternoon for a few hours. They don't sack much in this darn outfit. Damn silly! Unloaded a truckload of firewood for the ops fireplace.

Lemmens on alert tonight and tomorrow.

Show tonight was "In This Our Life" with Bette Davis. Good, heavy stuff. Snack bar again, Stearns is really on the ball. Bar was re-opened by Colonel Tacon tonight. Good.

Thursday, May 18: Wretham—Just like yesterday.

Sacked in late in the morning. I got up so four of us could relieve the Alert Flight so they could eat breakfast.

Big ball game with 369th in the afternoon, they won 6 to 4. Les Taylor pitched for us. After supper I watched the 368th play among themselves. Colonel Tacon and Shaw were out there and it was the screwiest, funniest game I've ever seen. Janney had us in stitches trying to catch. They played 16 innings and the score was about 25 to 20. Then Shaw and I whipped Randy and Homeyer's ass at bridge until 11:00 P.M. Read in bed until midnight.

[The US 5th Army captures Gaeta, south of Rome.]

Friday, May 19: Wretham—Haze and cumulus, warmer temperature.

Briefing at 0915. Our squadron is middle squadron, with Murphy, Taylor, Hipsher, and Wetmore providing target support over <u>Berlin</u>! Flying in over Heligoland thence southeast. Back out via Dümmer Lake, Egmond. I wasn't scheduled. Hell!

They hit 100 or so Me109s near Berlin. Wetmore got two, Bateman got one. No other action. The 369th got several.

We lost Laing, he bailed out. The 368th Red and Yellow Flights were bounced by 109s with Shaw leading. Smitty was shot down, and he had to jump. Janney got 11 holes. He dumped flaps and shot down his attacker. Nice work.

Baldy came all the way home from Berlin on the <u>deck</u>! Cater and Drake landed down at Manston. <u>Mosse</u> got one but is NYR and believed to have bailed out. Rough day!

[British troops capture Aquino airfield, located in the Liri Valley southeast of Rome.

Fifty Allied airmen are recaptured and executed by the Gestapo following their breakout from Stalag Luft III. Only three escaped airmen reach England.]

Saturday, May 20: Wretham—Briefing at 0715.

Start engines at 0935. Took off at 0945. Yellow Flight assigned low flight, led by me, with Newberg, Cal, and Andy. Tacon leading group east to Walcheren Island, on to a R/V north of Brussels, south to Reims, the target.

I lost group in a 360-degree turn at R/V. Proceeded south on course but failed to find them so we came home one-half hour early. Out Boulogne for 2 hours 20 minutes.

Ship ran beautifully. Have a new crew chief, Blanchard, from Algoma, Iowa. Very much on the ball. He'll be okay.

I sacked up in the afternoon. Some of 'em played ball, lost 4 to14.

Hollis and Ambrose fly tomorrow.

Party tonight but same as all the others. Went to show with Perk. Ate a lot, shot the bull with Major Wallace, had one lousy drink. Hit the sack before midnight. Nuts!

Sunday, May 21: Wretham—Day off so I sacked until noon.

All of 8th and 9th Fighter Command out in biggest strafe deal of the war: 303 locomotives, planes, towers, anything. Everyone fired and our group got 17 planes and 12 or so locomotives. Ran wild up in area northeast of Bremen.

We lost four men. Rodeheaver spun in (fuselage tank full). Baldy bellied in (hit by flak), they saw him run away okay, though. Bunky is missing. There's no report on him. Shupe flew into the ground but may have gotten out. Rough!

Strafing is damn dangerous work no matter how you look at it.

[Approximately 5,000 Allied aircraft bomb and strafe French and Belgian airfields and railways.]

Monday, May 22: Wretham—Briefing at 0845.

Lieutenant Clyde M. "Bunky" Hudelson Jr. *Photo courtesy of Ira J. "John" Bisher: Archived by Char Baldridge, Historian, 359th Fighter Group Association*   Lieutenant Arlen R. "Baldy" Baldridge. *Photo courtesy of Mrs. Helen Baldridge: Archived by Char Baldridge, Historian, 359th Fighter Group Association*

Took off at 1002. A Type 16 mission in the Beauvais, Compiegne area. In at Cayeux, out near Fecamp. Flight time was 3 hours 40 minutes. Over Thames Estuary coming home.

I led Yellow Flight, with Hammy, Cal, and Andy. Murphy led Blue Flight and Lane, Red Flight. Good formation but no action and no flak. Sore tails. I made a horrible landing.

Sacked in, in the afternoon. The ballgame with the 368th started at 1830 but ended in fourth inning when they broke all the bats. We were ahead 10 to1 on 8 errors and 2 hits. Wot a game. Went to the show, "Action in North Atlantic," which was very good.

I'm now on Detached Service to Group as assistant ops until Pezda gets out of the hospital. Smith goes to the 368th. Major Shaw asked for me. Happy.

Tuesday, May 23: Wretham—Group's 100th mission in the morning. Heavy cumulus clouds in area. Up at 0500. Plotted course with Shaw and Smith.

Briefing at 0600, start engines at 0655. Complete escort of B-17s to vicinity of Metz near Swiss border, for a 2 hour 39 minute actual escort, 4 hour 30 minute mission. I didn't go. Neither did Shaw. Murph was sore as Hell.

Breakfast 0700. Went to 368th and saw Gall, then to 370th at 1000 to censor mail.

Flights returned at 1145. Briefing at 1345. I had <u>no</u> lunch, was plotting again. Three flights of the 370th and 369th to glide bomb railway bridge at Hasselt, Belgium. Swanson leading 370th, I led Blue Flight with Siltamaki, Burton, and Grimes. Wetmore led Red Flight. Colonel left us to orbit at 13,000 feet, couldn't find target. We left the 369th and found target.

[This mission debuted P-51s as dive-bombers carrying two 500-pound bombs. Seventy-five of the eighty-nine Mustangs scored hits on the bridge, completely demolishing it.

The British 8th Army attacks the Dora Line in Italy, a fall-back position behind the Gustav Line.

At the Anzio bridgehead, the US 5th Army begins an offensive toward Rome.]

Wednesday, May 24: Wretham —Up at 0600, bite to eat, to plotting room to work on briefing with Major Shaw. He'll also lead group.

Briefing at 0715. Support for three wings of B-17s into and around Berlin, landfall Wesselburen (east of Heligoland).

Bad clouds up to 28,000

Captain Howard Fogg and Staff Sergeant Fred W. "Freddy" Gall (Crew Chief) with Major Clifton Shaw's P-51 Mustang. *May 24, 1944 photo courtesy of Anthony C. Chardella: Archived by Char Baldridge, Historian, 359th Fighter Group Association* feet and no big action. The 370th NIL. The 368th saw 60. The 369th bagged one Me109 and several locomotives. Five hours and 10 minutes flight time. No losses. Score for 8th Fighter is 31 for 11. Not so hot.

I hung around Group all day, "on duty." Had my picture taken with Gall by Shaw's P-51 mid-afternoon. It was about time. I wanted one of him. Show tonight but have 0730 zero warning order. Hell! I'm tired and head aches as usual. Th' Hell with it. "E" Flight on alert today but no scramble. Colonel was in charge.

Thursday, May 25: Wretham—Clear and chilly out.
Up at 0515. No breakfast, to plotting via Jeep. Plotted whole mission in 20 minutes. S-2 had wrong route drawn, the whole thing was wrong. We were supposed to brief at 0615, but no briefing. Ready at 0630. Finally took off at 0730. Wot a mess.

Me, Andy, and Hammy: Yellow Flight. Mac: Red Flight. Murphy: White Flight. One hundred thirty degrees to vicinity of Aachen thence south to Mulhouse.

Ettlesen hit in heavy flak at Aachen. He bailed out okay east of Nancy. Mac's oxygen hose came loose, he spiraled down, half out. Finally came to. Lane took over his flight and the seven of us came home. Clear across France to Cayeux. Four hours flight time. No enemy aircraft.

France looked beautiful. It was very hilly along the border with river gorge and mountains. Southeast Aachen also pretty.

I'm dead tired.

Friday, May 26: Wretham—Heavy middle clouds with a deck of low stratocumulus, broke in late afternoon.
Released until tomorrow at 0930. Spent morning at group pilot's meeting. Security. No leaves or days off, barbed wire stockades for planes at night. Helmet, gas mask, loaded pistol for all at all times. Wot th' Hell? Anybody'd think there was a war on.

Ten new pilots today. Hoorah. We got two but haven't met 'em yet.

To 370th at 1400. Murph talked competently about formation and tactics. A damn good man, sez wot's necessary and worthwhile.

Went to PX for rations then to Hall, supper, movie, and snack bar. Learned two good card tricks from Homeyer and McGeever in bar. Bed at 2400.

Saturday, May 27: Wretham—The most beautiful day yet, like summer, clear and cloudless. Over Continent, too!

Up at 0715.

Briefing at 0900. Major Shaw and I plotted course leisurely. Four hour 46 minute escort. Target, Mannheim, Strasbourg area railroad yards, communications, etc. No enemy aircraft for group. The 352nd got 13 on same division. Wot luck! France devoid of trains by daylight.

Major Shaw flew today. I fly tomorrow. Top cover flew at 32,000 feet today. Wow! We're top cover tomorrow.

Took pictures over to Gall this afternoon, they came out good. Took walk with Doc after supper through woods, fields behind Hall. Very lovely. Boy, it's darn near hot out today.

Had tea with Colonel Swanson yesterday morning and this morning. Wrote airmails to Margot, Mom. Sent photos of me with Gall.

Sunday, May 28: Wretham—Beautiful, clear day. No clouds, never better.

Up at 0800. Plotted mission for 1015 briefing. Targets for our four B-17s wings: Magdeburg, Konigsborn.

We took off at 1157. Me, Baker, Andy, and Newberg: Blue Flight, top cover. Picked 'em up at Dümmer Lake and stayed with bombers at 32,000 feet until 1530 near Frankfurt. Tough ride at that altitude but we held formation okay. Argued with 47s, dove on other 51s, but not a damn enemy aircraft in area. Disgusting.

8th Fighter only has 27 against loss of 10. Not so hot. We dropped tanks early to "engage" the 47s. Nuts! Made base with 10 gallons. Wot a ship. Amazing. Five hours and 10 minutes flight. Boy were we bushed!

England's coast sure looks good after a long haul and low gas. Had a nice flight. Sleepy!

[The synthetic fuel producing plants at Leuna-Merseburg are attacked by the US 8th Air Force.]

Monday, May 29: Wretham—Another <u>hot</u> summer day. Beautiful.

Up at 0700, to plotting at 0730. Took off at 0945. Me leading Green with Hammy and a pilot I didn't know. Late so joined squadron in air with me as Blue Four, and Hammy as Yellow Four. The unknown pilot was Red Four. Then White Two aborted, so I flew Murphy's wing. Nice pilot.

Targets: Politz, Stettin, and Poznan. We met bombers northeast of Hamburg near Stettin. The 368th (low flight) were bounced by 109s. We went down on 12 to 15 190s in front of bombers. Hit 515 IAS in formation! Murph got one in a left turn with me covering his right wing. A 190 came in on me. I broke hard up and left. Could have got around on him, but Wetmore came barreling down and got him (pilot bailed out).

We joined up at 2,000 feet. No one was in sight so back to 15,000 feet. Flew home via Kiel, Heligoland. Four hours and 35 minutes. Whew!

The 370th got eight, the 369th got two and the 368th got two. Hag got another. Wetmore and Lane each got two. But the 369th lost Brundage and a new boy.

[Pushing aircraft to their maximum range, the US 8th Air Force bombs aircraft production plants at Marienburg and Posen in Germany.]

Tuesday, May 30: Wretham—Up at 0630. Plotted course. Briefing at 0730. Scheduled as Red #5 with only 13 ships. My tail wheel blew and I didn't get off. Nuts!

A big show with 1,158 heavy bombers, 28 fighter groups, RAF, 9th Air Force fighter bombers, and mediums. Wot a day! Our escort was to Dessau then out through the old Dümmer Lake, Egmond funnel.

Hunter and Hawk shared a 109, Forehand got another up at 35,000 feet. Colonel Tacon flew with the 370th. They bounced some 109s low and Hipsher got one. We lost Dick Broach, though, of the 369th. Dammit. They think he bailed out over Holland. The 369th now has no captains. Rough. We've lost 18 men this month. Only have 32 total. Whoa!

Andy's brakes locked up when he was landing. He nosed the plane over onto its back but there was no fire. Boy was he lucky. We were simply paralyzed with fear watching and waiting and praying. By god he wasn't scratched! Took 10 minutes to get him out and he slept at hospital all afternoon but was back this evening all chipper and healthy. Whew!! Ship a total washout.

Major Hiles to Wing last week. Captain Shwayder here now as group surgeon. Seems very nice. Trigger made Lieutenant Colonel yesterday. Glad to see him get it. He's certainly worked for it despite any faults.

Got haircut. Big ballgame. We beat Group 19 to 9. The wildest, best game yet. Everything happened.

Skid marks showed Lieutenant Andrew T. Lemmens wheel had frozen upon landing, flipping his P-51C Mustang *Shrimp* CS-C 42-103294 onto its back. Lieutenant Lemmens was unscathed but the Mustang was fit only for salvage.
Courtesy of D. Page: Archived by Char Baldridge, Historian, 359th Fighter Group Association

Wednesday, May 31: Wretham— Another swell summer day. Not even any clouds.

Up at 0705. Briefing at 0800.

Mission: Escort bombers to target area in the Osnabrück, Hamm vicinity. Only four hours flight time and no action at all. Very few ships in commission in our group. Reese flew my ship and out near the enemy landing field he was hit with one .50 cal in each wing. No one knows how or from whence they came. Weird!! Pierced each gas tank so they'll have to be changed. A Service Group job dammit. Probably be a week.

Captain Andrew T. Lemmens.
Photo courtesy of Don Page: Archived by Char Baldridge, Historian, 359th Fighter Group Association

Got paid today and I sent $235.00 home. Sent Alumni a check for $50.00.

A <u>big</u> pool table (snooker) is being installed in bar tonight. Should be fun. Read Jack London's *Burning Daylight* all evening. Wot a man!

Excerpts from the May 1944 Informal Report of Morale for the 359th Fighter Group, submitted by "Chappie" Ziegler indicated that: "Much has happened during the month of May to shake the morale of our pilots. Yet they have come through once more with banners flying. It is hard for a ground officer like myself to fully appreciate exactly what has gone on within the minds and hearts of our pilots. I have been able to capture and record only a part of it. The reader must magnify what I have recorded many times to get the true picture.

"During this month this group changed over from flying the P-47 Thunderbolt to the P-51 Mustang. Ordinarily you would say this should improve morale to give the men a better weapon. Yes, except for one thing, it was a very unfamiliar weapon. It handled a lot differently; it had only half the number of guns. (Although early P-51s had only half the P-47's eight .50 calibre machine guns, by the introduction of the "D" model P-51, the number had increased to six.)

"Remember too that these men had flown the P-47 so long on so many missions that it had become a part of them. They knew exactly what it could do and how to get the most out of it. They knew you could shoot the plane and its engine full of holes and it would still get you back. They weren't sure just what the Mustang could do, how much punishment it would take and still bring them back. Remember, to a pilot these considerations may very well mean life or death.

"Another factor that has shaken morale has been the fact that during our first month of operation in the P-51 we have lost 18 pilots. Unfortunately two of these were lost during the transition period, when Captain Brown and Lieutenant Botsford crashed on consecutive days. No matter how easily the accident could be explained, whatever faith our men had in the P-51s was greatly diminished. Among the 16 men lost on operations were some of our best pilots; men like Captain Mosse, Captain Broach, and Lieutenant Rodeheaver: men with plenty of experience and courage. The one thing that offset the losses was the number of victories. For the first time our men were getting in where the enemy lay in waiting.

For the first time the scores of victories began to pile up. Lieutenant Wetmore for example now has 13. Lieutenant Booth has 6, Lieutenant Doersch, 6.

"I think the greatest blow to morale that our pilots weathered nicely was the order raising combat time from 200 to 300 hours before a man could go home on leave. You see, when those provisions changed two things occurred; you could hear men talking it over, yet when the new order on combat flying time came there was not very much talk. Each man was trying to figure it out in relation to his own plans, his own life. Can you appreciate what this meant to men like Lieutenant Wetmore or Captain Bolefahr and a few others who are expecting a telegram any day now telling them they are proud fathers? Can you understand what another 100 hours means to Major Irvine and the others who have not yet seen their children? It's like a man setting out to run a mile race. He gives all he can in that mile and then suddenly when he should be finished somebody waves him on and says it is now a two mile race.

"Well, those are the three factors that attacked the morale of our pilots. The way they responded has been a marvelous thing to behold. True, they faltered, but only momentarily. Now they are going on to finish the job they started. Those men are writing new pages in the book of courage and sacrifice. They are pages that must never be forgotten.

"Don't be misled though. This war has not left them unmarked. They came to England a bunch of exuberant kids, full of fun, wisecracks, practical jokes. I remember their first briefings had the atmosphere of a college football team at their last blackboard drill before the big game. Now five months later they are mature men. They have lost, temporarily at least, a lot of their exuberance and enthusiasm. They are much older, not in years but in the stuff of life. They are beginning to live more deeply, with more appreciation."

HEADQUARTERS 359TH FIGHTER GROUP
Office of the Group Historian
APO 637 / US Army
4 June 1944

History of the 359th Fighter Group, May 1944

Re-equipped in shining silver P-51s, the 359th Fighter Group fought a savage battle of attrition against the Luftwaffe in May 1944. These were the long grim weeks of air assault on the German designed to prod and lance and ferret out his invasion air defenses and hack them apart before the Battle of the Beaches began.

It was magnificent and it was war, but it was costly to the young pilots flying 500 miles into combat: more costly than most of them realized in the day-to-day excitement of new missions, new objectives, new tactics, and new records.

Eighteen men were lost in the 25 missions flown in 22 days of May. This was 125 percent of the total 13 lost in the preceding four-and-a-half months of combat flying in P-47s. And even greater tragedy, two other pilots lost their lives in transition training accidents in the sleek Merlin-motored Mustangs. From all causes the 359th Group had lost 15 men on 1 May, by 31 May, the total was 33.

Of the 18 lost in May, 13 were "originals" who had trained together in the States. Five were replacement pilots; one of them, Lieutenant Edward J. Maslow, was an experienced veteran of the Iceland Interceptor Command and PRU flights in England. The toll of the month included a squadron operations officer, six flight leaders, and three of the six West Pointers of whom it had been so proud, as well as the cherubic Clyde M. Hudelson Jr. whose application for appointment to the Academy was pending. Six, possibly seven of these men may have been shot down by enemy fighters. This estimate is generous to the Luftwaffe since it is probable that some of the seven were lost to engine troubles having no direct relation to combat. Eight others were knocked down while strafing. Two were killed in non-operation accidents. And one was hit by German flak at 25,000 feet and jumped. By a supreme irony, this latter victim of the wedding of trigonometry, electronics and ballistics was Captain Ettlesen, commander of the VIII Fighter Command's experimental strafing squadron and low-level attack specialist.

Thus, the casualties. The price paid by the Germans was heavy. In air combat, the score was 40-3-4. Ground strafing produced claims of 20-0-26, plus 41 locomotives, six barges, two tugs, and a variety of radar and signal towers, barracks, ammunition cars, and assorted targets on the ground. All of this in addition to the 359th Group's special mission in the war.

This basic job was the deep escort of heavy bombers into targets which the Germans believed to be unreachable. That job was done 15 times, including four long trips to and beyond Berlin, to the Swiss frontier, to Saxony, to Anhalt. The track weaves a web across the Reich and the bombers crawled round this lattice frame of protection to hurl thousand of tons of explosives upon the enemy's homeland.

With an audacity that defied every previous concept of the role of fighter aircraft, the Eighth was sent in May to beat up the railroads of Germany, and the 359th's assignments were Mecklenburg, on the Baltic, an area well covered on 21 May, and Baden-Württemberg to the south, on the shores of Lake Constance, to which, as the month ended, it still awaited dispatch.

In May, escort of the bombers along the penetration route to such a target as Brunswick in the heart of Germany, with direct support at the target and subsequent withdrawal cover, became commonplace: and it was a very different thing than the old 20 minutes of escort allowed by the huge petrol consumption of the P-47. The scoop-bellied Mustangs, IFF sets replaced by a fuselage tank and two 75-gallon tanks on the wing-bomb racks, permitted endurance of up to six hours. And endurance was the right word, as pilots cramped in the crowded cockpit, unable to move more than a cautious inch or two in any direction, soon discovered. "Dinghy tail," caused by sitting squarely on a Mark K dinghy with type C pack for six hours, became a recognized occupational disease, cause for grounding by the flight surgeons, even though the old seat-type parachutes were universally supplanted by the newer flat back chutes.

Even including such brief errands as the 65-minute bomber abortion of 10 May, the unsuccessful skip-bombing experiment of 23 May and three comparatively brief rides into France, the average time in the air for the 25 missions of May was 4 hours 18 minutes.

In summary, the month embraced 15 deep escort jobs, four more shallow bomber escorts, three area patrols modeled on Plan "Eye Que," the aforementioned fighter-bombing, one air-sea rescue search, and one "Chattanooga" strafe mission.

Maintenance was trickier on the P-51B than on the rugged Thunderbolts, the mechanics on the line were unfamiliar with the airplane and the battle loss higher. These factors resulted in fewer aircraft airborne: 1,014, or 40.5 per mission, and an increase in the number of early returns: 124, or five per mission. The 889 sorties flown accordingly represented 35.5 ships

a mission, or three 12-plane squadrons. Two factors make this figure arti-
ficially low: first, the fact that during transition to the P-51, only two
squadrons were operational for four missions, and, second, the special ASR
search flown 22 May, in which only four aircraft were put up.

From 15 May onward, the problems of maintenance were aggravated
by Command's decision to keep four aircraft alerted for local defense
against sneak German raids and/or suicide parachutist missions. This was
tiresome for the quartet of pilots elected for stand-by duty from half an hour
before first light until last light, but its more important effect was in decreasing the number of aircraft flown against the enemy. With 33 operational
groups in the theatre, the local defense of four planes each represented 132
operational ships, or three combat groups out of action every mission day.

The enemy was sighted in strength five times and was engaged in force
on four of these days. The scoring was concentrated in three of these en-
gagements and in the flashing ground attack on Mecklenburg on 21 May.
Similarly with the losses. With one exception, they came on each of the four
scoring days. The exception was the near disaster of an impromptu strafing
run by two flights of the 370th on the heavily defended Reims-Champagne
airdrome 11 May. Both flight leaders as well as Lieutenant Maslow were
lost, another pilot crash-landed in England, and Lieutenant Doersch did one
of those incredible things by pretzeling his propeller on the enemy airdrome
surface and somehow egg-beating his way to the emergency field at
Manston. For all of this the 359th got one enemy aircraft on Reims-Champagne airdrome.

These losses represented one operational loss per 3.75 enemy aircraft
destroyed, 1 loss per 55.5 sorties flown or .64 per mission. Including all
sightings, whether able to engage or not, the total of 401 airborne enemy
aircraft seen figured to 16 per mission, with an average mission score of
2.4-.1-1.2.

At month's end the casualties by squadrons were: 368th, nine; 369th,
nine; and 370th, fourteen. Of these, three were "routine" accidents, one a
detached service loss and 29 were operational. The scoreboard read: 124-
11-70, of which 46-8-39 were officially confirmed and 78-3-31 awaited
assessment.

The 359th Group learned during the month that both Captain Albertson
and Lieutenant Pino were POWs in Germany. The news left 22 unaccounted
for, of whom seven were known with varying degrees of assurance to have
successfully parachuted and two seen to safely belly in, with seven known
dead and two believed lost in the North Sea.

Of the 86 pilots brought to England, 24 had been lost to combat or accident by May's end, three had been transferred to other organizations, one was flying a P-47 in a recognition "circus," and four were on detached service with a special air-sea rescue search organization. The 359th accordingly had 54 of its old pilots at the end of the month.

These men were confronted with a new airplane in May, the P-51, with a new problem: the deep penetrations multiplied slight navigational errors geometrically, with a new enemy tactic, the massing of German fighters in "combat wings" of enormous shock strength against the bombers, harking back to decade-old US Air Corps pursuit ideas of massed firepower.

The result was that the American fighters were always outnumbered by the enemy at the decisive point of contact and frequently were sandwiched in between German striking force and German top cover.

But a change in doctrine to meet the enemy massing was inevitable and as the month progressed, the squadrons, which formerly had searched to front and sides of penetration and to side and rear on withdrawal, were stacked up, one atop another, with a stipulated combat wing of bombers that were the moving reference point for the whole show. Nasty experiences with the Hun top cover also resulted in sending the top squadron up to new levels, 32,000 feet being the usual briefed height. On the next to last day of the month, this top squadron was bounced from 36,000 feet and had combat at 34,000 feet, showing that the end was not yet reached. The objective was to break up the massed gaggles of Germans before they struck the bombers, in the conviction that proven AAF superiority in combat would do the rest, once the bludgeon stroke of the first assault was blunted. Defense by flight and section against the German masses was not possible. The US fighters were absorbed without checking the first massive blow.

On the ground, there was the weather which was magnificent most of May, after unseasonable chill and rain at mid-month. There was also the off-again, on-again theatre policy of permitting and rescinding leaves and passes, which made all "social life" haphazard, and, on 15 May, the announcement was made that the fighter tour of duty in the ETO had been extended from 200 to 300 hours. The deadline for application of the rule was 180 hours and no pilot had amassed that total, although Lieutenant Wetmore lacked less than 2 hours, and Lieutenant Hipsher lacked less than an hour. Had normal missions been flown on the 14th and 15th, many more men would have been over the line.

In preparation for the invasion, there was much practice of dive-bombing and much rehearsal of recognition factors in the intelligence program, which embraced preparations for transfer to the Army-Air 1/250,000 map series, use of the modified British grid instead of geographical coordinates, and emphasis on ship type recognition. As part of the anti-parachutist preparation, a special mobile defense detachment was formed and all personnel on the station were ordered to carry arms, ammunition, helmet, and mask. Aircraft were wheeled into barbed wire lagers every night, squadron ground personnel mounted special night guards, and construction of a reasonably elaborate "Tacon line" of defenses of essential buildings began.

The missions were long and frequent, and there was much to be done on the ground, but the daylight lasted until well after 10:00 P.M. and the one great non-combat interest was baseball. Gambling waned for no apparent reason, perhaps six months of it was enough, but softball flourished. The battery of Shaw and Tacon should have assured the HQ team an undefeated season but it was twice beaten, which was healthy for competition.

In all truth, England was beautiful, and there were days when Texans and Georgians complained of the heat. The heat, in fact, became on some evenings a problem at the new station theatre, which grew in popularity, and efforts were begun to install a blower there. Popular as the theatre was, the Red Cross Aero Club was the greatest single thing on the station for enlisted men. The officers' corresponding development, if there was one, was the remarkable food served at the now flourishing "Purple Shaft" Nissen Hut cantonment for ground officers, to which personnel billeted at Wretham Hall went for meals whenever they could contrive it.

At Wretham Hall there was comparative room because of the decision to move all, save flying, group intelligence, medical, and communications officers, to the Purple Shaft. The principal room at Wretham Hall, which had been the lounge, was converted into a game room, with a tiny boys' billiard table, Ping-Pong, shove-no-penny, and darts. A large air combat mural, by Sergeant Makosske, adorned one wall. At month's end, a 1350 snooker table, on loan to the club, was moved into the old study, and the old bar, repainted and refurnished, became a reading room. The results were excellent, especially in the new bar, which survived removal of its neon lights to their original signals truck, and which afforded pastoral views of Wretham Park from every window.

By all accounts, life was positively demure compared with other stations in England, but there was a satisfactory party on 20 May, the usual 100 girls riding down in trucks from Norwich, and an all-male celebration the Saturday before that was so vigorous that the bar was closed for four days. Colonel Tacon, who ordered the closing, told the officers he proposed to have no relaxation of the standard of conduct befitting officers and gentlemen, and there was, in fact, little drinking, save on the party night, which seemed clean fun.

As for morale and health in general, there are reports by two specialists, Chaplain Ziegler and Flight Surgeon Montimore Shwayder. Health was good and there was no question of the pilots' morale, although enlisted men and some ground officers perhaps had a harder struggle against the boredom of monotony. As for religion, it flourished. More than 450 men were regularly attending services, compared to the 100 communicants of all faiths the preceding fall, and the number was rising. By decision of higher authority, unexplained, prayers were forbade in the briefing room, which resulted in a more devout and voluntarily unanimous attendance by all pilots at prayers said after every briefing by Chaplain Ziegler from the running board of a pilots' truck outside the briefing room. Every pilot made it a point to be there.

The month was notable for completion of the 100th combat mission, and scoring of the 100th victory (as witness the teletyped congratulations from Brigadier General Anderson). General Anderson visited the station on Sunday, 14 May, and the 359th Group turned out in parade formation for the first time since Westover for presentation by the General of Distinguished Flying Crosses.

There was high excitement at the beginning of the month because of the impending changeover to the P-51s. Briefing on 1 May was very early to allow for 0740 take off on VIII Fighter Command FO 322. Colonel Swanson led a Crossbow area patrol that was snafued by the bombers remaining at 27,000 feet, apparently unaware that the base of the overcast was 25,000 feet. The 369th Squadron was off ops refitting, and only 30 P-47s were put up.

At noon, Wing ordered a deep reconnaissance of the Nancy area, and Captain Brown of the 370th Squadron was chosen to lead the eight airplanes dispatched. It was his last mission. They were away at 1315 and back at 1618. Meanwhile, FO 323 had arrived. Supper was early and 29 aircraft took off in a bad ground haze at 1803 escorting 1st Division B-17s attacking Troyes. The landing was late but by 2040 everyone was safely down. Twenty minutes later, there was news of a tragedy; the death at 1900 near Knettishall, the bomber station 10 miles away, of Captain Brown. He had spun in from 10,000 feet, witnesses said. A careful study of all available facts and an equally careful study of the wreckage led Colonel Tacon to the conclusion that Captain Brown had spun out of the top of a loop while practicing aerobatics in his new P-51, had tried to recover from the spin without chopping his throttle, and, in consequence, had gone straight in. There was, it seemed, no evidence of material failure.

This accident shook every young pilot and the loss of Brown affected all who knew him. Of the Class of '41 at the Military Academy, the deep-voiced, burly young man with the crew haircut was a leader, a fighter and a companion with a rare sense of fun. He had played a great role, whether as toastmaster of its first dinner in Manchester, NH, 54 weeks before, as table tennis master of Wretham Hall or as crack flight leader in a crack squadron. He was pilot, poet, and man.

Next day, fine and sunny, the 359th Group was released for training in its new P-51s. At 1330, Thetford police telephoned word that First Lieutenant Raymond L. Botsford of the 368th Squadron had been killed in another Mustang training flight accident. Botsford, a shy and smiling boy from the state of Washington, who neither smoked nor drank, was generally regarded as one of the best of the wingmen, as well as the finest type of clean and capable American young man. He had taken off on a training flight with Colonel Tacon and Major Tyrrell to fire in the guns on the new planes.

Colonel Tacon again made a personal investigation and found the apparent cause: one of the hundred minor things that can mean disaster for a pilot. By old habit, dating to his training days, Botsford had switched his fuel selector handle from right main to left main soon after takeoff. The notch on the selector panel had not clicked firmly and by a fraction of an inch too much, the selector had moved part way between right hand wing and left main tank. But the wing tanks were not hung on this practice flight. The deduction: petrol was drawn from the left main, air from the right wing connection, and an air lock had starved and killed his engine. The swathe through treetops showed how he had tried to get the airplane into an open field, missed a house and stalled in.

The same afternoon, Lieutenant Oliphint damaged a wing in landing in a gust wind at Wretham. Obviously, there was much to be learned about the new airplane.

Accordingly, next day, Colonel Tacon called a pilots meeting where he reiterated his opinion the P-51 was the finest fighter airplane he had ever flown, discussed the two fatal accidents of the preceding day, and called for reapplication of principles learned in flying school but overgrown by habit, perhaps, in long hours in the Thunderbolt. Lieutenant Colonel John C. Meyer of the 352nd Group talked about the performance of the P-51 in combat and there was a 90-minute question-and-answer period on the characteristics of the airplane and how it should be handled. The rest of the day was devoted to more transition training.

P-51s were flown over Europe by the 359th Group for the first time on 4 May, when the 369th Squadron put up 13 in a hybrid formation of 28 which flew into Holland on FO 326 only to find the bombers aborting because of thick cirrus. Genemuiden was strafed by a flight of the 368th as a parting gesture in their P-47s, but no enemy aircraft were found on the field.

On 5 May, rain all afternoon resulted in a release and there was a high wind overnight followed by rain at the 0715 briefing on 6 May, but by 0831, take off time, sunlight pouring through a break in the clouds bathed the field in a melodramatic glow of amber that seemed quite too sharply defined to be aught but artificial. The scene was theatrical but unforgettable, a crisp moment of golden glory in the drama of our times.

This was the first all P-51 mission, a Type 16 patrol of the Pas de Calais in another of the interminable series of assaults on the German secret weapon at Siracourt. There were 33 airplanes up and the mission was uneventful, no bombers being lost.

There was a rush briefing at 0715 on 7 May for the group's 88th mission and its first full, three squadron P-51 show: penetration, target and withdrawal support on Osnabrück under FO 329. Colonel Swanson briefed but returned early with his radio out and Major Tyrrell led the mission. The Continent was 10/10 and no enemy aircraft were sighted, although flak at the target was notably responsive to evasive action and followed the fighters closely.

Next day, 8 May, was a very different story. The 359th Group saw practically as many Huns in one formation as had been seen throughout all of April. The 359th's part began at 0545, when FO 331 arrived. Briefing was delayed until 0700 and, since start engine time was 0728, all went in a tearing hurry. It was Colonel Tacon's 50th combat mission. At 0725 the 369th Squadron still was servicing oxygen, but 43 ships got up at 0742, and rendezvous was at 0905 over Hasselt. The enemy struck 35 minutes later, bursting head-on at the bombers with rockets and time-burst cannon. The 359th Group intervened promptly and only some 30 bandits got through for a single pass. They never were allowed to reform but instead were fought from 24,000 feet to the deck.

This was the day that "Posty" Booth of the 369th Squadron scored his triple and came home to tell intelligence officers how beautiful the tulips were in Holland and how ugly the drably dressed people looked tending the lovely fields of blossoms. This also was the day that Pop Doersch, out of ammunition, hornswoggled a German into jumping.

The mission report that day, relaying to high authority Major Irvine's complaint that P-38s present had not helped out in the combat but instead had bounced his squadron, produced reverberations. Since the 20th Group took umbrage, there was an order by Colonel Tacon that a reporting policy be established of saying nothing critical about any other friendly force, whatever the circumstances. Major Sydney M. Rogers, Wing A-2, was among others concerned by the incident, suggesting that such difficult situations be adjudicated by telephone without any written record.

The total that day was 11-1-3 in the air, plus two locomotives. Two men did not come back.

On the 9th there was another early briefing for a freakish show which involved strafing of Laon-Couvron airdrome after the airfield had been bombed. This was an expedient designed to destroy dispersed aircraft (use of fragmentation bombs was another) but on this day it did not work out: Captain Mosse led the strafing section on its only run but a lapse in the bombing resulted in the run being made between bomber waves, almost literally between bomb bursts, and there was so much smoke and dust on the field no worthwhile targets could be found. The section strafed the shattered building anyway. A testimonial to very high frequency radio was the readability of Captain Swiren's station at East Wretham while the 359th was over the target, 250 miles away.

The afternoon of the 9th was devoted to dive-bombing practice on the Thetford range. After the bombers aborted over the North Sea on 10 May on FO 334, the 359th Group was recalled and there was talk of a dive-bombing mission by Wing, but nothing came of it, and a release was in at 1345.

The 11th was a confused day that turned out badly. FO 335 was preceded by a warning order at 2040 on the 10th that was canceled at 2357 and revived at 0410. The order itself was in at 0755. At 1030, Wing canceled the assignment and put on notice to support heavy bombers at 1700. At 1108, this cancellation was in its turn canceled, and 51 ships were airborne at 1325. A briefed preliminary sweep merged into an early rendezvous at 1507 near Besançon and support around the target at Mulhouse, where the 359th Group withdrew at 1555. Then came trouble. In obedience to an injunction in the FO, the Group had not carried wing tanks, and many men, especially the new pilots, had "a sweat job" to get home.

Worse yet, the debonair Kibler, slim, sandy, politely aggressive young graduate of the Citadel and US Anti-Aircraft office, and the equally nonchalant, black-haired Hodges both led their flights down on Reims-Champagne on the homeward journey. There was no cover for five miles. The Germans saw them coming and there was vicious flak all the way. The soft-voiced Hodges, chatting casually on the radio about it, bailed out at Péronne at 1659, and his chute opened. Kibler, sure, suave, married just before he left the States, did not come back, and there was no radio chatter to give clue to his fate. Nor was there any word from Maslow, who had applied for transfer to the 359th Group to get away from what he thought was a lack of excitement in unarmed photo-reconnaissance.

In addition to all this, Doersch almost flew into the ground and staggered to Manston with his propeller looking like four scythes; D.R. Tuchscherer crashed near Manston; Wetmore, the 359th's leading ace, landed away from base at Manston, and so did Lieutenant Robert M. Borg. For all of these facts, there was on the other side of the ledger, one enemy aircraft found and strafed on the field, an Me410 destroyed by Lieutenant Harold D. Hollis.

The whole episode strengthened Colonel Tacon's frequently briefed conviction that strafing was not profitable unless the targets were clearly juicy, and unless a satisfactory one-pass surprise attack could be planned and executed.

By some irony, 11 May was one of the loveliest yet seen in England, flowering into splendor after a chill morning.

At briefing on the 12th (the time was 0930 on FO 337) Colonel Tacon reviewed the losses of the 11th, and, without minimizing the courage and dash of the lost men who had led the attack on Reims, said he would hold flight commanders responsible for limiting attacks on fields where the targets plainly justified the loss of a man on these attacks, though that risk must be accepted if the aircraft were there to be destroyed. He also briefed on the growing necessity of frequently re-setting gyro compasses to protect men deep in enemy territory against a sudden compass failure, and on the movement of enemy aircraft in France away from our sweep whenever Allied planes penetrated near the "invasion air depots."

The show of the 12th involved a long-planned assault on the synthetic oil plants of Saxony and the Sudetenland. The 359th patrolled a 50-mile stream of bombers until the leader, Major Shaw, identified the B-17s bound for Merseburg, escorted them 'round that target and came out by way of Frankfurt. On the way home Captain Ettlesen took his flight down on Langensalza and scored 2-0-1 in a sudden, perfectly-executed attack that drew no flak but resulted in two battle damage cases. Ettlesen's own plane was hit by a .50 calibre slug from a wingman, and Lieutenant Burton wrenched a wing on a flagpole he didn't see in time to clear. Both these mishaps and the success of the bounce exemplified Colonel Tacon's convictions on the hazards and profits of correctly executed strafing.

13 May was the first time the 359th Group had found it necessary to brief on the 1/500,000 Order of Battle map instead of the larger 1/2,500,000 scale. FO 338 ordered withdrawal support for B-17 attacks on the Focke-Wulf plants at Poznan and nearby Krzesinki in Poland, which had proved

such difficult targets. This was a long ride, as is evidenced by the fact that four early returns logged four hours apiece, coming back from well past Bremen, and still they were classed as abortive.

Deep as the ride was, it was largely purposeless. The bombers saw cloud cover over the target area and turned back to their secondaries without entering Poland. The result was they were 40 minutes early, and though Colonel Tacon reached Dramburg on schedule, there was nothing to do but pursue the Forts up over the Baltic and into Denmark, leaving by way of Husum. Two bandits over Kiel were lost in the haze. The 359th came home in a bad haze, the last ship landing at 1837 with the red runway pundit light glowing through the gathering murk.

Next day was Sunday, 14 May, and the principal business was the afternoon parade for General Anderson and the DFC winners. It was chill, and a keen wind numbed the bloused and trusting officer who had shed their woolen underwear.

On the 15th, a FO was scrubbed by 0530. News of the extension of the tour was circulated that day, and the aircraft alert plan went into effect. It had its first trial on the 16th, when a practice scrambled out the 369th's quartet of planes 11 minutes from the time Flying Control got the word from Wing. The system was for the tower to fire two braces of flares as signal for crew chiefs to start engines, while simultaneously the pilots were ordered up by telephone. The 17th was another dull day, and it was still raining on the 18th. But from that point on the 359th Group had a mission a day, opening with its first mission to Berlin.

The first Big "B" day came on the 19th, with bad ground fog and haze, which persisted until an eerie landing at 1555 with pundits lit, despite flecks of blue in the overcast, and haze.

The FO was 342. Colonel Tacon briefed and led, rendezvousing at Henstedt at 1315. There was combat with more than 100 enemy aircraft trying to smash in at the bombers throughout the Pritzwalk, Wittenberge, Liebenwalde area. The air score was 11-0-1 for three NYR against shrewd and experienced pilots. Both Major Shaw and Captain Ettlesen had memorable adventures, and Lieutenant Cater barely survived the explosion of an ammunition car he blew up. Captain Mosse, the universally popular operations officer of the 368th Squadron, newly transferred to that job, did not come back. The Chaplain and Lieutenant Janney broke the news to Mosse's pretty little Scottish wife, whom he had married in Cambridge in the spring and with whom he had created a much admired idyll of life near the station. Lieutenant Smith, soft-spoken Georgian flight leader of the 368th, and Lieutenant Laing, another of the 369th's tall, bright replacement pilots, both parachuted over Germany.

All previous Jackpot areas assigned for mass strafing were canceled on this day, a blow to intelligence staff who had done much work on them, and new areas were assigned. And, in view of the havoc wrought by such train-busters at Etelsen, Command now also ordered preparations for assault on German railroads. The code-word was to be "Chattanooga," presumably in tender memory of the renowned Choo-Choo. S-2 officers worked that night preparing maps and target data on the new areas but the 20 May effort turned out to be a bomber smash at the same Reims-Champagne airdrome which had cost the 359th Group three pilots on the 11th.

Fog closed in on Wretham early but the whole show was pushed back an hour so that take off at 0940 was possible and the mission itself uneventful. That afternoon Command vetoed Colonel Tacon's proposed method of fighter-bomber attack on bridges (individual dives from 10,000 to 5,000 feet) and instead proposed skip-bombing with delayed action bombs, by element, at 300 mph from 500 feet, the method developed by the Ninth Fighter Command with success. Two bridges at Hasselt and three at Liege in Belgium had been nominated as the official "Eighth Fighter Command experimental bridges" and bomb runs on all were now planned.

Came 21 May and the Chattanooga in the area around Lubeck, northeast of Hamburg. The whole command did a staggering job, destroying or damaging 225 locomotives, a paragraph full of other ground objectives and getting 20-0-2 aircraft in the air and 102-0-76 aircraft on the ground for the expenditure of 26 pilots. The 359th lost four. One, the sideburned Homer L. Rodeheaver, 369th Squadron, was killed when he spun in from a gunnery pattern over a train.

Apparently he had failed to burn down his fuselage tank to the recommended 30 gallons on the ride into the target, electing instead to use wing-tank petrol. The result in the P-51, as all pilots had discovered in their two earlier major fights, was an alarming tendency to flick into a stall at the top of a turn, because the extra, unplanned weight of the fuselage gasoline changed the centre of gravity.

Two pilots bellied in that day after being hit by ground fire. They were Arlen Baldridge, 368th, a quiet, reticent analyst with the calm curiosity of a test-pilot. In the anxious days of spring, 1943, he had been a pioneer in the exploration by young pilots of what the P-47 would and would not do. Another to belly in was Second Lieutenant Joseph E. Shupe of the 370th, a new boy who had piled up a record of 7-0-4 and rapidly earned a place as one of the outstanding winners in the 359th Group. The fourth man lost was 20-year-old "Bunky" Hudelson, youngest and smallest, physically, of the originals. His red-cheeked, yellow-haired youth created a startling impression of adolescence belied only by the glint sparking like flinted steel in his blue eyes. "Bunky," as he was universally known after Billy DeBeck's precious child, was heard to call he was bailing out after a ground flak hit. So ended his hope of resigning his commission at the completion of his tour and entering West Point.

In exchange for these four men, the 359th exacted from the Germans a ground score of 17-0-24, plus two caught in the air, and, in the attack on the railroads, 31 locomotives, six radar towers, five signal towers, a transformer station and assorted other targets.

Early next morning, an intruder over the station shot down a Lancaster returning from Duisburg, the RAF plane crashing on the 39th Service Company area with six of its seven crewmen killed. The crashed ship was at first thought to be German.

At 1004 on the 22nd, 27 Mustangs were airborne to another Type 16 patrol of Picardy while the bombers attacked Siracourt once more. It was uneventful, as was a special mission of four P-51s led by Lieutenant Wetmore in support of B-17s dispatched on a long search of the North Sea off the Frisian Islands, apparently looking for crewmen from ditched bombers. At 1705, the alert flight was scrambled again. Three ships were airborne in 5 minutes 30 seconds, the fourth requiring 90 seconds more. Mission Number 100 was flown on the morning of 23 May. Up at 0713, the errand was to Metz, where nothing notable developed save for a single diving pass by eight enemy aircraft at the bombers at Lure. The enemy promptly broke for cover and could not be engaged.

That afternoon Colonel Swanson led an abortive skip-bombing mission to Hasselt. The Colonel went down on the wrong canal in the maze of Belgian waterways. His radio was weak and the result was that there was no positive control when flights eventually found Hasselt, or what they thought was Hasselt. One flight reported the bridge destroyed and someone suggested that the bombs be not wasted. This was interpreted as an order and everything went fubar. No bombs were dropped and the 359th Group returned home at 1754 to report the Hasselt bridge was done for, only to have the 361st Group come in on the same target 45 minutes after our departure and find the structure very much in being, as indeed it was after the 361st finished bombing. On the whole, all hands agreed, an extremely poor show.

The second Berlin mission was flown 24 May. Lieutenant Kruger made an emergency landing immediately after take off, and his airplane crashed and burned but he escaped with only slight injuries.

The mission itself produced little enemy opposition, the air score being

1-0-0, although two gaggles of 30 each were seen in the distance, too far to be engaged. But three flights of the 369th Squadron, with the Buzz Boy veterans in the van, did a satisfactory ground attack job, blowing up eight locomotives, six tank cars and damaging two tugs, three barges, etcetera.

Field orders had been arriving later and later, and the inevitable occurred on 25 May: the order came in so late that the 359th Group was 30 minutes slow getting away and could not execute the prescribed Zemke fan, a wide sweep of the type invented by Colonel Hubert A. Zemke of the 56th Group. The bombers were met leaving the target, Mulhouse, and later Captain Ettlesen was hit by flak at 25,000 over Saarbrücken. He nursed the plane as far west as he could and finally left it at 3,000 over Sarrebourg.

As usual, the radio conversation was memorable, the jewels being the anxious injunctions from his flight: "Remember what they told you," referring to the briefing on escape and evasion techniques, and the solicitous inquiries "Got all your stuff, Chief?" in reference to escape kit, purse, maps, dogtags. Ettlesen seemed, also as usual, only moderately disgusted by the turn of events.

There was no show on the 26th, but on the 27th a wild goose chase for bandits sent the 359th Group careering from Chateau-Thierry to Amiens, with the result that the 359th missed a rousing combat farther along the route, in which the 352nd Group scored heavily. By the time the 359th had obtained permission to rejoin the bombers the combat was all over, though our Group rendezvoused over the target, Mannheim, and took the B-17s out to landfall at Ostend.

The 359th again found no airborne opposition on the 28th, a long 5:23 mission to Magdeburg in which the return was by way of Frankfurt. A 368th section went down on Schönebeck but found no enemy aircraft there. Wetmore saw what he estimated to be 150 parked on Wittenberg but he was in the top cover squadron at 32,000 and could make no attack. A total of 1,125 fighters escorted the bombers on this mission into the heart of Germany.

But another major air combat of the month occurred on 29 May: a savage running series of fights north and east of Berlin from Malchin to Stettin. The action was by squadrons and the score for 12-1-0 for two; Lowell "One-Eye" Brundage, a sophisticated humorist, and Myron C. Morrill, a new pilot, both 369th. One of these was seen shot down by a veteran Luftwaffe expert wearing two chevrons on his ship. The German, our pilot and Lieutenant Butler of Bodney, went into a 12-turn Lufberry, and when our pilot broke, the German got him. Lieutenant Butler came over from Bodney to tell S-2 about it. Wetmore scored another double, raising his total to 13;

Colonel Murphy scored two, sharing one with Doersch, and the latter shared another victim with Robert W. Siltamaki.

Another victory was recorded by Posty Booth, his eighth, preserving his remarkable record of never having fired upon an enemy without destroying same.

A spasm of abortions came on 30 May. Of the 39 airplanes up, 12 came back early, leaving 27 to meet the bombers at Einbeck. There was a mix up here. The assignment was to pick up two wings at Dessau. These wings were on course, on time and happy, but they executed a sliding left oblique turn near the target which reversed their positions and put the lead wing over Dessau 10 minutes early. The 359th Group, which had been flying en masse on the starboard wing as guard against the expected attack, was surprised by the maneuver and could not get up to the target to clear the front for the bomb run, since the fighters had been watching the clock and knew they should have 10 extra minutes. They didn't have it, and so, when the Germans struck from the front, could only meet them coming through. The result was not satisfactory although several gaggles were fended off, and claims were limited to 3-1-0. Booth, incidentally, went down to strafe a Ju88 but saw no fire, claimed only a damaged and so ended his infallible gunnery record, although it remained valid for air combat.

Richard H. Broach was lost escorting an early return, Lieutenant Fong, home. Broach sent Fong out to sea, explaining he was going to hit a train and later was heard to call that flak had damaged his plane and he would have to bail south of the Zuider Zee. The 359th almost lost another pilot on the landing as Lieutenant Lemmens came in for a normal approach and flopped over on his back: his wheel had frozen, apparently from heated brakes, and did not make one revolution, as skid marks showed. Fortunately there was no fire, as it required 10 minutes to get Lemmens out. He was jarred but unhurt. The plane was fit for salvage only.

Colonel Tacon led a flight down on a field near Paderborn but the targets turned out to be dummies, and the attack was broken off. The dummies were well done and it was believed that real planes might be interspersed among them, but that was left for later investigation.

The month closed with a visit to the Ruhr, or the eastern fringe thereof, where the marshalling yards at Soest and Schwerte were seen well-hit.

There was news also that higher authority had allowed Captain Samuel R. Smith credit for the 24 hours of combat time he had amassed in B-24s before transferring to fighters. This put him over the 180 hour deadline, and his subsequent fighter time completed the stated tour of 200 hours. Accordingly at the end of May he was taken off ops while his application for 30 days home leave before beginning on a 100 hour extension was considered.

This, by and large, was the goal of almost every pilot. It was the core 'round which was wrapped the stern air discipline that gave them strength, coherence, and success in their outnumbered struggle against the German: the thought of home. There was little brooding about it; the demands of the crisis, hours of flight and combat did not permit that, but it was the dream that made all the hazards of present and future possible of acceptance. Sustained by that dream, they flew well and they fought well, and prepared for more of the same.

9.

JUNE 1944

Operation Overlord

Thursday, June 1: Wretham—Solid deck of heavy low stratocumulus that stayed all day.

Up at 0800. At 1300 released until tomorrow.

Shaw and the Colonel took a pick-up ball team down to Honington (364th) and won 4 to 1. I spent most of the day at the operations shack writing letters.

The new snooker table's a huge success, and it's a swell table. Saw the movie tonight, and that was about all to the day. A welcome day of rest.

> *[The British 8th Army captures Frosinone, southeast of Rome.*
> *Iceland severs ties with Denmark, becoming an independent republic.*
> *King Peter of Yugoslavia urges unity between the Serbs, Croats, and Slovenes until the war is won.*
> *Pope Pius XII broadcasts conditions for an enduring peace.]*

Friday, June 2: Wretham—Heavy cumulus and haze.

Up at 0800, released until noon.

Bombers hammering Pas de Calais all day. We got warning order at

1400. Took off at 1900, landed at 2215. Me, Baker, Andy, and Newberg: Red Section with Mac leading, middle flight. Down to Fecamp, R/V with bombers, then southeast to Chartres, then suburbs of Paris.

Bad haze and soup at bomber's altitude and we all got split up. Les Taylor (Yellow Flight) and I roamed, flew escort around the bombers and came back alone. We could see each flak gun fire, like winking lights or fireflies down in the towns. Quite a sight. No enemy aircraft.

Stearns had a nice bacon and egg feed ready for us in dining room at 2245. Damn nice!! Good guy! To bed at 2330.

> *[Out of Tripoli, over 100 B-17s of the US 15th Air Force attack rail yards at Debrecen, Hungary.*
>
> *Secret negotiations between the Rumanian government and representatives of the Soviet Union begin in Stockholm, Sweden.]*
>
> *Bulgaria discusses terms of surrender with the Western Allies.]*

Saturday, June 3: Wretham—Up at 0800. Readiness until 1600. Nuts! Sat around all day.

Two missions of B-17s pounded France again today.

They've changed the crystals in all of our radios.

0730 zero hour tomorrow. I wonder anew???

Shaw and the Colonel went to dinghy drill this afternoon. Ha ha, finally caught 'em.

The 368th and Group played a swell 10-inning game. Group won, 5 to 4. Snack bar as usual.

I had to hang around Ops all day so couldn't paint on airplane. Nuts.

Sunday, June 4: Wretham—Up at 0800. To line at 0900. I plotted the mission alone, a short two hour escort deal to Gravelines, Berck-sur-Mer so bombers could hit Boulogne, Le Tréport coastline. Me, Baker, Andy, and Hammy: Blue Flight, had low course. Colonel Swanson led us thru low stratocumulus clouds at 15,000 feet. Went okay.

Major Shaw was grounded. Said my courses were okay.

I had another job of plotting upon return. Only 30 minutes to calculate. Escort again for "A" Group (the 368th and 369th) and "B" Group (the 370th). Split escort from Le Havre to Paris area and back Le Havre.

McKee led the same "E" Flight in Blue slot. Nice job of escort. Down at 2205. Whew. Six hours and 20 minutes of flying and 2 course plottings unassisted. Good supper at 2230.

We lost Cater. His engine quit on the first mission and he bailed out in Straits of Dover. They <u>never got</u> him! His dinghy never opened.

Lieutenant Emer H. Cater.
Photo courtesy of Marvin Boussu: Archived by Char Baldridge, Historian, 359th Fighter Group Association

[The US 5th Army enters Rome.]

Monday, June 5: Wretham Hall— Dead tired. Hung around Ops all day. Released at 1600. Headed back to Hall. Sacked, ate supper, sacked again, got up at 2145. It was "E" Flight's turn to taxi planes behind the barricades. Our planes are all being painted with 12" black n' white stripes on wings and fuselage. I headed back to Hall.

At 2230 I was called down to Group Ops. This <u>was it</u>!!!!

Four thousand craft pulled out for Fortress Europe, changed course during the night, hit between Cherbourg and Le Havre.

P-51B/C Mustang with D-Day stripes at East Wretham Airfield.
Courtesy of Elsie Palicka, wife of Ed Palicka, 370th Fighter Squadron Photographer: Archived by Char Baldridge, Historian, 359th Fighter Group Association

Ops is a madhouse. Everyone is there, drinking coffee. Maps and documents are super secret. Briefing board covered with patrol areas, courses. Field orders everywhere. Telephones ringing. Group split into two units. "A" is the 368th and 369th; "B" is the 370th. We're to fly alternate, overlapping missions. An incredible scene.

[D-Day Order by General Eisenhower:
"You will bring about the destruction of the German war machine, the elimination of Nazi tyranny over the oppressed peoples of Europe, and security for ourselves in a free world.

"Your task will not be an easy one. Your enemy is well trained, well equipped, and battle-hardened. He will fight savagely.

"But this is the year 1944. Much has happened since the Nazi triumphs of 1940 and 1941.

"The United Nations have inflicted upon the Germans great defeat in open battle man to man. Our air offensive has seriously reduced their strength in the air and their capacity to wage war on the ground.

"Our home fronts have given us an overwhelming superiority in weapons and munitions of war and placed at our disposal great reserves of trained fighting men.

"The tide has turned.

"The free men of the world are marching together to victory. I have full confidence in your courage, devotion to duty, and skill in battle.

"We will accept nothing less than full victory.

"Good luck, and let us all beseech the blessings of Almighty God upon this great and noble undertaking."]

D-Day, Tuesday, June 6: Wretham—Raining and overcast.

Briefing at 0030. Worked right thru the night.

First take off was at 0240. Full night. Tacon leading "A" Group. Colonel gave us the whole picture and did a fine job. Group assigned areas ringing beach heads for patrols.

Chappie gave prayers on truck in moonlight. Gorgeous night. Inspiring. I'll never forget it.

Take off accomplished okay. Waited to rain until 10 minutes after take off. A miracle!

They ("A" Group) were out <u>six and one-half</u> hours!

"B" Group off at 0540 to relieve 'em. Each squadron left one hour apart to bomb and strafe area 770 (Le Mans, Tours). I went with the

370th. Mac led squadron. I led Red Flight with Hastings, and Connelly. Swell formation up thru holes in several cumulus decks. In at 20,000 feet then down to deck.

The eight of us first bombed roads and railroad tracks, then we found a train west of Le Mans and shot the Hell out of it. No enemy aircraft, no flak, no signs of anything. Got back together, came home in perfect formation. Swell mission.

Lousy cumulus over England with rain and low ceilings. Landed at 1630. No sleep, dirty. I plotted <u>five</u> missions unassisted. I was dead.

Tacon's "A" Group went out again at 1800 to patrol area 770.

I ate, took a hot bath, in bed at 1900 and was asleep by 1900:10!!

Tacon's "A" Group came back in full dark at 2330. Several landed elsewhere.

[Operation Overlord, the invasion of "Fortress Europe" by American, British, Canadian, Polish, and Free French troops begins in the early morning hours. After aerial and naval bombardment, five divisions, totaling over 156,000 men, land at Omaha, Utah, Gold, Juno and Sword beaches in Normandy. Twelve thousand paratroopers of the US 82nd and 101st Airborne Divisions land behind German lines. Over 14,000 sorties are flown by Allied Air Forces. About 50,000 men in German infantry divisions oppose the Allies, and in spite of heavy Allied casualties at Omaha Beach, the German defenders are overwhelmed.]

Wednesday, June 7: Wretham—Wakened at 0145.

Briefing at 0300. Me and Regan were the only ones there.

"B" Group, lead by Murphy, took 16 ships to bomb Le Mans (area 770) again. They took off at 0430 but the weather was too bad so they landed. They took off again at 0600 and knocked Hell out of an ammo train, blowing it up. Also several tanks and trucks in convoy were in the area.

At 1030 "A" Group headed out to cover heavies and Area 770 patrol.

Weather still a cumulus layer nightmare but it was good for landing troops. Breaks here and there. Practically no enemy aircraft. A few groups yesterday met 10 to 15 enemy aircraft southeast of Area 770.

The 370th and 368th out again at 1800 to patrol area of Rennes. Back about 2230. We lost Marcinkiewicz. He bailed out near Fecamp due to flak from strafing.

Didn't fly all day, chained to the plotting board!

[US forces that landed in Normandy join up with the British 6th Airborne Division south of Caen.

King Haakon of Norway delivers a speech on the rights of small nations to share in postwar decisions.]

Thursday, June 8: Wretham—We flew 12 missions from 0240 on June 6th to 2200 on June 8th, or 12 missions in 67 hours and 20 minutes.

Briefing at 0515. Whole group is to provide escort in Chartres area. Murphy led, I plotted. They took off at 0540.

I ate breakfast then sacked until 1000, then back to plot second mission. Whole group to fly with 500, 250, and 100 pound bombs in Laval area. I was Yellow leader. Mags *(magnetos)* dropped and I never took off. Hell!!

Back after test hop which checked okay. Plotted third mission in Nantes, Châteaubriant area. Took off at 1830, same bomb loads. Due back at 2230.

Another day with no flight time. Dammit!! I've plotted all but three missions so far!!

Hagan bailed out near Chartres, they saw him get out of his chute okay despite railroad flak. Sander of the 369th is missing.

Friday, June 9: Wretham—Invasion or no invasion, the weather won the toss today and we sat on the ground all day despite four briefings. Warm and cold fronts piled up to 26,000 feet with ceilings down to 400 feet in rain. We were standing by all day and actually got two flights off the ground as the group assembled for take off before finally scrubbing. This was at 1700. Very tough on the boys on the beach head, but we couldn't go.

At Group Ops all morning. Played bridge with Cally, O'Shea, and Vic all afternoon. Quiet tonight. Released until dawn tomorrow. Colonel Tacon still has a cold and hasn't flown since the first mission on D-Day.

Oliphint crash-landed in France last night. "Posty" Booth bailed out, hit by ground fire. Two good '69th boys gone. Boy, they only have about 18 left over there. Nuts!

[US forces moving forward from Utah Beach in Normandy capture St. Mere-Eglise.

*The Red Army begins an offensive against Finnish positions in the
Karelian Isthmus north of Leningrad.]*

Saturday, June 10: Wretham Hall—Up at 0315. Plotted for 0600 briefing.

Took off at 0710. Me, Kirby, Cal, and Hammy: Blue Flight. Mac leading us as we escort B24s over Evreux, Conches, Dreux area. Then we're to strafe area of Argentan for one hour. I'm to take Blue Flight down and find out what the target results of bombers were.

Lousy weather, with layers of cumulus. We all split up but managed to get together at 20,000 feet. Colonel Swanson all messed up as usual. Bombers were late and we tried to find the targets after last bombs away but it was hopeless thru 8/10ths heavy cumulus.

We flew down the Seine River to Nantes, west to Evreux, and hit an electric locomotive. Good strikes.

Came back at 2,000 to 3,000 feet in cumulus canyons. Damn good cover over Rouen, headed over Channel at 2,000 feet, then back to Group HQ to report. A wild combination of instruments, buzzing, and navigating. Fun but tiring.

Second mission: the 370th bombed a bridge near Dinan and the 369th

Captain Wayne N. "Bo" Bolefahr. *Photo courtesy of Ira J. "John" Bisher: Archived by Char Baldridge, Historian, 359th Fighter Group Association*

were sent out near Avranches. The 368th escorted four 38 FR4 (*photoreconnaissance*) ships to Antwerp on the deck. We lost Bo. He crashed, hit by flak.

Three others were battle-damaged. The base here was socked in. Returning planes landed all over England.

Third mission a composite of three squadrons, with Cranfill and McKee, three from the '69th, five from 370th, and eleven from the 368th, to dive-bomb and strafe railroad between Evreux and Nantes. Lousy weather.

Pop Doersch got a 109 and the 368th shared another. Lousy visibility. Some landed at 2230. Others are still coming back this morning. Drake is missing.

Typed up my suggested procedure for Spotter Flights:
1) Know at briefing what box bombs last and their call sign
2) Joins and flies with that box upon R/V
3) Number two man stand by on C channel for call "bombs away"
4) Pinpoint self on call and hit deck, or let down in overcast, still being in correct approximate area.

Mike Donohue phoned Wing, General Anderson said swell. He phoned 8th Fighter Command and it was on the June 11th T.O. including separate call sign for last box. They evidently liked the idea. I'm pleased. Wot a day!

[With a lack of armored reserves, German counterattacks against Allied D-Day invasion forces are unsuccessful.]

Sunday, June 11: Wretham—Two shows. In the morning they escorted B-26s *(Martin Marauder medium bombers)* to the Paris area, then strafed. Nothing exciting. Weather was pretty good.

In the afternoon we took off at 1355 loaded with 250 pound bombs. Warm front coming in, kinda nasty. Two squadrons, Cranfill led one, Forehand the other. Me, Hastings, Cal, and Hammy: Yellow Flight.

Cranfill kept us below the soup at 10,000 feet in nice formation. Let down our bombs near Falaise then broke into flights.

We found a six or eight truck convoy and Colonel and Hammy bombed and strafed it. Blew up three trucks and set fire to four or five.

Hasty and I bombed the railroad southeast of Vire. Nice hits and we knocked out both tracks then strafed some boxcars. Came home by twos at 30,000 feet in rain and soup.

Simmons gone. Flak.

Monday, June 12: Wretham—Best day of weather since D-Day, really good. So why we only ran one mission beats the Hell out of me.

Colonel Tacon led. They escorted B-24s to Chartres area then strafed near Paris. Flak and a few 109s cost the 369th Hess, Linderer, and Pherson. Tough day!

Spent the afternoon at line shooting bull with Colonel Tacon, Swanson, Murphy, and Shaw. I learned a lot. We got a new Major today from Panama, a friend of Swanson's name of Brown. We're also getting eight new pilots in about 15 days out of New York. Wow! 44-A really shoving 'em thru.

The 353rd (flying P-47s) were bounced at 3,000 feet by a nine ship squadron of Me109s. We lost eight. They said the 109s were really hot with great teamwork. So the 353rd went back in the afternoon and got nine 109s in the same place!! Regular storybook revenge.

> [The 326,000 men and 54,000 vehicles put ashore at the five Allied-held beach heads in Normandy link together.
>   The Czechoslovak Government in London calls on Czechs and Slovaks in the German and Hungarian armies to desert.]

Tuesday, June 13: Wretham—Up at 0500.

Briefing at 0530. Took off at 0630 on area patrol south of Rouen (Conches, Dreux, etc.) for B-17s hitting airfields.

Me, Andy, Call, and Hammy were Blue Flight with Murph and Tacon. Several layers of soup up to 20,000 feet due to warm front, but not too tough. No action.

On return, group was running low on gas and controller said Wretham pretty socked in so we landed all over. Call and Hammy landed at Manston. Me and Andy landed at Boxted ('56th Group). Had lunch, saw Sam White and Jack Bateman. Also saw D-25 (47s). Beauts!! Colonel Tacon and flight landed there too so we came back here together at 1400.

I headed back to Manston at 1645 in the AT-6 (North American Aviation Trainer) to get Hammy as he had a dented prop. But he, meanwhile, had new prop put on. We passed each other. So I had supper there and flew back. Really enjoyed it.

Second mission was an area patrol south and east of Granville from 1800 to 2300 with tanks.

> [The launch of the first V-1 buzz bomb from Pas de Calais kills eight civilians in London.]

Wednesday, June 14: Wretham—Good day, heavy cumulus.

One mission. Nuts!! Took off at 0615. Blue Flight led by me, with McNeil, Andy, Hammy, and Murphy. Top squadron. Flew an area escort to Brussels, Namur airfields. We encountered heavy flak at Namur but no trouble and no enemy aircraft. Flew at 26,000 to 27,000 feet in nice squadron formation. Really clear over the Channel. Back at 1000.

Foul headache. Tired. Lunch at 1115 then went to bed and slept until 1700.

I was told at supper of my transfer to the 368th and Taylor's transfer back to 369th. I'm glad yet sorry. Good to rejoin the old outfit, but the 370th flies better and has better engineering, etc. Sorry to leave Colonel Murphy, a wonderful pilot and leader.

Taxied my ship over to the 368th, moved flying equipment after supper. Major Brown, '40, Panama for three years, 1,200 flight hours, is the new 368th operations officer. He seems like a good guy. So I'm "home" again and it's okay.

[*The Royal Air Force launches heavy attacks against Le Havre and Boulogne.*]

Thursday, June 15: Wretham—Another good day of weather.

One mission. I guess the 8th is back to its old routine again. Nuts!

They went to Nantes, St. Nazaire, past Jersey and Guernsey Isles, an interesting trip. No enemy aircraft, no action. All okay.

I have "A" Flight, with Hunter, Ash, Lewis, and Olson, a good gang. Glad to have J.B. again.

Green Hornet P-51 with the 368th Fighter Squadron, A Flight. Clockwise from lower left: Lieutenant Wilbur H. Lewis (standing), Captain Howard L. Fogg, Lieutenant John B. Hunter, Lieutenant Paul E. Olson, and Lieutenant Joseph M. Ashenmacher. *Courtesy of Richard Fogg*

In room 208, best room yet. Whitey is flight chief. Bisher my crew chief. Good!! Wheeler, Hartman, Wilson, Scott, Roxby, lots of old "D" Flighters, a good deal. We have the Colonel's airplane. I'm very pleased.

Bateman takes my old 370th Flight. Doersch takes Taylor's. Callahan gets "F" Flight. A good gang of new fellas in 368th; Gilmore, Allen, Kosc, Kaloski, Hatter, all swell!

[There are heavy V-1 attacks on London.]

Friday, June 16: Wretham—Up at 0800. Nice morning. Briefing at 0910, mission scrubbed due to warm front.

Spent morning at line, talked to Whitey and Bisher. Attended talk on formation given by Trigger after lunch for the new boys. It was okay.

Briefing at 1500, took off at 1537, Type 16 in Beauvais, Ypres sector. Top flight about three hours, no action.

Wayne Philipps blew in, in a P-38 from the 370th. He's in group operations, never flies operationally. Seemed quite sad and lonely. Good to see him, we had supper. He left at 8:00 P.M. Seemed funny to me seeing that frail little guy wheeling that big ship around. His APO is #595, N.Y. at an old RAF base in Andover, southwest London. He doesn't like the P-38s very well, lots of engine trouble, heavy to wheel around, ceiling at 20,000 feet.

[V-1s are again launched against London, with over 240 strikes reported.
In Washington, the Finnish Minister and his counselors are asked to leave the United States.]

Saturday, June 17: Wretham—Up at 0800, to line at 0830.

8 to 10/10ths visibility with cumulus. Windy and cool.

Briefing at 1015. Escort area bombers (B-24s) to airdromes in Paris area. Take off delayed until 1210. We picked 'em up coming back out, brought 'em into Beachy Head okay. No enemy aircraft.

Colonel Swanson "aborted" on ground, called me to take squadron. Colonel Murphy to lead. Lewis, J. B., and Ash were with me. We only had 13 ships. Lane (Blue Flight), Mac and Perk led Red and Yellow Flights.

We headed thru the cumulus deck at 4,000 to 6,000 feet, came out behind Murph, but caught him okay.

A real responsibility leading a squadron, have to be on your toes every second, fly, look, think. Kinda fun though, and a real nice feeling of <u>doing</u> something. Came back with Murph's outfit thru nice holes.

Second mission due back 2200, escort same area.

Major Brown was killed. His plane exploded.

[German troops evacuate the island of Elba off the west coast of Italy.]

Sunday, June 18: Wretham—Briefing at 0630, took off at 0715. Me, Lewis, Keesey, and Gilmore: Red Flight. Tyrrell, middle. Lewis aborted, McGeever joined our flight. Escorted B-24s from Heligoland to Hamburg area, back on reciprocal clear to English Coast. Went to 32,000 feet thru some soup at 30,000 feet in one place. Beautiful day above cumulus layer at 2,000 to 4,000 feet over an all water route. No enemy aircraft. Flak was heavy around targets (oil and airdromes) to 32,000 feet. Swell formation.

Trigger did well, me too. Left him coming back (Mac's engine was cutting out) and went down to 18,000 feet to escort. Never saw so many bombers, estimate 1,400. Released until dawn.

Spent the afternoon loafing at line. "A" Flight getting green wheels.

Red Allen bailed out near Kings Lyn, engine quit over overcast when returning alone from Heligoland. Was he lucky! No radio and was two miles inland, not over water.

*[The US Fifth Army captures Perugia, Italy.
The US First Army cuts off the German forces defending Cherbourg.]*

Monday, June 19: Wretham—Day off. Stayed in sack until 1130. Really slept. Felt swell. At lunch we had strawberry shortcake.

Went to line, painted on the *Green Hornet.*

Today's mission: Bordeaux. Pop Doersch got lost, was up 7 hours 30 minutes!!

Some plane!! No action. Hawk is assistant operations officer now, good man.

Sam White is back in the squadron from A/S Rescue work. Good to have one of the old gang return. He's in "F" Flight with Homeyer. Slept in our room last night and tonight is just checking out in P-51s. Also, "Oscar" Fladmark from the gunnery flight is now in squadron. "B"

Flight with Bach. And Bach made his captaincy the other night. Good deal. <u>McKee a Major.</u>

After supper, took shower, shampooed, watched second show. Good.

[An Allied "Mulberry" artificial harbor at Omaha Beach is destroyed by a violent storm in the English Channel.]

Captain George A. "Pop" Doersch.
*Photo courtesy of George A. Doersch:
Archived by Char Baldridge, Historian,
359th Fighter Group Association*

Tuesday, June 20: Wretham Hall— Up at 0400. Briefed at 0530. Escort to Politz, Hamburg, etc. Oil refineries targeted. A really clear day over there, could see Sweden and Denmark. Mission nearly all over water, 5 hours 20 minutes. I started out as Blue Flight but all my boys aborted so I flew Yellow #3 at 32,000 feet with Mac, Bouchers. We were hit by Me410s but we couldn't catch 'em. Burton (369th) got one. A long ride over water!

Flew a second mission, to strafe rail yards east of Paris. Took off at 1715. I started as Red Flight, had to abort over Channel. Right mag shot to Hell.

Group hit some trains okay. Reports of Panzer Division moving in area. Lost Sansing (369th). Hit by flak, bailed out.

[The Me410 was a twin-engine fighter/light bomber put into service in March of 1943. Slower and less maneuverable than Allied single-engine fighters, it was reasonably effective attacking bombers but did not fare well in air to air combat.]

*Wednesday, June 21: Wretham—*Up at 0520. Briefing at 0630. Take off at 0715. Trigger led. Me, Lewis, Janney, and Kosc: Blue Flight. Solid deck of cumulus at 1,000 to 3,000 feet, went thru 'em by flights and assembled above. Mission: escort 1,350 bombers to Berlin! We picked ours up near landing fields near Kiel area, headed east to Stettin then south to target.

The sky was full of bombers. No enemy aircraft on ours. Lots of aborts, though; we had 13, the 370th had six and the 369th had eight.

It was overcast clear to the German coast so we never saw water. Berlin was <u>hidden</u> too, but by huge clouds of smoke. Terrific oil fires at Hamburg still burning from yesterday.

Colonel Tyrrell took White Flight down to strafe an airdrome 40 miles from Berlin. Can't understand it! Nuts! He was hit and had to bail out.

Lubien hit too but he made it back. Rough. Major Shaw becomes C.O.

I came home with five ships. Five hours and 40 minutes flight time. Whew!

[The US 8th Air Force carries out raids on Berlin and the synthetic fuel plants at Leuna-Merseburg.

Hermann Goering, the infamous head of the Luftwaffe, reportedly says, "the day I saw Mustangs over Berlin, I knew the jig was up."]

Thursday, June 22: Wretham—Cumulus deck. Released until 1200. Beautiful weather then.

Dive-bombed a bridge near Chateau Thierry in the afternoon. Didn't get the bridge, flak defenses were too heavy.

Lieutenant Colonel Albert R. "Trigger" Tyrrell, Commanding Officer, 368th Fighter Squadron. *Courtesy of Anthony C. Chardella: Archived by Char Baldridge, Historian, 359th Fighter Group Association*

The 370th lost Hollis and Grimes. Ambrose all shot up and landed at Manston.

I'm now acting operations officer with Forehand to group for a month. I like the job. Cliff is swell to work for. I'm making schedules, leaves, D.O.s, etc.

After supper, took Olson up to 25,000 feet. A nice ride on a beautiful evening. Chased around a bit doing rolls and dives. Olson, Britton, and Cook all okay to go tomorrow.

[In the east, 185 Soviet divisions begin Operation Bagration, a massive surprise attack on a 300-mile German-held front between Polotsk and Bobruysk. The German Army suffers 350,000 killed or captured, the highest German losses of the war.

The Luftwaffe launch a surprise night raid with 60 aircraft on the US 8th Air Force's shuttle base at Poltava in the Ukraine, destroying 44 B-17s and 500,000 gallons of fuel.

US bombers carry out a saturation bombing on Cherbourg.

President Roosevelt signs the G.I. Bill of Rights, promising generous benefits for returning servicemen.]

Friday, June 23: Wretham—Sat around all day due to heavy cumulus overcast until late afternoon. Volleyball, paperwork, and so on.

Briefed at 1645. Took off at 1815. Me, Olson, J. B., and Ash: Red Flight. Shaw, middle. Tacon led to area east of Paris to cover heavies bombing railroads, bridges, etc. They were late, then overstayed, so we all came back low on gas (no tanks). Landed at 10:10 P.M. (daylight only until 11:00 P.M.). Ash, Olson, Randy, and Lambright landed on coast. Everyone mad at the damn bombers.

Good squadron formation. Everyone back okay. Tired.

Leaves start again on Tuesday. Sam White sure seems glad to be back in our squadron. Full of pep like I've never seen him before. The 368th <u>still</u> a great gang!

Saturday, June 24: Wretham—Briefing at 0445. Wow! I slept!

They went to Paris area again as escort. We had 16 ships up and no aborts. Good deal! Back at 1100. A rare cloudless gorgeous cool summer day. No action on mission today.

Colonel Tacon to Flak Home tomorrow by order of Wing. Good idea, he's earned it by golly! Major Shaw is a swell C.O., boy, he's tops.

Training flights for Chatfield, Cherry, Cavanaugh, and Fladmark. No flying after supper, gave 'em all a rest. I like being in charge, being busy helps time to pass and cuts down on those lonely moments.

Sunday, June 25: Wretham—Wot a mission!

Briefed at 0530. Take off at 0615. Me, Olson, Randy, and Kysely:

Red Flight. Shaw middle. To escort B-17s way down near the Swiss border, Lake Geneva, Lyons, etc. Our squadron took two boxes of B-17s, others did the same but had different "targets." We went to the little town of Nantua, about 20 miles west of Geneva. The bombers descended to 3,000 feet, took the first section down with close cover. Our section stayed at 14,000 feet as top flight. Beautiful job of escort. The B-17s flew right down the damn valley, dropped not bombs, but parachute loads of supplies. Interesting. Wot a sight. Then climbed back up to 14,000 feet going home.

This was the most gorgeous mountain country, valleys, rivers, blue lakes, rock cliffs, a little lake near Nantua with sheer rock cliffs as walls, chalets, green pocket-handkerchief fields, railway viaducts. Not a cloud in the sky. And the whole vast greatness of the Alps towering out of the eastward haze to 14,000 to 15,000 feet, snow capped and dazzling, an unforgettable sight. Simply breathtaking!!

France clear as a bell, Cliffs of Dover visible from Rouen. Flew by Paris. Wonderful trip. Five hours and 30 minutes. No flak, no enemy aircraft, just miles and miles of scenery, the whole of France, its river valleys and towns like a relief map. Marvelous!

Second mission, took off at 1730. Three hour escort east of Paris. No action.

[The British Second Army begins a major offensive in the Caen area.
The Battle of Tali-Ihantala between Soviet and Finnish troops begins,
estimated to be the largest battle ever fought in the Nordic countries.]

Monday, June 26: Wretham—Heavy low and middle clouds.

Went to line at 0900, censored mail, played volleyball. Released until noon. At lunch, released until tomorrow.

We all took the afternoon off. I painted a train picture, the first one in a couple of months. Enjoyed it, but sure haven't much patience. A western scene, 2-10-2 type. That's all to recount today.

Randy and Hatter left on leave tonight, happy as Hell. Don't blame them! Nearly everyone went to the show tonight. Ash drawing women. Lew in sack. Sam White still bunks with us, good company. And so to th' sack m'self, with another *Perry Mason* to put me to sleep.

[Cherbourg is captured by the US 7th Corps.]

Tuesday, June 27: Wretham—Weather bad in the morning. To line at 0915. Censored mail, etc.

We lost four planes to the 9th Air Force. They brought us four of their wrecks from France. Nuts!

Thundershowers after lunch. Then the clouds broke up.

Briefing at 1545. Took off at 1655 with me leading middle squadron with Cook, Hunter, and White. Cook flew a perfect wing. Addleman led Blue Flight, Bach led Red. Picked up B-24s at Dutch Islands, south then west to Creil. Knocked <u>Hell</u> out of Creil! We escorted bombers by squadrons then by flights. Broke off to bring out stragglers. Me and Blue escorted two boxes to landing field at Dieppe. Left 'em in mid-Channel, skirted Manston and came home. Three hours and 40 minutes. Nice ride.

Good supper waiting for us. Weather darn nice here now.

Wednesday, June 28: Wretham—Early mission to Saarbrucken. Major Shaw led. Uneventful. Back at 1030. Bad wind on return. Hawk got a wing tip landing but he's okay. Kaloski landed at Leiston (357th) with coolant trouble, but came back after supper. Released until dawn.

We flew five missions without an abort. Gilmore had bad mags this morning and came back. Darn good record.

These old guys, Hunter, Hawk, Homeyer, Janney, Lane, Bach, Perkins, and Keesey, all fight like Hell to see who gets on flight schedule. Each wants to finish first and have a great time! What nuts!

Me, shower, sack, supper. Then bridge with White, Doc, and Keesey.

Then to second show, "The Desperados," a swell western in Technicolor.

Lieutenant John S. Keesey. *Photo courtesy of R. Hatter: Archived by Char Baldridge, Historian, 359th Fighter Group Association*

[The Vatican resumes diplomatic relations with the Netherlands Government-in-exile.

At the Republican National Convention in Chicago, Governor Dewey of New York is nominated for the Presidency.]

Thursday, June 29: Wretham—Up at 0500. Only qualified instrument pilots could fly so I had to change the schedule. Some mess waking up guys who didn't think they'd be flying.

Briefing at 0630. Took off at 0730. Me, Lewis, Homeyer, and White: Red Flight. Shaw, top. Thin stratus decks, no real instruments. Picked up B-24s in the area east of Münster; targets Oschersleben, Magdeburg, etc. Good escort. Lewis, Homeyer, and White were hot this morning! No enemy aircraft, heavy target flak. Near Zwolle we hit the front and a lousy "milk" haze, so switched to instruments at 25,000 feet. Lost Shaw, lost bombers, everyone split. We brought 10 B-24s back to the English Coast. Visibility was okay in England. Nice cumulus. Four hour and 55 minutes, beautiful flight. Tired!

A questionnaire at briefing room in the afternoon. Also, medals awarded by General Anderson. Murphy got the Silver Star. Good! Lubien made an emergency landing, nosed 'er up to avoid buildings. He's okay.

Friday, June 30: Wretham—Up at 0800. Heavy cumulus broke into beautiful warm, sunny summer day.

I got a new *(P-51)* D-5 today, "*Green Hornet II,*" a honey. #413602, lucky number! Painted name on 'er this afternoon.

Homeyer gets my old plane "*Green Hornet,*" still a damn fine airplane. Bach, too, got a D-5. Lane got his B-15.

Mission briefing at 1145, took off at 1300 carrying 100 pound bombs. We're to bomb targets of opportunity in Belgium after escorting one box of heavies who're bombing airdromes near Antwerp.

Forehand flew, led for the first time since he left the squadron. No enemy aircraft, no action. Let go of bombs from 8,000 feet but couldn't see results. Nuts!! Cavanaugh flew his first mission today.

Movie tonight, London tomorrow. Whee! I'm <u>tired</u>!!

Recapitulation—368th Roster:
Commanding Officer: Shaw
Operations: Captain Forehand (DS)
Assistant Ops: Perkins
"A" Flight: Captain Fogg, Hunter, Lewis, Ashenmacher, Olson
"B" Flight: Captain Bach, Lane, Kaloski, Keesey, Fladmark
"C" Flight: Lieutenant Hawkinson, Halter, Lubien, Kysely, Cavanaugh

"D" Flight: Lieutenant Janney, Randolph, Lambright, Allen, Chatfield
"E" Flight: Captain McGeever, Keesey, Gilmore, Cook, Cherry
"F" Flight: Lieutenant Homeyer, White, Kosc, Britton, Addleman

[The Royal Air Force launches a saturation raid on 2. and 9. SS-Panzer Divisions at Villers-Bocage near Caen.
The United States breaks off diplomatic relations with Finland.]

Excerpts from the June 1944 Informal Report of Morale for the 359th Fighter Group, submitted by "Chappie" Ziegler state that: "The month of June 1944 is one that will never be forgotten by any man in the group. The one big memory we will have of this month is D-Day. For weeks, rumors had been flying thick and fast as to when the invasion would start and what part we would play in it. These rumors kept morale high for a time, but then as the days dragged on a new and more persistent rumor crept into the picture. You heard it on the line, in the messes, in the Red Cross Club, wherever men gathered. So much good weather had been ignored that many were thinking that the invasion had been put off for another year. A man's morale went pretty low as he thought of another year away from home without any substantial gain toward victory. Things went along in that vein until midnight of June 5th, when everybody seemed to sense that "this was it!" Something electric went through the air with the news that the invasion was about to start. As in America, there was no great hilarity or celebration. Everyone knew this was going to cost many lives, but it was as if a load had been lifted. As a group we were like a fighter who had trained for his big fight. He had fought his way up through the ranks and earned a shot at the championship. He is nervous and tense as he awaits the bell for the first round. Then suddenly it rings and the tenseness leaves him. He's relaxed and confident. He knows he'll take some pretty stiff punches, but more than that he knows he can win. Well, I think that's the way we all felt. We didn't relish, in fact we hated the thought of the losses we would suffer. However, we knew if we were to win this fight we had to take it some time and the sooner we got in there the sooner we'd win and get out again.

"Briefing for the first invasion mission was called at about 0200 hours on 6 June. Naturally it was a very secret briefing, so I cannot report on the reaction of our pilots when they heard the news. When they came

out they were full of life, buoyed up with the nervous excitement of the realization that the greatest invasion in history was about to start and they were an integral part of it. I remember when they went into the briefing it was pitch dark outside and if I remember correctly it was even drizzling. In all, it looked like a poor send-off as far as weather was concerned. Then, just as the pilots came out to their trucks, the clouds parted and a bright cold moon lit up the whole field. The men stood gathered around the trucks for the regular post-briefing prayer. It was a moment that I for one will never forget. There wasn't a sound anywhere on the field or in the air. It was one of the holiest moments I have ever felt as I led those men in prayer. I remember Howie Fogg remarked about the same thing later on in the day. That was group "A." An hour later group "B" met for briefing and again we had that same experience of a holy moment. I'm a chaplain and yet I can't explain it. Perhaps it was the knowledge of the invasion, or the sudden clearing of the sky, or the knowledge that some of these men wouldn't live through the week, whatever it was in those two early morning briefings, we were at a holy moment in the history of our individual lives, our group, and our nation.

"Most of my time was spent with the pilots this month, but I can't close this report without recording the effect of D-Day on our ground personnel. It was a "shot-in-the-arm" to us all. All gripes, beefs, ill feeling seemed to have been momentarily forgotten, and they worked together as a team more successfully than ever before. They couldn't fly. They couldn't share the danger and risk their lives, but what they could do they did, and did it well. Our ground crews went without sleep hours on end. They stayed up night after night, stayed on the job hour after hour, to keep those planes in the air. Working with eyes red from lack of sleep, stomachs upset from irregular eating periods, bodies fatigued from lack of rest, the number of planes they kept in the air and the small number of abortions due to mechanical failure is proof of the magnificent job they did.

"It has been an expensive month. It has been referred to as a magnificent gamble. This is no gamble. If it is we had better quit now. This must be a transaction. We have paid the full price with lives, pre-aged youth, great sorrow. We who live on must now carry on and finish the task that they so magnificently have started. We must obtain full value for their sacrifice in peace, security, justice, and freedom."

HEADQUARTERS 359TH FIGHTER GROUP
Office of the Group Historian
APO 637 / US Army
4 July 1944

History of the 359th Fighter Group, June 1944

June of 1944 was the month that Eisenhower stormed and breached the Atlantic Wall of Festung Europa in the greatest short-range operation of war in the history of man to that time.

In the great scheme of assault, the VIII Fighter Command, forged and tempered as the peerless high altitude fighter team of all the world's struggling forces, was slung into the rough and tumble of ground attack. Only their airplanes had the needed range before the cannon and the tactical air forces could be disembarked, and only they could choke off support from the Wehrmacht at the chosen storming place, the Cotentin Peninsula of Normandy.

So simply, this is the story of June for the 359th Fighter Group. With the 14 other groups of the Eighth Fighter Command, they isolated Normandy, hacked and splayed the German plan of reinforcement and counterattack, and held off the Wehrmacht while ships and men tore open a bloody hole in Western Europe.

It was expensive. Fourteen pilots were lost on tactical missions, 11 of those in the first 7 days of crisis, and this was one-sixth of the 359th Group's normal pilot strength. Yet the total casualties for the month of 17 men, 16 operationally, was below the toll of May, and was well under the depletions suffered by other groups.

These are statistics, and they did not cushion the emotional shock of the grim second week of June, when 21 missions in 7 days cost 11 pilots, when foul weather, flak, fatigue, and warring enemy aircraft raised the normal odds against ground strafing to a great and nerve racking hazard.

Ten old pilots and seven replacements vanished from the mess at Wretham Hall, and new pilots fresh from replacement depots flooded in: faces changed and "originals" found themselves sitting at supper at tables where they knew no one. Of the 86 pilots brought overseas, 46 remained on flying status at the month's end. The cost in leaders was high too: a squadron commander, an operations officer and four flight leaders.

Yet the job, the most important task confronting mankind it was believed at the time, was done, done gallantly, on occasion recklessly, on occasion nobly.

236

Totting up a list of claims to balance such a butcher's bill is not possible. Though there was no large combat against the Luftwaffe, the damage done the enemy was varied, a table of statistics which runs to such items as 16 locomotives destroyed and 31 damaged, 18 armored force vehicles burnt and blasted and another 48 damaged, and two ammunition trains wrecked in flooding pyres of smoke and flame and noise. The 128,000 rounds of armor-piercing incendiary ammunition fired, with the 97 tons of bombs aimed and dropped, certainly harmed the enemy.

The more important fact was that this discourse of projection upon the German was achieved in an unrelenting snarling patrol of every highway and every railroad upon which his troops tried to move to their trapped and dying fellows at Caen, Carentan and Cherbourg. And that movement was blocked and crippled and delayed.

A summary of the work shows 43 missions in 25 days involving 1,469 airborne P-51s, 168 early returns, 1,301 sorties averaging 4:34, or about 5,900 combat hours. The invasion tactical work was not all; there were, for example, four escort missions to Germany.

This effort was of very great scope. On the mechanical side it was complicated by a number of factors. To begin with, and inevitably, there simply was not sufficient time allotted on some days for ideal maintenance or anything approaching it: some aircraft flew 10-plus hours of combat time on 6 June, D-Day.

The ground crews worked their hearts out in the critical days. But their job was complicated by deficiencies discovered in over-hauled engines: nuts loose, grease plugs wrongly inserted, mating surfaces on engine parts out of parallel, flanges warped, valve clearances wrong, cracked parts, all duly reported by Captain Hesser to higher authority. And at midmonth, the need of the Ninth Air Force for the best that could be had to fight the Battle of the Beaches meant that 80 of the best aircraft on the station were transferred out.

This entailed acceptance checks lasting perhaps 36 hours on the P-51B1s to B10s received in exchange for the B15s and C3s sent out. And these checks revealed insufficient oxygen tankage for our needs. TMI changes made in armament, gun sights, and shackles represented time consuming jobs that reduced the number of aircraft available for combat.

At the same time however, re-equipment began with the bubble-canopied, six-gunned, P-51Ds, on which all modifications were complete when delivered, and of which 15 were on the station at month's end.

Equipment otherwise was satisfactory, save only for the imperative need for RAF-type quick-release parachute harnesses, a need demonstrated once more in the loss of another pilot in the English Channel. Also, the dinghy flaps were flying open, it was believed, and those now were reversed so that the flaps faced in when the pilot sat on them.

Morale flamed high at the moment of test in the invasion. On the ground side, as the initial excitement subsided, there was some discontent at the limitation on leaves, which allowed furloughs only to combat personnel, and restricted all others to 24-hour passes within a 25-mile range. This may have had something to do with the minuscule rise in the VD rate, but it was generally balanced by steady improvements in the food, both in the rations provided and in the quality of the preparation. The mail stopped, or almost so, during the invasion but that was understandable, and letters flooded in a surge soon afterwards.

The weather required courage and competence of the pilots but on the ground it was, toward the end, a lovely if a rather damp June. The last converts from "long handles" donned cotton underwear as the days reveilled out to quite an incredible length of light. A soda fountain mirabile dictu was installed in the new Post Exchange, and although only "hand-made cokes" were at first obtainable, offered high hopes for the future. The calibre of motion pictures at the still-novel Post Theatre was regarded as excellent, and the Red Cross canteen continued to hold a high place in the affection of enlisted men. For those remote from the combat pilots, and there were naturally many such among the 1,600 on the station, the chief topic was the Russian advance, which replaced the flying bomb as a main source of conversation.

The 359th held its identity in the strain of battle and casualty, somehow molding the new men to a pattern in the old tradition. Perhaps the character of the group, its atmosphere in fact changing and shifting, was to be expected under the impact of new personalities with new backgrounds.

At the opening of the month the 359th was the second most experienced in average combat time per pilot, its average of 152.5 hours ranking only below the 78th's 156.2, as opposed to a Command average of about 120. This was logical, as the 359th had sent none of its veterans home for 30 days leave. In June, the first such leave was granted Captain Smith on the 200-hour basis, and the tempo was so forced during the month that several other men rapidly progressed toward completion of the new 300-hour standard. This fact, and combat losses, meant a constant stream of promotion and duty-assignment changes.

As for other rewards and official notice of brave work well achieved, there were two Silver Stars (Lieutenant Colonel Murphy for his fine 4 March performance and First Lieutenant Burgsteiner for the 11 April strafing), 17 Distinguished Flying Crosses and 15 Air Medals. The larger knowledge of duty done was in the hearts of the pilots fighting their lonely war in great hazard with great constancy.

With this preamble, here is June, 1944, at East Wretham, near Thetford, in Norfolk County, England.

This month began with a dull Thursday enlivened for duty personnel in the hours before dawn with a vivid electrical display in the southern skies that misled some too-eager citizens into believing they had first view of: a) the biggest German raid of the war; b) a novel battle; c) the invasion. The rumble of thunder broke this spell, and it turned out to be the only fillip of the day, a somber affair with a dull overcast in which a release finally arrived at 1355. The whole Eighth Air Force was grounded, save for 29 special sorties.

2 June was the same kind of day, with an early release to 1200, but at 1330, FO 359 arrived. Dinner was moved up to 1700, for a briefing at 1740, with 43 aircraft up at 1905 to escort 3rd Division B-17s to marshalling yards in the Paris area: part of the great scheme to cut the German links to Normandy. The job was uneventful save for the late return (2228) and the high VHF standard by this time taken for granted; contact with Lieutenant Dover, the Walcott Hall controller, was never lost although the extreme range was 275 miles.

There was no show on the 3rd, although Command put up 451 fighters on the Pas de Calais efforts. Colonel Tacon was summoned to AJAX at 0730 on the 4th to hear the plan from General Kepner, and secrecy or no, every single echelon seemed to be checking, by phone and teletype, with Captain Swiren to assure themselves he really was changing crystals so that the 359th Group could be controlled by "Oilskin" at the 66th Wing (Sawston Hall).

This was part of the scheme known as "High Flight," by which only P-38s, because of their distinctive silhouette, would be used over the invasion shipping. All P-38 groups were to be under control of the 67th Wing, which concurrently gave up control of its own P-51s. The switch in crystals was made on this Saturday night, 3 June.

First flight under 66th Control came next day, on the 4th, FO 367, with more of the diversion bombing used to pin Rommel's forces in Picardy. The 359th was up at 1345, and all was routine until Lieutenant Cater was forced by lack of oil pressure, long-time bogey of the 368th pilots, to bail out 20 miles southeast of Folkestone. Cater, former Navy air gunner, father of two fine children, a serious and mature man, had conquered stomach ulcers to stay at Camp Kilmer. He had been ill again in England and had given up his beloved cigars in the struggle with malfunctioning digestion.

Although, as an old sailor he should have had a better chance than anyone in the water, the last heard from him was his call at 1452, "I'm at 12,000 and gliding to 5,000 and I'm going to bail out." Lieutenants Perkins and John S. Marcinkiewicz followed his chute down until it hit the water and three Spits, four P-47s, a Warwick, and two launches were on the spot almost at once, but all they found was a seat cushion and half-inflated dinghy. Apparently Emer had lost his dinghy in the water.

That afternoon there was a second and hurried mission on FO 368, with Colonel Swanson leading the A Group and Captain McKee leading the B Group in escort of bombers striking at airdromes and marshalling yards at Paris. Up at 1916, the trip home was a race against gathering darkness, which was closing in at 2152 but at 2215 all were home. Bomb results were good.

Colonel Tacon came back to Wretham that night. While with the other group commanders in General Kepner's office, that Sunday afternoon the phone had rung with the news that SHAEF had postponed the great gamble another 24 hours.

June 5 opened with a chilly morning which succumbed later to a warm sun. Nine other groups were airborne but at Wretham the day was quiet until the alert flight was scrambled at 1242 for a test, to be followed at 1245 by a meeting of Colonel Tacon with his staff and the station commanders.

All passes and off-station traffic were stopped, phones leading off the field were cut off, 125 civilians building RAF installations were informed they would not be able to leave that night, the military police were alerted, and crews began painting the broad black-and-white invasion zebra stripes on the aircraft. In the midst of all this, Lieutenant Colonel Cecil Hahn, Eighth Air Force historian, arrived and decided to stay and see what developed on an operational station, though no one could give him any assurance this was not another of the innumerable tests, fakes, dry runs and assorted feints with which SHAEF had been tantalizing the Germans and testing its own preparation for so many months.

At 0930, intelligence officers were called to make up new squadron maps of the invasion flak defenses of England and to begin to put up "Plan Fullhouse" on the briefing map. The Colonel spent the evening briefing his squadron commanders. Before dark, the alert flight was airborne, since this, if ever, was the night for General Student's Nazi paratroopers to strike. The alert quartet was down at 2305, and the RAF took over the patrol.

At once, the ground crews were alerted and told to stand by their airplanes, but before that there was a memorable briefing by Colonel Tacon.

It began at 2400, 5/6 June, with the same momentous four words echoing that night through hundreds of stations over the island, "Gentlemen, this is it."

That briefing embraced the whole sweep and range of Plan Neptune, General Eisenhower's bold, simple, direct plan of attack interwoven with a hundred crafty tricks. No one, save the pilots who were to go on the first before-dawn mission and intelligence officers, were at that briefing, which lasted 105 minutes and scanned through the whole of the scheme of beach and sea assault and air attack, with recognition, rescue, evasion, and escape, with all the multiple directives from SHAEF, from Command, from Wing.

Aircraft were in short supply. So were pilots. The stock must be hoarded but some missions, the Colonel said, would have to be flown, and this was one of them. The weather was grim outside, and worsening, but go they must, even if they had to go to the allotted area at the southwest corner of Normandy individually. He said: "At 4 o'clock this afternoon, General Eisenhower pushed a button and the greatest assaulting force in history began to move. If this attack that is beginning tonight does not succeed, you all know the war may be prolonged three years. It must succeed. It cannot succeed without us. Air power will not get the credit if it succeeds, but you know and I know that without air cover, constant air cover, and air superiority, constant air superiority, the men in the boats can't win. They've got to win, we've got to be there to give them their chance. Tonight begins a time we'll tell our grandchildren about, and say: "I was there, I helped it happen."

The weather gods were kind . . . the clouds broke for take off, the moon appeared and the mission (33 pilots of the 368th Squadron and 369th Squadron) was off at 0242 into a glorious moonscape. But this was only local; a few miles away at Bodney, the weather was vile and a pilot took off into the control tower, and the 359th pilots had to fly through an overcast night slicing through wheeling and formatting bombers. By God's grace there were no collisions in the murky East Anglian skies for the 359th Group that night.

At Wretham, too, the clouds closed in immediately after take off and it was raining bitterly as the 370th Squadron pilots and the other pilots arrived at 0330.

A little earlier, at 0310, AJAX, had warned Captain Donohue that the second effort might have to be airborne earlier than expected. Colonel Murphy, who was to brief and lead this second show, accepted the news without emotion. He himself was drenched with the rain but he turned at the open door, stared back at the driving black night rain and said "I don't know how many can get through it, but we'll have to go."

Again, the weather cleared for take off, and the morning was beautiful with the afterglow of dawn at 0548 when Colonel Murphy took-off his aircraft. The briefing at which he had presided was unforgettable for the atmosphere created by the Colonel's moving intellectual effort to bring all the pilots into his mind and share with them the great concept of the assault. Part of it was very much in the normal mood of the Colonel, who was, in the great Gaelic tradition of the warrior, remote, polite, savage. As, in discussing the weakness of the force he would bring to the beaches, "If you think you have engine trouble, think of the men in the 4,000 landing ships, and make sure in your soul the trouble's in the engine." But the real drama of the briefing room that morning was summed up in a sudden curious surge of emotion at the end. "Fellows," the leader said directly, the strange word very normal and natural, voice suddenly abashed and weary, "I hope I've told you everything about this plan I should. I've lived with it for hours getting ready for this briefing. I want you to know what's at stake." He paused and looked at the faces of his men. What he saw there was good. There were no questions, and the briefing was over.

So the air umbrella was raised up. Perhaps the radar eyes were blinded. Perhaps the feints and the fakes had hypnotized the Luftwaffe into fear of a wrong move. Perhaps it was high policy not to attack the landing craft when they were most vulnerable. Perhaps the radar screens already wrote out the tale of the strength of the fighters patrolling the clouds and dark in the great aerial blockade of Normandy. At any event, the Luftwaffe did not fight, the beaches were isolated by air, and the landings were made. Thus the story of the Atlantic Wall.

For the pilots, it meant hearts-in-mouth dodging in the dark amid clouds of B-17s and C-47s, it meant hours in the dark, wondering what they would or could do against Hun night fighters, it meant the occasional far-off flash of the pre-assault final bastinado of the beaches, then the dawn, and the lifeless roads and railroads below. The first mission was up 6 hours 45 minutes, the second, 6 hours 35 minutes.

Back at base, the first news was the flash at dawn that 700 troop carrier planes had dropped their men successfully. This was raised to 1,000 soon after, and the whirling rush of fighter-bomber work then engulfed the station. Part of the Ninth Fighter Command was embarked. The RAF was assigned the beaches and the assault area. The weather was not right for the heavies, and it was left to the Eighth Fighter Command to blockade the roads, rails, and canals feeding the German lines.

There were four more missions on the 6th of June, and three were fighter-bomber attacks on roads in the south. The control sheet listing the work, the claims, the losses, does not catch the hurried atmosphere of one quick briefing after another, of the periodic counts of men and machines still fit for combat, of who was sleeping and who was ready. In the midst of it, Colonel Tacon fell ill of a cold, to be followed by Colonel Tyrrell, and both were sent to bed.

The bombing that first day was erratic. Used to dive-bombing with instant fusing, the attempts to skip-bomb lacked technique, and pilots were disheartened to see their delayed-action 500-pounder glance off targets without exploding, but they stopped everything that moved by day and they learned the new bombing way quickly, and there was always the madly ferocious strafing, repaying the Germans for Poland, Flanders, Greece, and Crete.

Everything was on the cuff: changes in plan, orders to go, to stay, reports. There were no mission summaries. Fighter Command issued no narrative. The Air Force summary, necessarily condensed, sketched only the outline.

The first mission was from 0245 to 0930, the second from 0550 to 1225, the third (ordered at 0724) from 1048 to 1450, the fourth from 1151 to 1603, the fifth from 1318 to 1646. All the last three went to the same area but the sixth mission of the day was Royal Flush; protection for airborne reinforcements. Colonel Swanson led that one (the 369th exploded a 40-car ammunition train near Beille) and take off was not until 1805, with landing not complete until 40 minutes before midnight. For some of the pilots, it was their first night landing in England and their first night landing in a P-51.

So D-Day ended, and though Command lost 26 pilots, the 359th Group had come through unscathed, fearfully tired, but proud of the job, their lives-on-the ground focused on sleep and the bomb line.

That first day amazing things were done by pilots and mechanics alike. The D-Day performance of Bob Pherson (11 hours 25 minutes in the air), John Oliphint (11:40), Herbert Burton (11:25) and Posty Booth (11:15). Only Burton was to survive the week. As for aircraft, IV-A of the 369th Squadron flew 16 hours on 6 June and that was topped by four aircraft in the 368th Squadron, where CV-U was airborne 16:55. The 359th Group as a whole flew 136 sorties in 6 missions covering 21 hours.

The drive continued on the 7th. Lieutenant Borg personally blew up another ammunition train and the 370th Squadron found its first tanks, discovering with joy that .50 cal API worked on enemy armored force vehicles. This again in the face of weather so bad that Sawston Hall gave permission at 0420 for a 30-minute delay, and at 0444 informed Colonel Murphy he could return to base even after take off if the weather, in his opinion, endangered the 359th Group. At 0502, the Colonel took up 16 aircraft on Part II of the Royal Flush cover, but they could not assemble or fly in the soup and they were back at 0544, finally getting away for keeps at 0638.

Still there was nothing moving on the priority roads, but the 368th Squadron, up at 1019 with the 369th Squadron, found nine locomotives to strafe, as well as goods wagons, a roundhouse, a 100-wagon marshalling yard and three trailers of ammunition, which last exploded with a bang.

And wherever the pilots went, whatever their targets, they saw French civilians oblivious of the snarling death in the machine guns, waving at the silver Mustangs, fluttering scarves at the airmen, unafraid of a mushing turn, a jammed trigger, a swung bomb. The pilots were thrilled, but for the danger to their friends, especially when the Germans began driving cars and trucks in-between houses to get away from the merciless gunfire.

It was on this mid-day mission that Lieutenant Marcinkiewicz, a new and promising pilot, jumped near Fécamp. He was perfectly cool about it, trimming his airplane for level flight after he turned it upside down and only then jumping. Debris from an exploding target (the ammo trailers) had damaged his engine, it seemed.

That night Colonel Swanson took the 359th out to cover the heavies attacking airfields and bridges in the western end of the Seine-Loire quadrant. There again was no enemy opposition but the pilots saw all the towns of France ablaze, with smoke to 15,000 feet over Falaise, Avranches, Vire, Argentan, and Domfront. The Germans were moving on the ground, but haze cloaked and veiled them.

So ended the second day, with the last plane in at 2227. And despite the tempo of the work there were 52 aircraft ready for new operations at midnight, a tribute to the sleepless ground crews and crew chiefs and their work.

On D plus 2, the heavies went after the bridges over the Loire, seeking to snap the fabric of the railroads there as medium bombers had previously chopped every line over the Seine.

There was a FO (377) but it was not in until 0425 and the effect was a hurried briefing at 0515 by Colonel Murphy.

Again the weather was execrable, haze and low ceiling, but Colonel Murphy discussed all that in a memorable line ("Weather is weather, and all weather is bad.") and by 0627, when 45 planes took off, the mist had in fact cleared, although scud and mist rolled back over the field for the landing at 1150. There was a great score for strafing, especially in the 369th

Squadron, which caught a German convoy control point at a crossroads and wiped out 26-odd vehicles.

But by now the Germans had light flak guns by the dozen at every vulnerable point, and there were two losses, First Lieutenant Benjamin M. Hagan III, one of the 368th Squadron originals, and Lieutenant Robert B. Sander, of the 369th. Sander was believed to have crashed in the woods near the control point but Hagan jumped after being hit in a wild strafing bee on a train southeast of Breteuil. The tall, lean, dour-faced jokester owned a questing mind, fortified by a rare depth of spirit. Aged 19 when he arrived in England, he had lived a curiously full life, although all of this was customarily masked in the prankery by which he was best known. He habitually explained he had become a fighter pilot to escape the perils of the explosives plant where he had been working and it was usually impossible to decide at what, if any point, his fantasies ceased to be fact. Two friends, Earl Perkins and Bill Simmons, followed him down and though his chute was afire when he jumped, both saw it later, empty, in a field.

There was bomb loading for the second mission of the 8th; low squadron to carry 500-pounders, middle squadron 250s, top cover 100s. Although the 359th had not yet encountered the Germans, there were Nazi hot shots roaming the edges of the assault area, bouncing flights intent only on bomb and strafe, and every field order and every briefing stressed and hammered at the danger of overconfidence, of forgetting that Germany still had 1,100 fighters in the west, even though he was hoarding them.

The bombing was better on this mission led by Colonel Swanson and all came home safely, but the third effort cost two splendid pilots. The afternoon mission (11th in three days) was down at 1643 and the next briefing was underway soon after that for an 1827 take off. Colonel Murphy told the pilots that the morning formation on the way out was the best he'd ever seen but that the pilots were tired, beginning to wear from fatigue, that this showed in tightening voices, in needless radio chatter, that each must protect all against this fatigue, that all must join in the conscious effort for better control.

The marshalling yards at La Flêche were bombed, and trains were bombed and strafed on this mission, again flown in wretched weather, so wretched that the recall went out after the 359th Group had been in its area 20 minutes. They stayed in to finish the job and came back at 2215 in the rain under a purple overcast to find the field only with the help of flares.

Neither Posty Booth, the shy killer who had destroyed all of the eight enemy ships at which he had fired in the air, nor John Oliphint, perhaps the ablest ground attack artist in the 359th, came back. Oliphint was short of coolant and knew it, but as his engine died he elected to go in and use his speed to finish his bomb run on a train near La Fléche rather than to abandon the attack, pull up, and bail out. Pilots thought he had cartwheeled after bellying in. Booth was hit by machine gun fire from the La Fléche yards. He called in the hit on the radio. Later, pilots saw a plane afire in nearby woods. Whether he got out, no one knew.

On this mission, the 359th Group fired 13,323 rounds, making a total for the day of 32,936. The pilots were tired men that night, so tired that some of them were beginning to think of Benzedrine to keep themselves going, if this pace of 12 missions in three days continued. But the weather intervened.

All day on 9 June, the 359th, like the rest of the Command, tried to get off and at the Wehrmacht. It was not possible. FO 378 was in at 0635 but the 1030 take off was delayed to 1130, then abandoned and a strafe-bomb show was listed for 1500. At 1650, Colonel Swanson marshalled for take off but there was solid cloud over England and the Continent and Major Stevens telephoned from AJAX to say that unless a take off was possible without going on instruments, to scrub the effort.

One flight got up in the rain but was on instruments before their wheels were cased and the whole job was scrubbed. The dispersed aircraft were left with their bombs hanging after a general scrub order came though at 1711, and at 2205, AJAX ordered bombs off and wingtanks on.

Early on the 10th (35 up at 0708) Colonel Swanson led an escort of heavies into Evreux. The bomb scheme now was simply to crater the landing grounds and runways and keep them unserviceable. The fighters were asked to spot and flash bomb results.

Captain Fogg led the spotter flight, didn't like the system, and suggested a new one, which was telephoned to Wing Intelligence. Colonel Rogers, Wing A-2, presented Fogg's plan to General Anderson, who rang up AJAX, and next day's Field Order stipulated Fogg's idea; thus the quick flow of tactical ideas from the field.

On this early 10 June mission, the only claims were an electric loco and several goods wagons strafed by Fogg and his flight. But this was the opening of an eventful day.

The only mission actively resented by the pilots as "a suicide job" came up next, escort on the deck of four Photographic Reconnaissance Unit P-38s to the Antwerp area. The PRU pilots said they had not been able to get any planes back from the heavily defended lowlands. The 368th Squadron was ordered to take them in. Colonel Tyrrell, briefing, warned of the flak and told the pilots they could do little good attempting to intervene:

keep the enemy off the PRU and let them brave the flak.

But the compulsion of the West Pointer's code of duty, honor, country, led Captain Bolefahr to do more than that. As the squadron swept in over the Scheldt with the four P-38s they came under a staggering barrage: there were automatic weapons emplaced everywhere along the winding coasts and the railroads, and the heavy guns were in motion at extreme slant ranges. Bolefahr, slim, dark, kindly, courteous, a soldier in whom the sense of duty replaced the killer instinct he totally lacked, felt compelled to intervene. He was there. The Air Force wanted the pictures. So all along that blazing route he flew in the van, firing at every emplacement, drawing the enemy flak while the camera-Lightnings went off to the side, making their low obliques. It was magnificent; it was also death. "Bo" survived until 1410, four miles north of Antwerp, when his aircraft flamed under a hail of hits and augured in from 100 feet.

McGeever's P-51 was badly clobbered, too, but he got back to Manston. All four PRU's came home with, the group hoped, pictures of whatever it was they wanted. On the way back four locos were destroyed and another damaged, but it was a saddened group of pilots who sat numbly in the lounge at Wretham Hall that night, and the impact of Bo's loss fell heavily on every man and officer who had known him. Of the seven Academy men with whom the 359th Group had come overseas, now one was left.

Before news came back that Bolefahr was gone, the 369th and 370th had been dispatched after bridges tying the southwestern tip of Normandy to the Breton Peninsula. Colonel Murphy led the 370th against a bridge south of St. Malo, getting good strikes, and Major Irvine led the 369th against the fabric at Avranches. Hits were seen on the span and on the embankment, and the hunting improved for the strafing which came after the bombing.

Lieutenant Tuchscherer survived a crash-landing at Exeter on the way home and much of the 359th was trapped by a sudden rainstorm which brewed up so swiftly that the 352nd was driven in to Wretham, within sight, almost, of their home field at Bodney. Meanwhile, weather or no weather, at 1705 Swanson ordered an attack on railroads in the Conches-Evreux area. Wholly because of the enforced lay-off on the 9th, the situation was becoming critical. The German build-up of strength was progressing and now the order was to cut the roads and railroads for sure. The order developed one of the finest performances in the 359th Group's history by Major Cranfill, but it took some doing, the first problem being where to find the aircraft.

At 1845, when Major Cranfill briefed on the show, news was still trickling in from the stations at which the afternoon mission had landed, but the sun came out then and 21 airplanes got up at 1950. At briefing Major Cranfill had discussed a tunnel he had found on the map at Canches, reputed bitterly defended, and announced he could order no one to attack it: but he made the attack himself and, although the flak was precisely as intense as expected, skipped both his bombs into the tunnel. His wingman, who had to break off because of the flak, saw them go in, and PRU pictures showed the blast marks.

The mission also developed the first aerial combat the 359th encountered since D-Day. It was an eerie business. Everyone was on the deck "strafing," as the order ran, "everything that moves." Visibility in the haze and mist under a low ceiling was very bad as the evening darkened, and Focke-Wulfs began flitting by at 100 feet. Pop Doersch got one (his sixth) and Lieutenants Drake and Chester R. Gilmore another while Vincent W. Ambrose damaged a third. Drake, one of the first two replacements pilots, did not come back. Flak had separated him from Gilmore, the latter reported. Bomb results that night were good, tracks reportedly out, hits on bridges and trestles and choke points. Mist covered the field as the last planes came back at 2235.

After impatient days off ops, Colonel Tacon was released by the surgeon for duty on 11 June. There was some discussion about using a shorter delay fuse to avoid the glancing non-exploding hits which had plagued pilots risking their lives to get in on targets, but the usual 8-11 second fusing was employed on a hybrid escort of B-26s to Paris (and their flak evasion, pickup and go tactics, were highly educational) followed by 250-pound fighter-bombing of transport. The bombing was fairly good on marshalling yards at Poix and at Grandvilliers. Compiegne flak got Lieutenant Gilbert R. Ralston Jr. on the way out and he jumped five miles off the enemy coast. An A/S Rescue Walrus went in to get him under coastal battery shell fire, after Lieutenant Samuel A. White Jr., on DS with the rescue people, had circled Ralston giving the May Day. The overloaded Walrus had to taxi back, being unable to take off. Ralston was the first man picked up from the water in the 359th despite intensive searches for Cater, and earlier, T.P. Smith.

Colonel Murphy led the second effort, which produced splendid strafing and bombing claims. Perhaps the mission directive should be quoted: "Estimate in yesterday's Field Order Number 379 that the enemy had seized upon Friday's bad weather to rush all possible armor, supply, and reinforcement toward the beach had proved correct. The approach roads and railroads on morning 10 June were heavy with traffic in several areas. The determined effort of this Command on Saturday disrupted much of this and inflicted very great damage. A large share of the credit for the fact that the enemy's front line strength has not been seriously augmented is given by High Headquarter to the fighters of the VIII Fighter Command."

Thus stimulated, the 359th Group used 64 250-pounders and 15,463 rounds of ammunition on bridges, railroads, trucks, troops, AFVs, horse-drawn caissons, motor transport, a radar tower, and much else. The job cost another original, Bill Simmons of the 368th. He was last seen south of Caen near Bretteville. Lieutenant Robert B. Hatter saw a P-51 crash and burn in approximately the same area.

Again, the early morning mission of the 12th was taken by Colonel Tacon. It turned out to be escort of heavies to Paris, the heavily defended suburban airfields which were the core of the Luftwaffe's strength, followed by strafing. The strafing was not especially productive and the 369th Squadron blundered into a confused low level dog fight over the rooftops of Paris. Three pilots did not come back, and only one enemy was seen to crash. The missing: Bob Pherson, stocky, calm, reflective, whose promotion to captain came through on the 26th; Howard Linderer, a curly-haired, firm-chinned replacement pilot already promoted to first lieutenant and slated for bigger things, and Lieutenant L. D. Hess, one of the new crop. This loss, whether it was to Paris flak, collision at rooftop level or enemy aircraft no one knew, was the heaviest of the month and raised to 11 the toll of the first week of the invasion.

This 0638 mission was down at 1140 and 35 planes still were ready to go that afternoon, the first time that Wretham had a blue sky that week. But nothing developed until 1855 and that was only a warning order for next day's go. This, (Mission Number 130) after some early morning cancellations, turned out to be another bomber ride to Paris with a rush briefing and take off at 0630 in a cold rain under a gray sky. The weather was bad, so bad that a recall went out at 1020, but the group finished escort and then had to set down at East Coast bases. But at 1200 all were accounted for and a brilliant sun flared in the afternoon, letting the outliers get back home, where Captain Swiren's radio men began recrystallizing back to 67th Wing control, "High Flight" being over. All hands felt better to be back under command of General Anderson, a combat pilot, and a staff which acted as firm supporters of its tactical elements.

This day also, the 359th Group learned that flying bombs had been launched overnight from the Pas de Calais platforms against England; and though the new, fresh torment for the longsuffering people of England seemed a cruel trial in the last hour before victory, the gravity of the new attack convinced the last doubters of the worth and value of their weary hours during the preceding six months on patrol over the Noball and Cross-bow sites while the bombers banged away.

When the 359th was finally home, the work was speeded, which was just as well since FO 387 came in at 1700, stipulating a rendezvous time that required a 1738 start-engine time. Briefing was called at once, began at 1730, was over exactly at 1738, but rather than rush and stumble, Major McKee set back all time 30 minutes. The assigned area was patrolled un-eventfully, though Caen could be seen under naval gunfire, and Sam J. Huskins Jr. of the 370th Squadron landed for oil check at an emergency strip on the beachhead, the first pilot to make a normal take off and landing in France. He brought back four letters given him by RAF airmen. They were turned over to RAF security for Norfolk, S.L. Mason, of Norwich.

The 14th was a beautiful morning, the dawn breaking through scattered cloud, changing to an azure sky with delicate puffy high cloud glinting in the sunlight. Briefing was at 0515 by Colonel Swanson for an uneventful escort of the heavies to Paris (flak being intense as ever).

At 1345 a release arrived until 1700 (these brief releases were very help-ful, allowing maintenance and new-pilot training) but a late show was scrubbed and the till-dawn release arrived at 1547.

A miscalculation in the briefing time on 15 June led to an unholy rush. The duty intelligence officer that morning misread his table of distances in the hurried tempo of plotting, reading '110' as 1 hour 10 minutes, instead of 110 minutes. Consequently, briefing at 0650 was hurried and Colonel Tacon, leading, "poured the blossom" all the way in a squadron race to rendezvous, which was reached on time, off the Ile de Ré in the Bay of Bis-cay. The bombers were early and were eventually picked up on the home-ward track off St. Nazaire at 0925. The mission was eventful only for the magnificent weather, which gave a sightseer's view of new country, since the route back was out across Brittany.

At noon, Wing notified the 359th Group that the four-plane alert flight maintained since May was abolished, the danger of paratroop intervention to block the air cover for the invasion being considered over. On the after-noon of the 15th, a long distance fighter-bomber effort (one tank and one bomb for a 455-mile run) was planned but abandoned by Wing at 1445.

The 16th presented the usual overcast with a bad ground haze. The con-templated effort was against Bourges and Avord on FO 392. At 0838, com-bat operations at Walcott put in a hold order but briefing was as planned at 0910, Colonel Tacon devoting most of it to an analysis of the fighting abilities of jet-propelled aircraft and rocket aircraft. He told his pilots once more that "no one was ever shot down in a vertical turn," discussed the danger of trying to dive away, described and diagrammed the acceleration curve of the jet planes. He recommended that if the new propulsion types were encountered, to turn in and up to capitalize on the Mustangs' turning circle and superior fighting ability at comparatively slow speeds. New weapons must be expected, he said, reminding the men of the flying bombs. The mission, as expected, was scrubbed and conversation centered on the announcement that the B-29 at last was in motion against Japan and had bombed steelworks on the mainland of Dai Nippon. Incidentally, there was much envious conversation in this period about air combat against the Japanese, the general feeling being that, compared to fighting the Luftwaffe it was pretty much like shooting goldfish.

In any event, a job of work turned up, area patrol in support of B-24s over Ypres under MEW control. This long-range radar did not work well that day, there was 10/10 cloud, the controller could not pinpoint the 359th, and vectors were uncertain. Colonel Swanson returned early with a rough engine and Lieutenant Janney acted as Chairman for the rest of the mission, which was down at 1910 after a 1547 takeoff.

The first mission of 17 June was a curiously mixed up affair. It began leisurely with a telephoned warning from Wing of a Liberator escort with zero at noon. This was amended at 0905 as a 1300 zero. The teletyped FO was in at 0927 with the original 1200 zero. By phone, Wing said, this should be 1300. At 1043, the teletype said to delay all times an hour. At 1110 Wing called to say there was confusion about times. Were we adding an hour to the 1300 zero? We were, so fine, said Wing. Half an hour later, Wing was back on the line to revoke this and explain that the teletype merely confirmed the earlier delay, so Major McKee took 45 aircraft off at 1210 and made rendezvous late at L'Aigle, but did shepherd two dozen Libs out of the Continent.

Meanwhile, Colonel Tacon was going over the briefing procedure with 20-odd new pilots, describing what he expected of them. Captain Swiren discussed R/T procedures and codes and Captain Donohue described what the 359th had done up to date. This was an all-day "cram" mission, interrupted at 1300 by news that Major Wayne W. Brown, a veteran of Panama who had joined up five days earlier as group operations officer of the 368th Squadron, had been killed near Coafield in southeast Anglia. The loss, fourth non-operational death on the station, was keenly felt since the quiet, assured new officer had made a splendid impression.

A second mission, area patrol of Evreau while bombers attacked Tours and Laval airfields, produced nothing save a freak target, a weather balloon shot down by the 369th Squadron over the orbit points.

18 June was a day of great disillusion for the people of Germany. The Eighth Air Force went back over the Reich, shattering the enemy's hope that the invasion would divert the hail of explosives from their homeland. It was quite a show: 1,160 heavies attacking with 2,938 tons and the bomb aiming, especially over resuscitated Hamburg, was extraordinarily fine. The 359th's part of the endeavor consisted of escort to the airfield at Lüneberg. Rendezvous was at sea off the Frisian Coast after struggling against a 90-mile an hour headwind all the way. There was thick cirrus from 26,000 to 39,000 just before the target and touch was lost for 10 minutes. Luckily, no enemy aircraft appeared before escort was reestablished and maintained to the English Coast. Colonel Tacon led. A brand new pilot, John C. Allen, who had arrived at Wretham only two weeks before, made an extraordinary solo trip home, bailing out just inside the English Coast, in a quite remarkable story. He got home with the help of his tiny escape kit compass, and his engine, which signaled distress over Denmark, lasted precisely long enough to keep him out of the water. He escaped with a fractured ankle.

That afternoon there was intensive local flying, breaking in the new men. At 1450, an accident was reported two miles southeast of Wretham Hall. It turned out to be a Bodney mid-air collision, killing a flight leader, and held breaths sighed in somewhat selfish relief.

A fine job and another epic individual homing feat both came up on the 19th. The mission (FO 399) was to Bordeaux. Heavy stratified cloud layers ran from the deck to 29,000 feet. Some bomber formations gave up and two fighter groups also abandoned the attempt to get through. Only one group actually reached the target area to see the bombing, and that was the 359th, the 370th Squadron, and two flights of the 369th. The other flights escorted their bombers back when the heavies aborted. In all, though no enemy put in an appearance, 16 fighters were lost, and for hours it was feared that Pop Doersch was one of them. He was disoriented, with a bad engine, no radio, no compass, and frightful weather. But, after 7 hours 30 minutes of flight in his single-seater fighter, he came home alone. The key to his homing was his decision to keep the beach off his right wing, realizing that he eventually would find a recognizable landmark, whether it be Cherbourg or Schouwen. Pop also found what he thought was a flying bomb site and offered to lead some bombers back to it but his offer, forwarded via Wing, was not taken up.

This all was a highly commendable show, but, it was succeeded in the calendar by a failure, one of the few in the 359th Group's combat history. The day was 20 June, the mission FO 402, the target the elusive oil works at Politz, northeast of Berlin, and the enemy, twin-engine, rocket and cannon-firing Me410s, got in and out with a vicious, slashing attack to knock down at least 17 Liberators in the Baltic northeast of Rügen Island.

Briefing that day was called for 0430 and the pilots were awakened at 0345. The briefing was planned to give the usual 90-minute interval between briefing and start engine, but it was decided to cut this interval, so briefing was moved back to 0530 (to the disgust of the punctual arisers) and then re-switched to 0515 when a headwind developed. Take off was at 0610 and rendezvous at sea, off Heligoland, 11 minutes early, at 0801. The Lib formation was extended, slightly echeloned, and, after the 355th Group joined at 0900 near Cape Arkona, Colonel Swanson, who had been covering the front of the force, swept to the rear and port to pick up two combat wings of unprotected B-24s flying nearer Sweden. Then all Hell broke loose. The starboard side of the Liberator formation flamed and twinkled with gunfire, and up to about 80 Me410s effecting complete surprise, came in for a wholly free swipe at the bombers. The 369th, with Colonel Swanson, was out of position. The 370th tried to get up, but Major McKee's wing tanks refused to release and by the time he had turned the squadron over to Paul Bateman, it was too late. And the 368th, flying top cover, never did see the enemy attack from 4 o'clock underneath.

Only Captain Burton, with a new wingman, Grant M. Perrin, scored. They got one Me410, chasing it down. The 355th Group, which was in better position, also could not block the first attack, but engaged the main enemy body, getting 13, while the 4th came up to knock down 10, and the 357th destroyed seven Me109s at Pasewalk. Of the 34 B-24s lost of the 358 dispatched, 17 were credited to enemy action, 11 to flak, two to accident and four (believed landed in Sweden) to unknown causes.

The enemy had gotten in for only one good pass, true, and had paid for it (the bombers themselves claimed 10) but the standard of fighter close escort now was so high that the 359th felt keenly the multiple bad breaks that had kept it from the usual 8-0-16 against 80 intervention. Bomb results at Politz were good and the preceding day's fire at Hamburg could be seen 100 miles away, which was one consolation, and there was an anecdote before the day was out.

That afternoon, the command was sent out to find and stop a German Panzer division supposed to be moving up to the battle area from the Paris area. The 359th Group, led by Colonel Murphy, did a bangup job. Only one armored force train was found, but Colonel Murphy led 10 aircraft in four passes at Chalons at 1900, and the 368th ran a gunnery pattern over marshalling yards at Chateau Thierry. The cost was their loss of First Lieutenant Virgil E. Sansing, a soft-voiced sad-eyed pilot decorated with a magnificent Polish-cavalry upturning mustache. Recently promoted, he had established himself as an able pilot, a fearless strafer, and a good companion. Hit by machine gun fire near Levignen he got out safely and his chute opened. On this mission they burned up 18,779 rounds of ammunition, peak total for any single effort in the month.

Back at Wretham, the station was preparing to play host to the Ninth Fighter Command's 369th Group. The plan was to bring up the Ninth's Groups from southern England to East Anglia and ram a tremendous show over Germany, to push three wings of B-17s into Russia on the first lap of a shuttle run. This had been expected for weeks and there was much envy of the 4th Group and one squadron of the 352th Group, elected to go all the way as fighter escort to Russia.

Preparations for the 369th Group were complete, a new homer on their frequency, billets in a double Nissen in the tech site, messing and transport, spare parts assembled by engineering—when, at 2005, Wing announced the visit was canceled. The weather was worsening rapidly and the strafing mission came home under a dull sky with scud at 800 feet.

This wet mist endured the night and there was doubt at 0600 briefing on the 21st if the 359th could get off, 10/10ths at 705 feet. Colonel Tyrrell was chosen at the last moment to brief. He prepared himself quickly and did an admirable job in presenting a highly complex effort designed to baffle the German fighter controllers. At 0640, the weather was still bad and Colonel Tyrrell asked Wing if he must take off at all hazard. Then the sun broke through the rain for a brief moment, and when Wing called back at 0700 to discuss scrubbing, Tyrrell already was on his way to his airplane, taking off into the scud at 0719. There were blue holes south of the field but the air was so wet that the runway dust rolled up into a brown cloud at the southwest corner, hanging there until all 41 airplanes were up.

The attack was the most successful of the AAF assaults on Berlin and the Fourth Force under our escort lost no bombers to enemy aircraft. Escort was uneventful and 6 hours 11 minutes long. Colonel Tyrrell had set his face against careless attacks on unprofitable ground targets, instructing his pilots in the 368th not to strafe defended airdromes unless they were ordered to. But on the way out of Berlin he saw aircraft on a field east of Wittstock and, whether out of boredom with the long ride or a sudden decision that the profits were worth the risk, he took his flight down in a steep dive. Flak began coming up to 10,000, so intense that McGeever, leading the second element, broke off, but the Colonel and wing man Lieutenant James J. Lubien, went on in. Lubien saw perhaps 30 gliders and at least one four-engined transport before a flak hit shattered his windshield. What the

Colonel fired at, Lubien didn't know. He did know that his own airplane was badly holed. He called for an assessment and Colonel Tyrrell looked the wing man's airplane over, pronounced it okay, and then flame spurted from his own engine. He called, "I am going to have to bail out." Lubien kept on going, trying to get more altitude. The Colonel had at least 5,000 feet when his engine flamed, was a safe distance from the strafed field, was not under fire, and presumably got out safely. Major McKee, leading the 370th Squadron, took over the group.

Colonel Tyrrell, commander of the 368th at Westover Field when the squadron was only a cadre of enlisted specialists, without either pilots and airplanes, had carried it through all the difficulties of organization, training, staging and combat orientation. He was an admirable briefing officer, an unflustered air leader, an analytical tactician, and as a combat pilot had contributed one of the fine individual performances in February when he climbed to 34,000 to engage and break up a superior German formation, destroying two of them.

His loss, the first field grade combat casualty, was keenly felt not only in his squadron but throughout the group. To take over his command, Major Shaw, who had gone through OTU as operations officer of the 368th Squadron, was sent back from his group operations post.

Before news came through that Colonel Tyrrell had jumped, Colonel Tacon had already called a meeting of all the pilots who had aborted on the mission. The list of aborts had been growing, 10 on the mission to Politz and now 16 on the ride to Berlin. This had left only 25 men over the target, and enemy attacks were invariably coming in formations of 60-odd, plus more as top cover. Colonel Tacon felt strongly that airmen were primarily soldiers, entrusted with a gun platform, and as bound to go where and when ordered as any soldier. Yet the problem was complicated by the fact that a pilot with his radio out was a liability to the whole formation, that the earlier a man who was worried about his engine aborted the better (since no escorts need be sent back with him across the water), and by all the delicate interplay of forces which decided an airborne pilot unsatisfied with the performance of his fighting machine. At any rate, aborts dropped off sharply for the rest of the month, averaging four per mission or 11 percent, better than May's record of 15.6 percent and below the Fighter Command May average of about 12 percent.

22 June opened an unhappy acquaintance with an embankment, long bridge, short bridge, and tunnel at Nanteuil, France. The 359th went out to attack it with 500- and 250-pound bombs, being informed there was no flak there. The attack proved that the flak was in fact intense and two of

the first four men to make skip-bombing runs were shot down. They were both veterans of the 370th, and were the first losses in that squadron since the invasion began; Harold Hollis and Howard Grimes, both were believed to have crashed under the hail of flak. The rest of the group dive-bombed without much success.

Next day, the 23rd, sent 28 B-17s against the Nanteuil bridge. These fiddled about over the target until the 359th's gas supply ran low and we had to leave, but the 13 Forts which finally attacked didn't hit the bridge either. Nor, later on, did Liberators that the 359th escorted to Nanteuil on 25 June.

Before this third attempt on the bridge, Colonel Tacon, on the 24th, led in one of the more weird escort jobs. The targets for Libs that morning were Melun and Bretigny, the Paris airdromes again. But the Liberators flew an erratic track to their secondary, then they headed for Paris, and finally wound up dropping on Conches. Colonel Tacon went down to strafe goods wagons and the 369th damaged a locomotive and some box cars near Abancourt in a post-bombing sweep which uncovered nothing moving on highway or rail line in the Amiens sector.

So there arrived the morning of 25 June what was, in many ways, the most satisfactory mission ever flown by the 359th Group. This was escort deep into France of three wings, 36 B-17s in each, freighted with parachute supplies for the French Maquis, the bushwhackers fighting the Germans. The bombers' load made it the most novel job yet encountered. The visible proof of the existence of a strong French underground movement (there had been cynics at Wretham) was stirring, and the change from bombing and strafing to spy story supply-from-the-air was a lift. Moreover, the country that was covered, deep down east of the Rhone Valley, was new, and flying down the valleys below the level of the Alpine foothills jutting to either side was pure exhilaration. The drop zones were marked by signal fires and smoke pots, trucks lined along roads, partisans running to the packaged supplies as these tumbled from the B-17s at 3,000 feet.

This mission had started in some hysteria. Briefing was at 0515 and waiters at Wretham Hall were slow getting up, so that breakfast was hurried. This was routine enough for some pilots but it bothered others who liked a leisurely start (for a pilot's reactions on the preliminaries of a mission, see Captain Fogg's essay). But the day was glorious at take off, 0614, and the set-course formation against a white-flecked blue sky was perhaps the most geometrically perfect one achieved in 146 combat missions. The pilots were down at 1225 from this one and went back with the Libs to Nanteuil at 1726, Major Shaw leading 38 aircraft out.

Rain scrubbed operations on the 26th, the weather clearing somewhat in the afternoon, and then the month spun out to end in four bomber escort missions the last four days.

Creil marshalling yard was the target on 27 June. Plotting was complicated by a prohibition against any flying over southeast England, meaning Kent and Surrey, then suffering the brunt of the flying bomb attack. Originally a "Diver Defense Area," a "Diver Gun Belt" had been set up, with a three-code system limiting flight below 8,000 feet. Hundreds of balloons had been moved in south of London, however, and after a friendly airplane had run into one, the Command's planes were told to stay out, no matter what the altitude. A circuitous track was plotted and the mission produced good bomb results but nothing more, save an improvement in the MEW controller's technique, this being judged now satisfactory.

Colonel Swanson led this one, and he also led the 28 June mission to Saarbrücken. Briefing was 0530, and the last plane was down at 1054. Rain and lashing wind developed under a dull overcast 15 minutes later and a release came through until the 29th.

The 29th was the day the Air Force sent out 18 combat wings of bombers to Germany and didn't lose one to enemy aircraft; a subject for much felicitation by higher authority. Yet Major Irvine, who led 36 P-51s off Wretham at 0727 found a highly-confused and shapeless stream of Liberators over the Zuider Zee, fighter escort spread so thin over so many targets it was non-existent in spots. And there was confusion when the time came to break down to squadrons to escort boxes over Magdeburg and Oschersleben. There were so many stragglers that at 1045 General Anderson ordered off another flight as a special straggler party.

For the 359th it was all "uneventful." Lieutenant Lane of the 368th decided to jump at 1205 when his engine quit but managed to get his gasoline feeding again and stayed in, and Gene Craig's late flight spent much time over a stranded ASR launch off Ijmuiden, but that was all except that Lieutenant Lubien, making an emergency landing, made an emergency stop and nose-over which was regarded as an exceptionally fine piece of crisis piloting, averting a worse crash.

The 361st Group, in roughly the same area, made a killing on the ground, however, and the 357th found bandits near Leipzig, and none of the Germans did get in at the bomber boxes.

That afternoon, Dr. Robin Williams came down from Pinetree to give an hour long questionnaire to 60 pilots on what they thought of their jobs, their airplanes, their assignments, their training, their food, and their leaves, a remarkably adequate opportunity for the discharge of beefs and bitches.

And immediately thereafter, General Anderson arrived to present Colonel Murphy with his Silver Star and distribute Distinguished Flying Crosses. The General told the pilots he was proud of them and the work they had done and knew they would "keep pitching."

The month ended with Mission Number 151 (FO 424), involving bomber escort to Le Culot, followed by fighter-bombing with 100-pound missiles. Transportation targets were assigned priority in the FO but the 359th found a luscious collection of barracks near Nieuport and flung 72 bombs into it. Nothing could be said with certainty without pictures but the results looked good, and AJAX was highly interested.

It was a good sign; the new boys were old hands now. And they still had an enormous job of work to do.

10.

JULY 1944

Deep Into Germany

Saturday, July 1: London—Rain all day. Group released at 1000. Caught the crowded train at 1535. Keesey went, too.

Saw a buzz bomb hit just before reaching Liverpool Street. Lots of people on roof tops observing.

Took bus then cab to May Fair 2000. Nice room, #306. Cleaned up. Phoned Len Barry. His wife coming in for lunch tomorrow, he'll be home later in the afternoon.

Had dinner, heard Jack Jackson, a blind pianist. Good. My Canadian friend bought me Scotch as usual. Funny little guy. Then to bed at 11:00 P.M.

Damn buzz bombs keep a guy awake, a weird sound. Dirty way to fight a war.

[Since D-Day, 920,000 troops, 177,000 vehicles and 600,000 tons of supplies and equipment have landed. In the 24 days of fighting, 62,000 Allied men have been killed, wounded, or are reported missing.]

Sunday, July 2: London—Up at 1000. Swell <u>double</u> breakfast in room. Tub, shave, letters.

259

Met Mrs. Barry in the lobby. Nice lunch. Took the bus to Putney to their house. Len came in soon after. His mother was there, also boyhood pal, Teddy, who flew a Camel *(biplane made by Sopwith Aviation Co.)* in World War I. Had tea, cake, good Scotch, and then supper.

Took underground back to London at 10:00 P.M., in bed at 11:00 P.M. Buzz bombs and sirens kept me awake. Nuts!

[German troops evacuate Siena, Italy
    Field Marshal Gerd von Rundstedt resigns as Commander-in-Chief of German forces in the West. He is replaced by Field Marshal Günther von Kluge.]

Monday, July 3: Wretham—Rained all day. Took the jammed 0820 train back to Hall. Ate lunch. Wrote letters. Was released until tomorrow.

Sat at the piano with Olson from 1930 to 2330. Some fun. He's good!!!

Wrote article on "Pilots Going on Mission" for Mike Donohue. Bed at midnight.

359th Fighter Group combat intelligence officers: Captain Maurice F.X. Donohue, Major John R. Fitzpatrick, Lieutenant Philip R. McTiernan. *Courtesy of Anthony C. Chardella: Archived by Char Baldridge, Historian, 359th Fighter Group Association*

Tuesday, July 4: Wretham—Weather fair to middlin'. Quite warm for a change. A mission flown in the morning but we weren't on it. After lunch we were told that our briefing was scheduled for 1815, so played a ball game. Cliff pitched one of his best games but they lost; no hits, and no pep. The 370th versus 368th, 8 to 2 loss. We just haven't got a ball club, never have had, never will have.

We were briefed to escort heavies via Type 16 around St. Omer, St. Quentin area. Mission was scrubbed while we were being briefed. So training flying instead. Les Hovden, our new "A" Flighter from Iowa, a nice guy, took his first hop in England alone. Nice landing.

Green Hornet II will be ready in the morning. I painted the crews' names on her.

I had cooks fix up eggs and toast at 10:00 P.M. when six returned from their local transition flights.

Wednesday, July 5: Wretham—Up at 0530. Briefing at 0615.

A nice summer morn. Some cumulus.

Our mission: A short escort of about 100 B-24s to targets north of Paris. We headed in at the beach head west of Le Havre, out near Dieppe. A three hour run. I led the squadron. Chatfield flew my wing damn well. His first trip. Janney and Ash good as element. Flew the old *Green Hornet* at 31,000 feet as top cover. She's still sweet as ever.

Flew the new *Green Hornet* this afternoon; Les flew the old one. Fired guns. Buzzed a few of the heavy 5/10ths cumulus. I like my new ship okay but it's hard to work the canopy. Les flew a perfect wing.

I felt lousy, though. My head ached again.

F-133 played Honington here. Shaw pitched. We won 6 to 5. Fed the boys supper at the Hall.

Charles Mosse is okay, a POW. Swell news!!

Captain Charles W. Mosse. *Photo courtesy of Paul D. Bruns, 369th Fighter Squadron Flight Surgeon: Archived by Char Baldridge, Historian, 359th Fighter Group Association*

Thursday, July 6: Wretham—A beautiful summer day. Warm. A few cumulus clouds. Lovely!

Two missions:

1) 0730 take off to Kiel. Escort led by Forehand. No enemy aircraft. Four and one half hours.

2) 1840 take off to Pas de Calais (Cambrai). Type 16. Major Shaw led. No enemy aircraft. Three and one quarter hours.

Lubien flew my ship this morning. Hunter took 'er up for the night mission. Both loved it. I'll go tomorrow. Early warning order.

Tested Joe Kelsey's (F) B-10 tonight. Had vibration at hi-speed. Been to steel hangar, checked, and rechecked. Finally took off radio mast. I dove her to 500 IAS, rolled her, etc. Beautiful. No vibration at all.

Hovden transferred to "B" Flight today. We have First Lieutenant Clark (the guy who took White's place at A/S Rescue has never even been here). Nuts!

Friday, July 7: Wretham—Up at 0445. Briefed at 0540. Escort B-17s to Lingen, Leipzig, back to Dümmer Lake. I led the 368th in top flight. <u>Very</u> hazy and we had trouble assembling. Got all mixed up east of Zuider Zee. Chrisman on one force, me on another, wound up in the same place. Six aborts. Flak scattered the rest in the haze. I wound up alone with Olson and Cavanaugh. A mess of a mission. Bombers all over! Lousy visibility! Out for five hours.

Flew *"Green Hornet II"* and she was very swell! Handles better than Bs at altitude. Up to 29,000 feet today just fine with tanks. Really a messed up shuffle over there, though. 8th Fighter got 70-odd enemy aircraft and we never even <u>saw</u> one. This goddam group is sure blind or somethin'!

Released this afternoon. Cloudy, showery, no flying. To station theatre for questionnaire on Pacific. Tired. Mad. Phooey!

> *[Four hundred and fifty Royal Air Force heavy bombers carry out a saturation raid on the German defenses in and around Caen, France.]*

Saturday, July 8: Wretham—Briefing at 0430. Wow! They woke us at 0345. I slept in since I wasn't on the schedule. Whew! They went to France, were back by 0900. No action.

It was a beautiful day here. A Texas cumulus sky. Cool with hot sun.

Delightful. Weather on Continent prevented a second mission.

Did some training flights this afternoon. Spent the evening on the range practice-firing our pistols. I was lousy, but it was fun lying around in warm sunlight for a change.

Received word from Nadine today that Smitty (J.B.) is a POW. Good deal! Wish we'd hear about Baldy and Hagan!

A lovely evening but a few showers at supper, however. Bridge is back in full swing here. A quiet day today for Howie.

Sunday, July 9: Wretham—Type 16 area support in Beauvais and Rouen. Briefed at 1115. Take off at 1201. Back at 1515. No action. Otherwise quiet. Weather socked in, so we were released.

Played piano with Paul until near midnight.

Pop Doersch and Ray Wetmore are all packed to leave for the States. Pretty swell. Won't be too long 'til we all get our chance.

Green Hornet II is running fine.

Dick Webb is in England. C.B. #28, Fleet P.O., MC-USNR. Located at Teignmouth, Devon. Sure would like to see him.

Hunter goes on leave tomorrow. Randy is still grounded with a bad ear.

Tom Raines P.R.O. *(Public Relations Officer)* read my paper on "Pilots Going on Mission," said he liked it very much.

[Units of the British 2nd Army enter Caen, bombed so heavily that it is reduced to rubble.]

Monday, July 10: Wretham—Heavy cumulus overcast with breaks in the afternoon at 1,500 to 2,000 feet. Clear beneath. Heavy showers. No missions flown all day. Had a warning order for 2030 but it was busted at 1630.

Played volleyball in the morning, Ping-Pong at lunch. Volleyball in the afternoon. Old versus new pilots. We beat 'em!

Joe Kelsey went to Flak Home in C-61 *(4-seat light transport built by Fairchild)* with Mac piloting. Lambright and Homeyer due tomorrow.

One of those goddam buzz bombs went right over the Hall roof last night at 0215. Woke me up. Hunter, too. Boy it was close! Whew! Dirty damn way to fight a war. London is increasingly unpopular with us as a place to go.

[The Red Army begins three offensives into the Baltic States.]

Tuesday, July 11: Wretham—Heavy overcast, scud-showers with base at 1,500 to 3,000 feet. Nuts!

Briefing at 0830. Escort B-24s to Munich (1,140 heavies) via Aachen, Mannheim, back via Strasbourg, Lille. Set course 1018 underneath the stuff. Climbed thru by flights. Group okay above 14,000 feet. Me, Cavanaugh, Janney, and Olson: Red Flight. Shaw, top. D-5s are nice instrument ships. One hour and 15 minutes out, the electrical system on my radio went out cold. Engine would quit when the battery was turned off. Nuts! So Ollie in the old *Green Hornet* led me home back down thru all the soup and heavy rain showers east of the field at 500 feet.

No enemy aircraft for group. <u>Heavy</u> flak at Cologne. Britton nicked in the wing but is okay. Everyone was split up by the heavy flak.

Janney has a D-5. Ollie got Janney's old B-7 which is good. A.G. is back. Lambright's a papa, it's a girl.

[The provisional French government of General de Gaulle in London is recognized by the United States as the de facto government of France.]

Wednesday, July 12: Wretham—Up at 0815. Briefing at 0930. Took off at 1110. Duplicate of yesterday's show in every detail but flight time. I led Olson, White, and Keesey. My #2 and #4 planes got lost in <u>very</u> rough air of overcast. Picked up Kosc for #2. Homeyer flew #4 later. Encountered heavy flak near Ruhr so everyone split up as usual. Major Shaw led. I became Blue Flight. We only had eight planes out of 16 for escort duty. Never saw the ground; went from here to Munich and back on instruments.

Couldn't release my left tank and it pissed me off highly. Then it <u>fell</u> off on my landing approach.

Sure was tired. Up for 6 hours and 10 minutes. A long ride. Plane ran fine, loads of gas.

Damn this lousy English weather.

Hunter is on leave. Ash set down at another field.

Thursday, July 13: Wretham—Briefing at 0600. Were to head to Saarbrucken but the weather was too bad. No take off. We were re-briefed at 0845. Shaw leading. Pick up bombers returning from <u>Munich</u> (for the third day). Cumulus and scud at 500 feet. Decks at 4,000 to 10,000 feet. Not too bad.

Tommy Lane went up in my ship. The goddam cam raised Hell and he had no power. He got within 10 minutes of Harwick at 150 m.p.h. and bailed out at 800 feet. A/S Rescue had him in 20 minutes. That damn plane!! Glad to be rid of her! The <u>old</u> *Green Hornet* still chugs along.

Heavy rains, cumulus, and overcast all afternoon and evening. Ollie headed to London.

Four new pilots arrived. "A" Flight, Barlett. "C" Flight, Boyd. "E" Flight, Barth. "F" Flight, Beal. Good boys all. 43-K P-40 time. We now have 38 pilots! Wow!

[The Curtiss P-40 Warhawk was a competent fighter in its day, but it was outclassed by the newer P-47s and P-51s. Although production of P-40s ended in 1944 they flew in combat until the end of war. As the newer fighters were rushed to the front lines, the P-40 also served a valuable role in USAAF flight schools.]

Friday, July 14: Wretham—Briefing at 0630. Took off at 0800. 8-10/10ths cumulus, low. Tops at 5,000 feet. Good above but hazy below. Same all day.

Mission: three wings of B-17s dump supplies for Maquis *(French resistance fighters)*, south and east of Lyons. Alps again, only in distance. Withdrawal from Moulin to mid-Channel. Shaw, top flight. I led Red Flight with Lewis, White, and Ash. Flew Bach's ship, a <u>good</u> D-5.

I now have Janney's brand new D-5, she'll be ready tomorrow. *Green Hornet III*. I have a hunch <u>this</u> one will be a winner. Seventy hours to go to my 300.

Janney finished his 300 today.

Lieutenant Raymond B. Janney III.
Photo courtesy of R. Hatter: Archived by Char Baldridge, Historian, 359th Fighter Group Association

Captain "Pop" Hesser is our new squadron engineering officer. Thank god they finally got rid of "Bull Shit" Stuart. Hesser <u>knows</u> his stuff.
   Tired!

Saturday, July 15: Wretham—No operations today due to heavy clouds. Some slow time flights. The four new boys all checked out fine. Beal and Boyd are outstanding. Cliff Barlett is from Manchester, New Hampshire. "A" Flight is still <u>all</u> Yankee.

   Wiley sent to Group. Stackler to us for captaincy. Wiley, naturally, is sore and wants a transfer. Kinda rough for him. Stack is okay, knows his oats.

   Good party tonight, some pretty gals for the first time. Weather cleared beautifully in the evening. I drank some Scotch, got sleepy, headed to bed at 10:30 P.M. with Ollie performing on the piano. All the pilots on schedule slept in the old station headquarters mission hut, holds 50 beds. The gals had the third floor to themselves. Pilots normally on the third floor slept in the beds of those scheduled to fly. Worked out fine.

   [The British 8th Army reaches the Arno River near Arezzo, in central Italy. The Italian government returns to Rome.]

Sunday, July 16: Wretham—One gorgeous, clean, warm summer day. Took off at 0700. Munich again. Five and one half hours. Bach led our squadron.

   Flew my new ship, fired guns. Barlett went with me. Then I headed to 30,000 feet alone. A sweet ship but something feels funny in the stick (elevation), otherwise sweet. Gun pattern beautiful.

   Lots of fun here at Hall, reminded me of house parties at Dartmouth. Gals in slacks, sunglasses, eating breakfast 'til 0900. Couples on sunlit terrace, pretty soft, wot a grand day. Very cheery interlude in life chez Wretham. Some of the dames were rough! Some good. Wild Bill Swanson had a queen. Wow!

   Ollie and I rode bicycles then played piano in the evening.

   [Allied forces make slow progress against German positions south of the Arno River.]

Monday, July 17: Wretham—Briefing at 0740, take off at 0850. Southeast Paris to escort bombers, then strafe. No action at all.

Five pilots are finishing up (Shaw, Hunter, A.G., Mac, and Bach). The rest of us were held back. Nuts!

Another gorgeous day! Back at 1400. Some slow time flying in the morning and afternoon for test hops. Another Pas de Calais Type 16 job took off at 1900. Landed at 2215. Eighteen ships.

Hesser has 22 ships in. What a man! Boy does he know his stuff, and really works. Mac flew my ship. They're gonna check that stick tomorrow. Hovden and Kasper went out; their first ride.

Kelsey is back from Flak House. Perk is on leave. Hunter will be back tomorrow.

This weather is wonderful. Been taking vitamin pills a week now and I'm feeling better. Test hopped Lewis' ship. Okay. Full day!

[While traveling by car to his headquarters at La Roche-Guyon, Field Marshal Rommel is severely wounded in an attack by a Royal Air Force bomber.

Fifty seven thousand German Prisoners-of-War captured in Belorussia are paraded through the center of Moscow.

The British 8th Army advances toward Ancona and Florence on the Adriatic Coast in central Italy.]

Tuesday, July 18: Wretham—Briefing at 0530. To Kiel on a four hour escort, target oil refineries. Back at 1030.

Rest of us to line at 0900. I test hopped Lubien's plane and it cut out at take off then ran swell and got off <u>fast</u>. Flew to Peterborough, Cambridge, Bury and so on in one-half hour at 500 feet. Sweet kite.

Released 'til dawn. Training flights and cross-country flights in the afternoon. Nothing after supper.

I painted my new ship, "*Moose Nose*," all afternoon.

Hunter is back from leave, Perk left on his.

Played snooker with Chatfield. Piano with Ollie.

Had a good air raid around midnight. Flak, lots of noise.

[The British 2nd Army begins Operation Goodwood, with the primary goal of removing the German Panzerkorps forces in the Caen area of northwest France.

The Egyptian government issues a request for a pan-Arab meeting.]

Moose Nose. Captain Howard Fogg's P-51D-5 Mustang CV-D 44-13762.
Courtesy of Ira J. "John" Bisher: Archived by Char Baldridge, Historian, 359th Fighter Group Association

Wednesday, July 19: Wretham—Briefing at 0615. Munich <u>again</u>. Back at 1245. Saw a couple of 109s but they couldn't catch 'em. Bodney got eight. Five hours and 30 minutes flight time.

I was up at 0830 and spent the morning at line, mixed paint for *Moose Nose.* Took out a four ship flight to altitude this afternoon. Me, Barlett, Ollie, and Barth. Went to 25,000 feet, flew formation. Rat raced back down to 2,000 feet, played tag with a B-17. They can really turn! Went thru very thin stratocumulus overcast going up to 3,000 to 4,000 feet. A damn nice flight. Both new guys were excellent. Ollie leads a nice element. We took it easy but it was <u>still</u> a good job.

Tired tonight. Headache again. Me for a hot shower and then the sack.

[The US 5th Army captures Livorno, a port city in the Tuscany region of Italy.]

Thursday, July 20: Wretham—Early mission to Leipzig, no action but heavy flak. Kosc got hit and it cut a hydraulic line, but he got back okay.

Training flights in the afternoon. Boyd landed at West Raynham RAF, a massive NF *(night fighter)* base. Had a rough engine and white smoke. Randy picked him up in the AT6.

Wrote letter and shot the bull all evening.

Colonel Tacon all pissed off at group, no victories, too many aborts, no guts. The Hell with that guy, he gives me a pain in the ass. He spent six months beating out all the spirit with his safety and conservatism preaching, then squalls cause Bodney *(home of the 352nd Fighter Group)* gets the jump on us. His own damn fault!

[During Hitler's daily noon time conference, a bomb explodes in the briefing hut at Wolfsschanze, Hitler's secret headquarters near Rastenburg in east Prussia. Hitler receives minor injuries, but Colonel Heinz Brandt, General Günther Korten, and a stenographer are killed, and several others are severely wounded, including General Rudolf Schmundt who later dies of complications from his injuries.]

Friday, July 21: Wretham—Early mission to Munich and (at last) there were a few enemy aircraft around our target. Colonel Murphy got a 109. Mac shot up a couple of trains. Gilmore bailed out west of Dover when his engine quit (coolant problem). May have been flak. He's in hospital. Mac down at Manston. Hunter flew *Moose Nose*, said she was okay.

Randy, in the AT6, took his crew chief to West Raynham to change plugs. Came back for me. Changed plugs, took off, then ditched it. Stinko! Leaking coolant internally so will have to change the engine. We had some tea, Randy brought Rinaldi back, returned and got me. I looked over a Moskie. Sure would like to fly one! Hungry; didn't eat supper 'til 2030. Tired.

[At one in the morning, Hitler broadcasts reassurance to the German people, telling them, "A very small clique of ambitious, dishonorable, and criminally stupid officers had formed a plot to remove me and at the same time overturn the high Command of the German armed forces . . . I myself am absolutely unhurt. I regard this as a confirmation of the decree of Providence that I should continue to pursue the goal of my life, as I have done up till now . . ."]

Saturday, July 22: Wretham—Released until tomorrow dawn. Lousy, cold, grey day. I let everyone sack in all morning. Forehand back as squadron ops officer, I'm transferred to Group Ops again. Nuts! Rather stay in squadron. However, who cares about what I'd rather do? Less work, more free time is one good factor.

Sunday, July 23: Wretham—To line in the morning, released until 1100. Went to church, Chappie was good. Got a pass from Major Fraley for Cambridge but didn't go. Lousy day again. Found an empty room in the Hall, #310, had a private bath. Made it into an "Art Studio" and painted a swell watercolour in winter grey, a train scene.

Group flew mission to Paris. Took off at about 1545. I remained in seclusion until about 9:00 P.M. Ate supper then Ollie came down. We played billiards until midnight, then piano. Went to kitchen with C.Q. for hot coffee, toast, and fruit juice. Swell time. Bed at 0300!

Better fun right here than going to Cambridge.

Monday, July 24: Wretham—Woke at 11:30 A.M. Ate lunch. Group off on a strafing mission to southwest Germany. They got some planes and locomotives. All made it back okay. Tacon led.

Ate lunch again, went up to #310 for the afternoon. Painted a large train, winter out west. Not bad, but not like yesterday's. Had fun though. That room is the nuts. Loafed after supper.

Captain Howard L. Fogg, Staff Sergeant Ira J. "John" Bisher (Crew Chief), Drozada (rank unknown), and Sergeant Creech (Armorer) with P-51D-5 Mustang *Moose Nose* CV-D 44-13762. *Courtesy of Ira J. "John" Bisher: Archived by Char Baldridge, Historian, 359th Fighter Group Association*

Tuesday, July 25: Wretham—Released all day again, my, my, vacation time. At line in the morning. Lousy weather. Good in the afternoon. We played the 369th a game of ball. Colonel pitched, me in short field. We won 7 to 5.

Talked to Bisher. "*Moose Nose*" is fine and has 52 hours now, a good engine. No oil leaks.

Tommy Lane back from Flak Home, seems fine. Hawk went down there this week. Must be quite a place.

Took a hot <u>bath</u>, ate supper, read, played piano, went to snack bar. Bed about 11:30 P.M. I gotta get more sleep. No brains!

[Operation COBRA begins, the Allied plan to break out of the Normandy area after D-Day.]

Wednesday, July 26: Wretham—Up at 0815. Good day, in fact one of those rare, good summer days. Released until 1500; there's bad overcast over the Continent.

At line all morning, wrote letter. Warning order in the afternoon, but mission scrubbed at 1600.

A very lazy day. Nobody at group did anything but keep a chair hot. Orwig left for the States today. He's a captain. Matthews also promoted along with Johnson, Ambrose, Hipsher, Perkins, Hawk, and Homeyer. Good to see them advance. Wish Hunter would get his, boy, he deserves it. No better guy on the field.

Captain John B. Hunter (right) and his younger brother Robert Hunter (rank unknown). *Photo courtesy of Anthony C. Chardella: Archived by Char Baldridge, Historian, 359th Fighter Group Association*

Loafed after supper. Sketched a C&O (*Chesapeake & Ohio*) 2-10-4. May paint it tomorrow.

[With months of fighting behind them, the Red Army recaptures Narva in the "Battle of the European SS," named that due to the large number of foreign troops in the German Waffen-SS who held the Narva line.

President Roosevelt is nominated to run for a fourth term by the Democratic National Convention in Chicago, with Senator Truman his running mate.]

Thursday, July 27: Wretham—Released again all day. No real news. Painted another train, darn good big one, C&O 2-10-4.
 Piano and billiards in the evening.

[US troops break through at St. Lo, forcing a German withdrawal from Normandy toward the Seine.]

Friday, July 28: Wretham—Beautiful day. Sunshine, etc. Up at 0400. Major Cranfill and I plotted (Pezda on day off). Briefed at 0530. To Leipzig for a five hour show. Took off at 0650.
 Tacon led. Saw jet-propelled fighters (Me163), the first reported in this theatre on ops. Four of 'em came in high to bounce our bombers. Tacon broke into their dive and they didn't attack. Went on down. He sez their speed is terrific, 600 IAS or more. Very small and pretty.
 A damn good party tonight.

Party at Wretham Hall Bar.
Courtesy of R. Hatter. Archived by Char Baldridge, Historian, 359th Fighter Group Association

Nurses from the 231st and 65th. All 50 of 'em American gals. A better, gayer, cleaner party with a terrific band from the 3rd Bomber Division. All the musicians played with orchestras prewar. Drum, bass, guitar, two trumpets, trombone, one sax. Piano player was with the <u>Hal Kemp</u> Band! Marvelous.

[US troops take Coutances in France.
The objectives of Operation COBRA are met.]

Saturday, July 29: Wretham—Up at 0500. Briefing at 0700. A milk run to Bremen with B-24s; water route. Pezda and I plotted. Took off at 0800. A front socked the base in at about 1200. Flights were due back at 1215 so they landed elsewhere. Only eight planes made it here in a hard rain with a 200 foot ceiling and 1,000 yards visibility. Lousy afternoon.

Wrote letters. Released until Monday. Ollie and I drank and played piano. Raided kitchen. Bed at 0100. Good "damp" evening.

[The final of a series of Royal Air Force bombing attacks on Stuttgart is launched leaving over 100,000 homeless.]

Sunday, July 30: Wretham—Lousy, damp, grey morning. Breakfast at 0830. Shaved. Went to church at 0930. Another good service. Chappie has a terrific personality. A truly fine Christian human being and regular guy. I like him!

Sketched in the afternoon. Weather cleared toward supper.

Loafed, showered, shampooed. Read in bed. A lazy day.

[Avranches, France is captured by the US 4th Armored Division.]

Monday, July 31: Wretham—Briefing at 0840. Took off at 1000. Pezda and Cranfill plotted. I flew. Blue Flight to Colonel Tacon. Me, Kysely, and Hovden (Lew didn't get off). We took off by flights at 300 foot intervals. On instruments from 2,500 to 3,000 feet and assembled okay above. To Munich again escorting B-17s. No action. A bit of flak over Belgium coming home. Colonel aborted so the 369th took over. Forehand took us in. I became Red Flight and Hunter joined me as #4. We escorted by flights. Wandered around from one combat wing to another looking for trouble but no enemy aircraft. CWs *(Combat wings)* all over the sky.

Up for 5 hours 45 minutes. Whew. Long ride after my layoff. *Moose Nose* just fine.

Ate a good lunch, had supper at 1700. Pork chops. Loafed all evening. Bed early.

[*US forces sweep past Avranches, France, forcing German troops to retreat east.*]

Captain Howard Fogg with P-51D-5 Mustang *Moose Nose* CV-D 44-13762.
Courtesy of Ira J. "John" Bisher: Archived by Char Baldridge, Historian, 359th Fighter Group Association

History of the 359th Fighter Group, July 1944

After the crescendo of June and the Invasion, July of 1944 was for the older pilots almost anticlimactic. The 25 missions of the month produced no large-scale air combat, strafing receded in importance, and the focus of interest shifted to the identity of the men completing their 300-hour combat tours. There were 17 of these on 31 July, of whom 11 were already in or on their way home to the Zone of the Interior.

But the complexion of the 359th Fighter Group had changed and the "originals" now were heavily outnumbered by replacement pilots for whom July provided pulsing excitement. There were eight long escort assignments to Munich, several in execrable weather, another to Leipzig, two to Merseburg and three to Kiel-Bremen. There was a strafing expedition to Leipheim, and another on French railroad targets. For the new men, this was a rugged introduction to combat flying.

In July, 31 more new pilots reported, and at month's end, strength was at a peak: 146 pilots, of whom 17 had finished their tours and were off ops, 2 were administrative pilots, 13 were in training, 9 sick, 5 on DS in England, 12 on pass, with 71 available for a mission.

The 25 missions include a freak job on 14 July, a four ship evening weather reconnaissance east of Paris with which Captain Janney of the 368th completed his tour. Disregarding this mission, the 24 jobs of the month resulted in 1,075 Mustangs airborne from East Wretham, with 193 early returns and 992 completed sorties averaging 5 hours 4 minutes each for about 5,400 hours of combat time.

The Luftwaffe still was hoarding its strength and enemy sightings dwindled. The total of 207 shown includes 100-plus seen in two gaggles by a single pilot on 20 July near Merseburg, the enemy obviously being late for a planned interception, and another sighting of 50 seen at 20-mile range over Munich on 21 July, when only Lieutenant Colonel Murphy's section could get in close enough for effective action.

Similarly, the 25 E/A sighted on 19 July in the Munich area were seen only by one section, which had dropped back on the task force trailing the lead assault elements, and the most profitable sighting of the month (three biplane trainers!) was made by a flight on 24 July, the flight driving all three of the antiques into the ground.

One sighting was, however, historic: the first operational use by the enemy of jet-propelled fighters, five Me163 Swallows being seen near, and driven off from, the bombers on the Merseburg show of 28 July, as Colonel Tacon's widely-circulated teletyped special report duly narrates. The same day four German daredevils, apparently Wild Boar night-fighters, got into a B-17 combat wing and the bomber's defensive cross-fire prevented our flights from following.

The aircraft claims for the month sank to 8-1-15, of which 5-1-4 were for air combat. All these claims were in the 370th (which also lost all five of the month's casualties) except for 0-0-4 twin-engines strafed on the ground by Colonel Tacon and a 368th section on 24 July.

As for strafing, the locomotive score was 11-0-12 but the most important achievement in this direction was the roaring fire started among 30 oil tank cars on a railway at Pont-sur-Yonne by Colonel Tacon and two sections of the 370th on 17 July. This elicited congratulations from Fighter Command but several other strafing jobs to be laid on after escort were abandoned because of weather; cloud also concealed Leipheim when the group hunted for jet-propelled targets on the ground 24 July. The month's ammunition expenditure of 37,670 rounds was only a quarter of the API burned up in June, and included such disappointments as the locomotive which hid in a tunnel from Colonel Tacon at Rouen on 8 July.

Of the five pilots lost, one was a victim of the weather, Lieutenant Bennie F. White who vanished in the Channel overcast returning from Leipzig on 7 July; Lieutenant Gordon M. Shortness was last seen in air combat over Gera on the 20th; Lieutenant Siltamaki and Flight Officer W.C. Reese were shot down on 21 July by Landsberg flak in making a triple-pass strafing attack there, and another, Flight Officer Walter W. Wiley, jumped south of Rotterdam on the 28th when he found himself out of gas. Siltamaki was growing into a flight commander, Reese had scored a probable in the 20 July combat, and Wiley was an enthusiastic strafer. White and Shortness both were at the beginning of their tours.

In addition to the eight long rides to Munich (one rendezvous, typical, being 30 miles from the Italian frontier, 260 miles from the Italian front line and 537 miles from Wretham), the month's errands embraced one visit to Leipzig, two to Merseburg, the Leipheim strafe-job and three to the Kiel-Bremen area. In France there were five Noball patrols as part of the counter-offensive against the flying bomb, three escort assignments on opportunity targets and airfields, the Janney weather hop, and one withdrawal support for bombers dropping supplies to the Maquis.

In addition to the five pilots lost, two others were forced by engine troubles to parachute. Lieutenant Lane had a fiendish time in the water off Bradwell Bay trying to inflate his Mae West and/or dinghy, but eventually abandoned his dinghy and got the life jacket opened and was picked up by A/S Rescue, in a testimonial to the worth of correct radio procedures. Chester Gilmore got back over England just before he had to jump. The bail-out was successful although again the dinghy arrangement, luckily not required, proved unsuitable.

Efforts to improve the bail-out equipment continued under the prodding of Lieutenant Colonel Swanson, and Lieutenant L.M. Major's report as equipment officer recites some of the steps taken in the attempt to get British quick-release chutes and a better dinghy fastening. Improved American equipment again was promised. Pilots also were measured for automatically-inflated Gee-suits.

Maintenance improved. Ignoring Janney's four-airplane mission, the 24 shows produced an average of 45 P-51s airborne, as against June's 34 and, although the number of early returns doubled (8 as against June's 3.9) the sorties per mission increased to 37, compared to June's 30.2. Part of this improvement was because of the continuing re-equipment with P-51D5s, and part of it was because of increasing familiarity by crews with the airplane and its Merlin engine. Airdrome dust and lack of potentimeters remained the principal problems.

As the new pilots flooded in, the problems of integrating them into the pattern of the 359th multiplied. The discussions on the group's history, techniques, tactical and weather doctrines, and briefing procedures were lengthened, flying control and communication lectures strengthened and the 370th Squadron produced its own special sheet for the new men. It was prepared by Captain Raymond B. Lancaster with the sections on formation flying written by Lieutenant Cunningham, R/T procedure by Lieutenant Lemmens and engineering by Captain Willis Dutton. Lancaster wrote the weather and combat paragraphs.

Colonel Tacon was dissatisfied with the number of abortives, mission totals reached 15 three times, 16 another day, 17 another, and said so, vigorously, but in the air the 359th flew better formation than it ever had, senior officers said, and on the ground pilot morale was excellent. Flak Home, offering seven days of complete rest and relaxation, was vigorously promoted by Captain Shwayder. Seven-day leaves were ordered more frequently and there was a resoundingly successful party at Wretham Hall for which the third floor was cleared to allow guests to remain overnight, thereby permitting invitations to friends in London. News trickled in slowly about casualties, although it was learned during the month that Charlie Mosse and Dick Broach were prisoners and that Bunky Hudelson was dead.

Morale among the ground staff, officers, and enlisted men improved with three developments: the Russian and American advances on the fighting fronts, withdrawal of the restriction of passes to a 25-mile zone, and a home-talent stage show, "Sack Happy." Another factor, less easily evaluated, was the extraordinary spate of rumors circulating among the enlisted men, sprouting at the rate of one a day and growing in fantasy. But for many men the problems inherent in the growing length of their absence from home had an aching reality, as Chaplain Ziegler's survey of some typical cases chronicles. At mid-month, classes in such subjects as map-reading were launched in a rehearsal of the military topics covered in OTU.

Although the weather summary tabulated by Lieutenant Platt shows a very high number of "Green" days, the sun in general was elusive during much of the day (the amount of sunlight for the month being counted in hours, it was so precious) and there was almost always much middle cloud.

1 July, in fact, produced rain throughout the night and early morning and there was no action, only nine of the 325 heavy bombers dispatched against the French flying bomb ramps getting in to attack. The 359th was not ordered on this show but next day spent an uneventful 94 minutes patrolling the Abbeville sector where 705 tons were dropped through cloud.

Three releases covered the 3rd, to 1000, 1500 and, finally, to dawn on the Fourth of July which passed quietly until 1410, when a FO led to a briefing at 1815 interrupted by news that the bombers had scrubbed, with a release soon succeeding.

On the 5th, another Crossbow attack developed nothing of interest. There was an early briefing for an 0735 take off. Wing notified Colonel Tacon in the air that the bombers were late so that the escort plan was lengthened and the combination of diminishing fuel and a low overcast canceled out a contemplated strafing of barges. This mission completed the tour of Captain Wetmore, the 359th Group's leading ace and first to finish the new requirement of 300 hours before home leave. He had refused several missions hoping to get a Berlin ride and a fight for his finale, but the bad weather and uninteresting assignments finally led to his accepting scheduling on this French mission.

Pop Doersch finished his tour next day, a Kiel escort on a beautiful day at base, with wisps of dainty cloud decorating a blue sky. The mission, off at 0739, was interesting chiefly for the herculean effort made by Colonel Tacon to save the crew of a Liberator he saw crash 40 miles northeast of

Borkum while on the way home. Nine chutes were seen spilling out of the B-24 and the Colonel and his section circled the area for 2 hours 40 minutes, calling up ASR help. The section dropped empty belly tanks for the crewmen struggling in the water and left when a Wellington came out and dropped a dinghy near the airmen. None of the bomber people survived to be rescued, however, and tempers were not improved by the fact that a flight of four 357th Group airplanes, which came out to relieve our section, found and shot down a Ju88 at 100 feet.

On this afternoon of the 5th, Major Shaw led an uneventful MEW controlled Noball patrol over Cambrai. The mission was not down until 2202, in the very apogee of the magnificent summer's night, blues lengthening into purple.

The weather held good, and after briefing by Major Irvine at 0540 next morning, the 7th, the bombers setting course to drop 2,383 tons of HE on Germany, could be seen wheeling in great spearheads over the field, sun glistening on aluminum as they headed east. It was the first time in months the bombers had been visible in such force, heavy cloud usually shutting them from ground view, and even on this morning there was a slight ground haze which cleared as the morning advanced. The target this day was Leipzig and, although the 56th Group found 12 Ju52s over Gardelegan airdrome and knocked down 10 of them, and the 361st encountered 34 single-engine enemy planes at various points for claims of 8-0-1, there were no Huns near our bombers and no sightings were reported by the 359th.

The mission of the 8th was slightly weird. Briefing was at 0430 on escort of two wings of the 3rd Division to attack two bridges. At 0505, these targets were scrubbed and Wing blithely announced the bombers would seek opportunity targets. Takeoff was at 0519 and there was much muddle in intercom with the bombers. A front with tops to 30,000 was seen moving north from Paris, further hampering the show. The final blow came when Colonel Tacon led his section down on a train and the locomotive popped into a tunnel near Rouen and hid there.

That night, ground crews worked late stripping the zebra invasion stripes from the upper surfaces of the aircraft, but next day produced only another undercast bombing of the flying bomb ramps, which provided uneventful area patrol, enlivened by the many RAF Lancasters and Halifaxes of the night force seen working in daylight with impunity, testimony of the air supremacy won over the Pas de Calais since the first Plan Eye Que of Christmas Eve, 1943.

During the late evening of the 9th, one of these same flying bombs from the Pas de Calais, using all its then-estimated 150-mile range, spluttered briskly over Wretham Hall, exploding 12 miles north in Covington Parish without casualties.

The sequence of attacks on Munich began 11 July, with wretched weather both home and over the target, although worse was to be encountered later in the month. Briefing by Colonel Tacon centered on weather procedure and setting course below the clouds. Going through the briefed three decks required 35 minutes, but nonetheless a new pilot, Lieutenant White, was lost in the undercast on the way home. On a sweep to Wiesbaden before the rendezvous at Germersheim on the Rhine, the 359th was under accurate flak fire of 300 guns for 6 sweating minutes. And this flak, in the Koln area, was to plague almost every Munich escort mission of the month. The precedent of an outstanding straggler support job was set on this first Munich show and was maintained throughout the month. On the way home, James J. O'Shea and Wilson K. Baker beat up trains in the Worms marshalling yard.

Another lowered overcast appeared on the 12th, again a Munich show. And once more there was a nerve wracking ride under well-pointed flak fire on the preparatory sweep, but all got home, one flight with a story of escorting a straggling Lib all the way to Luxembourg only to have it turn back there for Switzerland.

The weather on the 13th was even viler than the preceding two days at Wretham, rain in a wet mist with a ceiling down on the ground. It was the worst morning in months but briefing, again for Munich, went on at 0600. Wing, informed the cloud ran from the ground to 10,000 feet, could only say "pretend you're going to go," but at 0655, Major Shaw got through to Command and said take off was not possible.

The 359th Group went to "available," General Anderson declining to "push off" into the soup, and the 20th Group took over our part of the show. We eventually got away at 0925. Lieutenant Lund had to jump on this ride and Lieutenants Callahan, Baker and O'Shea did an extraordinary escort job on crippled Libs with wounded aboard, drawing flak in hunting out exit routes, furnishing headings by radio and acting as nurse-guardian navigators. The bomb people telephoned, and later wrote messages of appreciation and all three fighter pilots were recommended for the Air Medal. Another show, warned at 1300, was scrubbed 90 minutes later.

The 359th again missed a fight on the 14th. The mission was withdrawal support for B17s dropping supplies to the Maquis. At our rendezvous near Vichy, all was serene, but earlier on in the mission, the 357th Group had found 10 Me109s in the target areas and destroyed four of them.

That evening, a weather recco was ordered 40 miles east of Paris in advance of a 364th Group mission. Captain Janney took off four ships at 1648. The landing was due at 1908 which would have left Janney with not quite 300 hours. By a coincidence, his weather scouting was very thorough and he did not bring the flight back until 2002 which, by another coincidence, gave him enough time neatly finishing his tour. But in the interim, the weather report had been passed to the controller by radio so that all hands were happy.

Another Munich show came up on the 16th and although the weather at Anglian bases was generally miserable, Wretham had a beautiful dawn, marred only by a bit of haze, which vanished at take off at 0658. But over the Continent, 10/10ths clouds at 10,000 grew near Aalen into cloud towering to 29,000 feet. It was barely flyable for the bombers who became disorganized, but the enemy did not come up, there were no fighter claims, and of the 15 bombers lost, 12 were non-enemy.

Two missions on the 17th resulted in 8 hours 35 minutes of flying, including a morning strafing mission in which Colonel Tacon and the 370th burned up 30 oil cars and scored 1-0-8 in locos. The rhubarb part of this job was thoroughly pursued but there was no flak, light or heavy, throughout the enterprise.

That afternoon Colonel Murphy led a MEW Crossbow support job in which two pilots were officially "lost" although actually the 359th Group always knew where they were. Lieutenants Connelly and Caid of the 370th went into an emergency landing strip in Normandy and were so listed in the mission summary. Next day, the Group asked Wing for an official check on their safe arrival. That morning, the 18th, both Connelly and Caid came home, to be followed at 1500 on the 20th by word that Wing could extract from AJAX no information on the alleged presence of our two pilots anywhere in Normandy.

Also on the 17th, Lieutenant Robert E. Burton of the 368th led a special delegation of four pilots to Winfarthing, a bomber base east of Thetford, to be briefed on "Operation Aphrodite," a bizarre business of using robot B-17s. The show was scrubbed and all four pilots came back to their home station so thoroughly security-conscious they would barely admit to their own names. The Aphrodite experiment was still unmade at month's end.

After so much bad weather, an entirely glorious morning arrived on the 18th. Briefing was at 0530 with hundreds of bombers visible in the skies as far away as Norwich. It was the best ground-air visibility encountered in 10 months in England, and made an unforgettable spectacle as the dawn glittered like sparkling fire on the undersurfaces of the armadas of silently soaring heavies slowly merging into a great aerial train.

The targets were Kiel, the oil refinery at Hemmingstedt, Pennemünde, and Zinnowitz, with the 359th end of the show Hemmingstedt. Escort was maintained over the Kiel peninsula and back all the way to across the North Sea to Great Yarmouth.

There was "breathing trouble" again on this mission, a transmitter button being jammed (bugaboo of the first mission!) and this was repeated on the 19th, another Munich mission. There was action and air claims by other groups of 17-0-4, but the 25 enemy aircraft our pilots saw made one sweeping pass through the bombers and hit the deck so fast they were not caught, although our top cover squadron did see two of the enemy collide in their eagerness to get out.

There was an air score the next day, 20 July, on a mission to Merseburg for which Captain Pezda briefed. But only one section, led by Lieutenant Callahan, which dropped back behind the lead elements, was present when 20-odd enemy aircraft bounced the middle of the parade. Lieutenant Baker scored 1-0-1 and Flight Officer Reese got a probable. Lieutenant Shortness was missing from this fight. Actually, the pilots thought all three ships were destroyed but lacked the evidence to meet the formulae. It was uneventful for most, except for the constant increase in the number of early returns. By count, 23 came back before the mission was completed, but since two of these were for flak damage, with an escort for each and two others escorting a straggling bomber, only 17 were reported. Even so, Colonel Tacon took a vigorous line at briefing at 0620 next morning. The general tenor was that he wanted a more aggressive spirit, "the more of the bastards we shoot down, the faster we'll get home," and that he wanted decidedly fewer aborts, affixing very rough names to men who shirked their duty as soldiers and came home early if they were not in all conscience forced to do so.

The briefing had an effect; the aborts on this day, the foulest target weather encountered in 170 missions, shrank to two. The 359th split into two sections as briefed, and since the bombers also split into a solid stream of aircraft 15 miles long on a half mile front, definitely not as briefed, one group, led by Major Cranfill saw nothing except the weather. But Lieutenant Siltamaki, a jut-chinned Finnish-American boy new to his job, led a flight down on Landsberg, where 30 Ju88s were parked in rows and, in the intoxication of the attack, pressed home three separate strafing runs. The flak got him and Flight Officer Reese, but Flight Officer Wiley, who shot up a train in between bouncing the airdrome, got home to make claims of 3-0-10 for the flight.

The other group, led by Colonel Tacon, also was split by the weather and most of the flights were 20 miles away when an attack by an enemy force, variously estimated at 30 to 75, hit some bombers over Lake Ammer. All save one of the enemy promptly evaded attack but that one lingered to blow up a Liberator straggler and was itself shot down by Colonel Murphy, who came storming in with a section like the US Cavalry in a horse opera. Lieutenant Gilmore managed to stagger back to England where, at 1315, he jumped successfully under McGeever's calm coaching. McGeever, at the very end of his tour, celebrated by beating up two trains and destroying both locos near Sedan with Gilmore and Willis J. Cherry.

Another strafing do after bomber escort was listed for the 23rd after an all-day release on the 22nd but an undercast prevented. The weather again was frightful on the 24th, when jet-propelled jobs were to have been strafed at Leipheim, and neither the 359th nor 352nd could find the target. Thirteen of our aircraft could not even find the group above the overcast at base. Colonel Tacon, however, did locate a hole in Germany and strafed what he believed to be a glider-transition school for jet pilots near Ulm. Four twin-engine aircraft were strafed but did not burn. Nearby, Callahan's flight found and destroyed three biplanes and also damaged a train.

The 25th was a day off, a release at 0050 running until dawn on the 26th, and neither the 26th nor the 27th developed more than a succession of plans and cancellations. On the 28th, however, Colonel Tacon led the Merseburg mission, an early one, which resulted in the Jettie sightings. Flight Officer Wiley, who had shown so much dash, ran out of gasoline on the way home and jumped south of Rotterdam. Air-Sea Rescue plotted him and thought he was over land when he got out.

The weather was again sour on the Bremen mission of the 29th, and 27 aircraft landed at other bases after escorting all the way home to the English Coast. And the last ride of the month, again to Munich, on the 31st, found cloud over the target at 28,000 feet.

The 359th Fighter Group was changing, and after the interim period of readjustment passed in July, would increasingly take on the character of the new men. The "old timers" thought highly of them as pilots and believed they would also grow to be leaders.

11.

AUGUST 1944

Winding Down

Tuesday, August 1: Wretham—Same 500-foot overcast all morning. Briefing at 1045, took off at 1200. Me, Barlett, Lambright, and Chatfield: Yellow Flight. Maximum effort today! <u>Twenty-four</u> ships. Major Shaw aborted, Forehand took over lead, I took over Red Flight. Two groups of two targets in the shadow of Mount Blanc, St. Bernard Pass. Dropped supplies to Maquis from B-17s at 8,000 to 10,000 feet right down the rock-walled valleys. We didn't escort but instead patrolled the area where stuff was dropped.

A gorgeous trip, 20 miles to Italian border. Clear, a few cumulus. Mount Blanc is terrific, massive, and sunbathed. My engine ran rough, cut out, spit some smoke right over those mountains. Brrr! I headed for Geneva, but then she caught and held and I got her home. Very mad! A gorgeous trip though. Unforgettable.

Beal's prop ran away and he landed at a beach head. Cavanaugh's engine quit coming back (Perk's D-5) and he bailed out near Rivenhall okay.

Quite a day. I'm tired. Ten hours and 50 minutes of flight time in two days.

[The P-51 used a four-blade variable pitch propeller. If the controlling mechanism lost hydraulic pressure the blades would adopt a fine pitch, offering little resistance to the air, and the engine would speed up rapidly or "run away." If the pilot did not adjust the throttle setting quickly, the engine could over rev and destroy itself. Once a prop ran away the plane performed poorly and could not complete its mission.

President Risto Ryti of Finland resigns. He is replaced by Marshal Carl Gustav Mannerheim.]

Wednesday, August 2: Wretham—Same old 500 to 1,000 foot overcast all morning. Briefed at 1315. Escort in Paris area then strafe the railroad from Amiens to Rouen. Back at 2000.

Hawkinson was hit by flak while on deck, bailed out okay at 900 feet. A tough boy to lose.

A dull day for me, though. I plotted the mission, checked my plane in the hanger. Should be running by tomorrow.

Nuts on England.

[Turkey severs diplomatic relations with Germany.]

Captain Robert "Hawk" Hawkinson in front of his P-51C Mustang *Miss Janet* CV-N 42-103386.
Photo courtesy of Robert Hawkinson: Archived by Char Baldridge, Historian, 359th Fighter Group Association

Thursday, August 3: Wretham—Same morning as yesterday. Briefing at 1330. No strafing today, hence we lost no one.

Beal, that wonderful, coolheaded guy, stayed at the beach head. Talked 'em into a new engine and helped 'em put it in. They were only eight miles from St. Lo. and he was bombed out of his sack both nights by Jerry. He took off and slow timed it back, two hours over France today! Flew back here all alone this afternoon. Landed. No one knew nuttin' 'til he landed. Boy, he has what it takes. That's my idea of a pilot!!!!

Ten more new pilots. This place is a madhouse. Major Nelson in charge here and it's getting crazy.

Hunter and Colonel Tacon left for the United States. They drove to Liverpool in the colonel's car.

Friday, August 4: Wretham—Up at 0815. Briefing at 1000. Took off at 1125. Cranfill, Pezda, and I all plotted then I flew Red Flight for Colonel Swanson. I led Cliff, Addleman, and Olson. Joe Kelsey joined us later and we had a five-ship job. Flew 73 degrees to a landing field west of Kiel, by Heligoland. R/V east of Kiel. B-17s bombing GAF Station, etc. at Anklam, south of Sweden 60 miles. Beautiful weather. Excellent bombing. Nice flight. No enemy aircraft and few contrails. Bremen and Hamburg shows probably had all the fun.

Lancaster had power loss and he went to Sweden. The son of a gun sounded mighty cheerful.

Trip took 5 hours 35 minutes. Hot sun in our faces coming home at 13,000 feet. Boy, wot a headache. I ate a candy bar and Ole *Moose Nose* was right in the groove. Long ride.

[Florence is liberated by the Allies.
In Brittany, US Army forces capture Rennes.]

Saturday, August 5: Wretham—Briefing at 0850. Cloud deck broke at 0945 at take off. A beautiful clear hot day since then. Target: Halberstadt, escorting two wings of B-24s. The 369th saw 15 enemy aircraft and bounced 'em. Pezda, Taylor and two new boys each got one. Lambright (in *Moose Nose*) saw some, started to bounce 'em. Someone yelled a false break and he broke so hard he spun out at 28,000 feet. Had 35 gallons in the tank. *Moose Nose* okay, though.

Looked at a new K-14 sight with Colonel Bill this morning. Really some sight. Bendix built to British design.

Made a quick sketch of an A-20 here in the afternoon. Also got aboard a visiting Mosquito of Weather Reconnaissance Service from Walton. A quiet, warm delightful day.

Sunday, August 6: Wretham—Briefing at 0830. Berlin. No enemy aircraft although the 339th got a dozen or so.

Went to church again. Good as usual. Played billiards all evening. Bed at 11:15 P.M. A beautiful warm summer day.

Monday, August 7: Wretham—Up at 0610. Briefing at 0700, rescheduled to 0800 (so I ate) then rescheduled to 0825. Then the whole show was moved back one hour more. Took off at 1035. Nice day, haze layer down low and heavy towering cumulus operating at 18,000 to 22,000 feet.

Colonel Bill led. I led Green Flight with Britton. Swell fun roving all over. Guess I wore him out. We went way south to a target and R/V southeast of Bordeaux and south of Limoges, 80 miles from the Spanish border. Escorted three wings of B-17s. On the way back I joined Forehand's Red Flight of six ships. We came along at 5,000 feet. Went down on possible strafing targets twice. Looked for reported "bandits in area" with no luck. But fun. Came out over Normandy just west of Caen. Britton was low on gas so I led him into Manston and flew on back alone. Six hours and 20 minutes with 45 gallons left. *Moose Nose* was perfect! Some ride!

Tuesday, August 8: Wretham—Briefing at 0945. Heavy fog delayed our take off until 1121. To Fécamp thence into area patrol bounded roughly by Caen, Dreux, Le Havre, and Rouen. Forehand led, I led Red Flight with Ollie, Fladmark, and Cook. A good flight.

At end of patrol time, Bill started diving turn, and I followed. He said "drop tanks." I rolled out to dump and lost him. Here he was chasing 190s. No radio transmission on it that I could <u>hear</u>! Nuts and Hell! Keesey got one and damaged two 190s. Upwards of 30 were there. Red Allen got knocked off Bill's wing. Then we all tried to strafe north of the Seine River. I cruised around at 3,000 to 4,000 feet absorbing flak, saw no targets. We finally got fed up by being nearly hit so many times that we came home. Four hours and 35 minutes. Goddam the stinking luck and <u>damn</u> R/T chatter. Like a bunch of wimmin!

Cherry is missing. Strafing takes another.

Wednesday, August 9: Wretham—Munich again. 370th got five. Colonel Murphy got a 109. Four new fellas got one each. Keesey got another Fw 190 and Cook damaged one. 364th got 10 in the air, 24 on the ground.

A very good day with no losses.

Two Russian officers (AC) are here with General Anderson.

Visiting Russian officers inspecting East Wretham USAAF Station Number 133. Four men at front of photo, from left: Unknown pilot in flight gear, Captain Howard Fogg, Major Petrosky (Russian Interpreter), Major General Ivan Skliarov of the Russian Army; at back of photo: Colonel Linquist with his back to the camera, other two unknown. *August 9, 1944 photo courtesy of R. Hatter: Archived by Char Baldridge, Historian, 359th Fighter Group Association*

Nice rugged fliers. Good guys, spoke broken English. Keen. Drew little place cards for supper. Successful. Played pool all evening. Piano 'til 2:00 A.M. Off tomorrow. Steak and French fries with night run. Bed at 0245.

Looks pretty good for going home now. Major Shaw needs one more mission.

[General George S. Patton, leading the US 3rd Army, enters Le Mans.]

Thursday, August 10: Wretham—Mission to Metz. Dive-bomb and strafe. Went okay.

Slept until 1130. Went down to line after lunch. Test hopped *Moose Nose*. They found the trouble, the fuel enrichment valve in the carb was set cock-eyed. Now she's the best 51 I've ever flown. Terrific, smooth power. 55", 2800 RPM, 340 IAS at 2,000 feet. Really swell. Boy am I happy.

Wrote letters. Played some billiards. Went to the second show, "A Guy Named Joe." Played piano again until 0130. Pork chops and French fries with night crew. Bed at 0230.

Friday, August 11: Wretham—Slept until 1130 again. The most gorgeous day I've ever seen in England, and we were released all day. I spent all afternoon out in the pasture painting a picture of the Hall. Not bad, either. Swell sunshine. Really the best.

Spent entire evening reading *So Little Time*, Marquand's new book! Pretty good. Shot bull with Mike Donohue and Jeff, the RAF S-2 liaison officer. Bed at 2330.

[*German troops abandon Nantes, France.*

The governments of the United States, Great Britain, and Russia announce they will establish a joint commission for the administration of postwar Austria.]

Saturday, August 12: Wretham—Briefing at 0600. Escort heavies to Metz M/Y *(railroad marshalling yard)* via Caen and south of Chartres and Paris. Five hour 40 minute mission. Fox and I plotted. Second mission briefed at 1430. Dive-bomb and strafe in an area north of Paris.

Forty-two strafing missions were flown yesterday, just like D-Day week. Beating up the Seine Valley and Paris area.

I plotted second mission alone. Got back at 1800.

Ollie, Barth, Barlett back from two days in London. Really had a wild time. Wimmin. Liquor. Nuts!

Party last night. Lousy orchestra and equally lousy gals. We fixed up the terrace as a beer garden with tables and awnings. Looked darn nice. No drinking for me; I'm on the flight schedule tomorrow. Good snack bar. Bed at 11:30 P.M.

[*A German operation against Tito's partisan army in Yugoslavia begins.*]

Sunday, August 13: Wretham—Three missions for A & B Groups. I went on the first one. Took off at 0810. Me, Anderson (first mission), Chatfield, and Olson: Red Flight. Forehand led, plus Huskins with eight 370th ships. "A" Group to area including Dreux, Evreux, Chartres, etc. We dropped 500 pound bombs on double track railway cut at tunnel mouth west of Mantes–Gassicourt. Beautiful hits. Then strafed, but really nothing to strafe. I tore around above and alone for 20 minutes but no dice. Only saw a couple of ambulances, farmers, and hay wagons. We re-assembled at 4,000 feet over the tunnel. Andy went home early with a bad radio. Chatfield to beach head with a bad engine. Flak east of Rouen split up the rest of us so I came on alone. *Moose Nose* was wonderful.

Second mission, escort heavies in France.

Third mission, bomb and strafe same area. No action, no losses.

Monday, August 14: Wretham—Briefing at 0730. Another <u>gorgeous</u> day. Five hour escort to Ulm, Germany. No action, no flak, no losses.

Flights came back at 1430. I ate lunch with them.

I painted a sketch of the control tower. Good! Played some billiards with Callahan all thru supper. Lecture at 2030 by Oliphint (recently escaped from France). Damn interesting and instructive. Ollie crash-landed the week of D-Day, hit by flak while dive-bombing. Some experiences!

Lewis came back from leave so I sleep in #209 tonight. Chappie, Doc Shwayder, Kirk, and myself. Ron Major and Major Cranfill are supposed to come in but may not. Major Shaw will be leaving soon. Cranfill will get the 368th. Pezda made major today.

[Meeting in Quebec, the Morgenthau Plan is initialed by Roosevelt and Churchill. The Plan outlines the division of postwar Germany as well as its conversion into an agricultural country.]

Tuesday, August 15: Wretham—Briefing at 0630. Targets in Frankfurt area, escort B-17s at 25,000 to 27,000 feet. Me, Flack, Chatfield, and Barlett: Blue Flight then switched to White Flight when Perk aborted. High squadron. We (group) tried to cover 11 combat wings when the other groups didn't show up. Great sport in eight ship sections. We chased some bogies at 22,000 feet. I think they were enemy aircraft but we never caught 'em. Bounced some Spits at 15,000 feet in Belgium. Lancasters were in there beating up airdromes. A good but tiring five hour ride. *Moose Nose* was fine as ever! I had a beautiful flight. Those three guys were hot!

Slept all afternoon in #209 (my new room with Chappie, Kirk, and Doc Shwayder). A new captain is here (King) 42-J, Foster. Flew South Pacific P-38s. Has 150 hours in 38s here. Knew Bob Fox (he was shot down).

[A successful amphibious landing between Toulon and Cannes in France is achieved by Free French troops and the US 7th Army.]

Wednesday, August 16: Wretham—Briefing at 0630. Leipzig area. Colonel Murphy to lead an escort of B-17s. He nailed a jet job Me163. Jones, his wingman, also got one. There were several more in the area. AJAX and Wing all excited so Gilmore is flying the combat films down to AJAX tonight, a rush job. Major Cranfill got an Me109 at 30,000 feet. All smiles tonight. Good work.

I took it easy today. Moved my clothes. Got a haircut. A beautiful <u>hot</u> summer day. Almost uncomfortable here in the afternoon.

Perk is in F-133 hospital here, had a bad tooth (molar), the reason he aborted. Is having it out and will be grounded at least a week. Tough luck. Randy still grounded with bad head.

[Hitler orders all German forces in southern France to withdraw.
The United States government freezes Argentina's gold stocks held within the US.]

Thursday, August 17: Wretham—Briefing at 1100. Dive-bomb and strafe: "A" Group targeting Rouen, Amiens, "B" Group targeting Beauvais, Beaumont. Me in "A" Group with Major Irvine of the 369th, and eight of us. Took off at 1245. My goddam oxygen mask mike was busted and I couldn't transmit, so I flew over the bombing range and dropped my bombs. I led 'em up thru the cumulus, set their course, got 'em started, and then landed. Out for 45 minutes.

King took over and led our seven guys. His first ride in P-51s. They did okay. Shot up some locomotives, trucks, and bombed an airdrome.

Had an interesting escape lecture by Lieutenant MacPherson of the 321st, 352nd 42-F. He evaded over the Pyrenees and fought alongside the Maquis.

Doc Shwayder is turning my name in for Flak Home tomorrow, decided I could use the rest, week after next. Okay. I sure <u>don't</u> feel very eager of late. About nuttin'.

[In France, Orleans and Chartres are captured by US and British forces.]

Captain Montimore C. "Doc" Shwayder, 359th Fighter Group Flight Surgeon.
Courtesy of Anthony C. Chardella: Archived by Char Baldridge, Historian, 359th Fighter Group Association

Friday, August 18: Wretham—Up at 0815. Still swell weather. Released until noon. To line at 0900. Got a rush mission at 1000. Briefed at 1015. I plotted, didn't fly. Escort from Bayeux south and east around Paris to Saint-Dizier. Took off at 1130. Five hour 45 minute job. Cranfill flew *Moose Nose*, sez he couldn't trim her. Nuts!

General Anderson was here to give awards, but no dice, the mission was too hurried. He left. Pezda strafed the airdrome that the 17s bombed at Saint-Dizier. Two Ju88s destroyed. Three damaged <u>and</u> lost two of his flight to flak. One bailed out, no word of the other one. Pretty rough. Thought we might have a second mission but scrubbed the warning order at 1730.

War correspondent and an RAF Wing Commander talked to Murphy today regarding jets.

Saturday, August 19: Wretham—Bad weather arrived this morning. Rain, clouds, fronts, mist, the works. Released until tomorrow. Slept all afternoon. Got tight and played piano until 2:00 A.M. A dull day.

Sunday, August 20: Wretham—Weather bad. Released until tomorrow. Slept all afternoon. Read *Arrival and Departure* by Arthur Koestler. Mike Donohue recommended it. Very good!

Orders arrived. Perk and Thacker to Wing for three months. Lane, Callahan, Krueger, and Cunningham all made captain.

Went to church. Chappie had a swell service as usual. Really puts over a sermon in a nice, down-to-earth fashion. That's what's wrong with Christianity today. It isn't the basic text and doctrine, but the interpretation and application that's bad. They're 50 years behind the times.

[*The west bank of the Seine north of Paris is taken by US forces of the 79th Division.*]

Monday, August 21: Wretham—Released. Bad, <u>bad</u> weather.

Saw some Navy training films on dive-bombing. Old as Hell, though, and dull.

Everyone loafing, playing billiards, taking sack time. Cards, radio, piano, Ping-Pong, etc.

Major Shaw, Callahan, and Burton received orders directing them home for six months. That settles it.

Tuesday, August 22: Wretham—Released. Bad weather again. Whew.

Major Shaw, Kirk, and Callahan off to Liverpool in a C-61, weathered in at Peterborough. Hated to see Cliff leave. Hope he calls the folks in New York.

Saw "Standing Room Only" and it was pretty good.

Ollie and me on piano until 2:00 A.M.

Lieutenant Paul E. "Ollie" Olson on wing of his P-51B Mustang *Marihelen* CV-J 42-106917. *Photo courtesy of Marvin Boussu: Archived by Char Baldridge, Historian, 359th Fighter Group Association*

[Patton leads the US 3rd Army to Troyes and Reims in north central France.]

Wednesday, August 23: Wretham—Released again. Weather finally broke in the afternoon. Nice, but hazy. Everyone flew locally late in the day. First time we'd had a P-51 off the field since Friday. Some weather.

Perk and Thacker go to Wing for 90 days upon completion of tour. Tough break but better than Goxhill. And how! Nuts to that place! Major Cranfill to the 368th as C.O. Sam White joins Pezda and me at Group. Good deal. I like Sam!

Burton left today. Vic Cunningham got his orders. Same as Shaw's. Oh baby! Here's hoping.

[Goxhill, nicknamed "GoatHill" by the men stationed there, transferred from the RAF in August 1942. Known formally as USAAF Station 345 and used as a training base throughout the war, the facilities at Goxhill were less than desirable, with three wooden barracks supplemented by metal "tin can" living quarters, frequently surrounded by mud.

King Michael I dismisses Hitler's ally, Marshal Ion V. Antonescu, as head-of-state of Rumania. Rumania then allies itself with the Soviets.

Churchill confers with Pope Pius XII in Rome.]

Thursday, August 24: Wretham—Up at 0445. Ouch. Some jolt after the past few days. Then, of course, briefing was set back to 0730. I stayed up and shot the bull with Colonel Bill then rode to line in his newly acquired '38 Plymouth-Chrysler. Nice to ride in a real car. He can drive. Wot a guy, he's sure swell.

Mission to Leipzig area again. Pezda is leading "A." Cranfill is leading "B." Split target. Same route. Five hour job. The '68th had 22 ships up. Pop Hesser is some boy! A milk run, though, as they saw nuttin!

A B-24 489th Bomb Group Division "Special Delivery" dropped in to see some guys. Were going to Birmingham to see another friend and have supper. Invited me to join 'em. Got as far as Peterborough but hit heavy rain with zero visibility. Turned around, dropped me off here and beat it for Halesworth.

Pilot was Second Lieutenant Valentine. Brady's his C.O. Bright, the first lieutenant with 'em, had finished his tour and was just loafing. Three swell guys. Really got a kick out of that big, lumbering Pullman car.

[Fortified bunker positions west of Bordeaux are evacuated by German troops.]

Friday, August 25: Wretham—Briefing at 0845. To Peenemünde and Neubrandenburg, a long water hop. This is 359th Group's 200th mission. No action.

Sam and I horsed around Group all day. "Rebbie" Roginson, Special Service, took us with him in his Jeep to hear Glenn Miller at Knettishall, 488th Wing, B-17s, 3rd Division. Some base! Huge Officer's Club bar. Easy and informal. Any old uniform and everyone was full of pep. Makes us somewhat more disgusted than ever at Wretham Old Maid's Home. That gol darn "Snuffy" is a dictator worthy of Hitler, and is as out of place in a fighter group as Hitler would be in the Catskill Mountains.

[Already a famous big-band leader, in the fall of 1942 at age 38 Glenn Miller volunteered and was accepted into the Army so he could fulfill his desire to entertain the troops overseas. On December 15, 1944, while flying from England to France, Major Miller's plane disappeared over the English Channel. No trace was ever found.

Snuffy Smith is a cartoon hillbilly character first syndicated in 1919.

Secret cease-fire discussions begin between Finland and the Soviet Union.]

Saturday, August 26: Wretham—Paris has fallen officially. Last night French troops and Americans entered. What a wonderful day for France.

Up at 0515, then the damn show was set back two hours. Breakfast with Colonel Bill and Mike at the Purple Shaft. Good corn fritters.

Mission target is north end of the Ruhr Valley. No action. A five hour area patrol milk run. Lambright blew the *Moose's* tail wheel landing. Skidded, bent L strut. Service group is changing it.

Dick Gates was in for a while in the AT-6. He's fine. Fieg is home. Davis is MIA and Gerat not thru yet.

Went to bed at 7:00 P.M. for a nap, woke up at 7:30 A.M. this morning. Some nap! Felt good. I think I'll do it again. Sam White is in #209 with us now. Lane and Perkins are thru.

[Bulgaria declares its neutrality, withdrawing as Germany's ally and from the war against the Soviet Union.]

Sunday, August 27: Wretham—Briefing at 1020. Big B for a change. Pezda is taking 'em in over land all the way instead of the usual northern water route. A gorgeous, cool, sunny day. Even England can be beautiful.

The mission flopped. Weather. Never saw the bombers, they all aborted and hit targets of opportunity. Emden, etc. Group ended up strafing at Osnabrück and Münster. Cleaned house too.

This group is revitalized. Eighteen locomotives destroyed, 12 dams, 119 cars damaged, 3 tugs, and 12 barges damaged. "Colonel Bill" (*Swanson*) has humanized the base. Gonna have more liberty runs, parties, snack bar on line. A <u>pilot's</u> base instead of Snuffy Smith's infantry camp.

Monday, August 28: Wretham—Up at 0515. Briefing at 0630. Strafe rail traffic in Saarbrücken, Metz, and Bar-le-Duc. I was to lead the '68th but *Moose Nose* loaded up and wanted to quit so I didn't take off. Goddam engineering section thinks pilots are all liars. Lambright told them yesterday the ship was bad. Oh well.

Cold front came hootin' thru in the morning. Many of group landed elsewhere.

Perk is going straight home and Lane to Wing. Some joke! Lucky Perk. Poor Tommy.

[Free French troops enter Marseille.]

Tuesday, August 29: Wretham—Released 'til noon. High stratus deck at 10,000 to 15,000 feet. Low stuff at 6,000 feet. I test-hopped *Moose Nose* at 0900. Bisher reset the fuel enrichment valve. She runs fine now. Flew an hour, bounced some B-17s, P-51, had a swell time. Released 'til dawn. Weather over Channel. Good here in the afternoon.

I drew a pen and ink sketch and loafed.

Was fitted for a G-Suit by Lou Major this morning. Pretty clever. Air bladder around gut, thighs, and calves. A bit stiff and awkward, but RAF claims they do wonders toward improving shooting, what with no black outs.

Group has 20 new D-10s, came in yesterday and today. A re-arranged instrument panel and fillet to tail. Supposed to be a swell ship.

Wednesday, August 30: Wretham—Lousy, grey, rainy morning. Released until noon. Briefing at 1300, took off at 1400. Escort B-17s to Kiel above weather. *Moose Nose* raised Hell on take off. I slammed on the brakes, stopped on the edge of the field. Got stuck in a rabbit hole taxiing back with brakes on fire. Nuts!! <u>Now</u> they'll put in a new carburetor.

No action on the mission. They were out for four hours.

Olin Drake, the old bum, is okay and in an English hospital. He went down in France on June 10th. Also Sansing of the 369th. Must have been picked up in the present drive into France.

Fixed up Hunter's battle jacket. Never meant to fit him and is a bit big for <u>me</u>. I'll pay Randy, who picked it up for Hunter. Billiards with Raines and Jeff *(Geoffry)* Darlington the S-2 RAF wing liaison guy. Swell evening.

[Half of Germany's oil supplies are cut off with the capture of the Ploesti oilfields of Rumania.]

Thursday, August 31: Wretham —A gorgeous, clear, cumulus, <u>cool</u> day. Like San Francisco. Swell! More pep then I've felt for weeks. Then nuts. Released all day! Can't figure 'em out.

Lieutenant Olin P. Drake.
Photo courtesy of R. Hatter: Archived by Char Baldridge, Historian, 359th Fighter Group Association

Ship got new carburetor, valves checked, screws cleaned, tanks drained, and new brakes. *Moose Nose* ready for test hop at 1600. Left brake set too tight. Burned up taxiing out to take off. Took off and smelled it burning so lowered wheels and returned, hoping it wasn't fused and cracked. It wasn't. So we'll try again tomorrow. Engine seemed okay.

Perk and Lane and Thacker are gone, and Krueger. The old boys are a mere handful now. Oh, Cranfill and Oliphint too, left today.

[Bucharest, the capital of Rumania, is occupied by the Red Army, which begins to round-up members of the 'Fascist' Antonescu government.]

Excerpts from the August 1944 Informal Report of Morale for the 359th Fighter Group, submitted by "Chappie" Ziegler state: "The month of August has witnessed a tremendous improvement in the morale of our fighter group. This has been due to a number of factors.

"First of all, the tremendous successes of our armies in France has acted like a tonic to our men, both enlisted men and officers. Maps of France have suddenly appeared in offices all over the station. Each map shows the latest reported advance of our men. With the end seemingly in sight, our men are turning their eyes and thoughts homeward.

"The second factor that has improved morale is the return of furloughs, 48-hour passes, and 24-hour passes on the old basis used when we first arrived here. We are more isolated in this field than perhaps any other fighter group in this command. Under the restricted system of passes, cities like London and Cambridge were unavailable for days off. Only the smaller towns were really convenient. Many men spent their 24 hours in Thetford. Consequently, fewer and fewer men were leaving the base. Even though we have wonderful facilities on this base with our two officer's clubs, Aero-Club for enlisted men, 35mm movies, gymnasium, coke bar, 2 beer halls, and weekly dance, still a change of surroundings is always necessary. Now this is available with the return of furloughs, etc.

"The third morale factor and the one that I was tempted to place first in importance is the expressed interest of our commanding officer, Lieutenant Colonel Swanson, in the welfare of our men, both officers and enlisted men.

"They like Colonel Swanson as a pilot, a leader and a man. All this is leading to an enthusiasm or morale that is giving expression in the flying and fighting our men are doing. Slowly but surely this group is going to become the "hot" outfit it was destined to be, when we left the States as the best trained outfit to leave for combat.

"Each day is bringing us closer to victory and peace. Each day brings us closer to home and in doing that, each day raises the morale of our men just that much more."

HEADQUARTERS 359TH FIGHTER GROUP
Office of the Group Historian
APO 637 / US Army
4 Sept 1944

History of the 359th Fighter Group, August 1944

In August of 1944, the 359th Fighter Group became, for all practical purposes, a new unit. Of the 86 pilots who had come to England 10 months before, two were casualties during the month, 20 finished their tours and only 15 were left on flying status. And these 15 were almost all so close to the end of their 300-hour combat time that the greatest care was exercised in rationing them to the 29 missions flown in 23 days so that squadron and group leaders would continue to be available.

The result of all this was that the experience level of the 359th Group, which at the beginning of summer had been near the top of the Command, now sank to an average of 116 hours, with 61 pilots having less than 100 hours.

The new men were eager and there were remarkable prospects among them, but they were also green and 12 were combat casualties, while another, Lieutenant Lawrence A. Bearden, was killed on a training flight on 10 August. With Captain Lancaster interned in Sweden and Captain Hawkinson lost strafing, that meant 15 casualties for the month. Against this the 359th could show a phenomenal strafing score, locomotive claims, for example, of 62-0-47, excellent bombing, and 21-1-12 in aircraft.

New and senior pilot officers were posted to the 359th and there began to be doubt over just how many of the "originals," sent on 30-day leave to the States, ever would rejoin the 359th.

When Colonel Tacon left early in the month for his leave at home, he assumed that the pilots then finishing would return to his command with him. But on 7 August, Fighter Command limited the trip to the Zone of the Interior to the commanders and operations officers, plus one flight leader from each squadron. This was further modified on 22 August to mean that only 10 percent of the authorized strength could be absent in the States, and there were indications that perhaps 11 pilots, save squadron commanders, would be returned in the United States to a general pool for reassignment.

Inevitably, all this meant a radical change in personnel, especially since both Major Shaw of the 368th Squadron and Lieutenant Colonel Murphy of the 370th Squadron were finishing their second foreign tours and would ask for reassignment.

Something of a crisis in lack of trained leaders was approaching, and although this was partially alleviated by the decision of such men as Major Pezda and Captain Hipsher to take 25-hour extensions of their 300-hour tours, it was aggravated later in the month by the cutting of the tour to 285 hours, with every indication that the plethora of pilots ready for combat duty would mean further reductions in the stated operational time.

New leaders were developing. A combination of aborts one day had Lieutenant Hatter, a replacement in the 368th Squadron leading the Group, but the transition period was a constant worry of Lieutenant Colonel Swanson's, who took command on Colonel Tacon's departure.

Colonel Swanson was full of plans for the new pilots. He began construction of a snack bar on the line next to the ops block, reinstated movies at Wretham Hall, tripled liberty runs, and arranged weekly parties, while Major Aaron Hanson greatly improved the calibre of the mess and the serving, and with especially noted results, expanded the evening collation.

Another worry was the steady decay in the condition of the landing surface, especially Runway 22, the longest and best. Both the Flying Control narrative and the Technical Inspector's report for August are concerned with the pitted "turf" runway, both for the hazard to flying and the strain on maintenance created by the dust. Conferences with engineers produced plans to lay a steel-plank mat at the marshalling point, and the Alert Detachment was mobilized for emergency repairs. Aborts remained a problem, and the early return percentage of 15.8 was highest in the Wing. But the statistical summary shows an average of one less per mission than for the previous month, and a mass conference system instituted by Colonel Swanson to discuss the reasons for the abort promised to reduce the total still further. Despite the aborts, more than 1,000 sorties were completed and the total operation time of 5,468 hours was surpassed in the Wing only by the 20th Group, with 5,746.

And for the expenditure of 179,759 rounds of armor-piercing incendiary, .50 calibre bullets and 108,250 pounds of bombs, the 359th Group could be proud of its results, especially in the hawk-like strafing in which Major Pezda was a leading and driving spirit.

Colonel Murphy gained an international reputation by becoming the first airman to conquer the German's hush-hush new liquid-rocket fighter, the Messerschmitt 163, and the 359th Group was chosen by General Anderson as a model station for the inspection by Major General Ivan Skliarov of the Russian Army on 9 August. This was a full-dress affair, with the aircraft and all equipment shown the Soviet visitors, who spent an hour overtime in the briefing room with Colonel Swanson discussing escort and air combat tactics.

The first evaders returned, including Oliphint, awarded a Silver Star for his courageous decision to go in and bomb rather than bail out during the struggle to blockade the Germans from the Cotentin beachhead, a struggle now recognized generally to be as climactic as the fighter had known that it was.

Other Silver Stars went to S.R. Smith, Cal Callahan and T.P. Smith for their strafing, and to Major Cranfill for his June tunnel-bombing.

The 359th Group also for the first time lost men to internment, three of the 370th Squadron landing in Sweden on 4 August.

A list of all 76 casualties suffered since the first operation of 13 December, shows eight to be known as killed in action, five known killed non-operationally, 13 known POWs, four evaders, three interned, and 43 as missing in action, their fate not yet revealed.

Of the 22 originals lost in the month, 15 went directly to the Zone of the Interior.

The work of the month was varied, ranging from escort to B17s dropping supplies to the Maquis on the Swiss frontier below Geneva, through long range bomber strikes at Berlin and Munich, to savage clouting of everything German that moved, first 'round Rouen and then, as the tidal wave of khaki swept to and beyond Paris, up through the hills of Alsace and Lorraine.

One of the best days of all turned out to be a bomber mission which aborted, as Pezda had insisted on being routed across Germany rather than by the water track to Heligoland and consequently there was a juicy impromptu strafing score.

On the wave of the elation produced by the victories in France, with the simultaneous collapse under Russian pressure of Rumania and Bulgaria, morale generally was at a high peak among all elements, air and ground. Whether that mood would hold in the face of transfer to another theatre was not clear. What was clear was the growth of extreme chauvinism and a jingoistic sensitivity to every word printed in an English newspaper about the achievements of the American ground forces. This was not helped by the London tabloid's home morale-boosting attempts to deprecate the Bradley-Patton achievement, in the service of glory for the savage Anglo-German slugging on the Orne where the Wehrmacht was first bent and broken.

The weather held good for the first fortnight, then wavered and collapsed in mist and rain later in the month. But there was a mission a day for the first ten days and, in the final days of August, the weather was good enough to permit two consecutive days of brutal punishment of German road and rail transport.

With this preface, the blow-by-blow story of the month:

Plan Buick at that time meant airborne supplies for the FFI, the bushwackers of the Maquis who were playing so vital a role in the avalanche-engulfment of France. The month began with a long errand of this sort to the Annecy area in the mountains of southern France just south of Lake Geneva. This was Mission 177 on 1 August and the group divided in two halves, with Captain Forehand and Major Pezda leading. It was a long job (more than six hours) and an exciting one. The country was new, and going down in the Alpine valleys to watch the Resistance people running to the gaily-colored parachutes with their containers of weapons, ammunition, and supplies, was a welcome novelty and a change from both heavy escort and ground attack. No enemy aircraft were sighted but two pilots in the 368th had an exciting time.

Lieutenant Cornelius J. Cavanaugh had engine trouble on the route over north France. He turned back and managed to reach England, bailing out safely over Nuthampstead.

Slated to be processed at 63 Brooke Street in London as an "evader," Lieutenant Elby J. Beal nevertheless wangled repairs on the strip from a P-47 maintenance crew and flew back to Wretham after finding out how useful a foxhole is under air attack.

On August 2nd, the 359th Group lost Captain Hawkinson, leading the 368th, when he went down on two German lorries northeast of Rouen in what probably was a German fighter trap, since there were three fixed light guns emplaced nearby. The mission that day was notable both for the number of aircraft taking off, 55, and the number returning early, 18. One of the early returns, Lieutenant Ivan B. Holloman of the 369th, circled the landing ground for two hours struggling with an intractable landing gear. The squadron narrative tells how he finally made an extraordinary landing on one wheel. Major Pezda, promoted from Captain during the month, led his flight to a 1-0-1 score against locomotives.

The mission of 3 August was planned as a bomber strike at flying bomb dumps but bad weather resulted in a search for opportunity targets and bombing of Evreux airfield. Colonel Murphy, who led, landed with locked brakes and nosed over, one of two landing accidents that day. That evening, news came through that the universally-popular Hagan of the 368th, MIA on 8 June, was a POW.

The attack of 4 August on Anklam and Peenemünde cost the 359th

Group three good pilots, Captain Lancaster and Lieutenants Baker and Richard O. Rabb, all of the 370th. All three reached Sweden, where Lancaster safely parachuted and the other two landed with 15 gallons of gas each. On the way to internment, Baker and Rabb shot down a Do-217. All three collaborated on a saucy cablegram to the station, where, under the impression that the lieutenants had foolishly decided to escort Lancasters and had themselves run of gas, Colonel Murphy was much upset. Bomb results were excellent that day. On the way back, Colonel Swanson's flight shot up one of three twin-mast auxiliary schooners found off Terschelling.

The Luftwaffe came up to fight on the 5th, our end of the show being Halberstadt. The air score was 4-0-1 for no loss, and the indefatigable Pezda, who briefed at 0850 and led the group, got another locomotive, besides persuading an Me109 pilot to jump.

Next day was the only successful Berlin show of the month. Colonel Murphy had an inward course drawn south of Berlin, since the northeast and northwest approaches to Big B would be saturated with American aircraft at target time and he wanted to be in on the Berlin killing. But the enemy struck at the other task forces and his strategy was foiled, no Germans being sighted on the run into and out of Marienfelde. Fighters going on to Russia with a bomber shuttle run also found opposition and a score, but the 359th had to be content with two more locomotives, although there was consolation that night with the news, well-nigh incredible, that John Oliphint was back in England after a spectacular rescue from the crashed airplane in which he was trapped, an equally spectacular escape from the Germans and a successful evasion.

Mission 183, on 7 August, was an attack on targets in the Bordeaux area. FO 420 was in early and briefing was at 0700 but delays pushed the take off to 1028. Bill Forehand and his flight liberally splattered a tank with .50 bullets, and bomb results were good.

A large German concentration, 25 Fw 190s at 17,000 feet with 30 more as top cover, was encountered by eight planes of the 368th on the 8th, southeast of Caen during the saturation bombing of the Wehrmacht positions in front of the British lines. Radio calls for help were garbled, and the rest of the 359th Group went on to their briefed strafing, while the 368th section, led by Forehand, got a score of 1-1-3 for the loss of Lieutenant Allen, who had been so lucky on his lonely ride back from Denmark chronicled last month. Cherry, also of the 368th, was NYR on this mission, believed lost to light flak during the strafing. Of the air score, 1-0-2 was compiled by John Keesey, a mild-mannered, sandy-haired boy who began "to look like another Booth."

Keesey scored another victory on the 9th, as did six pilots in the 370th. One of these, Cyril W. Jones Jr., was on his first operational mission, the long ride to Munich, another, Robert M. York, was out for the second time. Both these, and Frank O. Lux, who also shot one down, had comparatively long turns as instructors in the States. This mission had an early start with an 0645 briefing by Colonel Murphy, with take off into a bad haze and wretched visibility at 0813. On the way back the 369th got two more locomotives.

An additional 16 locos were added to the score on the 10th, a bombing and strafing chore in the Par-le-Due area, which was part of the aerial blockade imposed by the Eighth Fighter Command on all attempts to relieve or reinforce the German armies being strangled in the west. There was a low scud at take off time, bombers floating under it from the B-17 stations to the east and south of Wretham, set course altitude to 500 feet, but target results, and the dive-bombing, both were excellent. Two pilots were lost and the loss of one of these, Lieutenant Lester W. Hovden of the 368th, never was satisfactorily explained. Flying on Colonel Swanson's wing, Hovden was the second man over the Bischwiller marshalling yard and his aircraft disintegrated at 15,000 feet without any apparent cause.

That made 10 missions in 10 days and at 0530 on the 11th, Wing warned to stand by with tanks but a release came through at 0915. Colonel Smith at Station HQ received word that afternoon that Broach, Laing, and Shupe all were POWs, while Chaplain was informed by the family of Lieutenant Stanley E. Sackett that he was listed by the War Department as killed in action.

A double do came up on the 12th. Major Irvine led an uneventful early morning escort of the heavies to Metz, and in the afternoon Colonel Murphy briefed for another railroad blockade job. The Colonel aborted, his radio was out, and Robert Hatter, reputed the best deflection shot in the 359th, led 33 aircraft into the Rouen area. He was the first replacement pilot to have that distinction, which was all the more novel since Lane had been slated to lead the 368th; Hatter became squadron leader only when Lane failed to get off. The area was devastated and targets were hard to find, but bombs damaged two marshalling yards and cut tracks, and there was effective strafing of four trucks and some 40 railroad cars.

The strangle strafing continued next day, split in two sections. One, led by Bill Forehand, was in the Evreux area at 0925, and dive-bombed but found that targets in this area were extremely scarce. Later that morning Major Cranfill took the rest out escorting 72 B-17s pounding the roads from St. Aubin to St. Valery. The heavies knocked down two bridges in the

Rouen-Louviers sector and started 15 fires. The third mission of the day was fighter-bombing; Vic Cunningham leading 24 aircraft off at 1704 down to Pacy-sur-Eure, where two highway bridges were demolished, 5 railroad intersections hit, and railway cars and motor transport strafed. There was some excitement as the mission ended, as one of Cunningham's 500-pound GP bombs hung up and dropped on the field at Wretham when Vic came home at 2015. The field was closed until the bomb was, with all due caution, removed.

There were no aborts on any of these three missions but next day, the early returns shot up again, to 13 of 46 airborne, on an uneventful run to Stuttgart with the First Bomb Division. A score of 1-0-1 in locos and some transport was recorded on the way out, with Major Pezda accounting for the loco destroyed. An hour before the group came back at 1430, a Liberator on a training flight crashed in the Thetford battle area near the station, luckily without fatalities. That night, the 14th, Oliphint told us as much as the escape authorities would allow him to of his evasion.

August 15 was the date of the monster pummeling of German fighter and night fighter stations in which 1,004-odd RAF Lancs and Halifaxes clobbered the Belgian and Dutch fields while the Eighth went on into Germany. The 359th's end of the show was escort 'round Frankfurt airdromes, where results were excellent. On the way out bandits got in on the last wing of the force, shooting down nine of the heavies before our group could get back from its assigned place at the head of the column. There was no engagement, but the 359th lost Lieutenant Frank E. Westall Jr., of the 370th, who called he was bailing out 30 miles below Dunkirk at 5,000 feet with low manifold pressure. There were 11 early returns on this day and Colonel Swanson ordered that a meeting of all aborting pilots be held on any day that exceeded five, so that all the pilots talked over the reasons for their aborts. Later in the day, at 1805, a red air raid warning was sounded for an approaching buzz bomb, but it exploded with a distant boom well south of the station, as did all the robots approaching Wretham during the month.

16 August was a reasonably historic day. Colonel Murphy became the first Allied pilot to destroy one of the new and still-mysterious German liquid-rocket fighters, an Me163. The Colonel damaged another, which Cyril Jones, his wingman, destroyed and Jimmy C. Shoffit, also of the 370th, engaged in a long and educational combat with a third, which was damaged. The story received a greater play in the world press than any other single story of an Eighth Air Force pilot.

Briefing on FO 518 was early, at 0630. Before rendezvous, tanks were dropped when the enemy struck at Erfurt, and Colonel Murphy left his

briefed course to rendezvous early. In addition, Major Cranfill and Lieutenant Lux each shot down a more orthodox 109. There was considerable
excitement in higher HQ at news of the first victory over the Me163s, and
some confusion on the station, since Colonel Murphy's film had been sent
to Honington to go up to Fighter Command by courier. The film was
retrieved and flown to Command by Lieutenant Gilmore that night. Earlier
in the afternoon, Colonel Swanson had his promised long talk with the 15
pilots who returned early from the mission.

An outstandingly good bomb-and strafe mission came up on the 17th.
Colonel Swanson led one split-group and Lieutenant Prewitt took over the
other when Major Irvine returned early. Both units found their assigned
targets in the Abancourt area overcast but stalked targets to the east,
destroying bridges, blowing up an ammunition train, damaging marshalling
yards and beating up 14 locos. The hunters split down into pairs, providing
four prowling Fw 190s a bounce of an element of two. Lieutenant
Theophalus A. Williams failed to return and his element leader, Jimmy Shoffit, could not release his bombs and could not stay to fight. Radio discipline
was bad on the mission, the chatter of two groups crowding A Channel,
and Lieutenant Dover, controller at Walcott Hall, also reported that straggling re-entry via banned air sectors into England of the fighters had bothered 11 Group in its attempt to spot and plot flying bombs.

The 18th was a crowded day. General Anderson came down from Wing
to present Distinguished Flying Crosses but arrived too late for the briefing
hurriedly scheduled at 1015 on FO 522, despite a release until noon received
the previous evening. Major Cranfill led the group off at 1112, on a wholly
admirable B-17 bomber show in which the Forts' formation, R/T procedure,
and reassembly technique were well-nigh flawless. Major Pezda took his
flight down to strafe Saint-Dizier between waves of the bombing, but
though he and Claude G. Crenshaw scored 2-0-3, both Rene Burtner and
Don S. Melrose were hit by light flak on their second passes. Burtner was
back at Wretham within a fortnight, having hidden near enough to the
Saint-Dizier airfield to help capture it when American tanks came up in
Patton's dash to Metz. At Wretham, word was received that Colonel
Murphy's Me163 film showed the enemy rocket-plane exploding, and was
so good technically they would be used to make new recognition pictures.
Also, eight British Armored Corps officers drove three Cromwell tanks to
the station for the instruction of the alert detachment, while Colonel Swanson and the combat air intelligence staff spent several hours discussing the
air war with the tank men. They came to Wretham Hall that night for more
talk, and two intelligence officers went to their hanger near the airfield

where the tankers were celebrating the end of a ten day bivouac. Both sides seemed to gain by the exchange of views.

Ensued now a lapse in operations, occasioned by rain which appeared to signal the end of a brief but beautiful summer. The magnificent weather of the first two weeks of August had sealed the fate of the German Fourteenth Army, and the respite was welcome, although it was interrupted by the compulsory evening showing on 20 August of a Navy dive-bombing film showing Navy technique with Navy aircraft. The same day, pilots chatting with friends in replacement depots sent back word that Gray, former commanding officer of the 369th, had a score of 11 aerial victories and 11 locos with the Ninth Air Force.

This lay-off lasted five days and ended with Missions 198 and 199, a double effort on 24 August. Half the 359th Group, led by Major Pezda, went to Kölleda, losing 10 of their strength of 25 on early returns, and the other half, under Major Cranfill, went to Weimar, where 129 B-17s did one of the great bombing jobs in their history, wiping out an armament works, a radio factory, and large segments of SS barracks. An armed trawler was believed sunk and a loco destroyed by Lieutenants Merle B. Barth and Eugene F. Britton on the way out.

The 200th mission of the 359th Fighter Group, on 25 August, was led by Colonel Murphy, the long ride over water to the Danish Peninsula and down to Neubrandenburg, which was well clobbered. Strafing on the way out damaged an airplane at Güstrow, a loco, and a corvette in the Baltic. Word arrived that both Colonel Tyrrell and Posty Booth were POWs. Again the weather had turned beautiful on the ground, with magnificent lofty cloudscapes floating in plenty of blue. The new mission century began with what seemed like a rough ride, to Gelsenkirchen in the Ruhr, but actually there was no flak damage in the group and the bombers, going in by elements of 12 at 30,000 feet, also got off well.

Towering cloud over Denmark forced abandonment of a scheduled large-scale assault on Berlin on the 27th, 10 percent of the bombers going after targets of opportunity on the German coast and the rest returning without bombing. Major Pezda, who briefed, announced he was bored with the overwater ride and so had plotted his course for a sweep into Ulzen. The result was that when the bombers aborted, Pezda swept via Hanover up to Stralsund on the Baltic north of Berlin, then swept back and finally sent the group down to strafe from Dümmer Lake west. The only air score in the Eighth Air Force that day was recorded by Lieutenant Lawrence Zizka of the 370th, who found and shot down a twin-engine bandit near Münster, and strafing results were extraordinarily good, 18-0-12 locos, plus tugs, barges, lorries, and a five-story factory riddled and set afire. Lieutenant Paul E. Sundheim of the 370th did not return, although he was heard asking for a heading after strafing near Münster. After briefing that morning, the pilots watched Lieutenant Gilmore, leading a flight of four, rendezvous over Wretham with three lifeboat-carrying Warwicks headed out to the North Sea to search for a bomber crew. They were back at 1351 with reports of a long and fruitless search.

Another extraordinary strafing job was accomplished on the 28th when Colonel Swanson led to the Nancy-Metz area. The locomotive score was 30-0-8, plus 18-0-18 in lorries, 29-0-173 goods wagons (including 10 exploding ammo cars), 0-0-35 passenger coaches, and a wide variety of other targets. The weather at base was execrable, and a driving rain at 0800, 15 minutes after take off, forced half of the 359th to land at other bases until the sun broke through in the afternoon. Lieutenant Ferris C. Suttle of the 369th was missing from this rhubarb, and Frank Lux, 370th, was injured after the mission was over, in taking off from Martlesham. Lieutenant John W. McAlister Jr., also of the 370th, made a dead-stick landing at Bentwaters when his engine froze. He was one of the two early returns on the mission and escaped injury in a category AC crash-landing.

On the last mission of the month, to Kiel on 30 August with Major Irvine leading, 10/10 overcast prevented observation of bomb results and also foiled Pezda and the other strafers looking for targets in the Emden area. Though they did not know it, freelance strafing for the P-51s was about to be banned by Command. Losses were making it unprofitable, but the hawk-like hunting spirit shown by the 359th Fighter Group, now practically reconstituted, and their eagerness to find, fix and strike the enemy, were welcome and encouraging for a future that became harder and harder to predict as the Eisenhower armies smashed steadily toward the German frontier.

The month ended with word that two more of the Invasion casualties, Virgil Sansing and Olin Drake, were safe—Sansing, after weeks of work with the Resistance movement near Soissons; Drake in the 74th General Hospital in England. It seemed a good omen.

12.

SEPTEMBER 1944

Changing of the Guard

Friday, September 1: Wretham—Up at 0600. Clear as crystal, cold as Iceland. A gorgeous morning and day. Briefing at 0730. Colonel Murphy's last mission. A wonderful record! Amen.

Escorted 1st Division 17s to Ludwigshafen via R/V south of Paris, thence east. Heavy weather, never R/Ved. Wing recalled the group. Four hours instead of five and one-half as scheduled. Kaloski's engine quit. Lousy prop ran away, no oil pressure. Bailed out in the Channel. No word of him, dammit! A swell Polack.

I test hopped *Moose Nose* again. Tried once but new left brake heated up. Bisher and Beck reset clearance, and now it's okay. She ran beautifully, simply perfect. 28-55" Hg. 2200-2800 RPM. 13,000 feet, IAS up to 450. Beautiful. Rolls, Split S, an unequalled ship when she's right. Here's hoping she stays that way now.

Saturday, September 2: Wretham—Bad weather.

> [*Finland breaks off diplomatic relations with Germany and demands German forces withdraw from Finnish soil.*]

Sunday, September 3: Wretham—Party. Gals from Cambridge.

[*Allied troops occupy Brussels.*
  Field Marshal von Rundstedt re-assumes command of the German armies in the West.]

Monday, September 4: Wretham—Left for Flak Home with "Lightnin'" McNeill. Spent the night at Ford's Hotel in London. Weather lousy. So are the trains!

[*British troops occupy Antwerp, Belgium.*
  The Finnish Army ceases hostilities against the Soviet Union.]

Tuesday through Saturday, September 5 through September 9: Stanbridge Earls—Heard Yehudi Menuhin play in Salisbury Cathedral. A wonderful experience. Salisbury a real, picturesque, English town. Like a page out of Dickens.

[*Considered a child prodigy, Yehudi Menuhin performed at the age of seven with the San Francisco Orchestra. After completing a triumphant European tour in 1935 he became one of the worlds most sought-after violinists.*
  The Soviet Union declares war on Bulgaria.
  Rumania declares war on Hungary.
  British and American forces capture Ghent and Liege, Belgium.
  General de Gaulle forms a provisional French government that includes communists.]

Sunday, September 10: Stanbridge Earls—Married 17 months today.

[*The US First Army occupies Luxembourg.*
  Russian and Iraqi diplomatic relations are established.]

Monday, September 11: Stanbridge Earls—No plane to get us.
  Group, led by Forehand, flew in the 8th's biggest day. Shot down 25 in the air, got 10 more on the ground. Some battle! Near Leipzig area. Boys landed all over. Brussels, Paris, Ghent. Several MIAs. Captain King got three in the air, one on the ground. Wot a battle. 8th Fighter got over 130. The 359th, 339th, and 550th got 100 of 'em. Some group!

[The US Third Army, led by General Patton, reach the German border at Trier.
    British troops in Belgium cross the Dutch border.]

Tuesday, September 12: London—No planes. Nuts. So we took the train to London at 1830. Stayed in Hempstead. Some dump of a hotel (Langorf). Phooey!

Forehand a major. Doc Shwayder a major.

[German troops evacuate several Greek islands in the eastern Mediterranean.]

Wednesday, September 13: Wretham—Took 1420 train for Thetford. Had lunch with Bill Kasper who told us all about Monday's battle.

Randy is going home.

Thursday, September 14: Wretham—I'm in charge of 13 new pilots being trained and flown out of Group Ops. A good idea. They'll be operational when they hit the squadron. But, oh, wot a headache and am I busy! The Fogg School of Aeronautics is in full swing.

Friday, September 15: Wretham—No mission. Middle clouds, scattered showers. I flew my "school" all afternoon.

Hawkinson and Drake are in London. T.P. Smith of the 370th is here after bail-

Captain Howard Fogg with P-51D-5 Mustang *Moose Nose* CV-D 44-13762. Lettering on fuselage reads:
PILOT—CAPT H.L. FOGG
CREW CHIEF – S/SGT BISHER
ARMORER – SGT CREECH
Courtesy of Ira J. "John" Bisher: Archived by Char Baldridge, Historian, 359th Fighter Group Association

ing out in April. Hodges, from the 370th, is now here. Captain Parsons of the 369th is okay. Les Taylor left for Liverpool. Randy got his orders. He leaves Monday!

[Howard's daily diary entries ended abruptly with the September 15th entry. We can only surmise why. Perhaps after keeping it faithfully for so long and being so close to going home he felt there was nothing more to say. We do know the war was not yet over for Captain Fogg. On September 21st he flew area support for the 1st Airborne's participation in Operation Market Garden at Nijmegen, the Netherlands. The next day he flew a 5 hour 24 minute mission escorting B-17s as they bombed a tank factory in Kassel, Germany. This mission completed his combat tour of duty.

Although his daily diary has ended, we are offered one last glimpse of this insightful, articulate man. Here, in an article written in July 1944, he describes the routine and the emotions of a fighter pilot preparing for a mission.]

Lieutenant Howard Fogg.
Courtesy of Richard Fogg

"PILOTS GOING ON MISSION"
by Captain Howard Fogg

It is 0700. The door to our room squeaks open suddenly and S-2 sticks his head through the opening.

"C'mon, you're goin' flying fellas, briefing at 0800," he bellows, loudly enough to be heard over at Bodney.

We wake up, resentfully. Still, this isn't so bad. Yesterday it was 0415. Our first fully conscious act is to check the weather out our windows. Never knew a pilot yet who didn't do this immediately when he crawled out of the sack. We dress after a quick splash in the wash bowl. Most of us shave before going to bed. Saves precious minutes in the morning.

A couple of the gang still sleep. They'll miss breakfast and catch the truck for briefing half-way down the drive. Most of us prefer a good hot meal and allow just enough time to gulp down eggs, toast, and lots of coffee. Others are already queued up at the toilet. Most of us can always relieve ourselves before a briefing. We won't admit it, but it could be nerves. There's never enough time, however.

The usual thoughts run through our minds at breakfast and on the truck to the briefing room. What position am I flying? Is my ship O.K.? Where are we going today? I guess, mostly, we wonder where we're going. It's old stuff to many of us. Some have been across 70-odd times. Yet still the same questions are on everyone's mind.

Still the same little "bubbles" in the stomach, perhaps we ate too fast or aren't quite awake. Maybe we shouldn't have slept those extra 10 minutes and gulped that egg so fast. But we always do, and anyhow, the "bubbles" always vanish in the briefing room. Nerves?

Most of us talk a lot at breakfast and on the truck.

"Gonna get one today . . .

"Hope it's a short haul . . .

"Hope it's long, I need time . . .

"Better fly in closer today, Joe . . .

"Oh, my God, is he leading the squadron . . .

"Pass the coffee . . .

"Where's that waiter . . .

"Wo't time is it . . .

"Gimme a light . . .

"Damn, I forgot my dog tags (this is serious when rushed) . . .

"Boy, what a swell day . . .

"Yeah, only 9/10ths heavy cloud . . .

"Nuts . . .

"Boy, my butt is still sore from yesterday . . ."

Much of the chatter is superficial, forced. We're trying to wake up, get a clear head. Talking helps.

Then we're at briefing. As we file in through the War Room every guy tries to look at the plotting map. Where are we going? How much time have we got 'till start engines? Or, is this another lousy milk run? Finally, everyone is seated. We all watch "Stormy" and his weather board. That is important to every man. If there is an overcast our first thought is always, how thick is it? We pay close attention to Stormy. He finishes and our eyes wander to the map, noting the courses, the flak, the apparent size of the show, subconsciously figuring on the chances of a fight along our route, how much water we'll have to cross, and the damn flak!

As for the show, we're impatient. Forget the other task forces, what's ours? What is it going to bomb? How many are there? Any other fighters on our bombers? How about that flak? Top cover 32,000 feet and wing tanks to boot. It's gonna be rugged.

We glance around the room. Who's leading the 369th? The 370th? They only have three flights. Have to watch aborts.

"In 45 seconds it will be 0816," that's it. Briefing's over. We know where we're going, what we're doing. Now let's get going.

"Hurry up, I want to check my Mae West, clean my goggles, get to the latrine." But first we have to catch Chappie's prayer. A solemn, very sincere moment when most of us realize as much as at any time that this is a serious business we're engaged in. That moment with Chappie is good. No more "bubbles." And let's get something today.

Unloading from the truck at the pilot's shack our first thought is of flying equipment. Coveralls, helmet, Mae West, parachute.

Next stop is S-2, a careful checking of all pockets. Some of us leave our rings, bracelets, wallets, pens, letters. Nothing written must go with us. "Gotcher dog tags? Hell yes! Do we look that dumb?" Then we duck without waiting for a caustic reply, escape kits in our pockets. S-2 hands us course cards and maps. We check the times again and stuff the maps in our overalls.

We note what plane we're flying; where it's parked, and mentally calculate our taxi procedure to the marshalling area. Important to note which plane we're to follow.

Somebody reminds us that our formation has been lousy and we should 'stick 'em in tight.' We promise this to ourselves. We have an unfortunate attitude of considering ourselves to be above instruction, w'ot the Hell, we're combat pilots, not OTU students. Among many faults this shows up in nearly every one who's crossed the Channel. It doesn't help anything but our ego.

Flying equipment, escape kits, maps, schedule of planes, O.K. We check the time again. Hell, let's have another cigarette. We've smoked a dozen already. They taste lousy, but it's relaxing. Some of us chew gum, makes your mouth feel better for those uncomfortable hours ahead with an oxygen mask creasing your face and parching your throat. Many grab wads of cotton from Doc. It helps the noise in the ears which can be as disconcerting as anything that happens in an airplane.

A couple of last drags on the cigarette. Time to go out. No use rushing. Everyone hates tearing out to his ship at the last minute. We run over the take off procedure mentally, check the weather for the thousandth time, grab our stuff and head for the plane after a final wise-crack or so at Doc or S-2.

Never say goodbye, just leave the shack casually. No fuss. Pilots hate any show of sentiment, emotion, even a handshake would be fiercely resented at the moment. After all, since 0700 we've been selling ourselves the idea that this is just another job. There's nothing to worry about.

We stop for a leak outside, then we go to our plane. Don't run, walk, take your time. Check the weather. "Damn, the wind's cross tee." Reaching the plane we hand our helmet to the waiting crew chief, look the ship over, noting the position of the tail-wheel. We usually chat flippantly with the crew chief if we know him well.

"Think she'll run?"

"Yessir, how many you gonna get today?"

"All depends on who cleaned the guns," we reply.

Five minutes to go. We climb up on the wing and wriggle into the cockpit. First thing is to fasten those dinghies to the backtype chutes. The dinghy is already in the cockpit. Next, fasten the Mae West lanyard. Assisted by the crew chief, we squirm and twist into as comfortable a position as possible. It's important to get set right now. Then the straps can be tightened if necessary. Finally we're as comfortable and secure as possible.

There follows a routine which no two pilots probably do alike. It includes: clamping the oxygen hose to our harness, putting on our helmet, plugging in radio; connecting and testing our oxygen masks, trimming the crate for take off; turning on radio, gun heat, often the pitot heat; setting the gyro compass, setting the altimeter; checking the ship's clock with our watch.

A minute to go.

"Is she cold, Sergeant? Brakes on?"

We check them anyhow. Flap handle is placed in "up" position. They'll come up as soon as the engine starts. The crew chief closes the canopy. We lock it.

"Chocks are out. Whenever you're ready," shouts the crew chief. We look over the switches and instrument panel again mentally rechecking all previous moves. It's time!

"Clear!"

We flick on battery and ignition switches; the fuel boost pump, main gas line. Suddenly the awakened radio makes noises in our headset. We prime the engine, at the same time flicking the starter button. The prop turns over reluctantly, shaking the crate. She spits, dies, we shoot the primer again. She coughs and comes to life in a whirlwind of noise and vibration. Lock the starter-switch off, flip the mixture control down, RPM 1300, O.K. She's running smoothly now.

Brakes off and we start to taxi out with quick glances at all engine instruments and a check of the flaps. The brakes feel good, but take it easy. They won't hold long against too heavy a foot. Watch the coolant temperature.

At the marshalling point there is usually a delay of several minutes during which time "mags" are checked, blower checked, fuel selector valve handle turned to all positions. The ammeter is read at high RPM (2000). Another final glimpse at the instrument panel. We roll into actual take off position. Flick the fuel boost switch to emergency. Push shut the sliding window of the canopy.

We're ready. No nervousness, no idle thoughts; everything is focused on the moment of take off, getting her in the air, shipshape, and into good formation as quickly as possible. We feel confident and at home in the cockpit, it's our office and we feel the best we have since waking.

Throttles go full forward. There's the roar, the dust, the rough bouncing and jolting. Suddenly we're in the air. That is the moment when our day, our job really starts. All else has been in preparation for this, all our thoughts, conversation.

Uppermost now in everyone's mind will be thoughts of flying good position; watching gas consumption on the long climb to altitude, checking and rechecking oil and coolant temps, RPM, manifold pressure, little else enters our minds until we're well past the English Coast. We check our radio transmitters by calling without pressing the throttle button. If anyone answers the set is faulty and we return to base.

We have varying amounts of pride in the appearance of the group as it heads out, whether the squadrons set course together and hold good position throughout the climb. We hate to hear the "aborts" start leaving the formation.

And as we get under way, there begins that peculiar practice which is common to most fighter pilots alone in their ship, talking aloud to themselves, muttering, humming, often ranting and raving like maniacs at some trite detail particularly if the going is difficult. Many talk to their planes, cursing them, praising them. It would make fascinating reading to record a five-hour mission in the cockpit of a Mustang, but it would be unprintable. Just let the leaders drop their air-speed too much and we start swearing. Let the weather be bad, let us get split up, the oxygen masks nearly melt with the heat of invective. This talking business is an odd yet satisfying outlet, a regular safety-valve.

We check our altitude and times and courses on the way out. Once to the English Coast we begin searching for other planes, the big friends, other fighters, and possible contrails. We wonder if the "damn bombers" will be "late as usual" and listen with interest to "Blue Two's report" to "Chairman." Radio chatter is a sort of diversion on the monotonous run to the enemy coast and eventual R/V.

Approaching that same coast our final thought is of flak and we almost automatically put on a couple more inches of manifold pressure, "let's get up some speed and get by the coast," is the feeling.

We go on until R/V, switching to wing-tanks as we burn down the fuselage tank to 30 gallons, watching for the bombers (and all other planes); studying the ground, if visible, for possible landmarks or recognition features.

Actually it's all pretty business-like and de-glamorizing. The details of flying proper formation, constantly checking the cockpit, listening to the radio, looking about, there are few if any divergent or idle thoughts. Details and facts follow the same general pattern on each mission and allow for very little individual reaction.

The big point of change in thoughts comes when we enter the cockpit. Once aboard the Mustang, heads clear, nerves relax, and the real job begins with no distractions. 'Til then there have been the questions, where, when, how long, the hurry of dressing, eating, getting to briefing, then the rush to get flying equipment, escape kits, last minute instructions by flight and squadron leaders.

All this creates a nervous tension in the oldest pilots as well as the new.

We can't escape it.

HEADQUARTERS 359TH FIGHTER GROUP
Office of the Group Historian
APO 637 US Army
4 October 1944

History of the 359th Fighter Group, September 1944

The "one big day" so long awaited by the 359th Fighter Group arrived 11 September, as the Group completed nine months of operational flying over Europe.

On that day the 359th destroyed 26 German aircraft in aerial combat, probably destroyed four, and damaged six, besides running up a score of 9-0-13 on the ground. That meant 35-4-19 for the day. Next afternoon, 12 September, the 359th scored another 10-0-3 in the air and 6-0-8 on the ground. The two-day total of 51-4-28 was one-third the total score compiled in the preceding nine months.

Ten men did not return from the missions on these two days, as a revivified Luftwaffe fought savagely against the joint Anglo-American attempt to make successful a final bombardment softening of the Reich for the ground assault.

The Germans fought only when the weather was right. The weather generally was execrable, so bad that it was a distinct achievement and a tribute to the ability of its pilots that the 359th could get up 22 times in the month, though one of these was a two-flight A/S Rescue affair.

On the 22 days on which missions were flown, 1,050 P-51s most of them now the model D, were airborne off the pockmarked, ragged turf at East Wretham, and 112 came back for a sortie total of 938, averaging 5:01 per mission. The total aircraft claim of 58-5-29 was opposed to 16 men listed as MIA as the month ended.

Though a slightly higher total had been scored in May, September generally was regarded as the most encouraging month in the 359th Group's history. There were two reasons: the grand slam of the 11th, and the emergence of new leaders. Fourteen men returned to the Zone of the Interior during the month as the tour was twice reduced, first from 300 to 285 hours, then to 270 hours. And permission to send men home whenever replacements became available brought the strength above 121, and made the tour even more pliable.

Of the 14 finishing, five were replacements who had joined in England during 1944, in itself a fact symptomatic of the change in the 359th Group's complexion. There were 21 new pilots arriving during the month and of these, one was a major, three were captains, two were first lieutenants, 12 second lieutenants and two flight officers. This meant that the 359th, in line with the policy of decreasing the number of pilots permitted to be in the States for rest and relaxation, would be reconstituted in the European Theatre instead of developing its own leaders from the pilots brought to England in October of 1943.

The experience level on 30 September was 128 combat hours per pilot, exactly the Wing average. And the experience was well distributed over the whole range, from men breaking into combat flying to the veterans still at it. The largest group, 50, were in their first 100 hours, 36 were in the second 100, 23 in their third hundred, two had more than 300 hours, and eight pilots had not yet gone operational.

The constant series of changes among flight commanders, product of time-expired men going to the States and promotions and transfers, created one bad result; a falling off in the standard of training of new men within the flights, heretofore the direct responsibility of the flight commanders.

The remedy experimentally tried by Major Pezda was to center within the 359th Fighter Group itself all training of the 13 new men who arrived on 8 September. Major Pezda took responsibility for the training, assisted by Captain Fogg, and finished the program of indoctrination before both Pezda and Fogg went back to the States; Pezda for rest and recuperation before returning, Fogg for reassignment.

But if the originals of 13 December, 1943, were streaming away as they completed their tours, the return flow from the States also began; Major McKee and Captain Doersch returning early in the month to the 370th, being followed by Captains Thomson and Matthews of the 369th.

They were eagerly welcomed, as was the growth of a great combat leader in Captain Benjamin H. King of the 368th. King, who had done a Pacific tour in P-38s and P-39s, getting three confirmed in fighting against the Japs, had transferred to the 359th from the 479th. He made an immediate impression in his squadron, where he became operations officer during the month, enlarged that impression by his behavior as briefing officer and group leader and clinched it with a 3-0-0 performance on the 11th and another aerial win on the 12th.

Eleven men led one or more of the 22 missions flown in the month, and five of these were replacement pilots.

Abortions remained a problem, the average mission figures were 45.73 up and 5.09 back for 40.64 sorties. On five missions the early returns reached double figures, but the abort percentage was nonetheless topped within the Wing by the 352nd Group's 12.3, indicating the problem was pretty general.

Morale on the whole was at a peak, so noticeable that Brigadier General Anderson commented on it when he came down to Wretham to present Distinguished Flying Crosses.

A snack bar in the Nissen hut next to the Flying Control Tower was opened by Colonel Swanson and proved the answer to many problems, especially that of some sort of lunch for pilots caught by 10-4 missions. It became a very popular place, as did the officers' PX and barber shop, which opened in the end of the building.

Chaplain Ziegler, discussing morale in his monthly report, mentions both this building and the Red Cross Aero club for the part they played in maintaining morale. So far as the pilots were concerned, the weekly tea-dances, now a fixture, and especially the thrice-weekly movies reinstated by Colonel Swanson there, were more important. On the ground side, the resumption of leaves and furloughs for non-flying officers and men, which came early in the month, also played a great role, more than overbalancing the now generally accepted conviction that the air offensive against Germany could not be finished in the fall of 1944 but must go through another winter.

In the circumstances, enlisted men concentrated on improving their quarters for what they learned 12 months before would be a bleak time in East Anglia. Darkness came quickly again with the elimination of one hour of summer time, but the mood generally was good.

The flying field, the turf sadly battered by nine months' flying, gave constant trouble and engineers for the First Bombardment Division, to which the 359th became attached on 13 September with the demise of the VIII Fighter Command, recommended removal to another station.

They suggested the B-26 bases in the Chelmsford-Colchester area but eventually left the decision to Colonel Swanson, and he, feeling that another move to the Continent in the spring was very likely in any case, obtained a high priority for the laying of steel mat on both ends of Runway 22, thereupon deciding to remain at Wretham for the winter. Negro engineers promptly set to work laying steel assembly areas at both ends of the longest and most used runway.

There was, nonetheless, some manufacture of crates for packing, but there was even more interior decoration of quarters and leisure rooms, notably in the handsome day-room of the 1101st Signal Company. Emphasis also increased on discussion groups, although some units criticized the program unfavorably, for instance, in comparison with the British Army's ABCA program.

From an operational standpoint, the statistical summary is notable because it has no fighter-bombing missions, and only one ordered strafing operation. The P-51 had proved too vulnerable on the deck, and a conference of group commanders called by General Doolittle early in the month produced an order to keep the Mustangs away from German light flak unless higher authority ordered otherwise. This was duly stressed at briefings, yet the damage done the enemy by ground attack had been so juicy that flight leaders repeatedly took their flight down anyway, resulting in a grievous series of losses.

This was notably so in the case of Cyril Jones, a lanky Tennessean and a remarkable aerial shot. He came to the 359th after a year as a gunnery instructor in which he had fired more than 100,000 rounds. He accordingly eschewed the A1 computing sight which was coming into general use and made a remarkable record before he went into the ground while strafing in defiance of orders on 12 September. His brief combat career embraced the first allied victory over a liquid-rocket Messerschmitt 163 and a total of 5-0-1 in the air and 4-0-4 on the ground.

Before the ban on strafing, however, the 359th Group, under Major Pezda's dynamic leadership, laid on a genuinely fine performance on 5 September. The weather that day was wretched, so bad that the P-47 strafing groups which the 359th was ordered to escort could not get through. Pezda led his people in, however, and most of the 48-0-15 claims on locomotives were made that day along with all the rest of the wide variety of targets. The ammunition expenditure for the month was 109,269 rounds, all armor-piercing incendiary.

Mission reporting was made difficult by the increasing number of pilots landing on fields in Belgium and France. Sometimes they did not get back for days and days, during which time they were listed as NYR, but investigation demonstrated that almost all had urgent operational reasons for landing and genuine operational difficulties in getting back. Ghent under shell-fire, Brussels at any time, and spots ranging as far as Bordeaux nonetheless provided memorable evenings and brilliant anecdotes for returning pilots.

Most harrowing story told by a returnee was that of Edward G. Kaloski of the 368th, who bailed out 35 miles south of Beachy Head on 1 September and was given up as drowned in the sea until the very end of the month, when he was reported hospitalized in England at Kingston. It was learned he had broken a leg getting out of the airplane, had "landed" in the sea five miles off the coast of France, managed to get into his dinghy, paddled ashore after long hours of struggle and lain on the beach for three days before he was found by French fisherfolk.

Six missions of the month involved cover for the Allied Airborne Army's fight for the Rhine bridges. Most of the others centered on the assault on German oil, Ludwigshafen being visited three times and Merseburg twice.

The weather was the great opponent in all these operations, and the month indicated exactly what it was going to be on its first day. There was a brilliant moon at 0130 1 Sept, when FO 543 arrived, but everything worsened steadily and when Colonel Murphy, flying the last mission of his brilliant tour, arrived with the 359th Group at Paris he found bombers milling confusedly at 20,000 to 25,000 feet. After 50 minutes of struggling against three layers of clouds, the bombers radioed that they were aborting. Of the 473 bombers dispatched that day, only one managed to bomb anything. Kaloski was lost on this mission and next day Captain King took six P-51s to look for him. They saw an empty six-man dinghy off Berck-sur-Mer and drew flak from Boulogne, but nothing more. Weather prevented any Air Force or Command operation. Meanwhile, however, both Virgil Sansing and Rene Burtner had come back to the station after hiding out with the Maquis. Burtner had gone in with the American light tanks that captured Saint-Dizier, the airfield where he was shot down. Sansing had lived for three months near Soissons and had watched the collapse of the German Army.

3 September saw the first September mission to Ludwigshafen. Lieutenant Albert E. Wolfe of the 370th went on towards Normandy, being stranded in Varades on the Loire, and was carried as NYR for six days before he finally returned on the 9th, a RON duration record later excelled by Captain James R. Parsons' difficulties in getting away from Bordeaux.

Weather again prevented any operation on the 4th, but on this day Bill Hodges, who had jumped after the disastrous attack on Rheims-Champagne May 11, telephoned from London that he was not only back in England but was determined to finish his tour. During the month, word was later to arrive that Maslow was a prisoner, and that debonair Kibler, the third flight leader lost at Rheims, had been killed.

Groups sweeping and bombing had a big day on the 5th, but the 359th's escort run to Ludwigshafen was without incident, save for three Me 282 jetties sighted in the target area. On take off, Lieutenant Eugene F. Dauchert of the 368th cracked up on the end of the runway, but he was unhurt. Major Pezda, dissatisfied with R/T procedure, called a meeting of all pilots in which he catalogued all the idle chatter he had been listening to and ordered it to stop.

The 6th was again a non-operation day, although the 359th was standing by until 1258 before the scrub came in and nothing happened on the 7th either. September 8, however, was a different story.

FO 556 was scrubbed in the morning and 557, arriving at 1111, stipulated fighter cover for three strafing P-47 groups, with the injunction "352nd and Groups will not strafe airdromes." In the event, although the 359th Group rendezvoused with the 78th Fighter-Bombers, that group had to turn back and both the 56th and the 353rd Groups reported trouble getting through the solid overcast to 18,000 feet in the Aachen area. So Pezda sent his 51s down to beat up the Koblenz-Frankfurt area and the pilots had a great day.

Lawrence A. Zizka of the 370th, left the area with large pieces of wire dangling from his wing but reached England safely, although he was for hours believed to be lost. Included in the claims were 5-0-1 in Junkers 52s found parked near Cronberg, NOT, as the 359th Group was careful to report, on the airdrome.

A more normal escort was flown on the 9th, an attack by 235 Libs on the marshalling yard at Mainz. The 4th Group, on the same show, saw two Me109s but there was no other excitement.

First Lieutenant Benjamin J. Vos Jr., a former instructor of whom high hopes were held, was lost on 10 September in what may have been a fighter trap. Fierce flak protected a field liberally decorated with dummies. The escort was to Stuttgart, and Lieutenant Kenneth L. Hobson of the 369th fought and shot down two bizarre aircraft, two fins on a single tail, single-engine, which was not satisfactorily identified as to type. There also was some strafing, including three locos.

The Command shot up 113-0-73 on the ground this day and, next day, the 11th, the Germans came up and fought. The strategic plan of the Eighth Air Force was to push 75 bombers across Europe on the shuttle run to Russia, under cover of a heavy assault on oil plants of the Leipzig area. This was done with the 20th Group making the long escort ride to Russia, but the Luftwaffe, up in strength, knocked down at least 20 bombers in the other forces (the total loss was 52) and itself suffered losses of 17-23-44 to the bombers, 116-7-23 to the fighters and 42-0-43 on the ground.

The 359th got itself 35-4-19 of these totals, and was officially commended for it by General Griswold. There was combat from 1115 to 1205 and the days' losses were five men.

There were several remarkable individual performances. Cyril Jones shot down four in the air over a landing field and also destroyed two more on the ground and damaged four others. Captain King got an aerial triple, Claude Crenshaw accounted for two in the air and another on the ground,

Grant Perrin, Louis E. Barnett, George F. Baker Jr., and Gilbert Ralston all destroyed two in the air.

One of the four men NYR got separated from his own outfit, joined up with the 4th Group and was seen by them to shoot down an Me109 in the air before crashing to flak on a landing ground. He was identified only by his 359th green nosed airplane.

The intelligence section was especially happy at the promptness with which the enemy had been engaged, since the section had accurately forecast where and how the Luftwaffe reaction would develop, and, through Flight Lieutenant G.S. Darlington, RAF liaison officer, had briefed Bill Forehand, the group leader that day, on what to expect. Accordingly, with Colonel Swanson's approval the S-2s now changed the briefing routine, with the duty intelligence officer briefing on the whole operation as it was planned, on the enemy and friendly situation, and the group leader briefing only on tactics. The result was lengthier tactical briefings and a refocusing of pilot interest on what the plan for finding and destroying the enemy that day was to be.

This briefing system was begun on the 12th, when battle with the GAF fighters was again joined in the offensive against German oil. Again there was a rash of landings in France, and 10 men were wholly unaccounted for, with 7 others believed safe at other bases, for several hours. The mission summary at first carried this total but was amended when it was established that the 359th had lost five men for a score of 16-0-9. Dick Connelly and Robert Hatter had doubles, and Cyril Jones, on the evidence of his wingman, was credited with three on the ground. But Jones, despite orders to stay off the deck, had gone back to an airfield he had seen the day before and had crashed there. The air combat developed in the Berlin area on the way to Breux. Barnett, Hughes, Hobson and Haas were the other men NYR.

In addition to the combat losses, Lieutenant Archibald of the 368th had washed out his airplane trying to get back in on the field with a bad engine. Benefiel had been forced to make a wheels-up landing at Woodbridge and Lieutenant Britton had bellied near Abbeville on a pole-protected field. These, with the aircraft NYR and those beginning to be scattered 'round the Continent, created an airplane shortage, which Colonel Swanson met by ordering the airplanes assigned to training new pilots to be readied for the next mission.

That came up promptly, next morning, and a resumption of the fight for air superiority over the Reich was expected. But the Germans were late forming up and, although Captain King, nursing a straggler home, saw 50

Me109s assembling, they were too late to hit the third force on the way home after bombing Merseburg.

There were claims of 3-0-0 on the 18th, but that was to be all for the month, as the two big days of the 11th and 12th had neatly rounded off nine months of combat. Now the job was to support the airborne landings. This began with area support for bombers ordered to plaster flak positions on the 16th. The weather stopped the heavies and 35 minutes after the 359th crossed in at Ijmuiden, the controller recalled the show.

The operation was carried through next day, however, in advance of the actual landings, and the 359th patrolled its area for 2 hours, passing the 1,000-plane airborne armada on the way home. Harold R. Burt of the 369th had coolant trouble and jumped, apparently into German hands, northwest of Antwerp. On this day also, news came in that Robert Siltamaki was a POW, while Bill Hodges reported that T.P. Smith, lost in the Silver Star airdrome strafing of 11 April, was in London and would come back to finish his tour.

The airborne assault on Eindhoven, Nijmegen and Arnhem continued on the 18th. It was a long (6:07) patrol under MEW control, and there were three scattered combats. A flight was bounced by 35 Fw190s in one of these, and in this fight Grover C. Deen and Edwin L. Sjoblad were last seen. There were three claims, by Crenshaw, Lieutenant Parsons, and another shared by John E. Keur and Thomas G. Bur.

The shortage of aircraft now had been mended and on both this day and the 19th, the 359th put up 57 airplanes. The weather, which played so large a part in this operation at Arnhem, forced the bombers to hit targets of opportunity along the Rhine on the 19th, and both this job and patrol of the drop zones immediately thereafter were uneventful.

Bad as this weather was, worse was to follow. On the 20th, the original orders were modified to insure that all groups would be down by 1930. The 359th again went out to patrol the airborne drop zones but as the weather worsened, a recall went out at 1750. Even so, most of the group stayed to their briefed withdrawal time. The recall code of that day was "Tulip Time" and there were characters cheerfully inquiring "where is this Tulip Time we're supposed to go to?" with the result that the mist was down on the tree tops and the field was thoroughly socked in when the last men got down at 1936. Keur had coolant trouble and jumped three miles off Lowestoft, being promptly gathered in by Air-Sea Rescue. That night there was a major reunion at Wretham Hall as Ettlesen, Drake, Hawkinson, Doersch and McKee returned simultaneously, the first three from months in Europe under cover, the last two from 30 days home leave in the States.

Ensued much confusion on the 21st. The other groups in the wing could not get off to support an attempt to drop Polish paratroopers in the Arnhem area. At noon, Wing said that the 359th would go but would be recalled in time to get home before dark. At 1400, Wing amended this to say not to take off unless ordered to do so, and to cut the schedule to the eight or twelve most experienced pilots in each squadron, this in turn being limited to eight pilots per squadron at 1412. Pilots were put on stand-by in their aircraft and they were then ordered off, getting up at 1449. Five of the six flights assembled under Major Pezda, but Major Irvine, leading, found cloud up to 13,000 feet north of the field and the MEW controller refused permission to Pezda to go on with the 20 pilots he had. Finally, at 1805, informed by Major Irvine the weather was still horrible and he was having difficulty breaking out, the controller at Walcott recalled the show.

An uneventful escort to Kassel was led by Major Irvine on the 22nd. Lieutenant Magee's brakes froze and he nosed over on landing, without injury.

There was rain overnight, but the dawn of the 23rd was clear and crisp with a blue sky. So, a release till 1100 arrived the night before, and the 359th Group was released for the rest of the day at 0940.

Aviation petrol was then in short supply, and economy had been ordered, but General Anderson approved a good will visit to North Weald, a RAF Spit station whose Czech and British squadrons expected to be re-quipped with Mustangs. The station had been visited earlier in the month by Darlington and Donohue of the Wretham Intelligence Section, who had toured RAF fighter, night fighter, and sector stations. Accordingly, Colonel Swanson, Captain King, and Lieutenants Hatter and John F. Lauesen went down to spend the afternoon and talk over the P-51. That afternoon, Pop Doersch lead a practice escort mission, enlivened by a stuck landing wheel on Lieutenant Marshall's aircraft, which wheel finally came out in a dive, and a practice strafing of Wretham. And that night, the gun crews were alerted for flying bombs, now being launched rather erratically from He-111s off the Dutch Coast.

Rain and high wind on the 24th resulted in a release. It was a Sunday, and despite all hazard of the weather, a record number of girls arrived for the tea-dance from the Norwich, Cambridge, Wisbech area, so that the parties, it was felt, had proven themselves a success. Meanwhile, official transfer of the 67th Fighter Wing to the 1st Bombardment Division, with a change in APO to 557, had been announced, along with dropping of the old escape procedures, photographs, and purses, since the Germans now, save for Holland, were driven back within the Reich, and no longer could pilots expect to have eager help from underground organizations if they were shot down.

The next operational day was a ride to Frankfurt on the 25th, which resulted in the much regretted loss of Lieutenant Lauesen of the 368th, last seen in a vertical dive from 26,000 ft near Wiesbaden. One of 11 brothers, several of whom were also pilots, his parents still were in Denmark, and the tall, shy, yellow-haired man lived only to help free them. He had flown 150 operation hours with the RAF in Spits, had transferred to the AAF, been grounded because of nose medical troubles at altitude, had gone then to the gunnery flight and, by dint of hard work, gotten himself transferred back into combat status. Anoxia or flak seemed the only explanation for his loss.

Major McKee started his second tour in the ETO on the 26th, but the mission to Osnabrück produced nothing of interest. Captain James K. Lovett led the job on the 27th to Düsseldorf. Pilots again saw the trail of a Big Ben 40-ton rocket launched in the general direction of England, but as usual were too far away to pinpoint its launching site, although it seemed to come from near Düsseldorf. Captain Hodges, one of the original Flying Tigers, had to return early soon after take off but promptly took off again in an effort to catch the group, eventually coming back after crossing in over the Continent alone.

There was some difficulty with the rendezvous on the 28th, since the bombers bound for Magdeburg were 14 minutes late and the 359th was to make a preliminary sweep along their route in. Eventually the bombers were found, although one squadron latched on to the division going to Merseburg, but no enemy opposition developed. Howard E. Steussy of the 370th was lost on the mission. He was last seen near 15,000 near Koblenz and there were no theories as to what happened to him. It seemed worse for some time, since six men landed on the Continent and were at first reported as missing.

The last mission of the month, to Münster on the 30th, produced sighting of three jet-propelled German aircraft but they did not attack and could not be caught. Otherwise, there was no action, even though Captain King sent one section sweeping as far as Steinhuder and Bremen for some sign of the enemy. The 359th Group was definitely looking for the Germans, sure of its own ability to handle anything it found.

In three weeks the 359th Fighter Group would celebrate the first anniversary of its arrival in England. A lot had happened in the year, but the pilots knew that there was still plenty of excitement left in Germany before the Luftwaffe was destroyed, and precision bombardment of the enemy homeland, as the tacticians dreamed of precision bombardment, began.

*Upon Howard's return to the United States he made
this final entry in his diary:*

Diary Memoranda:
The Original "Overseas" 368th Status

Tyrrell:	POW
Shaw:	USA
White:	Group HQ, NYTT
Botsford:	Killed on Local Hop
Bolefahr:	KIA
Simmons:	MIA
Taylor:	369th, NYTT
Perkins:	USA
Fogg:	USA
Baldridge:	MIA
Janney:	USA
Randolph:	368th, NYTT
Cater:	Killed, Bailout
Downing:	Goxhill, Instructor
Hagan:	POW
Kibler:	KIA
McGeever:	USA
Pino:	POW
Smith:	POW
Hawkinson:	MIA, okay
Hyland:	KIA
Keesey:	368th, NYTT
Hudelson:	KIA
Lemmens:	370th May '44, USA
Lane:	Wing HQ
Burton:	370th May '44, USA
POW:	Prisoner-of-War
KIA:	Killed in Action
NYTT:	Not Yet Thru Tour

13.

OCTOBER 1944–AUGUST 1945

OCTOBER 1944

October 14: The Allies liberate Athens, Greece.

October 21: The US 1st Army captures Aachen, the first German city to be occupied.

October 25: Russia invades Norway.

NOVEMBER 1944

November 2: Belgium is liberated when Canadian troops take Zeebrugge.

November 4: Axis forces in Greece surrender.

November 24: Strasbourg is liberated by the French.

November 29: Allied troops liberate Albania.

DECEMBER 1944

December 16: The Battle of the Bulge begins in the Ardennes region.

JANUARY 1945

January 17: Warsaw is liberated.

January 26: Auschwitz is liberated by Soviet troops.

January 27: The Battle of the Bulge ends.

FEBRUARY 1945

February 2: Ecuador declares war on Germany.

February 8: Paraguay declares war on Germany.

February 12: Peru declares war on Germany.

February 23: The American flag is raised at Mt. Suribachi on Iwo Jima.

February 25: Turkey declares war on Germany.

February 28: US Army troops liberate Manila, the capital of the Philippines.

MARCH 1945

March 28: Argentina declares war on Germany.

March 29: The Red Army enters Austria.

APRIL 1945

April 4: The Ohrdruf death camp is liberated.

April 10: The Buchenwald concentration camp is liberated.

April 12: On the morning of April 12th, Roosevelt mentions that he has a terrific headache. Later that day he dies. The doctor diagnoses that the President has suffered a massive cerebral hemorrhage. Harry Truman is sworn in as the 33rd President of the United States of America.

April 15: In Millville, New Jersey, where he is in charge of ground school, Captain Fogg continues to teach young pilots while also keeping current on his own flying. He is honored when asked to join a handful of pilots to fly a special mission: to overfly the interment of President Roosevelt.

Interment of President Franklin Delano Roosevelt. Second 330 of video clip U.S. Government Archive Number [208 UN 151 FGMC] from funeral ceremonies held at Hyde Park, New York.
Courtesy of CriticalPast

Fly-over at the interment of President Franklin Delano Roosevelt. Second 378 of video clip U.S. Government Archive Number [208 UN 151 FGMC] from funeral ceremonies held at Hyde Park, New York. *Courtesy of CriticalPast*

April 28: Mussolini is captured and executed by Italian partisans.

April 29: The Dachau concentration camp is liberated by the US 7th Army.

April 30: In his bunker in Berlin, Hitler commits suicide.

MAY 1945

May 2: German forces in Italy surrender and Berlin falls to Soviet troops.

May 4: German forces in Holland, Denmark, and northwest Germany surrender.

May 7: Germany surrenders unconditionally to the Allies.

May 8: Victory in Europe. Ceasefire takes effect at one minute past midnight.

AUGUST 1945

August 6: Flying at 31,000 feet, the crew of the B-29 *Enola Gay* ushers in the nuclear age when they drop "Little Boy" on Hiroshima.

August 9: "Fat Man," the second nuclear weapon used in war, is dropped on Nagasaki from *Bockscar*.

August 14: Emperor Hirohito announces Japan's unconditional surrender. Victory in Japan.

SUMMARY OF ACTION:

Captain Howard Fogg

Captain Howard Fogg flew 76 missions and completed his combat tour with the Army Air Corp in September 1944. He was discharged from the Army in August 1945. Along with the ribbons he earned while with the 359th Fighter Group, Howard was awarded the Air Medal with three clusters and the Distinguished Flying Cross with one cluster.

Well respected for his leadership skills and his focused demeanor whether flying escort or strafing trains, Howard was also tasked with teaching young pilots how to fly, both in England and upon his return to the United States. During his combat tour his commanding officers relied on him to accurately and swiftly plot numerous missions. Many inquired whether he would take up a career flying commercial aircraft following the war, but that was not where his heart led him. Instead, he pursued his art, and decades later was regularly acknowledged as the world's foremost railroad artist.

At the height of his artistic career, when the waiting list for one of his paintings was measured in years, Howard casually mentioned to his son Richard how honored he was to have been selected to fly at President Roosevelt's interment. He had never spoken of this before and in his typical modest fashion, Howard said, "you could tell which plane was mine, it was the one slightly out of formation." But Howard rarely flew out of formation, either in his plane on that long-ago day in 1945, or throughout his life. He married the woman he loved. He and Margot raised three fine sons and sustained numerous life-long friendships. And Howard succeeded beyond his wildest dreams in the artistic career he first envisioned in 1938.

SUMMARY OF ACTION:

359th Fighter Group

During its 17 months of operation, members of the 359th Fighter Group, comprised of the 368th Fighter Squadron, the 369th Fighter Squadron, and the 370th Fighter Squadron, excelled at escort missions and at the very hazardous jobs of "killing" trains and destroying aircraft on the ground. Although often frustrated at the restrictions placed on pursuing enemy aircraft that endeavored to lure them away from protecting their "big friends," the bombers, the pilots of the 359th faithfully fulfilled the escort missions that comprised approximately 75 percent of their flights.

The 359th Fighter Group was awarded a Distinguished Unit Citation as well as numerous battle ribbons, including:

The Air Offensive Europe ribbon, awarded for preparation for the invasion of Normandy;

The Normandy ribbon, for invasion support and subsequent break out of the beach head areas;

The Northern France ribbon, for support for the drive across France;

The Rhineland ribbon for supporting the airborne invasion of the Netherlands as well as the drive into the Rhine;

The Ardennes-Alsace ribbon for support during the Battle of the Bulge;

And the Central Europe Ribbon for supporting the final actions across Germany.

There were 13,455 sorties flown by the pilots of the 359th. In addition to guarding the "heavies," they shot down 241 enemy aircraft, with an additional 33 probables and 69 damaged. Another 122 were destroyed on the ground plus 107 damaged. Almost 500 locomotives and 1,400 railway cars were destroyed or damaged. Other ground attacks supported troop movements and targeted infrastructure. To do all of this, 1,000,000 rounds of .50 calibre ammunition was expended along with nearly 900 bombs of varying poundage.

The Fighter Group lost 121 pilots.

368th Fighter Squadron P-51s in a post-war lineup. *Courtesy of Stephen Almasy, Crew Chief. Archived by Char Baldridge, Historian, 359th Fighter Group Association.*

EPILOGUES

On May 21, 1944, Lieutenant Arlen R. "Baldy" Baldridge, as part of Blue Flight, attacked an airfield in the Wismar-Rostock area. Hit by flak, Baldy crash-landed, was quickly captured and taken to Bad Doberan. There, he was severely beaten and then shot through the heart when allegedly trying to escape. Postwar, the Bad Doberan area reported the greatest number of atrocity cases involving pilots, and by September 1948 the remains of 22 American and two British pilots had been unearthed.

On June 10, 1944 while on his 62nd mission, Captain Wayne N. "Bo" Bolefahr overflew a heavily defended marshalling yard in Antwerp. Bolefahr distracted the gunners by attacking the main flak emplacements resulting in his P-51 being hit numerous times before disintegrating when it hit the ground. A posthumous Distinguished Service Cross was awarded to Bolefahr in honor of his courage.

Lieutenant Emer H. Cater lost oil pressure and bailed out of his P-51 over the Straits of Dover on June 4, 1944. Lieutenants Perkins and Marcinkiewicz followed him down to the water. Almost immediately, eight planes and two launches reached the site, but they found only an oil slick, seat cushion and partially inflated dinghy.

Major George A. "Pop" Doersch flew 158 missions in two tours. With 10-1/2 aerial kills credited to him, Pop was one of the Fighter Group's Aces. He retired from the Air Force in 1967 as a colonel and worked for the Hughes Aircraft Corporation until 1989. Pop passed away on December 1, 1994.

While attacking a train on June 8, 1944, Lieutenant Benjamin M. "Hag" Hagan III was hit by flak. His P-51 caught fire, burning his face and right leg. After bailing out he was captured and hospitalized for a week, his burns having temporarily blinded him.

On August 2, 1944, Captain Robert W. "Hawk" Hawkinson bailed out northeast of Rouen, breaking his ankle on landing. The mayor of nearby Vieux Manoir and his two young nephews carried Hawkinson to a family farm where he was hidden. The next morning, covered by hay in the back of a horse-drawn cart driven by the mayor, Hawkinson was taken through a German checkpoint to a farm near Cauricourt. In late August a Canadian Army medical unit picked him up.

Hit by flak on May 21, 1944 and with his engine smoking, Lieutenant Clyde M. "Bunky" Hudelson Jr.'s P-51 disappeared over a hill near Wismar. He was reported as killed in action.

Captain John S. Keesey flew 68 missions, destroying at least two Fw190s and damaging three others. He completed his combat tour with 270 hours of flight time.

Lieutenant Ralph E. "Kib" Kibler perished on May 11, 1944. Hit by flak while attacking an airfield at Reims-Champagne, Kib's fighter hit the ground at high speed.

Flying two tours, Major Andrew T. Lemmens served with both the 368th and the 370th Fighter Squadrons. He completed 133 missions, flying more than 500 hours in combat and scoring three aerial kills. Major

Lemmens ended his tours as the 359th Fighter Group's Commanding Officer.

Shot down about 50 miles north of Berlin on May 19, 1944, literally moments after shooting down three enemy fighters, Captain Charles W. Mosse was a Prisoner-of-War until the war ended.

Lieutenant Paul E. "Ollie" Olson was brought down by flak on December 18, 1944, and after treatment at a hospital in Hoffmonstahl he became a Prisoner-of-War in Stalag IIB, which was liberated on April 16, 1945.

Major Clifton Shaw completed his combat tour in August 1944 and returned to the United States.

Shot down near Berlin on May 19, 1944, Lieutenant James "J.B." Smith was captured and became a Prisoner-of-War.

Colonel Avelin P. "Hardtack" Tacon Jr. commanded the 359th Fighter Group from January 1943 through November of 1944. A career officer, he served with distinction and retired from the USAF with the rank of major general in 1967.

Lieutenant Colonel Albert R. "Trigger" Tyrrell, the 368th Fighter Squadron's first commanding officer, was flying his 63rd combat mission when shot down on June 21, 1944 while strafing an airfield east of Plau, Germany. He spent the remainder of the war as a Prisoner-of-War.

"Chappie," Captain Wilber C. Ziegler, the well-respected station chaplain at East Wretham was awarded a Bronze Star for meritorious service. Until his retirement in 1980, Chappie continued in the ministry. After retirement he taught for three years at the Boston University School of Theology and also served as interim district superintendent. Chappie died on April 29, 2003.

In 1949, Wretham Hall, the three-story structure that housed the officers of the 359th Fighter Group, burned to the ground.

THE POSTWAR CAREER
OF HOWARD FOGG

August 1945: With Howard discharged from the Army and Margot expecting their first child, the Foggs move to Summit, New Jersey, to live temporarily with Howard's parents. During the many discussions with his father about the future, Howard discovers that during the war, Howard Senior met famed public opinion pollster Elmo Roper, whose son was also a pilot, flying B-17s out of England. The two fathers hit it off and Roper tells Howard Senior that his son should call him after the war.

November 1945: Despite skepticism that it would take him closer to his goal of painting trains for a living, Howard contacts Roper's office and schedules an appointment. When Howard describes his career goals to Roper, the pollster laughs and says, "I've heard everything now!" But Roper stops laughing long enough to contact his friend, Duncan Fraser, President of the American Locomotive Company (ALCO). Howard takes three sketches and one painting to Fraser's office and Fraser purchases them on the spot.

March 1946: With ALCO in the midst of converting from steam to diesel locomotive production, Fraser makes the decision that launches Howard's artistic career. Hired as ALCO's new company artist, Howard begins painting their locomotives in the livery of prospective customers.

September 1946: At a three-day gala hosted by ALCO at the Waldorf Astoria Hotel in New York City, Howard's paintings are on display, and Lucius Beebe attends. A journalist with the New York *Herald-Tribune*, Beebe is considering leaving New York to pursue freelance writing and publication of railroad books. Lucius seeks out Howard and a long-term relationship is born, with Beebe buying a number of paint-

Howard Fogg. ALCO artist in the cab of a New York Central "Niagra" class 4-8-4 steam locomotive at Harmon, New York in July 1946. *Courtesy of Richard Fogg*

ings over the years. In 1947, Beebe's book, *Mixed Train Daily*, is the first of many to use a Fogg painting on the cover.

August 1955: While Howard focuses primarily on his commissions from ALCO, with their permission he also continues freelancing. After two summers vacationing in Buffalo Creek, Colorado, Howard, Margot, and their three sons move to Boulder, Colorado, where Howard sets up a home studio and paints primarily watercolors.

1957: With commissions from individuals, authors, publishers, railroads, and related industrial firms increasing, Howard ends his formal agreement with ALCO, although he continues to paint periodic commissions for them for a number of years.

1961: Friends for several years, Howard does his first painting for Ed Trumble, who would go on to found Leanin' Tree Publishing in January

Howard Fogg and Margot Fogg, Boulder, Colorado.
August 1967 photo courtesy of Richard Fogg

1965. While Leanin' Tree does not purchase every original of the 90-plus Fogg paintings they include in their line of western art cards, some of those they did acquire are on display in their Gallery of Western Art.

During the decades: Thanks to his artistic ability and engaging personality, Howard developed numerous friendships throughout his career, from the humblest rail fan to railroad presidents, from fellow painters to artists in music and film.

When railroad president and lifelong friend John Walker Barriger III introduced Howard to William Withall of the W.H. Miner Company, a 44-year business relationship was born. Miner, a manufacturer of freight car components, now possesses the most comprehensive collection of Fogg originals known.

Magazine articles featured Howard and his work. Limited edition prints were issued periodically. Jigsaw puzzles, porcelain plates and mugs, playing cards, calen-

Richard Kindig and Howard Fogg with Union Pacific Railroad 800 class #8444, La Salle, Colorado.
July 28, 1979 photo courtesy of Richard Fogg

dars, and greeting cards featured his art. His illustrations graced the covers and contents of multiple railroad books. In later years, books were written about him and his artwork, the most recent being *The Railroad Artistry of Howard Fogg*, written by two of Howard's most valued friends, Ronald C. Hill and Al Chione.

While there is no formal accounting, it is estimated that Howard completed more than 1,200 paintings over the course of his 50-year career. A number of these images continue to be printed in calendars and as greeting cards, but the majority of the original paintings reside in offices, businesses, museums, and the homes of those who loved his ability to capture the emotion of railroading.

October 1, 1996: Howard Fogg loses his battle with cancer at the age of 79. A few months later his ashes are scattered along the Union Pacific railroad tracks at Sherman Hill in Wyoming by his sons Richard, Peter, and Howard III. A high-speed freight train thunders through soon after.

Margot Fogg and Howard Fogg
in Boulder, Colorado.
1990 photo courtesy of Richard Fogg

POLITICAL CARTOONS
BY HOWARD FOGG

"I Thought I Warned You Fellas Last September!" April 18, 1939 cartoon by Howard Fogg. *Courtesy of Richard Fogg*

While at Dartmouth, Howard began drawing cartoons for the under-graduate magazine The Jack O'Lantern *as well as for the student news-paper. His sense of humor and innate drawing talent seemed to point directly toward a career as a political cartoonist. These examples suggest he would have been successful in that endeavor had he not dedicated himself to railroad art.*

"Bragging or Apologizing?" February 19, 1940 cartoon by Howard Fogg. *Courtesy of Richard Fogg*

"Education of A Nazi," February 20, 1940 cartoon by Howard Fogg. *Courtesy of Richard Fogg*

"The Inevitable Winner," February 21, 1940 cartoon by Howard Fogg. *Courtesy of Richard Fogg*

"Better Make Up Your Mind F. D. Or There'll Be A Wreck," February 24, 1940 cartoon by Howard Fogg. *Courtesy of Richard Fogg*

"It Won't Be Long Now!" March 4, 1940 cartoon by Howard Fogg.
Courtesy of Richard Fogg

"All For One And One For All," April 5, 1939 cartoon by Howard Fogg. *Courtesy of Richard Fogg*

"The Modern Frankenstein," April 11, 1939 cartoon by Howard Fogg *Courtesy of Richard Fogg*

"John "Ferdinand" Bull,"
February 18, 1940
cartoon by Howard Fogg
Courtesy of Richard Fogg

"Information Please,"
February 19, 1940
cartoon by
Howard Fogg
Courtesy of Richard Fogg

"If He Hurries It'll Be A
Battle To The Finnish,"
February 24, 1940
cartoon by Howard Fogg
Courtesy of Richard Fogg

"Spring Training,"
February 27,
1940 cartoon by
Howard Fogg
*Courtesy of
Richard Fogg*

ROUGH SKETCHES
BY HOWARD FOGG

Howard would often create a "rough sketch" for a customer to ensure that his vision for the final painting matched their expectations. Depending on the circumstances, the sketches were done in either pencil or watercolor. These examples, courtesy of Richard Fogg, are presented with Howard's original notations.

PLEASE RETURN   10/9/74

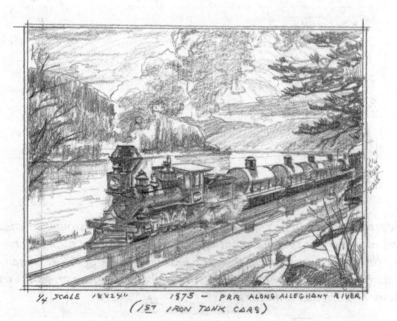

1/4 SCALE 18x24"   1875 — PRR ALONG ALLEGHANY RIVER
              (1ST IRON TANK CARS)

1/4" SCALE (18 X 24")   WELDED TANKERS - U.P., OREGON - 1925

"HOT DOG" CAR IN MONTANA ROCKIES - G.N. RY. 1956

¼" SCALE (18 X 24")   MADISON (ILLINOIS) BELT RY. 1893

"CEMENT PICKUP ON THE N&W" -1965   3-9-75

Here we have an unusual example where differing perspectives of the same scene were offered for review. The customer, Union Tank Car, selected "B" for the final painting.

ACKNOWLEDGMENTS

Well, there you have it. Thank you for allowing us to share my father's diary with you. I hope you consider it time well spent.

This was a difficult project for me because it raised so many questions I wish I had asked when I had the chance. Like so many men and women of that most remarkable generation my father rarely talked about his wartime experiences. In fact, I didn't even know this diary existed until he passed away and my mother asked my brothers and me if we'd like to read it! On the rare occasions when he did talk about the war he was neither boastful nor bitter. The only time I remember any strong emotion was when he told me about the day he grounded himself, Brown took his place in *Clumpy II*, and didn't come back. That has to leave a man asking unanswerable questions.

Most of the time, his stories reflected his wonderful sense of humor. He found it amusing that much of the action he saw involved bombing and strafing trains, given his love of railroading and subsequent career. He laughed about the time he buzzed a train to give the French crew time to get off and saw the engineer give him a wave of approval from a nearby field as he came around to strafe the train.

My father and fellow pilot Paul "Ollie" Olson kept in touch after the war and the Olsons and Foggs became lifelong friends. Paul was shot down late in the war and a German surgeon put him back together. My father appreciated the irony in shooting down a plane and then ensuring the pilot's recovery and good health. Of course, not everyone was as lucky as Paul, as evidenced by "Baldy" Baldridge's tragic death. My dad never talked about the danger, focusing instead on the good times and how relatively easy they had it at Wretham. I was shocked to see just how dangerous his "easy" job was when reading his recapitulation of the original "D" Flight pilots.

When I think about the art my father created during his distinguished career it helps put in perspective the tragedy of war. Had he died in the ETO, those paintings, and the pleasure they have given so many people, would never have existed. You can't help but wonder what all the others who died there, on both sides, might have contributed to their respective societies. And yet, for us to have ignored the Nazi threat would have been an even greater tragedy.

Although the veterans of World War II are all but extinct, their legacy surrounds us. Every time we read an uncensored newspaper, practice the religion of our choosing, cast a vote, or do any of a hundred little things we take for granted, they are there, looking over our shoulder. Let us never, ever, forget Pop, Baldy, Hag, Bo, Kib, Brownie, Ollie, my father, and all the other members of the armed forces who put themselves in harm's way then and continue to do so today. We owe them so much.

This book exists thanks to the efforts of my beautiful and tenacious wife. She had the inspiration to take my father's diary and format a book around it, spending literally hundreds of hours painstakingly transcribing the diary, trying to decipher his writing with words like Wittmundhafen and Mantes-Gassicourt. There were times when I questioned the viability of the project, but she remained steadfast in her commitment. She is a truly remarkable person. My father always said that if we ever divorced he would disown me and keep her. I think he meant it.

—*Richard Fogg*

Collaborating with Richard on this manuscript has been an honor and a joy, an exceptional, memorable experience. The opportunity to share in Howard's life as a young pilot raised countless questions about the war and a fervent desire to learn more. But even more importantly, when Richard read our first rough draft and had to hold back tears, I knew that we had succeeded in preserving his father's voice.

To those of you who have aided in this journey, thank you for your thoughtful suggestions and assistance. Laura Deal, Karen Robinson, Zhenille Robinson, Paul Flanders, Shirley Wilsey, Shannon Baker, Jim Hester, Julie Kaewert, and Karen Albright Lin, you are all such talented writers and special, supportive friends.

Richard, while this book commemorates your father, I know he and Margot were inordinately proud, as am I, that you chose to follow in Howard's footsteps by serving our country in the Air Force, especially for the year you served in Vietnam. So this book is also for you.

And to Howard and Margot who welcomed me into their hearts so many years ago, you will be remembered forever with love, respect, and an abundance of delight.

—*Janet Fogg*

Special thanks from both of us to Captain Rene Burtner, Squadron Commander of the 369th Fighter Squadron; Peter Randall, webmaster of the www.littlefriends.co.uk/ site; and most especially to Charlotte (Char) Baldridge, sister-in-law of "Baldy" Baldridge and Historian for the 359th Fighter Group Association. Char's tireless efforts to preserve the 359th's history and boundless enthusiasm in sharing those efforts can only be described as gracious and awe-inspiring. For the countless emails, numerous photographs, and varied documents, including the illuminating transcripts of Chappie's monthly "Informal Report of the Morale of the 359th Fighter Group" and Maurice F.X. Donohue's "Monthly Narrative Histories of the 359th Fighter Group" that Char transcribed from archived material in the history files at HQ USAF Historical Research Center, Maxwell AFB, we can only say for the thousandth time, "Thank you so much, Char. Mission accomplished."

We also want to take a moment to remember Janet's father, William F. Perry, who served on the USS Jenkins in the South Pacific half a world from Howard.

Other veterans who have touched our lives include our friends Jack VonEschen (Korean War), Jerome Gloss (World War II and the Korean War), Barry Gallucci and Rick Carver (Vietnam War), William Stanford, who retired after a career in the Air Force, Ed Trumble of Leanin' Tree, who served in the 99th Infantry Division and was wounded at The Battle of the Bulge, and Janet's brother William G. Perry who served in the Army.

Ultimately, of course, this book is for Howard. But it is also for every man and woman who has served or is now serving our country. We hope that *Fogg in the Cockpit* reminds readers of both the cost and value of freedom and liberty, and why they must always be protected for future generations.

—Richard Fogg and Janet Fogg

Richard Fogg, with a little help from his father, assembles a 1948 puzzle which featured one of Howard's early paintings for ALCO. *Courtesy of Richard Fogg*

ART BY HOWARD FOGG

Early in his career Howard painted almost exclusively in watercolor, and although it remained his medium of preference, he did complete approximately 200 oil paintings at the behest of both corporate and private customers. This representative sample begins with prewar watercolors and concludes with oil paintings completed late in his career.

New York Central #1167, a class T-2b electric built by General Electric in 1917.
1940 watercolor by Howard Fogg. *Image from the photo archives of Howard Fogg*

1940 watercolor by Howard Fogg. *Image from the photo archives of Howard Fogg*

Above: Santa Fe Railroad 4-8-4 "Northern" type. 1940 watercolor by Howard Fogg.
Image from the photo archives of Howard Fogg

Below: Canada Pacific 5900 class. Scene painted while at East Wretham and inspired by a photograph in the English book *The Wonder Book of Railways* purchased by Howard in London in 1943. Spring 1944 watercolor by Howard Fogg. *Image from the photo archives of Howard Fogg*

Above: A P-47 shooting down an Fw-190: the painting mentioned in Howard's April 8 and April 12, 1944 diary entries and described in the Informal Report from the Office of the Chaplain dated 1 May 1944 as hanging in the bar at Wretham Hall. Major Aaron Nelson, Executive Officer of the 368th Fighter Squadron brought the painting home at war's end. 1944 oil painting on canvas duck (from the 359th Fighter Group's parachute department) by Howard Fogg.
Archived by Char Baldridge, Historian, 359th Fighter Group Association

Below: A "Thank You" painting presented to Elmo Roper.
1946 watercolor painting by Howard Fogg. *Image from the photo archives of Howard Fogg*

Above: One of Richard Fogg's proudest possessions, this watercolor was a Christmas gift from his father. With snow cover and low hanging clouds obscuring much of the scenery, it allowed Howard to finish it quickly without taking too much precious time away from his backlogged schedule. December 25, 1978 watercolor painting by Howard Fogg. *Courtesy of Richard Fogg*

Below: Prior to the publication of *Fogg and Steam* in 1978, consideration was given to a very special limited edition in which each book would include an original, and unique, painting. This 7" x 10" watercolor is one of two test paintings for the project. Unfortunately it was deemed to be economically unfeasible. 1978 watercolor painting by Howard Fogg. *Courtesy of Richard Fogg*

Above: Although this 7-1/4 x 9-1/2 inch rough sketch was, unfortunately, never used as the basis for a painting, Howard was particularly pleased with the unusual and moody setting he had captured. Watercolor painting by Howard Fogg. *Courtesy of Janet Fogg*

Below: This whimsical image of a caboose is one of a series done for Leanin' Tree. 1968 watercolor painting by Howard Fogg. *Image courtesy of Leanin' Tree, Inc.*

Above: Chesapeake & Ohio Railroad 2-8-4 along the New River Gorge east of Charleston, West Virginia. 1994 watercolor painting by Howard Fogg. *Courtesy of Howard L. "Tex" Fogg III*

Below: Seaboard Coast Line diesels, part of the Family Line System of railroads. Painting by Howard Fogg. *Image from the photo archives of Howard Fogg*

Above: Texas & Pacific Railroad "Texas" type 2-10-4 steam locomotive.
Watercolor painting by Howard Fogg. *Image courtesy of Leanin' Tree, Inc.*

Below: On occasion Howard would create a scene with a fictitious railroad.
This 4-4-0 steam engine in an 1880s New England setting is one such example.
1979 watercolor painting by Howard Fogg. *Image courtesy of Leanin' Tree, Inc.*

Above: Santa Fe Railroad passenger train in the famous "Warbonnet" livery, climbing Glorieta Pass near Santa Fe, New Mexico in the late '40s. Painting by Howard Fogg. *Image courtesy of Leanin' Tree, Inc.*

Below: Four Colorado & Southern narrow-gauge engines push a steam-powered rotary snowplow toward the tunnel at Alpine Pass in Quartz Creek Valley, Colorado. 1970s watercolor painting by Howard Fogg. *Courtesy of Richard Fogg*

Above: Pittsburgh and Lake Erie Railroad Company locomotive shop at McKees Rock, Pennsylvania. Painting by Howard Fogg. *Image from the photo archives of Howard Fogg*

Below: Southern Pacific Railroad "Daylight" 4-8-4 in the special 1976 Bicentennial colors. The train toured the country from April 1975 through December 1976 and carried items of Americana as diverse as the original Louisiana Purchase and a moon rock. 1976 oil painting by Howard Fogg. *Image courtesy of Leanin' Tree, Inc.*

Above: Western Maryland Railroad and Pittsburg & Lake Erie Railroad diesels share an interchange in the Dickerson Run Yard, Pennsylvania. 1964 watercolor painting by Howard Fogg. *Image from the photo archives of Howard Fogg*

Below: Pennsylvania Railroad GG-1 electric locomotive. This is the locomotive Howard refers to in his diary entry on October 2, 1943. 1974 painting by Howard Fogg. *Image courtesy of Leanin' Tree, Inc.*

Above: Denver and Rio Grande Western #3707 along the Colorado River in Glenwood Canyon, Colorado. Jim Matthews, a Boulder realtor and friend of Howard's, received training at Camp Hale, Colorado, as a member of the Army's 10th Mountain Division. With fond memories of the big Denver & Rio Grande Western articulateds that thundered through nearby Glenwood Canyon, Mr. Matthews commissioned this oil painting in 1971. Oil painting by Howard Fogg.
Courtesy of Richard Fogg

Below: Denver & Salt Lake Railroad passenger train exiting a snow shed at the top of Rollins Pass, Colorado (prior to completion of the Moffat Tunnel). Watercolor painting by Howard Fogg.
Courtesy of Richard Fogg

Above: Great Northern Railroad 4-8-2 pulling the Oriental Limited passenger train in the Montana dawn. 1972 oil painting by Howard Fogg. *Image courtesy of Leanin' Tree, Inc.*

Below: The Alaska Railroad was finished in 1923 and owned by the US government until 1985 when it was purchased by the state of Alaska. Mount McKinley looms in the background. 1978 oil painting by Howard Fogg. *Image courtesy of Leanin' Tree, Inc.*

Above: Denver & Rio Grande Western Railroad's California Zephyr climbing the foothills westbound out of Denver in the early '50s. 1983 watercolor painting by Howard Fogg. *Image courtesy of Leanin' Tree, Inc.*

Below: Union Pacific Railroad "Big Boy" 4-8-8-4 with a load of "reefers" (refrigerated freight cars). Only 25 of these legendary articulateds were built for the Union Pacific by ALCO between 1941 and 1944. 1985 oil painting by Howard Fogg. *Image courtesy of Leanin' Tree, Inc.*

Above: Denver & Rio Grande Western Railroad 2-8-8-2 on Tennessee Pass in the Rocky Mountains of central Colorado. 1968 watercolor painting by Howard Fogg. From the Al and Bernadette Chione collection. *Image courtesy of Leanin' Tree, Inc.*

Below: Denver & Rio Grande Western Railroad freight train on the downhill run to Denver after the 6.2 mile journey through the Moffat Tunnel under the Continental Divide. Painting by Howard Fogg. *Image courtesy of Leanin' Tree, Inc.*

Above: Denver & Rio Grande Western Railroad "Mikado" type 2-8-2s double-heading
in southern Colorado circa 1940. 1987 oil painting by Howard Fogg.
From the Al and Bernadette Chione collection. *Image courtesy of Leanin' Tree, Inc.*

Below: Denver & Rio Grande Western #3615 takes on a load of water as a westbound passenger
train steams by on Tennessee Pass in the Colorado Rockies. 1993 oil painting by Howard Fogg.
From the Dave and Jean Gross collection. *Image courtesy of Leanin' Tree, Inc.*

Southern Pacific #4294 headed toward Cascade Summit, Oregon, circa 1948. This was one of Howard's favorite paintings. He was fond of the Southern Pacific 4-8-8-2 "cab forward" design and thought this painting was particularly successful in capturing the setting, and the need, for this unique steam engine. Operating in the Sierra Nevada mountains, the numerous sharp curves, long tunnels, and snow sheds presented problems for a traditional configuration with the cab at the rear. Visibility around the curves was restricted, and with the smoke stack in front of the cab the lengthy tunnels and sheds created serious breathing problems for the crew. By placing the cab at the front these problems were eliminated. Here, cab forward #4294 is seen approaching a snow shed, with additional "helper" engines to cope with the steep grade.
1991 oil painting by Howard Fogg. *Image from the photo archives of Howard Fogg*